er

1888	*Carried timber from North America across North Atlantic. Based - Belfast, N. Ireland*
1893	*Hospital isolation ship, Southampton*
1923	*Bought by the Admiralty, re-fitted at Irvine, became a Royal Navy training ship, then a WWII accommodation ship. Name changed to HMS 'Carrick'. Berthed James Watt Dock, Greenock, Scotland*
1948	*SV 'Carrick', brought to Custom House Quay, River Clyde, Glasgow as Royal Naval Volunteer Reserve Clubhouse*
1978	*Floods at her mooring, Custom House Quay, River Clyde, Glasgow*
1989	*Floods at her mooring again*
1990	*Clyde Ship Trust takes ownership. Towed to Prince's Dock, Glasgow*
1991	*Sinks in Prince's Dock*
1992	*'Carrick' raised from Prince's Dock and towed to new owners, the Scottish Maritime Museum at Irvine*
2001	*Campaign to save 'Carrick' from deconstruction. Reverts to original name*
2010	*Ownership transferred to 'Clipper Ship City Of Adelaide Ltd' group*
2013	*Towed from Irvine to Rotterdam for final voyage to Adelaide on heavy-lift ship MV 'Palanpur'*
2014	*Arrives Adelaide, becomes a floating museum at Dock 1, Port Adelaide*
2019	*Planned move to permanent site at Dock 2*

Sources: Ron Roberts 'The Ship That Won't Die'
https://en.wikipedia.org/wiki/City_of_Adelaide_(1864)

Clipper Ship
City of Adelaide

BENEATH THE SOUTHERN CROSS

RITA BRADD

'City of Adelaide' by G McMillan, 1991
is reproduced by kind permission of the Scottish Maritime Museum

CrawsNest Press
Frizzels Wood House
Dunbar
East Lothian EH42 1RN

www.ritabradd.com

First published in hardback by CrawsNest Press in August 2019 in Great Britain

Designed and typeset in 9.5 point Berthold Bodoni by Bob Randall
Printed in Great Britain by Latimer Trend

A CIP catalogue record for this book is available from the British Library

ISBN 978-1-9998376-5-5

CONTENTS

INTRODUCTION

IN RESPONSE TO my set of questions posed to HRH The Duke of Edinburgh in April 2015, I found he had become a Trustee of the National Maritime Museum at Greenwich in 1948. Soon after that, he was informed by the Director that the then owner of *Cutty Sark* could no longer maintain her. He felt very strongly that she should be saved and put on display. They formed the Cutty Sark Trust, the ship was fully restored and is now owned by the National Maritime Museum, open to the public. While all this was going on, it occurred to the Duke that there might be several other historic ships that ought to be saved. The Maritime Trust was set up and the search for such ships began. The remains of several ships were found, including Brunel's *Great Britain*, in the Falkland Islands; HMS *Warrior* in Pembroke Dock, and HMS *Carrick* (originally *City of Adelaide*) that had been used as the Royal Naval Volunteer Reserve (RNVR) Club Headquarters on the River Clyde, Glasgow, Scotland. *Carrick* sank at her dock but was raised in 1992 and towed to Irvine, to the Scottish Maritime Museum as a preservation project. Fate was again against her, and she faced demolition. In 2001 The Duke of Edinburgh formed a committee to save *Carrick*. The bid from Sunderland, where she was built in 1864, was unsuccessful; however, he was relieved and delighted that the ship is now in Adelaide, South Australia. His hope then was she would be restored to such a condition that she could be put on display to the public by successful bidders 'Clipper Ship City of Adelaide Ltd'. He was disappointed at that stage that *City of Adelaide* had not found a permanent home, but was hopeful a site would be found for her. His Royal Highness stated he would do it all again.

I do not quite know where to start in sharing with you how 1864 clipper ship *City of Adelaide* has impacted my life since I discovered her in 1999 at Greenock. At every turn, something made me home in on her. She wriggled herself under my skin and cropped up under my radar in random ways. She hijacked me away from a book about my adventures to ports around Europe and beyond where the annual Tall Ships Race was visiting. I shelved that to devote myself to follow *City of Adelaide*'s Fate. I had no idea just how much both our Fates were to intertwine.

I have always been a sucker for the underdog. I could not fathom that a ship of her age and remarkable survival was under threat of deliberate deconstruction in Scotland. Compared with the gleaming *Cutty Sark*, *City of Adelaide* was Cinderella. She became my obsession. I tracked every move that was happening with her. I began to make connections, make enquiries. I withdrew from my own life into *City of Adelaide*'s. Whatever I had to do and wherever I had to go to be with her and see for myself what was happening with her, what was being done to save her, I would do it, be there. I was uncontrollable. I felt compelled to raise awareness of her plight, to try and fight her corner, to let the whole world know she existed by the skin of her teeth. I did not expect to accompany her half-way round the world on a heavy-lift cargo vessel! I did not expect to voyage through time on the device of a diary kept by twenty year-old

Sarah Ann Bray on *City of Adelaide*'s maiden voyage in 1864. I did not ever expect I would abandon four generations of family to go on a mysterious journey.

I have learned and grown so much in researching and writing this intriguing story. I have crossed barriers of shyness in approaching people from all walks of life, in sharing accommodation with an all-male crew of fifteen Ukrainians and two Russians on a huge cargo vessel, and arriving in a country that fascinated me from a young age to be welcomed with tremendous warmth into the bosom of what I now call 'my *City of Adelaide* family'.

The group 'Clipper Ship City of Adelaide Ltd' has been determined, ruthless, passionate, selfless, astute and bold in their ambition to bring *City of Adelaide* home as the most significant symbol of heritage for South Australia. They have done so as volunteers and without funding, apart from help with transportation costs. HRH The Duke of Edinburgh's vision for her has been realised. Thousands of visitors of all generations from around the world are fascinated by her, going aboard to discover her varied history and the brave souls who went out on her. A variety of events and entertainment take place within her on an ever-increasing scale. He will be proud of the team effort that brought the ship home. Disappointingly, she remains on a barge and will not now return to Fletcher's Slip as her permanent home, ironically due to housing development in Port Adelaide.

As for me, I may not be the best qualified person to have undertaken this adventure, but I am so, so grateful and privileged to be the one chosen to enjoy this absolutely marvellous, unique voyage with my heroine, Sarah Ann Bray and our beloved ship, *City of Adelaide*.

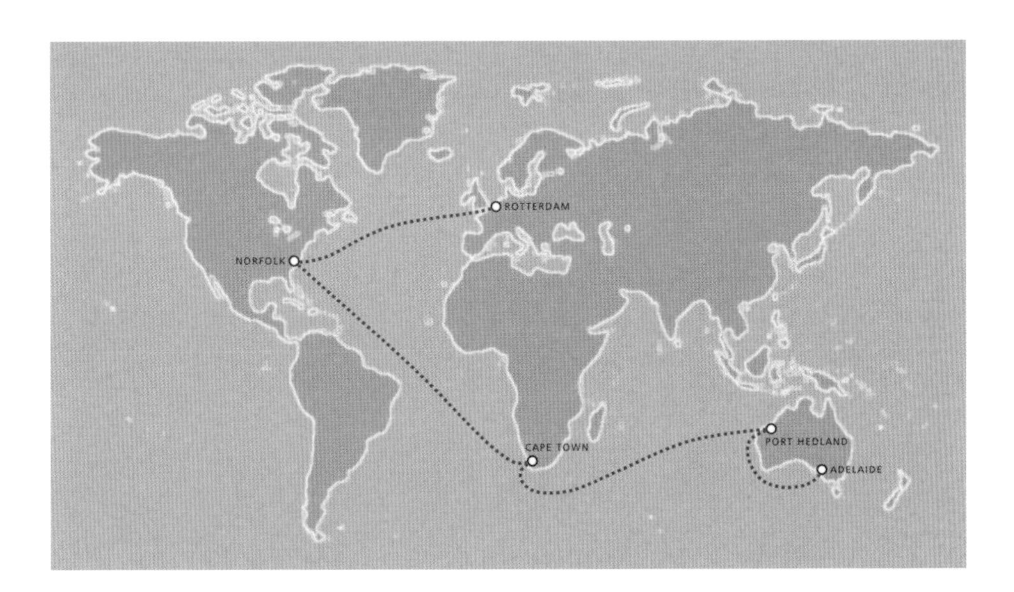

City of Adelaide Bleeds

The Red Ensign bandage frays
at the edge of the seeping wound of Adelaide
stricken by failed sutures.
Rain lances lashed her armour
till fireballs blistered and shrivelled her skin,
let barrages of subzero cannonballs batter into her.
The Atlantic wind howls at the stench
of her gangrene, lifts her skirts,
licks death into her.

Glory days gone. Glory days gone.
She was spawned in Sunderland by William Pile
in the womb of tough men proud
of scars earned in the growing of her.
Rivets sweated into her iron ribs
through wooden skin shielded with copper
and sealed against the wet
with black and white and red,
and nails scraped grime away from caulk
that drew her long and tall and rounded
till her umbilical cord was severed
and she broke free.

Captain Bruce was first to try her,
riding on her belly filled with emigrants
on a quest for Aboriginal land
and prosperity in the spring of kangaroos,
the climb of koalas, the rush of gold
and the fat of the land where Ned Kelly waltzed
with Matilda in the shadow of Ayers Rock,
till the kookaburra sent her home stuffed
with wool, wheat, copper, reunion.

Sold! to transport coal.
Sold! to transport timber.
Sold! to isolate the sick.
Sold! to party in Glasgow
as *SV Carrick* and drown in Princes Dock
till resurrection and a one pound ransom
clipped her wings, slipped her pride for all to see.

Glory days gone. Glory days gone

but see her young sister

how she shines in her Cutty Sark.
How she shines.

PROLOGUE

UNTIL I SAW two sailing ships moored up in Scotland's Port of Leith in 1982, I thought they were confined to films and pages of stories about pirates, slaves, people trafficking, battles, exploration, transportation, stowaways, romance. There is a photograph of me taken on that sunny day by my husband, Alan. I am crouched down, facing the ships; I am smiling back at the camera. My brand new daughter is in my arms, my toddler son stands beside me.

I was not to see another tall ship until we visited Newcastle as a family in 1993 when our youngest child was nine years old. We found the River Tyne spanned by the criss-cross of a green-painted iron bridge and awash with an array of tall ships. I gasped, stopped in my tracks, breathed in the sense of adventure that bobbed on the watery highway that led to the freedom and exhilaration of the North Sea. Hundreds of sailing boats, large and small from all over the world with a matching diversity of crews, swamped the River Tyne for the start of the Cutty Sark Tall Ships Race. I had never heard of it. Thousands of people came from far and wide to see them. There was food, entertainment, music by the quayside, dancing, all topped off in the late evening dark with a spectacular fireworks display. I absorbed history, adventure, youth, maturity, wood, hemp. I heard wavelets slurp at hulls, voices twitch out commands, laughter, singing from decks and from the quayside, tears from small children cramped into a forest of adult legs. Dogs barked. Ropes creaked. I craned my neck and saw masts soar into the stretch of blue above. Young mariners and old ones too, stuffed toes into ratlines as they scrambled up to the rigging to fix this, adjust that. Some crew members were dressed in smart blue or black naval uniforms of trousers and jackets that obscured starched white shirts, their throats choked by Windsor-knotted ties, their feet hutched into jet-gloss shoes. Others looked like castaways, their sun-bleached hair coiled down bare backs like rope, their skimpy, washed out clothes fluttered in the breeze like bunting. The air was filled with expectancy, confidence, curiosity. African drums beat a thrill into the crowd. I watched eyes squint as they measured the height of tapering masts. Fingers pointed, etched rigging onto the canvas sky, worked out the function of each of the ropes whose lengths were tethered on truncheon-like *belaying pins*, hanging redundant until they were loosened at sea to control the running rigging, or lines, of hoisted sails. Ropes coiled on decks like doormats, they were so closely wound, and brass fittings were trophies that gleamed out the pride of the crew. On the wharf, vessels had their gang-planks lowered to seduce people to scramble up them. I could not wait to go aboard and explore the mysteries of a tall ship. We stood in queues, and spent the whole afternoon dredging for treasure aboard the ships and amongst tents and marquees set up to house food, drink, trinkets, books, t-shirts, hoodies, tea towels, caps, paintings, prints, drawings, carvings. It was endless. Our children were captivated by all of this, but when they grew weary, the promise of fireworks revived them. Darkness fell. We ate hot dogs and burgers, grease oozing between our fingers and onto paper napkins each time we took a bite. I retrieved a sliver of onion from the prow of my jacket. The anticipation was intense. The crowd thickened. I did not think that was possible. Soon there was no way out. We were jammed in a flow of human lava. By the time the first firework hit the sky we were all pieces of a jigsaw puzzle pressed together and trapped in an unlidded box. A spark shot right into me and lit a fuse. A passion for tall ships exploded within me that night. I suffered an inexplicable emptiness, a sense of loss I could not explain as we left the ships behind and headed home. I knew I would have to find those ships again.

And I did. It did not occur to me in 1995 when Alan, as Sub-Lieutenant, and our son as Watch Leader of Dunbar Sea Cadet Unit helped crew the Sea Cadet tall ship TS *Royalist* that they were actually participating in the Tall Ships Race whose vessels were moored in the Port of Leith on the north shore of Edinburgh. They were promoting the Sea Cadet organisation, holding hospitality fundraising events on board around the Firth of Forth. My heart swelled with pride to see them at work as the ship was welcomed into the Port by loud cheers and applause. The crowd was thrilled by the sight of cadets lined along the spars like swallows gathered on telephone wires as they motored in to moor up. That evening Alan and I were at a reception in Leith Sea Cadet Unit in honour of TS *Royalist*. Captain Gordon Paterson offered me a strawberry dipped in chocolate as his invitation uttered from his lips. We were to join TS *Royalist* on Sunday for a sail beneath the two bridges on the Firth of Forth, and have lunch on board. I was speechless. My cheeks flushed at the prospect.

The weather was fair two sleeps later when we drove to Leith and found TS *Royalist* where we had left her. I was fascinated by proceedings as the new crew of cadets showed off their fresh-found skills and cast us off to envious eyes of people on the wharf. Soon we were out in the depths of the River Forth. I loved being on board with the wind powering through my hair, the sun on my face, and spray and salt tingling my lips. I was fascinated by the crew hoisting sails to the call of *two-six-heave* that kept them pulling ropes in rhythm for maximum strength. I loved the helm, all brass and wood, and held it tight as I learned how to manoeuvre the ship and read the compass. We were served chicken in the crowded mess below decks where cadets took it in turns to eat. Politeness and manners were the order of the day. I had no problem with sea sickness. I devoured the meal and thanked the Cook. All too soon this memorable day was ended.

I got hot under the collar in 1996 and 1997 because I was not able to go to the races. I was aware I was becoming a tall ships groupie. In 1998 I was determined to see the ships. I arranged with my parents to take care of our children. I reserved two seats on a flight to see them on their visit to Dublin. It would be a weekend away, a surprise for Alan. When he said he did not want to go, I went to the computer and logged in. My face and ears burned, my lips were pursed. Blood pounded in my temples. My finger hovered over the booking. I looked at the number in the box and swapped *2* for *1*, and pressed *Enter*.

I was launched.

Part One
THE SEED IS SOWN

'It filled me with an overwhelming sadness to see a once magnificent ship reduced to a hulk on a lonely slipway, stranded and neglected like the driftwood that lay at her stern.'

CHAPTER ONE

GREENOCK 1999

An Encounter with SV *Carrick*

SHE THRUST HER bow into the palm of my hand on the quayside at Greenock in July 1999. Her captain, a Sea Cadet aged around 13 years, disappeared into the West Coast of Scotland sunshine as I clutched the shiny paper that drew my eyes away from a spinning merry-go-round, where gaudy wooden horses grinned glistening tombstone teeth at the crowd, as their riders grew dizzier and dizzier. I drew breath at the desolate image of this Sailing Vessel called *Carrick* on the Scottish Maritime Museum's flyer. It filled me with an overwhelming sadness to see a once magnificent ship reduced to a hulk on a lonely slipway, stranded and neglected like the driftwood that lay at her stern. I was bewildered by the state of this clipper ship that had been built in 1864. There could not have been greater contrast between her and the cared-for, manicured ships that strained at their tethers in Ocean Terminal before me. She ran aground in the bay of my heart. I tucked her sadness into my backpack out of sight. I no longer felt like taking a ride on the merry-go-round.

I was particularly excited to be at Greenock for this Tall Ships Race. This was my second complete immersion of a long weekend on my own to drool over tall ships. Dublin had been wonderful. I had stayed with a friend of my neighbours, and spent most of my time by the River Liffey and on its many bridges pigging out on tall ships and pints of Guinness. Each morning as I took the bus from my hostess's home, I could see into pubs. There was sawdust on wooden floorboards to sup up any alcohol that frothed or spilled over the lips of glasses. Dublin was gorgeous. O'Connell Street was full of musicians and street performers, Bewley's coffee and steak pies that oozed with gravy drunk on beer. I had met sweet Molly Malone, the prettiest bronze of all, and sang of cockles and mussels in my head. I had seen The Dubliners cosseted in Arran sweaters, filled my ears with their sea shanties clambering out from rigging on board the Irish Sail Training Vessel, *Asgard II.* I had met victims of the Irish Potato Famine, set in bronze. I had been soaked in a cloudburst that turned the streets into rivers, and splashed my way to meet new friends in a pub for lunch.

Alan was forced to resign himself to this new passion of mine. He had brought me across central Scotland to Greenock from Dunbar on the east coast on the back of our Yamaha Ventura 1300 motorbike. We were cooked in our leathers as I clung to him while he drove solidly along the M8 on a glorious morning behind our friend, Eric Laird, who rode solo, before heading south to Largs. We took the ferry from there across the water to the island of Great Cumbrae. We would watch the Race fleet of tall ships glide over the mirror of the Firth of Clyde on the way to the Port of Greenock. We hoped to see swathes of sail hoisted. Eric had brought everything but the kitchen sink in his panniers. We soon had a disposable barbecue glowing where sausages fizzed and spluttered over charcoal, and basked in the rays of the sun that blazed in the early afternoon. There were rolls, cakes, biscuits, and even ice cream that had somehow withstood the shoogles and heat of the journey. Hot coffee was poured from flasks into plastic cups to wash everything down. It seemed ages before a tiny dot was spotted on the horizon to the south. It tantalised our eyes. We scrambled for binoculars and verified…yes! It was indeed a tall ship. Soon it was joined by another, and another, and another, and as they cut through the glass of the Firth of Clyde like skaters on ice, they grew larger and larger, and we could make out the number of masts each had, barely swaying in the calm. I was enthralled. I leaped from rock to rock, holding up to my eyes first, my binoculars, then my camera. I pressed the button that would beach each image onto the film inside it. There were all sizes of hulls, from very large ones to smaller yachts. My ears could not pick up the sound of engines that had been engaged to propel them through the water. Not much sail was hoisted, there was little blow for them to be of any use. Every now and then I would join my companions and discuss the ships, and try to make out their names, flag of country, and figureheads. When the last of the ships became a small speck to the north, we packed up and ferried back to the mainland in search of bed and breakfast accommodation for me. Just for me. We got on our bikes and I fell into a reverie behind Alan as the engine hummed us along the road. I was jolted back to the now. The bike had stopped. We had arrived in a small town; we drove round and round to find accommodation. Everywhere was full: there were *No Vacancies* signs in windows. In the end all we could find was a tired, classic Scottish stone-built house with stepped gable ends and grey slate roof, right at the seafront and a convenient half hour or so by train from Greenock. The price was reasonable so I booked in for three nights, to begin the following night. We left, kicked the motorbike engines into action and headed for Falkirk almost fifty miles away for another barbecue, at my brother's house. Things were in full swing when we got there. I was plied with red wine by my sister-in-law as she spoke of what was to come the following day. Stuffed with more sausages and burgers, Alan and Eric left for the journey home. I had more red wine and listened to the plan. We would drive to Rosneath early in the morning to meet up with her sister and brother-in-law. We would sail on their yacht across the River Clyde to Greenock where the Race fleet was moored up. The red wine I had knocked back was my saving grace for a decent sleep that night.

We awoke early to a blue sky and the promise of glorious weather, and headed for Rosneath. The sunshine contrasted with the sinister grey of Faslane Naval Base that we passed on our way. We arrived after about an hour, packed food for the voyage and cast off, penetrated by the blue, beady eyes of a large grey plastic owl whose job was to keep seagulls and their corrosive poo off the boat. We were short on breeze, so fired up the motor to get us across to the ships. We passed the half-submerged wreck of a boat seabirds swirled around. Some were perched on the section of hull that stuck out of the water. Cormorants spread their wings like vampires engulfing their prey, their wings heavy cloaks as they proffered them to the sun. This was *Captayannis*. She was a sugar boat that had anchored at the Tail of the Bank on the River Clyde to offload her cargo at James Watt Dock in Greenock, on 27 January 1974. A severe storm had broken out. She dragged her anchor. Before her engines could be started for her to head for more sheltered waters, she drifted into the taut anchor chains of an oil tanker. Her 121 metre hull was holed. Water gushed in. Rather than let the ship sink, her captain made for shallower waters and beached her on the sand bank with all hands saved. She keeled over the next day and remains as she was then. Confusion had prevailed as to ownership and insurers, so she could not be removed. Blowing her up was not an option because of the sensitivity of the nearby bird sanctuary. I loved that nature had claimed her for herself.

When we reached Greenock, the port was hoaching with people. Families ambled round the quayside, their tongues lapping at blobs of ice creams melting in their cones. Babies and toddlers rattled across the cobbles in prams and buggies. Mariners showing people round the vessels posed for photographs in the click and whirr of cameras. The general clamour was interjected with the sharp bark of dogs. We were out of all that mayhem. We were on the yacht, manoeuvring round mooring lines. Our motor hummed the same tune as the dozens and dozens of other craft filled with people. We first feasted our eyes on the massive Class A 40+ metre hulls that were like floating tower blocks dwarfing us, then dropped them to caress the smaller, less than 40 metre sleek fibreglass, steel or highly-varnished wood of the modern fast and fleeting Class D boats, and traditional clinker wooden craft, and tenders that bookended the Class Bs and Cs. To top it all, there was the complete range of rigging and sail plans a body could wish to clap eyes on. We made short-shrift of lunch, washed down pizza, quiche, salad, sausages and chicken with copious amounts of wine and beer. I pinched myself, thought, *How many people get this rare opportunity to be up close to the hulls of these magnificent giants?* I could not get my head wrapped round why Alan had turned down this opportunity and gone home.

When the day was weary and the others faced the sail back to Rosneath, the yacht was manoeuvred close to the quayside. I grasped hold of a vertical steel ladder fixed to the walls with both hands, straddled a narrow expanse of water with one foot welded to the yacht's hull, the other clamped onto a rung of the ladder. I hauled myself off and abandoned ship. I scrambled up to join the throngs on shore and waved my sailing companions off, before I took an evening train south to my accommodation for the first night amongst the faded carpets and furniture that could speak volumes about the last forty years or more. As I closed my eyes, I could see images of the day etched on the back of my eyelids – the drab quayside transformed, painted with dancers, buskers, revellers, magicians. My ears were cluttered with sounds of drums, flutes, accordions, guitars, banjos, sea shanties. I saw myself below the clown with curly, yellow hair, squashed tomato-red nose, sad down-mouth, big ears sticking out from under his bowler hat. I had looked beyond his oversized boots, up the stilts covered with shiny trousers striped in silver and black. He had squirted water at me from the big dayglow pink flower fixed in his lapel. A warm thrill spread through my body from my toes to my head with the knowledge that I would be back the next day. I giggled and fell asleep to the taste of salt and a final chuckle of seagulls.

Each morning I got up and had a hasty breakfast before taking an early train to Greenock. My face reflected pleasure in the windows of the railway carriage as it sped past the tangled coastal scenery and the contrasting order of concrete and brick houses, flats, garages, sheds, industrial buildings and pasture. Each day I pressed myself through the crowds to get on board the vessels that invited people to feel a wooden or steel deck beneath their feet, touch hemp ropes and massive chain links, to scramble across decks and talk to crew members who were always happy to answer questions. The uniforms worn by naval personnel were spick and span, as were their manners. I gave my camera to a passer-by and posed with an officer for a photograph. There were Mexican mariners who stretched bright, white smiles that echoed the dazzle of their uniforms; there were tall, slim cadets in black trousers and white shirts, their high cheekbones jutting from beneath white caps with deep, black peaks; there were young men and women in bohemian attire, t-shirts, shorts, short skirts, sarongs, with hair unilaterally bleached by the sun and blown unkempt by the breath of many winds along their voyages, their feet bare, or toes otherwise clinging to flip-flops. There was freshly-washed underwear, tea towels, towels, jeans, hoodies that dangled from makeshift washing lines, or were draped over any part of the vessels that would accommodate them. Sometimes they were pegged down, other times they were left to the vagaries of the breeze. I picked up foreign sounds that fell from international mouths, as well as different ambiences amongst the various ships that perhaps reflected the country they had originated from, or maybe the discipline imposed on crew by their officers, or even the contrast of affluence of some ships with the necessary frugality of others. Some ships had a rubber stamp in shapes of circles, ovals or squares bearing an outline of the vessel, its rigging and its name. Crew members sunk these into ink pads of ship's choice of colours in shades of blue, red, maroon, turquoise, black, green that were impressed onto magazines, leaflets, pages of diaries, paper handkerchiefs – anything people presented them with, even skin. I remembered you could buy official programmes that gave details on participating ships, general information on the festival, and advertisements. I went looking for one to collect stamps of ships I would visit, as a souvenir. I bought one from an official merchandise stand, and could not resist a navy blue sweatshirt with *Greenock 1999* embroidered on it.

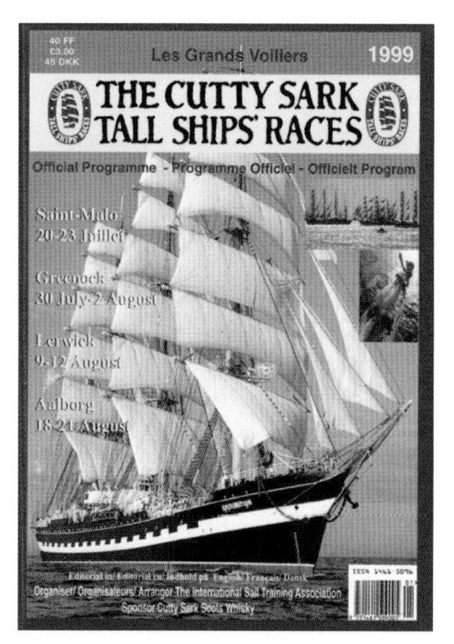

I was thrilled to see the three masts of *Christian Radich*, a full-rigged ship that starred in *The Onedin Line*, the television series from the 1970s, and the *Alexander von Humboldt* from Germany with her green sails, made famous in the Beck's Beer adverts. They became my first trophies, followed by sister ships *Sir Winston Churchill* and *Malcolm Miller*, the magnificent Mexican naval ship *Cuauhtemoc*, *Glenlee* from Glasgow, Clydebuilt in 1896, known as *Galatea* when a Spanish Navy Training Ship; and *Oosterschelde*, a former cargo ship I later sailed on in 2014 on the River Thames during the Tall Ships Regatta. There were boats from Ocean Youth Club; *Swan* from the Shetland Islands where the Race fleet was headed next, and *Kruzenshtern*, the huge Russian ship; *Asgard II* I saw in Dublin was there (she sadly sank in the Bay of Biscay in 2008).

Not every vessel opened its arms to the public. Some preferred instead to rest, carry out repairs to sails and rigging, splice ropes, polish brasses, prepare food, sup a beer or two. At these times and when ships were closed to the public, a sign saying *Crew Only* was slung across the entrance at the bottom of gangplanks, forbidding general access. There were times when the larger ships hosted receptions and corporate events on board, so earned valuable income. These were attended by women in glamorous attire and jewellery that sparkled, and men in suave dinner suits, their throats adorned with bow ties. I felt a bit smug that I had been a guest of a captain and been spoiled in this way. Crew members served canapés, champagne, wines, and intermingled with the guests to ensure their every need was attended to.

I feasted on the ships the whole time until they left Greenock on 2 August when something called *The Parade of Sail* was to take place. I did not go to the Port to see them leave. Instead I based myself in front of my bed & breakfast house and sipped red wine amongst throngs of families. We waited…and waited…then the most magnificent sight filled our eyes. The Tall Ships fleet appeared, gliding down the river, sails up, the wind tumbling through them. There were white sails, red sails, green sails, square sails, triangular sails. The whole fleet passed by in sun and breeze.

Captain David Bruce

It was like an armada. I raised my ceramic mug and toasted them safe voyage. As the last vessel became a tiny dot again, I gathered my belongings from my temporary abode and headed to the station for my train home. I was full of elation, full of envy. I flicked through the pages of the programme on the journey home, and ruminated over everything. I got home and unpacked. The flyer from the Scottish Maritime Museum with that sorry image of *Carrick* fell from my backpack. My eyes, my heart, my soul burned. I began a search for her on the internet. I found she was a clipper ship originally named *City of Adelaide*. She was commissioned to be built by quarter-owner Captain David Bruce, a Scotsman born in Perth in July 1816. He wanted a bespoke *clipper ship* – so called because of their swiftness due to being narrow for their length and having a large sail area that enabled them to clip over the waves rather than plough through them. This ship would be superior in size, speed and comfort than his previous ship *Irene* that he had captained for the previous eleven years and given great service to the South Australian trade with. Joining him as fellow quarter-owners of the ship were Adelaide butcher turned copper ore miner Henry Martin; brothers Joseph and Daniel Harrold from England, who settled in Adelaide as ironmongers and shipping agents, and Joseph Moore of Devitt & Moore, London ship-brokers, who became managing owners of *City of Adelaide*, the first ship to be built for their line that later included *Cutty Sark* amongst many others.

The ship was built in 1864 by William Pile, Hay & Co, who had a reputation for quality workmanship, materials and fittings, at their shipyard on the River Wear at North Sands, Monkwearmouth, Sunderland, to an innovative and at the time experimental composite hull design of iron ribs with timber planking, topped with a sheathing of copper to keep the hull sleek and streamlined for speed and protected from weed, barnacles and worm infestation that would slow her down and make her less competitive in the trade races. All of this made the ship stronger, lighter and faster. David Bruce was first to captain her, from 1864 to 1867; his elder son John Bruce from 1867 to 1873; Llewellyn W E Bowen from 1873 to 1875; the younger Bruce son Alexander from 1875 to 1876 then finally Edward Alston from 1876 to 1887. She carried migrants, emigrants and goods from Great Britain and Northern Europe from London to the new expanding City of Adelaide in the State of South Australia. She returned with copper, wool and wheat from both Adelaide and Port Augusta.

I discovered funding for the restoration of *Carrick/City of Adelaide* at the Scottish Maritime Museum had ceased. She was destined instead for scientific deconstruction. I had to know why.

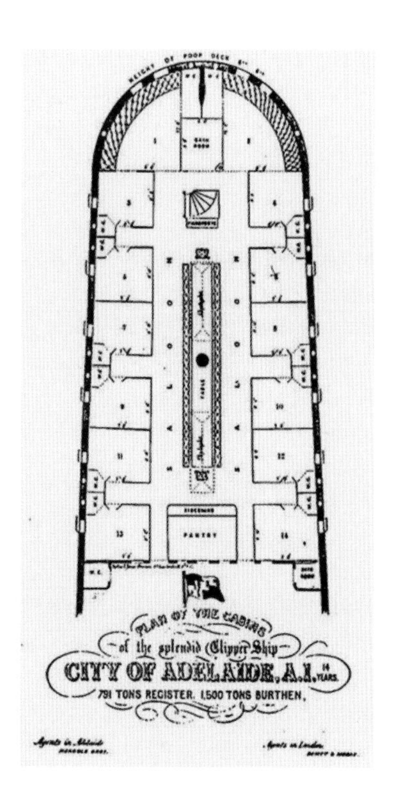

A SHIP WITH TWO NAMES

IN 2006 I was writing a book, *Tall Ships Groupie*, about my travels to see the tall ships races in ports they visited in Europe, Britain and beyond over many years. I approached Jim Tildesley, the Director of the Scottish Maritime Museum at Irvine at the time to *expert-read* what I had written about *Carrick/City of Adelaide*. His prompt reply stated he would be very happy to help with information on events relating to the ship over the last twenty or so years. He also mentioned Dr Alan Platt, a very good friend and expert on the ship's history who was based in Scotland. As I carried out research, my mouse found itself more and more drawn to any information I could find about *Carrick/City of Adelaide*. In October 2006 Alan and his friend Eric had taken a trip on their motorbikes to the Scottish Maritime Museum. Eric took great delight in phoning to tell me they were aboard her. I was green with envy. Alan gave me his entry ticket when they got back and I was fired up to find out more about the ship's plight. I found on the World Ship Trust website that they had classed her as a *vessel in peril*, her case being the most urgent at the time. Bold letters jumped out at me from the screen – *RESCUE POSSIBLY UNDER WAY.* I juddered with excitement. Perhaps she would be spared her undeserved fate of being deconstructed after all. I revisited the website dedicated to her, registered in Australia, where I found there was a group of South Australians known as 'Clipper Ship City of Adelaide Ltd' (CSCOAL) who were trying to rescue *Carrick/City of Adelaide*. She was a National treasure to them. They made a claim that a quarter of a million South Australians had descended from people who migrated on the ship from the United Kingdom and Northern Europe between 1864 and 1887, leaving London and Plymouth, arriving in Adelaide in search of new opportunities. Few people would make the return journey, so the ship's holds would be stuffed with wheat, copper and wool that also acted as ballast to keep the ship steady.

VESSELS IN PERIL & VESSELS IN NEED

VESSELS IN PERIL

This page is dedicated to drawing attention to the plight of some of our member ships in urgent need of support to secure their preservation. Although many vessels are able to support themselves, others are struggling to survive. The most urgent case at the moment is the ***CITY OF ADELAIDE (ex-Carrick)***.

RESCUE POSSIBLY UNDER WAY

THE CITY OF ADELAIDE

(Ex-Carrick)

CITY OF ADELAIDE

www.worldshiptrust.org

I found that His Royal Highness The Duke of Edinburgh had formed a Committee in 2001 to save *Carrick/City of Adelaide* from deconstruction. Her name was changed when she was bought in 1923 by the Admiralty to be used as a training ship, because the Royal Australian Navy had commissioned a ship on 5 August 1922 during King George V's reign that was named *His Majesty's Australian Ship City of Adelaide.* To avoid confusion between the two ships, *City of Adelaide* was given the new name of HMS *Carrick* on 16 May 1925 by the Marchioness of Graham, who later became the Duchess of Montrose. Young men were trained on her up to and including WWII for service in the Royal Navy, and on Defensively Equipped Merchant Ships.

At the Committee meeting in 2001, it was decided the ship should revert to her original name, *City of Adelaide.*

HMS Carrick, RNVR drill-ship, at the Great Harbour, 1931.

CHAPTER THREE

REACHING OUT

Making Connections

JIM AND I did not have any further communication until I emailed him on 22 May 2007. This was the day after *Cutty Sark*, built five years after *City of Adelaide*, had been on fire at Greenwich, London. Work was being carried out on *Cutty Sark* when a blaze broke out. The images of the inferno had been all over the breakfast news, and I wept. Jim was interviewed on the teatime news with *City of Adelaide* in the background. He highlighted the difference in conservation investment between the two composite-built clipper ships. In my email I asked him whether he thought the tragedy of what happened to *Cutty Sark* would somehow give a lifeline to *City of Adelaide*. I also wondered whether *they* would come hunting for body parts for *Cutty Sark*, as *City of Adelaide* had been under threat of deconstruction for several years at that time.

By coincidence, on my birthday in 2011, I received a generic invitation to a fund-raising dinner for *City of Adelaide* in Adelaide, South Australia. It was impossible and impracticable for me to attend, but I was so excited to have been on the invitation list as someone who subscribed to the website. I discovered *City of Adelaide*'s builder William Pile and I share the same birth date, but of course, not the same year! The invitation included information on *City of Adelaide* that I was not aware of.

'With the announcement by the Scottish Minister for Culture and External Affairs, Fiona Hyslop, that South Australia is the preferred bidder to obtain the world's oldest clipper ship City of Adelaide, we invite you to join us at a dinner to raise additional funds to transport the clipper to South Australia.

The dinner also commemorates the 147th Anniversary of the first arrival of the City of Adelaide in South Australia in November 1864 under the command of Scotsman and quarter-owner Captain David Bruce. The clipper ship City of Adelaide was purpose built to serve South Australia. Launched on the 7th May 1864, the City of Adelaide is a few years older than the world's only other surviving clipper ship, the Cutty Sark.'

ADELAIDE ADVERTISER 15 Oct 2011

Clipper won't get here for birthday

STUART INNES

THE arrival of the historic clipper City of Adelaide has been delayed until next year.

The Clipper Ship City of Adelaide Preservation Trust needed luck and more funding to get the world's oldest clipper ship here for the State's 175th birthday on December 28.

But as neither of those were forthcoming, it is now likely to arrive in Adelaide around the middle of next year.

An officer from the Australia Quarantine and Inspection Service is in Scotland today completing his inspection of the iron-framed, timber-hulled ship that was built in 1864 and now sits on a slipway.

AQIS checks any wooden items coming into Australia and looks for unwanted pests, insects and diseases.

The inspector's trip has been paid for by the trust. "The Scottish Maritime Museum previously funded a biological cleaning of the ship," preservation trust director Peter Roberts said yesterday.

In Adelaide, work is nearing completion on a 100-tonne steel cradle that will be sent to Scotland and placed under the ship in the first stage of its transport to bring it to Adelaide.

It's envisaged the clipper will be centrepiece of a maritime history display at Port Adelaide.

It was clear *City of Adelaide* was not letting me forget about her. She kept shoving her hull into my heart.

I noticed the Tall Ships Race was returning to Greenock in July 2011, and that the race route would take the fleet from Waterford, Southern Ireland past Irvine en route for Greenock. I contacted both Jim Tildesley and Peter Roberts, one of the Directors of CSCOAL, suggesting it would be grand if some sort of acknowledgement of the existence of *City of Adelaide* at the Scottish Maritime Museum by the Race fleet might be organised to draw the attention of the young Race crews to this iconic clipper ship that spanned the 19th Century to the 21st. She was, after all, on the list of the top twelve most important vessels in the United Kingdom. I copied in the Tall Ships Race organisers and Fiona Hyslop, Member of the Scottish Parliament and Scottish Nationalist Party Minister for Cultural and External Affairs at the time. Peter advised me of potential media coverage of the proposed salute by BBC Scotland and Australian Broadcasting Corporation who were considering making a two-part documentary on the transportation of *City of Adelaide*. Despite our best efforts the salute did not happen.

On 9 December 2011 I was burning the midnight oil. I emailed Peter Roberts and asked him about the documentary he had mentioned. I had a composition, *City of Adelaide : Farewell To Scotland* that might be of interest to the producer. Beads of sweat seeped into my clothes as I further asked whether it would be possible for me to accompany *City of Adelaide* on her final voyage. I talked about writing a book, I talked about sponsorship for the voyage with proceeds going to *City of Adelaide* in her new life as a museum, I talked about my past fundraising efforts, I talked about a percentage of my book sales being donated to *City of Adelaide*.
I wanted Peter to be instrumental in realising my ambition. I was grateful that the ship's departure from the United Kingdom had been delayed for a number of reasons. My stomach lurched as I clicked the *Send* button and watched my Fate go into the ether.

I thought I would never hear from Peter again. Six days later my hands shook as I opened his response. My eyes could not move fast enough to read the words. My stomach heaved with butterflies. Peter apologised: his internet had been off-line. He told me there were no firm commitments in place with any documentary makers. He gave me an idea of what would happen with the ship before a shipping-line could be booked. It would need to be jacked up and weighed, and it would be April before anything further would be known. Even worse, there was no guarantee that the shipping-line would be willing or capable of taking fee-paying passengers. Peter attached an image of a bright-yellow heavy-lift ship on the high seas to his email. If he intended that to put me off my quest, he failed.

I had been feasting on information about *City of Adelaide* on the CSCOAL website that Peter managed, when I came across the Donations Page. People from all over the world had sent money to help recover the ship back to Adelaide, South Australia. Some donated birthday present money, another gave a portion of proceeds from the sale of a motorbike. From several dollars to even thousands, each amount was precious. The huge affection and support that people felt for the ship came across in many comments from people who had known her in Glasgow when she was the clubhouse for the Royal Naval Volunteer Reserve moored up on the Clyde, and from people in Australia whose ancestors had travelled out on the ship, or similar ships. Relief that the ship was to be saved from deconstruction was evident. I trawled through the comments and when I saw a graduate of Adelaide University looking for paid work in research/writing/archiving I felt panic. What if that person approached CSCOAL and they were given the task of what I planned to do – voyage with *City of Adelaide* when she finally left Scotland, and accompany her all the way to Adelaide. My finger spun the wheel on the computer mouse, and I scrolled down the pages. I was agitated. Then I saw this –

Image of vessel from Peter Roberts

Ruth.Currie *United Kingdom* *Glasgow Scotland*	*I am so pleased that the City of Adelaide is being rescued from its sorry state. I am a great granddaughter of Sarah Bray mentioned on this web site and have known about and watched the ship's sad decline all my life. As Scotland couldn't raise the money to restore her I am so glad she is going back to Adelaide, where she is of huge importance.*

I read, and read again this lady, Ruth Currie's comments. Her great-grandmother had a connection with *City of Adelaide.* A rush of blood flooded my brain. I saw she lived in Glasgow...Glasgow! This lady lived just 70 miles away from me! I had to get in touch with her. Something inside told me it was vital that I meet Ruth Currie. I had to find out all I could about her great-grandmother. I immediately emailed Peter Roberts on 31 January 2012 and asked him if he could track Ruth Currie down and give her my contact information. I could not wait. I looked up an on-line telephone directory and made a list of all the Ruth Curries that came up. I began dialling each one with the Glasgow pre-fix – 0141. There was no reply from the first one. The second one was not the Ruth Currie I was looking for. The third one drew another blank. By this time I was nervous. I did not want to be disappointed again. I got up from my desk and made myself a cup of coffee. I came back to my room and dialled. A female voice answered. *Yes,* I thought to myself, and was about to speak when she screamed, 'Go away' in my ear and slammed the handset down. Surely this could not be her, I prayed. I had exhausted my list. All I could do now was wait, wait until I heard from Peter.

The next day I received Peter's response, *'Sorry but we do not have a Ruth Currie on our website'.* I was crestfallen. I could not accept she had just disappeared into thin air. I repeated the request in an email on 7 February, stating Ruth had been a donor. I heard nothing back, and gave up hope. Then, out of the blue on 15 March I was sent a copy of an email Peter had sent to Ruth Currie at 2.36 am on 16 March (time slip of Adelaide, Australia being 10½ hours ahead of Greenwich Mean Time at this time of year). I was ecstatic. He had passed my information on to her. Next morning Ruth emailed me, giving me her phone number and address. She also echoed my own thoughts about *City of Adelaide*'s destiny...'I am sorry Scotland could not raise the money to restore the ship but she is really much more relevant to South Australia'.

I emailed Peter Roberts:

'You are a star! Ruth Currie and I are in touch! Thanks for all your efforts.'

Part Two
IRVINE

'From the moment I discovered Sarah Ann Bray, I was fascinated. This young woman had voyaged to the other side of the world on 'City of Adelaide' when she was twenty years old. I felt my cheeks flush with the zing of excitement, and blood flooded my brain.'

CHAPTER FOUR

TRAIN TICKET TO IRVINE

I HAD NEVER seen *City of Adelaide* in the flesh. All I had seen of her was that flyer at Greenock that had started this whole thing off, and computer images of her forlorn self on that desolate slipway in Irvine. I had to do something about this. I felt her pull. She was beginning to dominate every thought in my head from the moment I awoke till the moment I fell asleep. I had stayed overnight with my eldest daughter in Edinburgh on 5 March 2012. We took the bus into the city centre. I headed for Waverley Station to catch a train to Glasgow and then onwards to Irvine. I could not contain my excitement as I bought my ticket.

I was like a young lass going on her first date, high as a kite. I smiled at my reflection on the train. I bought a coffee when the trolley came round, and sipped it with satisfaction as green field after green field slipped through my line of vision. As we approached Glasgow after around fifty minutes, stylish red sandstone buildings juxta-posed with ultra-modern concrete and glass ones replaced the openness of the countryside. It was sad to see some in a state of decline, their beautiful ornate architecture submitting to roots of plants that dislodged gutters, and scratched and scraped their way into pointing that eventually let rain in. Green rivulets of moss tumbled down from roof to ground. Dampness was everywhere. When I got off the train in Glasgow Central, I went to a booth to have a passport photo taken before taking a train to Irvine. Four of me dropped out of the tube. I inspected the images. *Good enough*, I thought. I got on the train for Irvine and spotted John Fardell, a children's author/illustrator I had met in the past, so went to sit with him. He was on his way to do an author event at a school near Irvine. I was glad he had missed his earlier train due to unforeseen delays, because we had great chats that ranged from emotional trauma to Scots Language on the half-hour journey. It was good to have his company. As we approached Irvine, the huge, dark hulk of *City of Adelaide* jumped out at me. She was silhouetted against the sky from the train window. She had taken me by surprise. Just as quickly as she had come into my eyes, she fell out of them again. My heart leapt. I was impatient when we got off the train. I could not part from John soon enough, our goodbye was ethereal as I watched him disappear from the platform.

First things first. It was almost sadistic to delay going straight to *City of Adelaide*. I headed for a supermarket where I bought a pair of scissors, and had some breakfast, savouring what was to come. That morning I had received a package. It contained everything but the photograph I now had for a make-it-up-yourself identity card. I opened the package, freed the scissors from their blister pack, cut out one of the four images from the booth at Glasgow, stuck it on the card, signed it, and slipped it into the self-seal plastic wallet that had been provided. Voilà! My new identity as a *Member of the Freelance Writers Association*. I went for a pee before making my way down to the Scottish Maritime Museum. This was an impromptu journey. I had not contacted Jim Tildesley to say I was coming; by now, he was retired. I stopped at the Museum café and looked at some of the exhibits before coffee and cake; then I went out and made my way to get as close as I could to *City of Adelaide*. She languished behind a steel barrier at the back of the café at the end of a series of workmen's huts. I checked the barrier for any weaknesses, but could find none. A chap with a big bushy beard and skip cap passed me. I asked him how I could get close up to the ship. His grudged reply advised there was no access to the slipway because it did not belong to the Maritime Museum, there were forklift trucks going about and it was a hard-hat area; access was prohibited. He walked away, leaving me empty. I had locked my glazed eyes back onto *City of Adelaide* through the steel fence when I heard a car draw up.

Two men got out. They carried some sort of cooker, maybe a microwave oven, between them. They went through the gate and into the rundown porta-cabin closest to me. When they came out I asked about site access. I introduced myself and explained what I was about. The two volunteers, Ricki and Norrie, who also volunteered with the *Glenlee* in Glasgow, suggested I speak to the chap with the beard who was working on the Puffer, *Spartan*, an old Victualing Inshore Craft (VIC) similar to *Vital Spark* that had featured in the legendary television series *Parahandy*, starring Gregor Fisher. I told them I had already had a 'conversation' with him. They then suggested someone called David Mann might be in the Museum Office and offered me a lift to see if he was there. We all bundled into an old car and drove out of the café area and across the road, a distance of several metres, and got out. They ushered me upstairs. David Mann, Operations Manager was on the phone when I arrived. He gestured for me to sit down. Someone brought me a coffee, and I felt at ease. Ricki and Norrie left. We parted company like old friends.

David was very helpful. He reiterated the site access issue. The Scottish Maritime Museum did not own the land *City of Adelaide* was on. It was classed as a building site because of the work that was going on, hard hats and hi-vis jackets were a requirement. He gave me the run down on the cradle that was being built in the yard, and a rough outline of the plan. The cradle would have to take all the weight of the ship. Australian companies had donated steel for this and it was being assembled by volunteers from Scotland and Australia. David told me Mike Edwards, Co-Founder of Travelsphere Ltd established in 1977, had had ambitions for *City of Adelaide* to become a tourist attraction. He had pulled out because after he commissioned a full marine survey of the ship it was found costs to put her into a condition where she could be used by the public were prohibitive. Furthermore health and safety requirements would have meant altering her interiors significantly. This would ruin her authenticity, and he did not want this. He spent a large sum of money to provide cover to protect her top deck that it was claimed to be of the same material as the Millennium Dome in London. David spoke more about the cradle that was being constructed in the yard beside the slipway where *City of Adelaide* was, and the process that was being gone through to get her ready for her voyage to Adelaide. There had been tests and re-tests, the ship had been jacked and weighed. A barge with a 1.5 metre draught would be brought in; the weight of the ship would determine the choice of barge. *City of Adelaide* would be taken on the barge then would likely be lifted off it and be put inside a cargo ship hold. I felt a thrill run through me. She might be shrouded in plastic after fumigation. I could not imagine this. This ship was the size of a Boeing 737 airplane. David told me Richard Smith, one of the Directors of CSCOAL would be on site with *City of Adelaide* until 1 April. There would be an educational and cultural exchange with Australia over the next three years as part of the Scottish Government's financial assistance in the removal of *City of Adelaide* from Irvine to Adelaide, South Australia. David Mann indicated that Ricki, one of the volunteers, was coming round to the realisation that *City of Adelaide* is going home. He asked me how I felt. I responded that I was delighted and relieved she was not to be demolished, and happy she was going to Adelaide where her history and future well-being are important, and she will be cherished. He knew I was serious about my interest when I mentioned Peter Roberts' and Fiona Hyslop's involvement in this ambitious project. David said the barge would be on standby for the spring tides to float the ship off on. I spent about half an hour with him before he pointed me in the direction of where I could best view *City of Adelaide.* I asked if I could keep in touch with him by email to be kept informed of progress. We exchanged cards and shook hands.

I went in the direction David had pointed me in and got a fabulous perspective of the huge hull of *City of Adelaide.* David had said she is in better condition than *Cutty Sark,* although the fabric of her is not maintained. I was overwhelmed by the size of her. She was huge. She was like an enormous mussel shell turned up towards the sky. I felt a thrill run through me that I was so close to her, I drank in her lines, I shed tears at the state of her, felt mysteriously drawn to her. She looked so forlorn with bits of black plastic stuck on her hull that blew in the wind like rags on a scarecrow. I began taking photos with the disposable camera I had bought earlier from the supermarket, having forgotten my digital camera in the haste of this impromptu adventure. To me *City of Adelaide* was simply glorious.

I was flabbergasted when a figure appeared at a window, not a porthole, in the ship's hull. He pushed something through the window. I was astonished to see a Red Ensign flag unfurl before my eyes. I waved in acknowledgement and the mysterious person disappeared. I mulled over the ship, imagined her in her glorious heyday. The figure appeared again. He shouted a mobile phone number to me and asked me to send a message to it to say he was low on mobile phone battery. He told me his name is Peter Maddison, he is an elected representative for Sunderland. He told me he was occupying the ship in protest at her going to Australia. He is Chairman of a group known as *Sunderland City of Adelaide Recovery Foundation* (SCARF). He told me the group wanted to recover the ship to Sunderland, where she had been built in 1864. He said it was cold and damp inside the ship, but he is happy. He asked my name and where I had come from. I explained my connection with *City of Adelaide*, and where Dunbar is located. I suggested he get a PO Box set up because he said he was in this for the long haul. We laughed. I saw nothing of the dilapidated state of *City of Adelaide* as I photographed her. She is of remarkable beauty and stature. I imagined her masts clad in full sail, and her slice her way over the waves with settlers for South Australia on board.

Darkness was falling; with reluctance I turned my back on the ship. It was time to go. My feet dragged me back to the train station, wrenched me away from this ship that had captured my heart and soul.

I missed the first train back to Glasgow Central because I stopped to take a photo of the ornate wrought-iron external gates leading to Platform 1. Just like John Fardell earlier that day, I saw the back of the train disappear like a mirage. I was excited, elated and on the way home in slight disbelief at my luck, but very aware that *going for it* was definitely a philosophy to hold. I felt this ship was becoming my destiny. I knew something special was happening between us. I drew a picture in my notebook of me with a big banana smile. I was famished by the time I got to Edinburgh. Instead of going straight home I went to a Chinese buffet near Waverley Station and stuffed myself with a good couple of plates of food, a small plate of fresh fruit and some wobbly jelly stuff in flavours of mango, coconut and coffee. It was good to take the extra time to indulge myself and reflect on the events of this fantastic day before I headed back to the reality that was home.

CHAPTER FIVE

AN IMPROMTU TRIP TO SUNDERLAND

I WAS AT home when I phoned Peter Maddison on 13 March. My call was diverted. I spoke to someone called Kenny who told me how he helps Peter on board *City of Adelaide*. He swaps phones and charges them up for Peter. He gave me another number. When I dialled it, Peter answered. He was on his third cup of coffee when he told me how lucky he was. 'It is a very happy, wonderful experience,' he said. I felt a pang of envy. He was awestruck by 'this amazing thing'. He mentioned his friend who comes by cover of darkness and keeps him in supplies of food, water and other essentials. I said I was jealous of him being on the ship. He invited me to bring a sleeping bag and join him. I laughed, and said I would not mind. He said it was not that difficult to get on board. He said he hoped to occupy the ship till 31 March 2012, and asked me to keep this confidential. This date was the deadline for removal of the ship from the slipway onto a barge. He said he had had both positive and negative reactions from people to his being on board. He outlined the preferred bidder process and the criteria Australia would have to meet in order for *City of Adelaide* to be accepted into their country. I was puzzled as to why he was occupying the ship at this stage. It was clear she had been given to CSCOAL, the group of South Australians and would soon be heading 'down under'. Peter told me he is an ex-merchant seaman, and an ex-councillor for Sunderland City. He said *City of Adelaide* is in remarkable condition for her almost one hundred and fifty years of age. He told me there was to be a meeting about the ship in Sunderland the next evening. I said I would try and attend this. I needed to glean every morsel of information I possibly could about the ship, her history, and current situation. I felt a swell of empathy for this group, but suggested to Peter that the deal was done and dusted. He asked me why I thought this. I replied it seemed the Australian group had a strong case and a great deal of support, and that *City of Adelaide* had been specifically built to take migrants to South Australia in 1864. I suggested as a second choice he might consider town twinning with Adelaide, South Australia. He said he already had plans to have a fund to bring two youngsters from Australia to Sunderland to train as shipwrights. He gave me the phone number of someone who was to chair the meeting the following night and outlined his background. I said again I would try and go. I had no idea how long the journey would take, but I felt the drive to attend the meeting to find out what was going on, why this group from Sunderland was continuing to fight to have her for their City against all the odds.

Despite feeling fluey and having to attend a dental appointment I was determined to go to the evening meeting in Sunderland. Alan tried to reason with me, but I was adamant. I booked my rail travel to Sunderland, a round-trip of over two hundred miles. Alan had not yet grasped how important *City of Adelaide* was becoming to me. She was filling a hole in my life I did not know was there. I drove to Berwick station and was soon on the train swishing south as a spectacular, bright orange ball bounced the day below the horizon. The Metro from Newcastle brought me close to the meeting place, and I found it with ease. Word had gone round that I had come a long way to be at this meeting, and their welcome was warm. This turned out to be

SCARF's second open meeting. The first one had been held in 2007 in the aftermath of the fire on board *Cutty Sark*. The significance and importance of preserving *City of Adelaide* as the oldest surviving composite clipper ship in the world, built in Sunderland, had been breathed new life by this tragic incident. I found out that this second meeting had been called in the wake of the announcement in a letter to Fiona Hyslop from John Hill, Minister for Culture in the South Australia Parliament that stated the recovery of *City of Adelaide* was a private venture, there could be no partnership with the South Australian Government, there would be no public money available to help bridge the Aus$2million/£1.25million funding gap for shipping *City of Adelaide* to Australia now or in the future. They already had several historic vessels that merited funding. I could feel the mood of the meeting lift. Here was the prospect that if CSCOAL were denied financial assistance with funding the transportation of *City of Adelaide* to South Australia, then there was a strong chance Sunderland might win her after all. There were also further 'significant issues' that needed to be resolved before the Australian plan could be realised, and guarantees would be sought from CSCOAL that they had sufficient funds to restore *City of Adelaide* before she was given a permanent berth in Port Adelaide. CSCOAL's aim was to preserve the hull, not restore it. I felt the excitement in the room and was swept along with their renewed hope that they might get the ship. It seemed an impossible task that CSCOAL would have to meet a thirteen-point list of conditions drawn up by National Historic Ships before the ship would be allowed to leave the United Kingdom. Ben Borland, Deputy Editor (Politics) of the *Scottish Sunday Express* at the time, corroborated this news story that was to appear in the October 2011 issue of *Classic Boat* magazine. The newspaper suggested Scotland may have to foot the bill for *City of Adelaide*'s removal to Australia, but it was more likely a renewed effort would be made to find a new, permanent home for her in the United Kingdom. Most comments on this article on the internet supported the return of *City of Adelaide* to Sunderland.

So SCARF had a second bite at the cherry. There was a presentation where various points were made as to why SCARF should fight to get the clipper ship for Sunderland, such as: she would inspire young people to learn trades and get apprenticeships, she was built in the town, the town needed work not a tourist attraction, she was the crown jewel of the merchant fleet, she is in better condition than *Cutty Sark*, even before the fire. The reason for her great condition was because she was in the Northern Hemisphere. Worry spread through the room that if *City of Adelaide* went to the Southern Hemisphere, the atmosphere would cause the natural oils to be sucked out of her, and she would warp. I was fascinated to learn more of her history, of her being built in William Pile, Hay & Co's shipyard, and that there is even a bust dedicated to him in Sunderland Museum & Winter Gardens reflecting the high esteem he was held in. Discussion took place on the importance of the ship, her design, her cargo, her Scottish Captain, David Bruce. I listened as plans were made to publicise *City of Adelaide* and the desire to bring her back for Sunderland that was once the greatest shipbuilding city in the world, with the necessary population to make it so.

Some of the reasons put forward to keep *City of Adelaide* in Sunderland were that it was the preservation of an important symbol for the city, it would provide industry, it represented a link between Britain and the colonies, it is a valuable antique. Opportunities would present, such as work for young people, teacher training, maritime construction, history, social, adventure, a conference centre. Actor Steven Langley could see opportunities for performances of music, theatre, dance, light shows and so on. There would be great acoustics because of the teak wood. It would be a terrific venue, theatre space, perhaps with a restaurant on the mid-deck. He felt it would provide a platform to restore civic pride to Sunderland.

I learned more about the history of *City of Adelaide* as her 'Seven Ages' were outlined:

- her life on the high seas as a passenger ship with Devitt and Moore between 1864 and 1887, homeport: London
- her life as a cargo ship carrying coal around the British coast (1887-1888) and cargo ship carrying timber from 1888 to 1893, homeports: Dover and Belfast respectively
- her life as an isolation hospital ship after she was de-rigged, from 1893 to 1922, homeport: Southampton
- her life after being bought by the Admiralty, renamed HMS *Carrick* to avoid confusion with the newly commissioned HMAS *City of Adelaide*, and used as a training ship between 1922 and 1948, based: Scotland
- her life with the RNVR (Royal Naval Volunteer Reserve), after being donated by the Royal Navy for use as their Club's headquarters, from 1948 to 1989, homeport: River Clyde, Glasgow
- her life with the Clyde Ship Trust from 1990 to 1992, under whose watch she sank in Princes Dock, Glasgow
- her current life with the Scottish Maritime Museum from 1992.

The original plan as published in the 'Third Annual Report on the Sanitary Condition of the Port of Southampton, 1894'.

Further discussion brought forward the 1999 Map of Britain that marked places worthy of visit by people from overseas. *City of Adelaide* would be to Sunderland what the Eiffel Tower is to Paris. The *Trincomalee* had not been built in Hartlepool, yet she had put that town on the map. Martin O'Neill, Business Perspective Small Retailer of the Year, thought *City of Adelaide* would be the catalyst to start off a tourist industry with spin-off for souvenirs and so on that could provide work for local people. Mention was made of *City of Adelaide*'s condition inside. There were pigeon carcasses, eggs, droppings, every crevice and crack was full of micro-organisms. The Australians had said they could make the ship acceptable to meet stringent restrictions for import to Australia, but one member present could not see how this could happen without destroying the ship. Expressions of fear were heard of her preservation in private hands. Another member pointed out the Australians had a big funding gap. People were asking what SCARF was doing. The Australians had had the steel for the cradle donated, they had used charitable laws to zero out expenditure. One member in the room had been following the ship for five years, another for twelve. I heard assurances had been given that the ship would come to Sunderland. Sunderland was gathering momentum with a petition they had raised amongst local people that had grown from 500 to over 2000 in three days. If they could reach 100,000 signatories, the matter would have to be debated in Parliament. There were pledges of over £200,000 from private and commercial sources they would start to collect as soon as the green light was given by Historic Scotland that *City of Adelaide* would be going to Sunderland. They had the promise of a berth in the South Docks for two years, with a promise of future permanent accommodation on the River Wear. The Australians on the other hand had no money, they had identified a site for the ship twelve miles from the sea that only real enthusiasts would visit, and they had no support from the Government of South Australia. It was not sustainable.

Discussion took place over the financial burdens the presence of *City of Adelaide* at the Scottish Maritime Museum caused. There had been a dilemma. The Scottish Maritime Museum had rescued *City of Adelaide* in 1992 after she had sunk in Princes Dock, Glasgow the previous year. She was towed down the River Clyde to Irvine. In 1993 the museum began to preserve and restore the ship. After Scotland gained Devolution in May 1999 previous United Kingdom funding for the clipper was stopped. A funding application for another major project by the Scottish Maritime Museum to the Heritage Lottery Fund was rejected. This had the knock-on effect that other organisations supporting the preservation and restoration of *City of Adelaide* reduced their funding. The Scottish Executive responded to an appeal by the Museum for support. This was granted, but with a recommendation that *City of Adelaide* be sold, and a condition that no government funds would be spent on her. Further to this, Ayrshire Metals, the owners of the slipway where *City of Adelaide* languished, had received an agreed peppercorn rent of £1 a year from the Scottish Maritime Museum. When Ayrshire Metals gave notice to quit the slipway in April 1999, the agreement in the contract that a £50,000 penalty per annum would have to be paid if the Museum was not able to vacate the slipway was triggered. Facing these demands and being unable to find a buyer for the ship, the Museum applied to North Ayrshire Council for listed building consent to deconstruct the ship. She would have to be got rid of or broken up. This produced an outcry from governments and maritime heritage organisations around the world. The Museum's application was refused by the Council. It was said that £500,000 had been pledged from National Historic Ships UK for the deconstruction of *City of Adelaide* to anyone who applied for the money. The Australians still needed an export license, the fourth deadline extension was looming. SCARF had stood back after Peter Maddison boarded the ship. They felt his occupation of her would secure her for Sunderland. Supporters would be there to welcome him off the ship on 31 March 2012. The protest was not over. A production crew that had received an offer from the BBC for a documentary would be present filming the occasion. A covert reconnoitre had been carried out to find a gap in the fence that would provide access to the ship because a sustained legal battle over the slipway was going on *sub-judice*.

Several questions were asked by those present in regard to what was being done to get the public involved in bringing the ship back to Sunderland. Discussion took place over the bidding processes on each side, and how these had been looked at by Sir Neil Cossons, former Director of Greenwich Maritime Museum and former Chairman of English Heritage. There was further talk of how *City of Adelaide* could be kept on a dry dock barge anywhere on the River Wear; that it would take two years for restoration work to stabilise the steel from inside out, and that if she was in Sunderland she would surely attract visitors and boost numbers to other tourist attractions in the City.

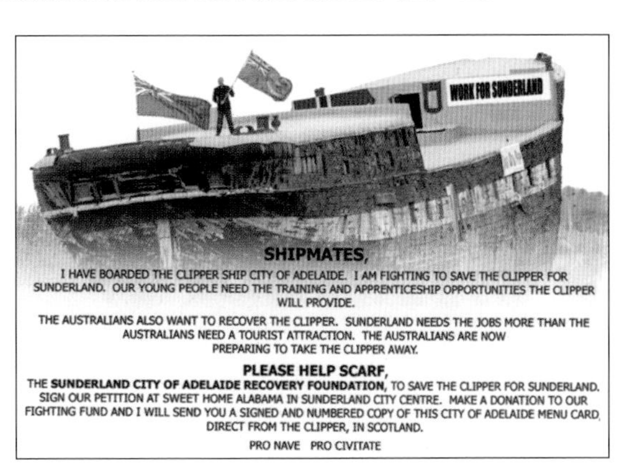

After the meeting I took my leave of the company. They were the lovely people Peter Maddison had said they would be. I left with leaflets on the *Trincomalee* and some *City of Adelaide* material. On my way back home the Metro was delayed between Sunderland and Newcastle due to a power failure on the tracks. I was in danger of missing the last train home. The driver tuned in to my panic and received clearance to press on. I arrived in Newcastle to find Platform 3 busy with people. My train north was three minutes late.

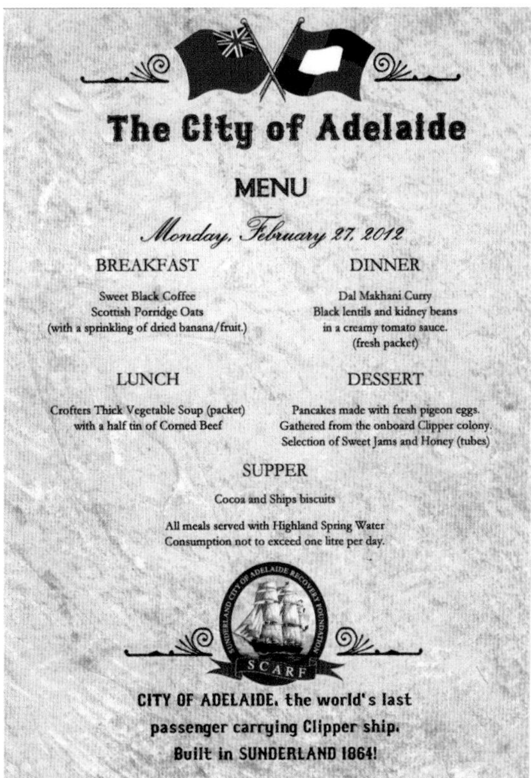

When I got home I searched for further information on the decision by the Scottish Government that CSCOAL had become the preferred bidder for *City of Adelaide*. I found that Historic Scotland had announced in a Press Release on 28 August 2010 that Fiona Hyslop, Minister for Culture and External Affairs had made a decision that might at last secure the future of SV *Carrick*. She had arranged an appraisal of options available for the ship's future by real estate advisers DTZ. One was removal to Sunderland; two, removal to Adelaide, South Australia; three was staying in Scotland at a different location, and four was managed deconstruction with significant parts of the ship being retained at the Scottish Maritime Museum. DTZ concluded the only viable organisation with the financial capacity and necessary engineering expertise to manage the project was CSCOAL. There was massive support for the ship's return in South Australia from individuals, businesses, community organisations, and the Government as well as the large Scottish community. CSCOAL had paid for the Australian Quarantine Inspection Service to inspect the ship in Irvine late in 2011. I contacted Fiona Hyslop in connection with *City of Adelaide* and was referred to Historic Scotland. A meeting was arranged with an official but unfortunately at the last minute he changed the venue from Edinburgh to Glasgow and I could not make it. The meeting was never re-arranged.

So many thoughts butted into my drowsing that night it took ages for me to fall asleep. At least now I understood the background to *City of Adelaide*'s sorry situation. At least now I had the answers as to why her death warrant had been signed. But now I was torn. Both groups so strongly wanted *City of Adelaide*. I wanted her to go to Sunderland for all the aspirations and passion Peter Maddison and SCARF had. I wanted her to go to Adelaide because she had been built in 1864 specifically to carry people there who wanted to have a different, improved life building the new State of South Australia. I felt the claimed quarter of a million descendants from people who voyaged on her deserved their heritage. I felt more and more that *City of Adelaide* belonged in the place she had sailed to twenty-three times. If the ship had not been commissioned in 1864 for this purpose, she would not have been built. The determination of CSCOAL to bring back the ship to Adelaide and the amount of thorough, comprehensive research and planning that existed on their website could not fail to impress.

Something pervaded my sleep that night. I woke up next morning with a strong sense that my journey with *City of Adelaide* was only just beginning.

MEETING RUTH CURRIE

The Diary of the Maiden Voyage of *City of Adelaide* kept by Sarah Ann Bray – 12 August to 7 November 1864

I RECEIVED A phone call from Ruth Currie early on Saturday morning, 17 March 2012. My heart began to pound and my mouth went dry. My ears pricked up and I felt my eyes blur. Ruth said she was delighted to learn of my interest in her ancestor, Sarah Ann Bray. I was bowled over by her invitation to lunch. I set out for Glasgow with my cartwheeling stomach to meet Ruth the following Tuesday, taking an early morning train. I recognised her right away as she stepped out from her car. 'I'll be the one with her hair in a bun,' she had laughed in her phone call. We hugged, stepped back and looked hard at each other before we got into the car and drove through endless, unfamiliar streets. We chatted in excitement until we got to her tenement. The climb to the top was a challenge, and I wondered how she coped with the stairs and shopping she would inevitably have to carry up them. From the stairwell window the rooftop view to the River Clyde and beyond stunned me. Church spires prodded the whole sky like umbrella points puncturing holes for frequent west coast rain to dribble through. Ruth invited me in. She introduced me to her husband Andrew, and their stripy cat, Pushkin. We had a light lunch of homemade soup, a selection of cheeses, and tasty morsels to put on bread, crackers and oatcakes. Ruth told me Andrew had been on board *City of Adelaide* when she was the Royal Naval Volunteer Reserve clubhouse in Glasgow, and her other name, *Carrick*, means 'Rock' in Scots. She and Andrew had met there socially, they recalled their dances on the sloped decks: one minute her husband was higher than her, the next she looked over the top of him. We talked about how ghastly it must have been if you did not have a cabin on board *City of Adelaide*. As a Third Rate passenger you would be in 'Steerage', even possibly, she thought, amongst the animals that were carried on board for food, e.g., cows for milk, hens for eggs and meat, and so on – and all that accompanied their presence. It could not have been very pleasant. Ruth said she has been revitalised into sorting out her family archives, and after we had eaten she took me to a room where she had laid out a number of items. I floated on air at the feast of papers and photographs before me, amongst an array of brown furniture. I wondered if any of this had been inherited from her great-grandmother. I shook myself out as a shiver ran through me. I wanted to find out about Ruth's family, whether there were descendants in Australia. Did she have any information that could help me with Sarah's voice? She pulled out a lovely group photo of her great-grandmother and great-grandfather, their three daughters and two sons, and a little pug dog, taken in a studio. It was a calotype image in many shades of grey. I could see the strong family resemblance in Ruth. As I pored over the seven handsome faces in the photograph, Ruth told me normal practice was for subjects to have supports to hold them steady from the back whilst the image was taken because it took so long. My eyes searched the photograph, took in the Victorian dresses in silks and taffeta, some velvet and serge, perhaps. Sarah was seated to the right of the photograph, the little pug at the hem of her dress. I stared at her face and felt I knew her. I wished I could slip into the scene. I wished I could sit opposite Sarah at the occasional table and sip tea with her poured from the china teapot on the tray. I wished I could ask her about her voyage on *City of Adelaide*: what it was like on board; how long the journey took; was she comfortable? Was she ever cold? Was it ever too hot? What was the weather like? Did she see any whales? What wild sea life did she see? What route did they take – did they round Cape Horn or did they go round the toe of Africa, via The Cape of Good Hope? I was bursting to have answers. I was bursting to know how she coped with that maiden voyage in 1864. I could almost smell the brand new ship, the freshly-hewn wood, tar, oils, leather, ropes, animals, cooking aromas. I wanted to be Sarah.

Ruth's voice broke into my reverie. She told me none of the three daughters married. Sarah's father Tom, born in 1815 was trained as a cordwainer, a maker of shoes. He married Sarah Pink in 1838. This qualified them for assisted passage to emigrate to South Australia later that year to find a better life, one that would sever them from their known lives. Ruth reckoned he went into property speculation as he had become so wealthy he could travel back and forth to Great Britain, and his daughters Sarah and Blanche went to school in Kensington. Ruth gave me a family history booklet compiled by Sarah's great-grandson. There were further images of Sarah and her family in it. I felt thrilled to see her as a precocious young woman, and was struck by her elegance and obvious affluence. Ruth talked about her great-grandfather who was depicted in an image taken at Greenock, with him amongst other traders gathered round a mound of sugar.

Then she pulled out a wad of A4 paper. She unfolded it calmly, teased me as she peeled out each page. She pushed the document towards me. I did not know what it was, yet I saw my hands quiver. Ruth purred, '...and this is a copy of Sarah's diary from the 1864 voyage...you may borrow it if you like.'

My head swirled.

I felt an urge to escape the flat before Ruth could change her mind.

DESCRIPTIVE ORDER FOR BOOKSELLER.

Letts's Diary,

No. 8.

6s. 6d.

IRVINE AGAIN

Up Close and Personal with *City of Adelaide*

ARMED WITH THE copy of Sarah's diary and all the other family documents Ruth lent me, we drove to Central Station. I got out of her car and thanked her very much for the lovely day, and for the treasures I carried. Once inside the station I scanned the *Departures* board to find the platform number for the train to Irvine. I raced across the station and dug deep for my ticket, but it was too late. I was annoyed to see the rear of the train disappear down the track, but there was another one in half an hour. I checked my mobile phone for messages. Nothing. I had only contacted David Mann before I left home to let him know that I would be in Irvine that afternoon, so unsurprisingly there was no response to the email or the text I had sent him. As I waited for the next train, I took out Sarah's diary. It was a photocopy of a photocopy and some parts were barely legible as staccato ink scrawled in nevertheless beautiful handwriting across the many pages. I could not believe Ruth had loaned me it along with the background genealogy prepared by her great-uncle. From the moment I discovered Sarah Ann Bray, I was fascinated. This young woman had voyaged to the other side of the world on *City of Adelaide* when she was twenty years old. I felt my cheeks flush with the zing of excitement, and blood flooded my brain.

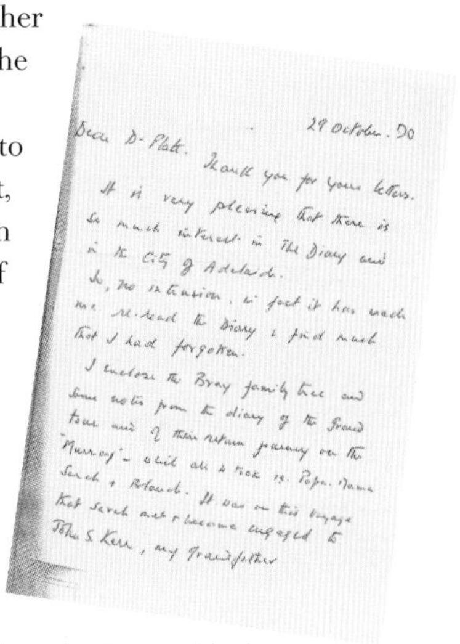
29 October. 90
Dear D-Platt. Thank you for your letters.
It is very pleasing that there is so much interest in the Diary and in the City of Adelaide.
It, no intrusion, in fact it has made me re-read the Diary & find much that I had forgotten.
I enclose the Bray family tree and some notes from the diary of the Grand tour and of their return journey on the "Murray" – which all took [illegible]. Papa. Mama Sarah & Blanch. It was on this voyage that Sarah met & became engaged to John S Kerr, my Grandfather

On arrival in Irvine, I phoned David Mann. I detected an unfamiliar coolness in his voice as he agreed to meet me. I knew he knew I had met Peter Maddison on my previous visit, and wondered whether he thought I had a 'Sunderland agenda'. I planned to see *City of Adelaide* after meeting him, and this meant a possible further encounter with Peter Maddison. When I met David my suspicion was confirmed. I reassured him, reiterated the basis of my interest in *City of Adelaide* was purely research for the book I was writing about her. He relaxed, and updated me on the cradle that was being assembled in the yard from steel donated by several South Australian engineering firms that would hold the ship steady in transit. It was built on the principle of an egg box holding fragile eggs. It was to be stress-tested the next day and assembly should begin on the following Monday, when Fiona Hyslop would be in attendance. David said there was no way *City of Adelaide* would be off the slipway by 31 March 2012. The hull and cradle had to be weighed, the merchant ship that would take her to Australia had yet to be identified, and a whole lot of other details needed to be organised. I recalled the image of the bright-yellow heavy-lift ship Peter Roberts had sent me, and felt a thrill I could not share with David. I asked him why the ship had been left all this time. He explained she needed £5,000,000 spent on her, and this was not forthcoming from the Scottish Government. I was baffled. Why would you not want to preserve this very special vessel?

Afterwards I went round to behind the flats where the best view of *City of Adelaide* was. As soon as I arrived Peter Maddison was at a window in the hull of *City of Adelaide*. He called over, 'Is that you Rita?' I said, 'Yes,' and phoned him. He told me the Australian engineer and three workers, young men, who were stood around the pieces of steel for the cradle that was being assembled to support the hull of *City of Adelaide*, would be leaving soon: daylight was fading. Peter suggested that after they were gone I should come over to see the ship close up, from the port side. He spoke from the starboard. I bottled it, my heart thumped at the thought. But I knew I could not resist this chance. It would mean a climb over a low wall that had a greater drop on the other side. I would have to cross the yard where the sections of steel were being assembled, then squeeze through the gap between a steel mesh barrier and a high wall. I explained to Peter I needed to remain neutral for the sake of my book and aspirations. He encouraged me to go for a wander. He would phone me when the four men went away for the day. I walked away, looked at the old boats littered around the harbour-side that also longed for tender loving care. I marvelled at the Bridge of Scottish Invention that was split in the middle. There was no way you could cross this bridge and get to the curious mound on the other side on the Ardeer Peninsula that was *The Big Idea* museum built on the site of Alfred Nobel's dynamite factory. Both these constructions were opened in April 2000, at a cost of £14 million. Both failed to attract sufficient visitor numbers and were closed just three years later. Would that some of that money had been spent on *City of Adelaide*! I did not know then the significance of the gap in the middle of the Bridge of Scottish Invention that remains open until closed by operating a chain drive running it on rollers mounted on piers mid-river, and on rails on the north bank. When closed the movable span docks with the fixed span on the harbour-side.

Just before 5 pm as the street lights began to glow above me, Peter called. I was to meet him at the boundary wall of the yard. My heart raced. My hands would run over *City of Adelaide*. I could caress her. I would press my nose into her planks and smell her, smell where she had been since she was built. I would stand in her shadow. I would defy the Scottish Maritime Museum's strict Health and Safety rules. They had said there was no way I could get up close to the ship. I was prepared to risk everything for this chance. This ship and I were becoming more and more entangled.

Peter was waiting at the steel barrier. When I arrived he skulked across the yard and I climbed onto and sat on the wall. I jumped, and he steadied me as I landed where brand new steel from Australia rubbed shoulders with rusty old boilers and bits of engine, broken concrete, scrub grass. We ran across the yard to the break in the barrier and squeezed through. It reminded me of ringing doorbells and running away

as a child. Then I was with her at last! She towered above me on slabs of wood that kept her off the ground, where the steel rails of the slipway that had dragged her to dry-dock from the element she loved rusted in puddles steeped in green sludge, mud and rotted wood. I felt so very small beneath this giantess. She made me feel so very safe. I could feel her warm embrace. I could hear her breath. I gulped it down and with it, her soul. I felt dragged into the past. I lost myself within her. I could feel her age. I could feel her life. I was carried away to the sounds of William Pile & Hay's shipyard, felt every blow from the hammers of musclebound, sweaty men. My ears filled with the clank and clamour of iron on iron as rivets were buried into ribs. Sadness misted my eyes at the terrible state this ship was in. Some of her timbers looked rotted and slimy from the Atlantic wind's phlegm. Some of her planking had lifted away from the hull. There was a mysterious metal plate fixed to it. I wondered whether it was a repair to a holing. Once, the gleam of copper dressed her below her fine water line to keep her sleek and free from sea worm infestation, barnacles and weed from the sea, to keep her fast and clean to cut through whatever King Neptune threw at her. Now it was dull, peeling off and diseased with verdigris. The band of white paint going all the way round her hull at the window line was faded and dirty, and whole areas of timber had lost any remnants of the smart, black paint she was once covered in. Her rudder was missing. Some of her caulking dangled from between the planks where once it was hemp, looped and tapped solid with a blade into the gaps so tight daylight could not squeeze through. Tar was then used to seal the hemp in and make the whole hull and decks watertight. She was undernourished, forlorn. I pressed my cheek against her and stroked myself back one hundred and forty-eight years in time. Here was *City of Adelaide*, this magnificent lady, this pride of William Pile, of Devitt and Moore, of the two Harrold Brothers and Henry Martin who were quarter-owners with Captain David Bruce, who commissioned her build. Here was the clipper ship whose belly had been filled with migrants from Northern Europe and Britain who would sculpt the new State of South Australia with their skills as builders, shoemakers, childminders, bankers, lawmakers, miners, educators, nurses, joiners, cabinet-makers, doctors, dressmakers, pharmacists, milliners. The list was comprehensive. Everyone, everything was needed to make the new State thrive. It would be the only State in Australia that was not built on the misery of blood, sweat, tears of convicts, petty criminals and the often undeserved misfortune of poor people transported for minor offences from Britain. I thought of all those people and animals that had travelled in her from London and Plymouth to Adelaide. I thought of those she had kept safe as much as was in her power, that no one lost their life through anything she had caused. I thought of the copper, the wheat, the wool she had brought back to the United Kingdom. I thought of how much coal she had carried, and in doing so, how she had inadvertently facilitated the demise of herself and fellow sailing ships as steam became more and more popular. Those ships did not rely on the vagaries of winds and seas. They had in-built power that brought a steadiness that enabled scheduling and forward planning of voyages for seafarers, cargo pick-ups and deliveries. I thought of *City of Adelaide* crossing the Atlantic, taking people to Canada and back again as a by-product of her going there to bring timber to the United Kingdom to fill the gap there. I thought of her as an isolation hospital for people with infectious diseases moored off Southampton, where she had windows cut into her hull for ventilation, and had her masts, rigging and figurehead stripped away before she was bought by the Admiralty and taken to Greenock in the west of Scotland. There she had 20mm Oerlikon cannons fitted to her decks for sailors to train as gunners. She would have been broken up after her war service had it not been for the group of men who saved her to be used as a floating clubhouse for the Royal Naval Volunteer Reserve in Glasgow, Scotland.

I agonised over the two floodings she had suffered, and her final sinking in Princes Dock, Glasgow in 1991. This ship was a *people's ship*. This ship had a history far more interesting and important than *Cutty Sark*. This ship was of a pioneering design not yet accepted by Lloyds Register at the time of her build in 1864, a design adopted for *Cutty Sark* five years later. This ship had been absolutely paramount and fundamental in populating and advancing the State of South Australia. Yet here she was, being treated like an outcast, something disgraced, something despised. It was pitiful. She had been undergoing preservation. Why had the funding for this ceased? It had to be more than because responsibility for her had been devolved to the Scottish Government.

Clyde Ship Trust 1990-92.

CHAPTER EIGHT

INSIDE THE BELLY OF *CITY OF ADELAIDE*

I BEGAN TAKING photographs and listening to Peter Maddison. When he received a phone call, he walked away from me to the stern of the ship. He looked like a fly in the shadow of an eagle, the ship was so long and vast. When he came back he gave me three verdigrised nails that had pinned Muntz Metal (copper/zinc brass) sheets, to the oak and elm wood, from the waterline of the ship to the keel to ensure sleek, efficient clipping of the waves, as in the days of the tea clipper races. I was ecstatic. I felt a thrill run through me, and tucked them into my purse for safety. I noticed an aluminium ladder propped up and tied against *City of Adelaide*'s hull that fed into a window in the ship's side. I asked Peter about it. I asked him if there was a chance for me to climb up that ladder and go on board. My fingers curled and pressed my nails hard into my palms as I waited for his response. He looked me up and down. I thought he was a bit cheeky, or maybe he thought I was a bit cheeky. The penny dropped. I realised I was being sized up. He asked me if my legs were flexible. 'Last time I used them they were,' I smiled. He explained going on board would mean a climb to the top of the ladder where I would need to squeeze myself in through the window in the hull that looked like a postage stamp from where we stood. Like Jack facing the prospect of climbing the beanstalk, I knew that all danger must be put to the back of my mind. I would never get this chance again. This was my golden goose moment. I would climb that ladder and get inside this ship that had become my obsession, come hell or high-water. Peter sensed there was no point in argument. I was beyond reason. He went up the ladder and came back down. There were some people on board. He had mentioned them earlier. He had gone up the ladder to ask them to make sure I would land safely once I passed through the window.

I began the climb while Peter remained on the ground to steady the ladder. At the top I followed his instructions: *hold onto the frame, put your left leg through the window first, straddle the window opening, slide over.* Then I reached for and grabbed with my left hand a strong secure rope that hung on the inside of the ship. I dropped my left shoulder, pulled my head through and steadied myself against the opening with the other hand. I was overwhelmed as I felt with my left foot to find a secure hold on the promised iron rail. I then pushed up and twisted my body till I could drag my right leg through the open space, and placed that foot onto the rail before moving my right hand onto the rope. There was a bit of a drop to the deck of the ship, and I manoeuvred to face the hull. I lowered myself towards the planks of the 'tween deck. I felt a rush of blood. My spine tingled. A deafness filled my ears. I froze, became absorbed by the ship as I absorbed her. I felt transported to *Elsewhere.* An inexplicable sensation, a lightening round my head, a sense of relief overcame me. I could not believe what was happening.

Unfamiliar arms caught and steadied me as I landed on the deck beneath the *weather* or *top* deck, and the cargo hold.

Peter soon joined me and introduced me to the film crew that was making a documentary about the ship and his occupation in protest at *City of Adelaide* being given to South Australia and not Sunderland. I noticed candles, lit against the fading light, tents, cooking utensils, plastic bags containing food, water, normal items that make up a campsite. Peter took me on a tour of *City of Adelaide.* Flags. Flags hanging everywhere, towards her bow. Australia, Red Ensign, City of Adelaide, Devitt & Moore, Sunderland 1864 all sagged in the stagnation of this grand ship. I could not believe her size. On the outside she measured up against a Boeing 737 aeroplane, including her missing bowsprit. The vastness of her interiors echoed the large and imposing qualities of a cathedral. I thought of Jonah being inside the whale. Here were her ribs, strong iron, exposed between the decks. Here was the housing for the mast that I could barely put my arms around. We went across the 'tween deck, watching for odd bits of rotten timber. There was pigeon poo everywhere, but it was worst on the quarterdeck. Peter told me he was cleaning the ship, and pointed to wire mesh that had fallen away from openings in the hull that pigeons got through. I cringed as now and again Peter stabbed *City of Adelaide*'s timbers with a marlin spike, a metal tool used in marine ropework. 'See how sound her timbers are,' he boasted. *Not if you keep stabbing them,* I thought to myself. The bow post was immense, a solid block of oak. This too, he stabbed. I felt the thrust as if he had stuck the marlin spike

into my heart. I wrapped my arms around myself. I felt my eyes screw up, my breath draw in through clenched teeth. He showed me the locations of crew quarters and First Class accommodation where Sarah and her family stayed. I felt a thrill as I realised I was standing right where Sarah must have written her diary, the very diary I had in my bag, freshly received from her great-granddaughter, Ruth. I reeled at the realisation that something really special was happening, something spiritual.

Peter pointed out prisms set into the top deck that amplified light that filtered through to the 'tween deck to improve visibility down there. I went up some wooden steps and poked my head through the access to the Poop Deck and saw the material that David Mann had told me had been provided by Mike Edwards to protect the ship, when he had been interested in having her to turn her into a tourist attraction for his travel company. The ship was in great condition, mostly dry and quite warm, and even though paint was peeling off from the rusting iron making it look in poor condition, the iron itself seemed sound. We made our way back to where Peter and his visitors had pitched their tents. Candles flickered. It looked very cosy. The planks on the decks were quite solid in the main, and even some varnish in Second Class had endured.

The film crew asked Peter and I to have a conversation around the makeshift camp. Peter conjured up a galvanised steel pail from the darkness, brought it over and placed it upside down beside another. He put a tea towel over it and gestured for me to sit down on this poshed-up version of Oor Wullie's traditional seat. I found out this was not the first time Peter had occupied the ship. He had spent a week aboard her in 2009. The cameras went into action and we chatted about the ship in general, how Peter is so obsessed with her that his daughter is named Adelaide. I told him of the book I was writing about my tall ships travels, and that *City of Adelaide/Carrick* would occupy the last chapter. Before I left, Peter asked me to write an article for the Sunderland Echo about my visit. I signed release papers for the film footage that had been taken. One at a time Peter and I reverse-squeezed through the gap in the ship's side and reconnected with the outside world. I descended the

ladders with *Cloud Nine* supporting me. Peter escorted me away from the ship. I did not want to go. As I began to take my leave, I explained my own dream of travelling with *City of Adelaide* to Adelaide, South Australia. He said he shared this dream. He was a merchant seaman and knew berths could be bought on cargo ships. He would love to go with her to Australia, if that was indeed to become her destiny.

I got back to the wall, hoisted myself up and took a last, longing look at *City of Adelaide*. I knew I would see her again. Something had taken hold of me even before I was inside her belly, and that something had become my essence. But I knew it was more than that.

I walked to the train station with my head buzzing and my feet springing off the pavement. I realised my hands were cold. In my excitement I had lain my red leather gloves somewhere inside *City of Adelaide*. I took the next train to Glasgow. If all went well I would be in Dunbar at 10.41 pm. Phew! What a day.

CHAPTER NINE

THE LONG WAIT

Written in the Stars

BY NOW I was becoming increasingly excited over my ambition to voyage to South Australia with the clipper ship on whatever cargo vessel would be selected to transport her. I had no idea what to expect. I wrote to Peter Roberts again saying I had met Ruth. I thanked him for his time and effort in connecting me with her, and told him she had provided me with a wealth of her great-grandmother's papers, including a copy of her diary. I knew then it was even more vital that someone should accompany the ship back to South Australia. Someone had to record her final voyage. I knew that someone had to be me. An unknown force was driving me towards the ship. I was not going to put brakes on what seemed more and more to be my destiny. I reiterated to Peter my determination to make the voyage, and asked if it was possible, when the contract was negotiated, that a clause might be included that would allow me to accompany the ship to chronicle her final journey home to South Australia. Peter had been my linchpin, and I wanted him to keep me informed of developments. He replied instantly, expressing concern about me managing expectations, but he was delighted by my response – 'I would be disappointed if I do not try my utmost to make it happen'.

Peter Maddison remained on board *City of Adelaide* until the end of March 2012. In an email he acknowledged Alec Renwick who had been present at the meeting in Sunderland, as the person who took steps to save *City of Adelaide* for Sunderland, and as someone who supported him during his occupation of her.

In August 2012 it was reported that *City of Adelaide*'s rudder would be arriving in Adelaide 'soon'. This was a huge 9-metre timber replacement rudder, fitted on Fletcher's Slip in Port Adelaide in 1877, after the original one was swept away during a fierce storm off Kangaroo Island, South Australia. It was made from Eucalypt, or grey ironbark timber. New cast-metal hinge-pintles were made to hang the new rudder from the ship's stern, making *City of Adelaide* ready to set sail once more. The rudder was authenticated by the Queensland Department of Primary Industries and Fisheries in 2005. It arrived on 22 December 2012 to undergo tests that would ascertain whether the ship itself would withstand the rigorous import regulations of Australia. These confirmed the timber treatment processes it had undergone met with Australian quarantine import regulations and procedures, and the future of the hull's acceptance into Australia was secure. It was a vanguard for the export of the ship itself. When Peter Maddison

noticed that the rudder was no longer on site at the Scottish Maritime Museum, he sought to challenge the legality of the export of the rudder.

I spent most of my time in 2013 writing scripts in Scots for local community radio, East Coast FM. Following the broadcast of the first script inspired by the ditty *Three Craws Sat Upon A Waa* in December 2012, the Station Manager requested I produce a script each month for broadcast. Somehow I managed. It kept me distracted from becoming ill over the fact that each day brought *City of Adelaide* closer to leaving Scotland. I was determined to make the voyage with her to Australia, but there was nothing I could do that would guarantee that. My destiny was not in my hands. I looked for guidance, reassurance. I began to chant mantras in earnest to remove objects that might prevent the realisation of my burning ambition. I began to check my horoscope daily throughout the summer of 2013. It said I was ready to strike in a new direction, my senses had become dull due to doing the same thing day after day, and a change of scenery would be refreshing. I should plan a trip to a place that had always captivated my imagination.

Australia. I had been fascinated with the Continent since learning about it in primary school – its size, the indigenous population, the animals, the colourful birds. Aborigines fascinated me, their art, their ancient tribes, their oneness with nature. My horoscope continued. I would begin painting or writing, dancing or playing music again. I was on the brink of a tremendous breakthrough. I needed plenty of stimulation to stay engaged with the world. It said I was making much progress on the professional front and that my family was not very supportive, some members feeling that my dreams were impractical. I was to tune out of the negativity and continue to follow my star. My persistence would pay off. I was a natural leader, that if I was not happy working for others I should launch my own business that would be a success, especially if the work involved restoration. I would be able to handle just about any situation that was thrown at me, I should have more confidence in my abilities and that if I was invited on a group holiday, I should accept. Sometimes who you know is just as important as what you know. My excellent conversational skills could make inroads with big wigs. I was being inspired by fellow artists. My work could lead to an exciting career opportunity. I was stunned by this:

17 July 2013 – Daily Tarot – There could be contact with Australia.

My horoscope continued to advise me not to fall under the influence of well-meaning relatives who would draw me away from chasing my dream. Any venture or enterprise based on my own talents would be successful. If I was a round peg in a square hole or unappreciated I should move on to a career or position that would bring out my true talents at last. I thought this was hilarious, since I had just been let go from a company for being a square peg in a round hole, but I was buoyed by the prediction that success, honour and self-esteem awaited my decision.

By the beginning of August my horoscope continued to inspire me. Reference was made to a long-term plan that was slightly eccentric or unusual. I was not to delay any longer. I should get my plan off the drawing board and into action. I was to be sociable, for friends could bring me luck, I should not be swayed by an overly emotional friend's opinion, I should not need anybody's permission to make change. Some people who were afraid of transition would urge me to reconsider my plans. But I needed constant stimulation to be happy, I should obey the occasional impulse, I was told. Also, financial limitations would be an issue, but I would find a way to fund my pursuit. I would need to be matter-of-fact and distance myself from people or circumstances that would upset or worry me, I should push ahead progressively.

I was aware of being snippy at home, even resenting being disturbed when a cup of tea was brought to me while I was writing, or the call that a meal was ready for me. All this well-meaning invaded my world of dreams. I had stopped cooking lunch. I had stopped cooking dinner. I had clammed up. I answered in monosyllables and rarely tried to make conversation. My garden was neglected. I was doing the absolute minimum of housework that I could get away with. I was conscious that Alan was taking on more and more. The only thing I kept up was shopping for food and household items. I pushed my guilt to the bottom of a mineshaft and filled it with muddy water. I was drowned in the chrysalis my horoscope said I was. I was facing the total transformation in my life when the old me would be reborn into someone stronger and wiser. I would alter the way I expressed myself and reacted to loved ones. And that was so very true. I was beginning to put my own needs and wants above those of my family. I was expanding into the world of creativity, taking part in poetry events in Edinburgh and sometimes Glasgow. People appreciated my work, I felt myself glow and grow in confidence, and this was noticed. My horoscope advised I was to take time to think, to stay away from large crowds and have quiet time to make a decision about a family matter. It said that breaking away from my kin would not be easy, but it was critical to my personal growth. Spending time on my own would be enlightening; it would be hard to sort out my feelings when surrounded by a lot of strong minded people. I should make time for a private retreat and tune into my inner voice, my best guide. If I was thinking of launching a writing project, this was the time to get started; the words would flow like a mighty river to share with the world.

In the last week of August the tarot cards said that international, cosmopolitan or continental concerns called. I was to expand my horizons. Someone from another creed, country or culture could completely captivate me. Unorthodox people, places and pursuits also appealed. I should travel to find my fortune now, I should not rule out a move to another town, county or country. It could be the making of me. I was not to believe all a politician or VIP told me, and that even a legal matter may not be the truth.

I did not live or shape my life according to these predictions. Often I would look at them retrospectively and was astonished by their accuracy. I found myself placing photographs of my deceased grandparents in my writing den. I found myself speaking with them, imploring them to bring about my ambition, sometimes with such intensity that I found myself trembling with tears streaming down my face.

On 30 August 2013 I drove a long way from home to Logan Botanical Gardens for a poetry event. Being on the west coast, I could not miss the chance to visit *City of Adelaide*. I was not up-to-date with what was happening. Despite taking a wrong turning, I got to Irvine in time to see *City of Adelaide* in daylight. I passed the new Maritime Museum yard and found myself in the car park near the mouth of the River Irvine. I could see her in the distance on the slipway. I had not seen her from this angle before. I switched off the car engine. As I opened the door to get out, a storm blew up from nowhere. I struggled to open the car door, but succeeded and got out to brave the pelting rain and wild wind for long enough to take a few photographs, and captured my hair plastered across my face in my first ever selfie, with *City of Adelaide* in the background. I wrenched the car door open and got back inside, breathless, battered and worn out. I was soaked. I started up the engine, grateful for the warmth blasting through the grills on the dashboard and on to my feet. I headed for the other side of town for a closer look at the ship. I parked my car in front of the flats I had known about since my visit there in March the previous year, when I had met Peter Maddison, and been inside her. I got out. There was a security guard on duty. A 24-hour watch had been organised as soon as Peter Maddison left the ship at the end of March 2012, and higher fencing had been installed. I called over to the man. He was a bit cagey at first, but when I remarked at how good the ship was looking and made conversation about her with him, he dropped his shoulders and spread his feet apart. His face relaxed and he spoke. The ship had had a makeover. The raggedy, loose paintwork was gone. The festering scab of copper was picked. She had been power-washed.

A white van arrived and a man got out. 'Is it possible for me to get inside and take photographs of the ship? I was just passing by and thought I would take the opportunity,' he asked. I noticed the logo on his van with *Photographer* slapped in the middle of it. I admired his tenacity. The security guard replied in the negative, but their conversation enlightened me more as to the schedule for *City of Adelaide*'s departure. I could see by the groundworks that were taking place all around her hull that things were imminent. A JCB was working in the dusk clearing that horrible, green-slimed stagnation that signified the past twenty-plus years of her life. This ship, this *City of Adelaide*, this *Carrick*, was on her way out of here.

CHAPTER TEN

OFF THE SLIPWAY

I WAS AT Callander Poetry Weekend on 7 September 2013 when I found out *City of Adelaide* was on the move. A fellow poet knew of my interest in the ship and had seen things were happening at Irvine. 'Your ship's going to Australia,' she said, and put the screen of her mobile phone in my view. My guts wrenched. Sure enough, there she was being loaded onto a barge. All this time watching and waiting; now my dream was disappearing before my eyes. I was crushed. My armpits became clammy. The skin on my forehead baked. My immediate thought was to abandon Callander and run away to my ship. I was shrivelled. I was too far away from Irvine to go, it would be all over before I got there. I tried to focus on what I had come to do despite my agitation. Kevin Cadwallander, who was born in Sunderland just as *City of Adelaide* had been, would read my poem *City of Adelaide Bleeds* whilst I played *City of Adelaide : Farewell to Scotland* on my pink clarsach that afternoon in the church hall, across from King's Bookshop on the High Street. We had prepared for this rendition of what he had made into a Filmpoem, using some of my images of the ship. It was so ironic that as we performed, the ship was moving for the first time in twenty-one years.

I was too upset to write much of a comment in the document I record my horoscopes in. The horoscope told me that *a fabulous career opportunity is on the way, so be sure to grab it.* It was no comfort that my tarot reading for the day told me to *hold on to my heartstrings, for cataclysmic events are about to have an overwhelming and profound effect on your emotions. A loving liaison could end overnight or a creative dream may be shattered, but good will triumph in the end.*

Good will triumph in the end. I would cling to these words.

At the same time as the move of *City of Adelaide* off the slipway onto the barge on the River Irvine, the formal handover of the ship by the Scottish Maritime Museum to CSCOAL was happening. Fiona Hyslop performed the ceremony in front of a small gathering of people, including those involved from Scotland and South Australia. I found a YouTube video of the preparations for the departure off the slipway. At *City of Adelaide*'s bow, the Sarens Self-Propelled Modular Transporter (SPMT) was being manoeuvred in sections into place for it to be rolled under the cradle she sat on. They worked in daylight and in darkness. A farmer from Lincolnshire had even donated a month of his time and machinery to help release the ship from her gungy fetters. The bucket of one digger repeatedly punched into the pile of concrete rubble at her stern that it scooped up load-by-load, and dumped it amongst the driftwood that had long been the ship's prison guard. They were constructing a firm base to support a ramp that would be put down between Hebo Vanderwees Netherlands barge *Lastdrager 28* and shore for *City of Adelaide* to be wheeled over. On the water, the barge was slipping up to come behind her to meet with the stern of the ship in readiness to receive her. She was about to feel herself afloat again. Inside she had been braced with scaffolding to help support her frame during her voyage to Australia. Daylight streamed through the many gaps that have grown between the planking since her caulking had fallen away. Stood around her was a garden of hardhats in white and blue and yellow. It is amazing to see a 600-ton load move on the SPMT and not see a single horse or ox, tractor or other vehicle tow it. It is amazing to see how obedient the trailers are under the control of a hand-held computer. It is like watching a collie dog round up a flock of sheep to the coded whistle of the shepherd. They are multi-wheeled platforms used to carry extremely heavy loads that are too large or heavy for trucks. They can be linked together both lengthways and side-by-side for extra-large loads such as buildings. They have a grid of axles ranging from two across to four to eight axles long that are controlled individually by computer to distribute weight and steer accurately. They can turn, be moved forward, sideways, backwards, diagonally and each axle can swivel through 360 degrees and they can even spin in place. The platform is kept level when passing over rough or uneven surfaces by the axles telescoping independently of each other, thus keeping the load steady. A single person can operate the whole from a cab or from a hand-held device, and a power pack driven by an internal combustion engine can be attached to the SPMT to provide power for steering, suspension and drive functions. I had seen an SPMT before, when Concorde was brought along the A1 north to become an exhibit at the National Museum of Flight in East Lothian, Scotland. I had waited for hours in my car in freezing rain to witness the unique transportation of her. She had come out of pitch-black, her nose cone piercing the night as she was manoeuvred round Spott roundabout at Dunbar. It was both spooky and surreal.

Now my beloved ship was travelling off the slipway onto the barge without incident. The final hurdle to her taking to the open sea again had been overcome. Mark Gilbert, one of CSCOAL Directors, later spoke of these being *beautiful machines* that were perfect for the task, each of the wheels took an equal load and kept the ship level whilst she was riding over the lumps and bumps off that slipway forever. *City of Adelaide* was bound for South Australia, and I would not be going with her.

I was dejected by what happened while I was at Callander. I had no appetite to look at the CSCOAL website where I could have found out the latest news on the ship. *City of Adelaide* had left a cavity in my chest when she slipped away. No one would now record her final voyage from Irvine to Adelaide, South Australia. No one would write the voyage up in tandem with the diary from 1864 of Sarah Ann Bray. I took a little hope from my tarot for 16 September that indicated I should take a chance and discover a new side of life, I should be adventurous and luck would smile on me, and that cosmopolitan connections would be worth a small fortune. Over that summer *Libra* told me spending time alone, such as in solitary pursuits like reading, writing and meditating would make me less dependent on others and would boost my self-worth. I would be in touch with my own wants and needs, I would trust my own impulses instead of looking to others for direction. Again, this struck me. I was always prone to seek approval, permission to do things, but with this bond with the ship, more and more I was sharing less and less of what I was doing. *Libra* said I was riding high emotionally and positive thinking would bring positive results. I was to make the most of my increased insight and intuition and dividends would be paid. Developing a project for pure pleasure would put a sparkle in my eyes and a spring in my step. At the beginning of September my horoscope said that a rebellious newcomer would admire my work and offer to showcase it. I should accept this generous offer. I was on the brink of being discovered for my artistic talent, I should not be afraid of criticism for it would help me learn and grow. The following day told me my current high spirits, sincerity and sheer joie de vivre made me stand out from the crowd and would attract plenty of admiring glances. This was an excellent time to get projects off the ground or impress people with my super personality. I should connect with my instincts and make some changes to my daily routine. I was tired of people influencing my decisions all the time.

I had things to keep my mind occupied. I had entered a poetry competition to commemorate the Battle of Flodden in 1513. I had been shortlisted. This meant a journey to the Scottish Borders on 12 September to read from the anthology *A Set of Ribbons* at the historic Bowhill House. The following day I flew to Paris with my troupe, *The Three Craws*, for a long weekend to perform at the Bayeux Museum, Normandy, France to highlight the visit to the Bayeux Museum of The Battle of Prestonpans Tapestry designed by a friend, Andrew Crummy, that tells the story of the Jacobite Rebellion of 1745. We were met at a Paris airport along with a group of musicians and battle re-enactors, and accommodated in a stunning chateau. My troupe performed the script in Scots, English and French to tell the story of the Tapestry through its stitchers in the streets and the Museum Courtyard. We enjoyed wonderful hospitality, and were fascinated by the Bayeux Tapestry that depicts the Norman Conquest by William the Conqueror. We arrived back in Scotland on the evening of the following Monday, after a sumptuous farewell banquet.

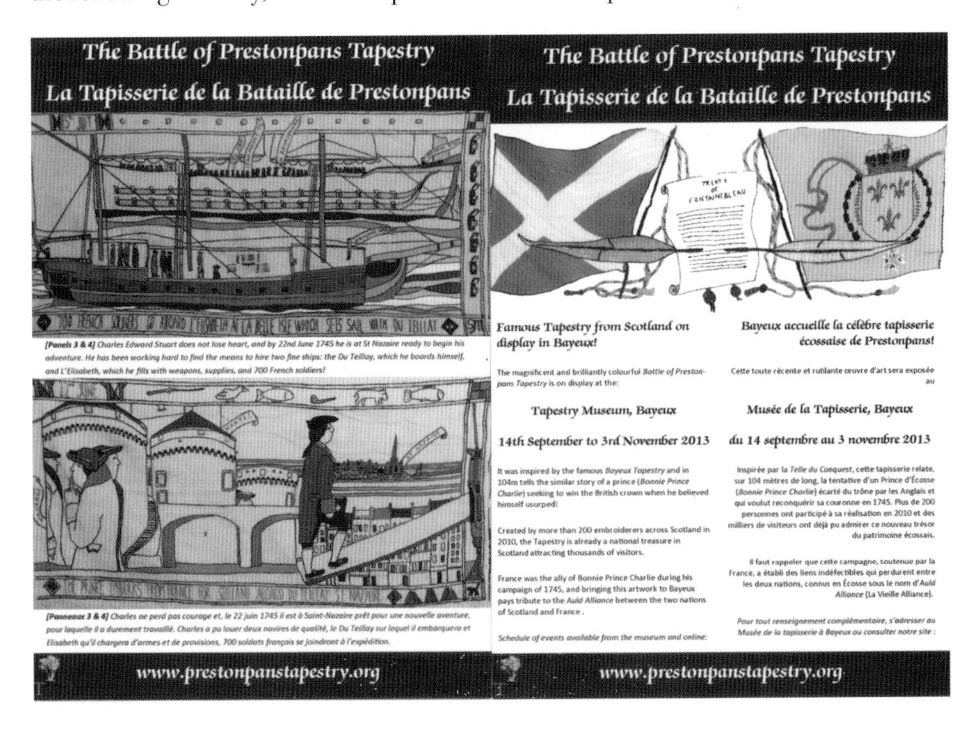

Leer, the 7th. 10.1954

My dearest little Ritalein!
In few days you will be already two years old. On the day of your birthday your Oma will think of you and you will be very much in my thoughts. I would love to be with you my sweet little doll! Your Oma thinks so often back to the first six month in your life, when she was so lucky to be like Mummy to you, it was so lovely for your Oma.
My Ritalein, with all my heart I send you all my best wishes, most of all, stay healthy, so that you will grow to be splendid and beautiful.
May your Daddy's and Mummy's wishes and hopes for your future be in rich measures fulfilled, that will make me happy as well.
These are my wishes for you my beloved little treasure.
Your loving Oma.

Letter to me as a two year-old, from my German grandmother, translated by my mother

PICKING UP THE THREADS

ON WEDNESDAY 18 SEPTEMBER I opened my laptop. I was still in my dressing-gown at 10.30 am and unwashed. Whatever made me type in the *Search* box for *City of Adelaide* is a mystery. The home page appeared. I pointed the cursor to the words, *News Release*, and a bulletin popped up:

City of Adelaide will be leaving Irvine today between 12 and 2 pm.

I read it again. And again. I checked the calendar. Wednesday 18 September. What was this? When it sank in that the ship was still at Irvine I almost screamed with joy. I had no choice. I have never moved so fast in my life. I tore off my dressing-gown, dived into the shower, got dressed and was in my car within half an hour. I left Alan standing with his mouth open at my words, 'I have to go. *City of Adelaide* is leaving today. I've got to do this.' I garbled something about my misunderstanding as I high-tailed it to Irvine. I had no Satnav, I had not been able to find the map I had taken out of the car a few days earlier. I could remember something about Biggar, and something about Troon. I had a change of mind about route at one point and added on goodness knows how many miles and minutes to my journey, for I ended up in the traffic jam I had heard warning of on the car radio and intended avoiding.

I drove past the new Maritime Museum yard and into the car park where *City of Adelaide* was moored. My heart forgot how to beat, then lurched to catch up with those lost flutters when I saw her sitting proud on the barge she had been floated onto those couple of weeks earlier when I believed she was already on her way to Adelaide. She was away from all that driftwood, rusting remnants of bits of maritime memory, aged portacabins, wild grass, mud, stale water skinned with green algae, the nearest she had been to being on water for over twenty years on the slipway near the Maritime Museum café. I arrived half an hour after the start of the time window of two hours she would be towed away on the barge in. I was so excited. There was a reasonable-sized crowd gathered and I joined them on this cold, strong-winded September afternoon. We stood waiting. Waiting. Waiting. Cameras flashed. I spoke to a few people, some had known the ship in Glasgow, others since she had been brought to Irvine. I could detect a strong affection for her, sadness sagged the air that she could not be saved to remain in Scotland. She held memories for these people. She had been their landmark. For some who had been in the Royal Naval Volunteer Reserve she had been their clubhouse in Glasgow from 1923 to 1948. She had given some people a sense of purpose and pride, in their restoring of her.

The crowd grew restless, began wandering around, stamping feet, rubbing hands or clapping their arms around themselves to stave off the chill. But the strong off-shore wind defied the will of the tug, *Dutch Pioneer*. Her mission was postponed. She would wait for a lesser blow, try again tomorrow. I was distraught. Coming back the next day was not an option for me. I was to look after my little granddaughter. I would not subject her to the 2½ to 3-hour journey it would take to get from her home to Irvine, and return after a long stand about in very cold, possibly wet weather. I drove to Gottries Road and looked for somewhere I could get a takeaway or a cup of coffee. I had not eaten or drunk anything that day. I found the Old Town Café was open and went in to see if its slogan *The Friendly Café* was true. The couple who owned it told me they had moved here from the newer part of town. I told them why I was in Irvine and bemoaned the fact that I would not make it back the next day. They said there was a couch upstairs in an area they were not using yet. They also told me of a well-priced bed & breakfast a few doors along. My mind was chugging. I stabbed at the macaroni and cheese with my fork and drank my coffee. Their son, amusing himself at the end of the school day in the livelihood of their parents, drew me back to tender memories of my own childhood in my parents' café they had opened, when their days of driving round the countryside selling ice cream from vans were over.

I had a strong feeling of Fate as I drove away from Irvine. I thought of my German grandmother who came over from her home in 1952 to look after me for the first six months of my life. There was not a great gap in age between my older brother and me. I saw the letter from her for the first time in 2011. I read it often, each time I feel her presence. It thrills me to hold the same paper she touched and penned these words on to, left her hopes and good wishes for my future folded inside an envelope that had been lost for almost sixty years, till my mother rediscovered it.

It was as if she was reaching out to me from her grave. If ever I needed her wishes for my fulfilment, it was now.

The next day I took my granddaughter to her playgroup, our normal activity on a Thursday. After playgroup we went to her home as usual, to chill out after all the stimulation. I checked the CSCOAL website. News release:

Departure postponed to 20 September 2013 from 2 pm.

Someone was definitely looking out for me.

CHAPTER TWELVE

CITY OF ADELAIDE : FAREWELL TO SCOTLAND

THAT FRIDAY MORNING I rose early. This time I was prepared. I packed my poem *City of Adelaide Bleeds*, the extract from Sarah Ann Bray's diary from 20 September 1864, exactly one hundred and forty-nine years ago, and my pink harp *Gypsy Rose* into the boot of my car. I headed for Irvine once more. I parked my car right in front of *City of Adelaide*. There was a crowd of people being disrespected by a strong, cold wind that flattened their hair against their scalps and forced them to put on warm headgear, keep billowing skirts in check, whilst people strained backs into the wind as it pushed them from behind. I watched goings on for about half an hour from inside the shelter of my car. The tide was rising. I once again felt I was being watched over, that I had made it there in time in the most unlikely circumstances to see my obsession make her way out of Scotland at last. It was now or never. I got out of the car, opened the boot and took out my harp from the shelter of her case. The wind tried to blow the boot shut and bowl me and *Gypsy Rose* over, but we held firm. I checked the tuning, I am not sure why, because in these weather conditions it would not hold, and people might not notice anyway, with the howling in their ears. I took her two legs from the case and made my way to stand in front of *City of Adelaide*. I fitted the legs into the holes in the base of the harp and sat on a concrete platform that I might have stood on, but decided against it. The wind sliced an eerie sound from the strings, a wail that muffled itself into the hulk of *City of Adelaide* whose timbers had stood in forests more aged than her almost one hundred and fifty years, and were now bolted to the iron ribs of her. I leaned against the concrete platform, cradled my harp, and faced the crowd with trepidation. 'Gather round everybody! Do you want to hear a poem…about *City of Adelaide*?' I called. Heads turned. I began to strike the strings of *Gypsy Rose* with fingers sticking through fingerless gloves. More heads turned. I called again. I thought to myself, *What am I doing?* But I looked over my shoulder and saw *City of Adelaide*. This was for her. This was my farewell to her, my wish for her safe voyage to a new life. This might be the last time I ever saw her.

When a good number had gathered, I was about to begin playing when a man with a video camera on a tripod rushed over. 'Dae ye mind if Ah film ye?' he asked, and introduced himself as Hugh Loney. I felt warm. I recognised his name from copy emails from Peter Maddison. 'Not at all, I'd be delighted,' said I, sparkling inside from the dust from wings of butterflies beating inside my belly. It was pretty daunting facing a camera whilst trying to find the right notes on a span of thirty-three harp strings on a gusty day in front of strangers. I was unfamiliar with my newly-built instrument, and not used to playing standing up. It was freezing, my fingers were already beginning to stiffen. This was a risk. But it was for my beloved ship. I pulled two pieces of paper out from my jacket pocket. On one, the extract from Sarah's diary for 20 September 1864:

> *'A lovely day. The sea is much smoother and we are going about 6 knots. I practised and read in the morning. For the first time all the passengers (24 in number) dined together in the Saloon.'*

I fought with the wind to put this first piece of paper behind the second, whilst trying to support *Gypsy Rose*. A hero in a woolly hat stepped forward from the crowd and came to my rescue. 'Would you like me to hold it for you?' 'That would be lovely,' I said through a wide grin. I read *City of Adelaide Bleeds* as he clutched it against the thieving hands of the wind and held it up for me to read. I finished playing *City of Adelaide : Farewell To Scotland* and thanked the audience. Several people voiced their appreciation for paying tribute to the majestic ship that had been part of their lives and landscape for so many years. A few said they thought more would have been made of the occasion. Why was there not a formal farewell ceremony? A good number told me of their association with *City of Adelaide* when she had been moored in Princes Dock, Glasgow as a social venue for several clubs. I took note of a few of their names with the resolve to track them down when the time came to hear these anecdotes. I thanked Hugh Loney, put *Gypsy Rose* back in the car and returned to the flanks of *City of Adelaide* to wait for what was to come.

Cameras were everywhere. The *Dutch Pioneer* came from afore the pedestrian bridge, the Bridge of Scottish Invention that split in the middle and allowed *City of Adelaide* to pass through from the slipway that had been her prison for so many years. There had been millimetres to spare between each side of the bridge as she passed through. It was this manoeuvre I had missed while at Callander Poetry Weekend when I thought the ship was already on her way to Adelaide and I might never see her again, and then found all that had happened was she had been put on the barge in readiness for good weather and the full spring tide that would allow her weight to be taken without the barge touching the bottom of the River Irvine. That time had now arrived, and I was here, here to see *City of Adelaide* begin the first leg of her voyage back to South Australia, where she had been built for. I was in awe of the precision of planning and engineering, generosity and

determination that had been in the mix to make this final move happen.

I waited with the crowd, watched the movement and actions of the teams of people on board various craft and on the quayside as they made ready for the shift. The small *Red Countess* arrived from Troon, south of Irvine, to help tug the barge carrying *City of Adelaide* out from the River Irvine. Another boat helped control the setting adrift of the barge. There was intermittent discussion on the barge between several men. I saw Richard Smith, the CSCOAL Director who had supervised the build of the cradle and strengthening of the hull for the journey, in the huddle. All three vessels kept the barge *Lastdrager 28* pressed against the wall of the quayside. The gangplank was drawn back aboard the barge. You know when this link with *terra firma* is removed things are imminent. Then *Dutch Pioneer* took *City of Adelaide*'s bow position facing upriver on the barge, their sterns facing to sea. She reversed back and clamped herself to the barge by a chain dangling from the telescopic arm that reached out over her stern. Every breath was hushed. First the steel hawser at *City of Adelaide*'s stern, then the steel hawser and rope at the bow were cast off to the men on the barge. The light stern line was cast off, then another lighter rope tied towards the forward of the barge went. The tug *Red Countess* took up the slack of two ropes that had already been prepared, one tied at a bollard on one side of the barge, and one on the other. The two lines were joined to make one, to form a y-shape leading from the barge. She came forward of *City of Adelaide*'s stern and began to tug. The little boat on *City of Adelaide*'s port side was all this while pushing *Last Drager 28* back against the quayside walls, controlling her release. At last the main rope at the starboard stern was thrown off with great vigour from the bollard on the quayside by the stevedore in a pirate bandanna.

A train of boats made their way out into the Firth of Clyde: *Red Countess* in the lead, *Lastdrager 28* with *City of Adelaide* on her deck and a lifeboat beside her, *Dutch Pioneer* being dragged behind looking back to land. The little tug *Red Empress*

latterly brought in to assist, emerged from behind the convoy to take up the rear as *City of Adelaide* departed Scotland forever. I thought this was her finally on her way to Australia. I was not distraught. Someone told me she was only headed to Chatham, near London to be prepared for an official ceremony by His Royal Highness The Duke of Edinburgh when he would rename her back from *Carrick* to *City of Adelaide.*

You could hear *City of Adelaide* fill her lungs with relief at freedom from her shackles. She visibly swelled with pride. She was in her element, breathing again in the bosom of King Neptune. Everyone's eyes strained as the vessels diminished stroke by stroke of *Dutch Pioneer*'s engines till she was a tiny speck on the horizon.

The crowds dispersed. I mooched around, found myself unable to tear myself away. I found an empty half of a muscle shell in the grass and noted how its shape resembled *City of Adelaide*'s hull. I put it in my pocket. I spoke with one or two people that had been on board the ship when she was a clubhouse for the Royal Naval Volunteer Reserve in Glasgow. I added their contact details to the others who had stories about *City of Adelaide.* I said, 'Thank you' again to Hugh Loney, and promised to keep in touch. I looked at the great gap *City of Adelaide* had left on the river. I noticed two brooms lying on the quayside where they had landed after being thrown from the barge by a seaman. A man came over and we discussed them. I needed a new yard brush for home. He needed one for the Salvation Army Centre where he was a volunteer. I bundled him and the two brooms into my car and delivered him and his esteemed new broom to said Centre.

With the sweepings of *City of Adelaide* in the bristles, I drove home with Greenwich on my mind.

Part Three
GREENWICH

'I felt connected to the ship in a way I could not explain. I just knew that I needed to be with the ship on her final voyage home.'

CHAPTER THIRTEEN

GREENWICH, MEANTIME

16 - 22 October 2013

AFTER SHE WAS towed away from Irvine on 20 September on the barge *Lastdrager 28* by *Dutch Pioneer*, I kept a close watch on what was happening with *City of Adelaide*. I watched her progress on the Marine Traffic website as she made her way down the west coast of Britain, round into the English Channel towards the River Thames and Chatham. I pounced when I saw on the CSCOAL website that the Renaming Ceremony was a fundraising event being held on 18 October 2013. I could not find my wallet quickly enough and my fingers fumbled to pull out my bank card. My hands shook as I sought the keys on my keyboard to fill out the on-line form and make the payment. I pressed the *Register Now* button and became one of the limited number of people who would witness this historic event. This was another last chance to see *City of Adelaide*. After this ceremony she would be heading towards the last phase of her preparations before going to Australia. If I could not go with her, I had at least to be there to see her go. My laptop pinged. The electronic ticket arrived almost before I could draw breath. In an instant I had printed it off and stuck it in a poly-pocket on my wall like the trophy it was. I did not expect to receive a direct invitation to the event from The Chairman & Directors of Clipper Ship City Of Adelaide Ltd and the Agent General for South Australia, Bill Muirhead AM, that arrived a few days after this. I savoured it all over again, and digested the regurgitated words of the website that stated the purpose of the Renaming Ceremony: the old colonial clipper *City of Adelaide* had been bought by the Admiralty in 1923 and had been towed from Southampton where she had served as a hospital ship, to Irvine in Scotland where she was converted to a naval training ship. I found it fascinating that she ended up there many years later. She was then towed to Greenock to be commissioned as a Naval Drill ship for the Clyde Division of the Royal Naval Volunteer Reserve. Because a new cruiser completed the previous year for the Royal Australian Navy had been named *City of Adelaide*, it was decided to rename the clipper to avoid confusion between two British Empire ships. She became known as *Carrick*, meaning 'Rock'. After the Duke of Edinburgh's conference convened to save the ship from demolition in 2001, it had been agreed to give her back her original name, *City of Adelaide*, because it was under that name that her significant activities had taken place. Now a traditional mariner superstition was to be adhered to, to avoid bad luck prevailing her on her first time at sea since 1923, and her first international

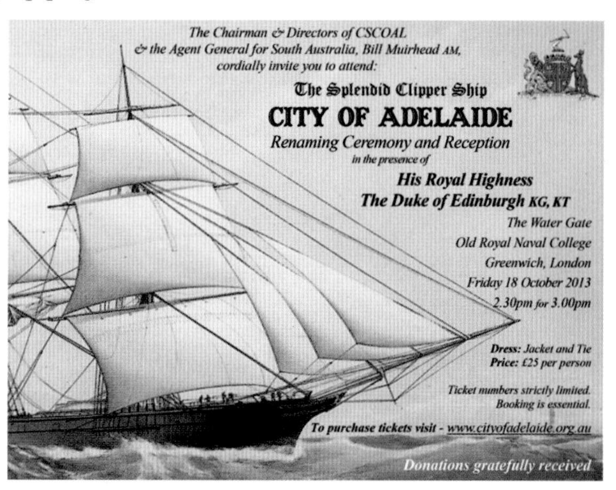

voyage since 1893. The old name *Carrick* would be purged from King Neptune's personal record of the names of vessels, his *Ledger of the Deep*, and from his memory. *City of Adelaide* would be entered in its place. A final ceremony to appease the gods of the sea and winds would complete proceedings. This would be the last ever voyage of a 19th Century clipper ship.

I still clung to my ambition to go with *City of Adelaide* to Australia. As long as she was within British waters, there remained hope that it would happen. I had emailed Peter Roberts on 30 September to say how proud he must be that all the long-term planning for the stricken *City of Adelaide* was coming to fruition. I congratulated him on the wonderful website he was master of, and told him I had been at Irvine on the day of the ship's departure. I referred to my pop-up harp and poetry performance dedicated to the ship, and said that if there was ever an appropriate event for the poem and music to be aired, that was it. He responded with his customary speed and warmth. He said he had arrived on the wharf just as I had finished playing, but did not know who I was. He explained ceremonial activities around *City of Adelaide* at Irvine were diminished in case protestors might affect the involved and hugely expensive process of removing the ship.

I asked Peter if there was any news of what shipping line and which ship would be commissioned to take *City of Adelaide* to Australia, and asked about the clock clicking down second-by-second towards the departure date on the website. He told me it reflected the departure date from her original home port of London. From there she would be taken out of public view to another port where she would be fumigated and shrink-wrapped in opaque white plastic. The departure date from that port on the heavy-lift ship after fumigation was estimated to be sometime between December and February. I reminded him he had suggested I contact him after the clipper's weight had been confirmed. He went on to explain to me what I might expect as a passenger on a heavy-lift ship. He told me I would have to sign a letter of indemnity as well as provide a health declaration stating I was fit for the voyage. Since it was likely we would pass via the Suez Canal, they would insist I took out insurance against piracy, kidnapping and so on. This could incur a cost of US$3500. Pirates! Kidnapping! The thought of these threats had never entered my mind. I could see my dream slipping away on just the cost, but now I had to think of my safety too. I shrivelled. Peter went on to point out that the cargo ship could take any route it chose, to collect additional cargo along the way. It could go via Cape Horn, Cape of Good Hope, the Suez or Panama Canals. The length of the voyage could be two to three months depending on what route was taken. My heart began to sink. How could I go away for such a long time? How would my family cope with what I would be asking of them? So much was an unknown, and the costs seemed to be mounting up. The daily rate for 'lodging', bedding and so on was U$50; in all, I was looking at a minimum cost of $5000. CSCOAL would need to ask approval from the shipping firm and the contractual relationship would be directly between me and them. Peter asked me to confirm I was still interested in the heavy-lift voyage. My reply was an instant, resounding 'YES!' There was nothing else for it. This was my obsession. I had to make this utterly unique voyage with this ship that had possessed me. No one else in the world – ever – would have this chance. Money could not be an object. I would find it by whatever possible means. I would get round my family – of course they knew of my obsession, my passion, how involved I was with the ship, and they knew of my dream, but none of them really knew just how close I was getting to realising it. I was working on the basis that there was no point in sharing developments until my passage on the heavy-lift ship was confirmed, minimising whatever speculation might bring.

I thanked Peter again for his support especially at this very busy time for him. I told him of the thrill and gratitude that rippled through me as I read his email. My two-year ambition looked like it might be fulfilled. I told him I had bought my ticket and booked my train and accommodation for arrival in Greenwich on 16 October in good time for the Renaming Ceremony. I intended to see *City of Adelaide* glide up the Thames to sit beside the younger composite clipper ship *Cutty Sark*, at Greenwich. I told Peter I hoped we would meet at last. He made one last attempt to curb me from packing my bags, but in doing so he also asked me if I would take their video camera with me to capture plenty of footage on the voyage. He asked me if I was Scottish. Curious about this, he responded to my question and told me one of those involved with the clipper ship, Rosemary McKay, was born in Glasgow. He said it was she who had traced information on Sarah's great-granddaughter Ruth and forwarded my personal information to her, that prompted her to get in touch with me.

Within days of the euphoria of booking my place for the Renaming Ceremony, I was horrified to discover that with the recent change in Federal Government, a review of the £500,000 grant towards the transport of *City of Adelaide* to South Australia was being undertaken. This would mean CSCOAL would not be able to book the heavy-lift ship. There was *City of Adelaide*, sitting on a barge at Chatham docks waiting to be renamed by His Royal Highness, The Duke of Edinburgh before making for home. The Australian contribution to the cost of her voyage home had been frozen. On top of this the land set aside for the clipper's permanent siting was criticised as being a 'backwater', five kilometres from the centre of Port Adelaide, somewhere people were unlikely to visit. These two factors were a threat to the agreed thirteen conditions that had been set for the preservation plan for the ship. They could potentially provide grounds for appeal to the Arts Council to refuse an export license for an historic artefact. Now that *City of Adelaide* was outside Scottish jurisdiction, it would be easier for such an appeal to be made. Sunderland may still have a chance to recover the ship for their City.

My travel plans to Greenwich had been made. I received another email from Peter Roberts to say that leading South Australian *7News* presenter, John Riddell who was flying over to the United Kingdom for the Renaming Ceremony wanted to interview me, having heard about my aspirations to travel to Australia with *City of Adelaide*. In the email, yet another emphasis from Peter that the ultimate decision on whether I would be permitted to make the voyage rested with the ship's carrier.

This. This is what I have been waiting for. This. This rail journey to Greenwich and *City of Adelaide*, and *Cutty Sark*. 'Splendid,' said the man, as he handed back my ticket he had perforated. Splendid indeed.

I was reading Penelope Shuttle's book *Redgrove's Wife*, particularly *Running Out of Time*, and *Peter's Shoes*. These two poems are very poignant. Time is running out. Death comes ever closer. I am driven to do as much as I can with what is left to me. I was putting myself into the shoes of Peter Maddison. I thought how desperate he would be as the time for the ship to be taken to South Australia came closer, how miserable and unhappy. I wrote a couple of my own poems in this frame of mind.

Notes from the train journey to Greenwich 16 October

'This morning milk is overflowing from my glass. I feel full, full of richness. There is a thin-ness about the air that does not reflect the fatness I feel in my heart at the start of this journey to Greenwich. I am totally happy with all the decisions I have made for this trip, down to finally stopping procrastinating about should I, should I not take my Australian opals, and I have. To hell with it, if they go missing, so be it. But they may yet be a way towards funding the trip I have been working towards for over eighteen months now, if I can pull it off. I have other stuff I can sell to make the journey possible. I am feeling a bit tired as I was up till 3 am just footering about like I always do when I am about to take off on my travels. Passing York I see the National Rail Museum and think of my father-in-law. I think of his visit there with Alan and our eldest daughter. I see allotments. They remind me of a special journey I made with my mother in 2007. My mother had always wanted to take me back to her roots, to show me where she had been born and where she grew up. When Szczecin in Poland was a host port for the International Sail Training Association Tall Ships Race in 2007, we got the opportunity. This is the town she was born in, known then as Stettin. We took the ferry from Newcastle to Amsterdam, then travelled onwards by train. We passed through Holland into Germany, to Berlin where we spent three nights. We pressed on. Only the steel rail tracks that rattled us along in our carriage prevented us from being engulfed by the pine forests on either side. We arrived in Poznan in Poland and spent four nights in this former German town of Posen she had lived in for several years as a child, until the advancing Soviet Red Army forced them to leave. My grandfather had to remain behind to defend the town. It was the last time my mother saw him. He was killed soon afterwards, in January 1945. We traced the communal grave where he is buried. I sat and wept, left him flowers. It is difficult to fathom the bond I felt with this man I had never met. I am certain if it had not been for my passion for tall ships, my mother and I would never have made this memorable journey together.'

I made a smooth connection from Kings Cross to a DLR (Docklands Light Railway) service to Greenwich. There was a group of school children in my carriage, playing I-Spy. 'L' was for *litter* and... *lumbrella*! I sent a smile to them. My accommodation turned out to be a little out of Greenwich on the way to Woolwich. I took a bus to the Angerstein Hotel and was told by the driver to look out for East Central Library, a landmark across the road from it. I found it to be a quaint building wrapped round the corner where two streets converged, with some pink stone blocks visible that had escaped being covered by the pale grey paint of the rest of the building. I went in and registered with the barman, and was grateful that he carried my pink, cabin-approved suitcase up four flights of stairs to a charming room where the skyline spilled through the window. I had booked to stay here for the whole of my visit, but changed it to have the first three nights here and the final three in a six-bed female dormitory with shared external bathroom in Greenwich when I realised the Angerstein was some fifteen minutes by bus from where *City of Adelaide* was to be moored. The change meant I would be right in the heart of things. I did not want to be worrying about buses there and back to my accommodation. I did not want any hold-ups or pressures during this important time with the ship. It was getting late. I unpacked, and went for a drink at the bar. Armed with the knowledge that the Number 129 bus stop that would take me back into Greenwich was just metres away, I went to my room and tried to sleep.

I have been sixty-one for a week now. It is the morning of 17 October. You can spend your time finding out who you are or you can waste it worrying what might happen if you step out of the box, or what people think of you. Today I am to be interviewed for *7News*. I will say who I am, but who am I? I thought of what questions John Riddell may ask. He has made me think of reasons why I want to go to Australia with *City of Adelaide*. Ever since that day I saw the stricken ship on the flyer at Irvine, she got under my skin. At the time I discovered her in 1999 I was writing a book about my travels visiting the International Tall Ships Races since 1993 in ports around Britain, Europe and Bermuda. Whenever I was carrying out research on the various ships and ports I had visited, I found my computer mouse hovering over *Carrick*, as she was known then, to see what was happening with her. I could not believe the state this historic, marvellous ship was in. I could not believe she had been undergoing restoration and that funding had been withdrawn for this. I had felt her seeping through my skin, like osmosis. She had captivated me. When I found out there were campaigns to save her, that bidders were making a play for her from around the world, I was relieved but sorry that she would not remain in Scotland. When I found the CSCOAL website, I was astounded by the information on the ship, how much research had gone into her history, how comprehensive it was and how well-presented it was. There were lists of passengers, lists of crew members, lists of cargo she had carried, even down to two Scottish Deerhounds. There were newspaper cuttings, diaries, dates and details of the various lives of the ship, her stranding, the story of the loss of her rudder in storms off Kangaroo Island in 1877 and how her Captain had battled seas using a jury-rigged rudder and dragged her away from reefs then finally to Semaphore anchorage with the use of heavy chains and trimmed sails. When I found out about Ruth Currie's donation, something had stirred within me. When she gave me the copy of her great-grandmother's diary, I felt my spine quiver and the hairs on the back of my neck prickle up like a porcupine ready to shoot its quills. When I met Peter Maddison and he snuck me onto the ship in the dusk in March 2012, I knew something special was happening. I felt something take hold of me. I felt something at my side. I felt something inside. I felt connected to the ship in a way I could not explain. I just knew that I needed to be with the ship on her final voyage home. I knew Sarah's diary from the maiden voyage in 1864 must be complemented by a record of the final voyage. I knew I had to be bold. There could be others out there better qualified than me who might chase my dream and steal it from me. I could not let that happen.

I set out for Greenwich after having made myself a coffee and eaten a pack of two plain biscuits from the tray in my room. The staircase down was steep and narrow and I left by the back door. Within minutes a bus arrived and I was on my way. I got off at the *Cutty Sark* stop and got my bearings. Then I saw *Cutty Sark* resplendent, buoyed up by a glass bow-wave. Shiny, admired, sparkling in the sun I felt a pang of deep sadness in my heart for *City of Adelaide*. How I envied those masts for her. How I envied the fuss, the funding, the interest. I would see this ship close up later. For now, I was content just to have this preview from behind the Old Royal Naval College fence, with a bronze cannon between us.

I was overawed by the grandeur of the buildings of the College. I was touched that here was what had been known as Greenwich Hospital, a permanent home for retired sailors of the Royal Navy. Queen Mary II had been moved at the sight of wounded sailors returning from the Battle of La Hogue in 1692, and set up The Royal Hospital for Seamen at Greenwich, an equivalent care facility to what existed for veterans of the army at Chelsea Hospital. The Foundation that operates the hospitality for retired naval personnel and their dependents still exists, with sheltered housing being provided on different sites. Greenwich Naval College on the site once provided assistance and educational facility for orphans of seafarers from both the Merchant and Royal Navies that still exist today but again, on different sites. Within the grounds were actual medical hospital facilities where pensioners were cared for, before it became known as the Dreadnought Seamen's Hospital where sufferers of tropical diseases were looked after.

I went into the Painted Hall that had been rarely used as its intended pensioners' refectory because it was considered too magnificent, but it had been used for the lying in state of Lord Nelson's body on 5 February 1806 prior to being taken up river to St Paul's Cathedral for a State funeral. I found two memorial tablets here set into the floor of the Painted Hall, commemorating twenty-two volunteers from America who came to serve in the Royal Navy to fight to maintain the freedom of Britain from 1939-1941. Up several stairs into the Painted Hall itself there was much opulence. There scrolls crowning the brown-painted columns were gilded. There was trompe l'oeil, making garlands and drapes look three-dimensional. There were medallions marching round the arched windows looking over table after table resplendent with silver triple candlesticks packed with tall, white candles with flickering flames at their tips. Naked and near-naked figures, cherubs, horses, harps, sailing ships, flags were painted on walls and in recesses. But it was the ceiling that was most striking. You did not have to crane your neck to see it. It was reflected by a mirror in a glass case that several people were looking into. Clouds and a burning sun are backdrop to a mess of people, both heavenly and earthly. A huge fireplace stood beneath a monochrome painting with yet more angels, bare-breasted women, horses, trumpets and in the bottom right-hand corner, a dragon being trampled to death under the hooves of a horse ridden by a soldier in armour carrying a standard and shield. To crown it all there was a golden organ on a balcony overlooking the Hall. On it there was a plaque that read, *Praise him with the sound of the trumpet, Praise him with stringed instruments and organs* (Psalm CL). There was yet another memorial, to those who lost their lives on HMS *Orpheus*, one hundred and twenty-two souls that perished on the Manukau Bar, New Zealand on 7 February in the year 1863 when *City of Adelaide*'s keel was laid down, and four further survivors who later died on duty. I was moved by all these tributes to people whose lives had been taken by service at sea. I stepped back outside and wandered through the grounds of this impressive College. From the front of one of the massive buildings the sound of flutes, cellos, violins, jazz juxta-posed with angelic voices streamed out from windows set high up above me. I felt tears prick my eyes, and sat down on a bench to reflect on what had brought me to Greenwich and to this new experience that fascinated me. My passion for tall ships was taking me on travels I never anticipated. Suddenly a rainbow spanned itself right from the other side of the River Thames, across it and over the buildings of the Maritime College. I felt it was a welcome for *City of Adelaide* whose arrival was only hours away. I saw it as an omen. I phoned my son for an Estimated Time of Arrival for *City of Adelaide.* 8.13 pm. She was past Canvey Island at 6 pm. She was on her way! I decided to have something to eat, drink a coffee and go for a pee to be comfortable before I found a suitable spot to start my watch for her arrival.

I went out of the gates and headed towards *Cutty Sark*. I entered the sales building where tickets to see her beneath the glass wave could be bought. I browsed the shop selling all sorts of merchandise related to the ship, models of her, mugs, tea towels. What caught my eye was a bottle of *Cutty Sark* blended Scotch whisky that had been named after Robert Burns' poem *Tam o' Shanter. Cutty Sark* got her name from that famous poem; it means *short slip, skirt* or *shirt.* The legend is that Tam was riding home after a night of drinking when he noticed lights in the ruin of Kirk Alloway in South Ayrshire, Scotland. He decided to investigate, and spurred his horse, Meg towards the sight. He saw a witches' coven in action. He becomes mesmerised by a girl wearing a short skirt. When she dances in a frenzy he cannot contain himself. He shouts out, *Weel done, Cutty Sark.* Immediately the revelry stops, and everyone comes out and goes after Tam. He is chased by the incensed throng until the witch Nanny Dee almost reaches him. But she cannot keep up the pursuit when they come to a bridge, because witches cannot cross water. She reaches out and grabs Meg's tail. She yanks it, it falls off. So Tam and his horse get away. *Cutty Sark*'s figurehead depicts Nanny Dee holding Meg's tail.

I sometimes wonder whether *City of Adelaide* would have fared better if she had had a more captivating, exciting name. John Willis was *Cutty Sark*'s first Captain. I was asked to write a poem in 2015 about *Cutty Sark* for a project called *Scotia Extremis* because of my obsession with tall ships.

'Weel Done, Cutty Sark
Family Motto – *Where there's a Willis away*

John – 'Jock' – 'Old Stormy' – Willis
ran away from his Eyemouth home, aged fourteen
stole over the Scottish Border, headed south to London
and sailing ships, scrambled up ratlines, slithered along courses,
raged at the sea with all his might, untied gaskets, hoisted sails
hauling hemp rope to the 'two-six-heave', rode the bowsprit,
scrubbed the decks, caulked to the rhythm of the melody
in his throat responding to the call of the shantyman,
worked in a pub in New India Dock – 'Canary Wharf' to you –
fixed musical instruments for jolly jack tars, saved his wages,
weighed his anchor, became a Sea Captain and builder of ships.

Junior John – 'Jock' – 'Old White Hat' – joined with his father
and their union spawned me at Dumbarton on the River Leven.
My design echoes *City of Adelaide*, also known as *Carrick*, the first
composite clipper ship, built in Sunderland, my iron ribs fleshed
with finest Rock Elm fetched from Canada and North America
and Teak from East India and Burma. My bottom is silken,
like Kylie Mynogue's in *those* hot pants, gleaming in copper
making it smooth, sleek to slice through wild waters
in peak performance. I broke the back of Scott & Linton,
was completed by Denny Brothers. They were all there
when they named me *Cutty Sark* in November 1869,
and I was towed to Greenock for my rigging –
twenty-nine sails to capture the breath of uncertain winds
in 32,000 square feet of canvas. I pranced at my tethers like Meg
with Tam o' Shanter on her back at Kirk Alloway till they fled
from that 'unco sight' and crossed Brig o' Doon, left her tail
in the snatching hands of Nannie Dee, the witch trapped now
bare-breasted in my prow in her short slip that gave me my name.
Our ceilidhs with the winds and seas were legend as we made
for China, raced back with the new season's teas. We danced
hornpipes, jigs, strathspeys and reels together, eight times.

But the week I was launched was the week the Suez Canal
opened up, gave a shortcut to shipping, an access that cut out
the need to round the Capes of Good Hope or Horn.
Steam ships rose to hot favourite, odds-on to win, hissed
down my neck – they were not reliant on the whims of the winds,
never ended up in the Doldrums so I was given a new life
beating back from Australia, with wool in my hold.

There is more. I have carried cargo, trained cadets, survived
two fires at Greenwich where I find myself stuck high and dry
in a glass wave with Nannie Dee shaking Meg's tail at Canary Wharf,
as though she and Tam had just escaped across the River Thames.
I never thought I would be stranded like this. Cup of tea, anyone?
Or a wee dram of Cutty Sark blend, perhaps?'

I came out from the café and saw a huge anchor in the sky. *How appropriate*, I thought: first a rainbow, and now a cloud heralding *City of Adelaide*'s arrival. I twitched, watched time here in Greenwich, meantime. I was so excited anticipating the grand appearance of *City of Adelaide* in the capable, trustworthy wake of *Dutch Pioneer*. This was a ship grown by William Pile, Hay & Co from a forest of trees that had become a docker that worked her way carrying tons of coal around Britain, brought hectares of trees from Canada, had served the healthy by isolating infectious people, had trained gunners for WWII and danced with the Royal Naval Volunteer Reserve at Glasgow; all this after her service bringing hope of a better life to people migrating from Northern Europe and Britain voyaging on her from London and Plymouth to South Australia, and returning with copper, wool and wheat.

There was word going about that a contingent from Sunderland was to arrive the next day with a diminished replica of the 9-metre rudder in time for the Renaming Ceremony as a protest to the ship going to Adelaide. I had no right to this ship other than that I was becoming part of her history. I must see her through, for Sarah Ann Bray's sake. I would have loved to see *City of Adelaide* go to Sunderland to rekindle shipbuilding skills in what had been known as the largest shipbuilding City in the world. I would have loved to see her bring pride back to the area through the retention of old shipbuilding skills and the passing down of them to the hope-bereft youth. But the bid to bring her to Sunderland had been weak, it had been *not technically feasible nor properly costed*, according to the Scottish Maritime Museum and Historic Scotland.

There had been no word from John Riddell of *7News*. As the night drew in, activity in front of the Queen's Gates of the Royal Naval College increased. People were beginning to migrate along the riverside walkway across from Canary Wharf, once known as India Dock. Tripods began taking up prime locations for cameras that would crown them, ready to capture what everyone was anticipating. I bathed in the atmosphere and stayed rooted to my excellent viewpoint. I was like a cat on a hot tin roof, but there was no way I would move and jeopardise my position. I could see Peter Maddison down on the riverside. The tide was out. It was dark. He had a video camera. He looked forlorn and my heart went out to him. We shared the same obsession. He had known the ship longer than me. He had fought for her and given everything up for her. I feared he would be lost now *City of Adelaide* was on her way out of the country.

The crowd was getting restless. I was squashed against the railings by bodies stretching to look to our right, or east of where we were. The Millennium Dome blistered up like a huge birthday cake covered in lit candles at the kink in the River

Thames that would give the first sighting of the ship. Press and TV film crews had holed up in the Trafalgar Hotel bar. Someone was listening in to reports on the progress of *City of Adelaide* as she was towed up the River Thames. There was a pontoon where *City of Adelaide* would be moored a little way off from the banks between me and Canary Wharf. The night and the river were black as oil. Only the lights across the water and around me and their rippled reflections interrupted the muffle. Then, a beam of light shone from behind the bend in the river. She was here! With stealth, speed, and silence apart from the sound of the *Dutch Pioneer* engine and the cut of her bow through the water, *City of Adelaide* sneaked up right in front of us. No longer a silhouette, I could see her ribs were swollen with relief and pride that she was at sea again, albeit with the aid of crutches. She was glad to be away from dry land with a future again, one where no matter who gained her, she would be cared for and admired for her wonderful history. She was towed beyond the pontoon in bright emerald light and a spotlight shining from the back of the wheelhouse of the tug. I held my breath as she was manoeuvred with great skill to face the opposite direction she had come from. On the deck of the barge men were working, they tethered the barge, and prepared to drive piles into the bed of the river to make all secure against drifting in the current of the river. Personnel in smaller boats helped to make the whole operation a success. *7News* arrived. Photographers and film-makers were everywhere, each trying for the best, most unique angle. My camera was on night mode. I kept my fingers crossed it would capture images, at least good enough for mementos. I jostled with people who tried to get into my prime viewing position. I hustled closer to newsmen with cameras, overheard a telephone conversation that funds to help finance the ship's transportation to Adelaide had been sanctioned by the new Federal Government. CSCOAL had done it! This was the last hurdle that sealed the ship's fate. Nothing stood in the way of her going now.

As the man on the phone disconnected the call, I approached him. He was undoubtedly Australian, and I recognised him from the CSCOAL website. I asked him if he was Peter Christopher, and introduced myself. He was warm and very welcoming, as though we had known each other for a long time. When all was settled with the ship, Peter and I walked into the night together. We exchanged business cards at my bus stop under the canopy of trees across from *Cutty Sark*, and he continued on to his hotel. I cast an eye over *Cutty Sark*. I swear she groaned at the disgraceful, pitiful sight of the neglected *City of Adelaide*.

CHAPTER FOURTEEN

CARRICK/CITY OF ADELAIDE RENAMING CEREMONY by HRH The Duke of Edinburgh at Greenwich, London

MY OVERFLOWING EMOTIONS were a tidal surge that overwhelmed my chest and caused me to gasp, to sob when I got to the Angerstein, elated. The next morning I woke at 7.05, and wondered what day it was. 18 October. The Renaming Ceremony! It was today!

I showered. Started dressing, pulled on my skirt made of two tartans, a warm black jumper and threw over my long black coat. I felt so fresh, and my face was wrapped in an uncontrollable smile. I sprung my way to the banks of the River Thames and went in by the Watergate where I had stood the previous evening. I was so elated to see *City of Adelaide* out there on the barge, in daylight. There was a sense of anticipation about her. She looked magnificent, quite at home in waters she had been familiar with nearly one hundred and fifty years ago. She would not recognise this place with the multitude of changes that had occurred in all that time, the old blackened buildings of East India Dock now replaced by shimmering glass and marble towers of Canary Wharf that last night looked like they were cargo on *City of Adelaide*'s deck. She had a banner in front of her that read *Bound for South Australia*. There was also something on her starboard bow where the ship's name should be. I could just make out beneath white opaque material the name *City of Adelaide*. I asked a man who was painting window frames of Greenwich College to take a photo of me with *City of Adelaide* in the background. I wandered over to the stand being erected for the ceremony, and headed for the Media tent where I found Peter Christopher. I recognised John Riddell, who said he was delighted I had turned up and said he would film me immediately if I was in agreement. He briefed me on questions he would ask, and suggested I read an extract from my poem *City of Adelaide Bleeds* where Captain Bruce is referenced, as they had been talking about him. Peter confirmed what I had overheard the previous night, that the money had come through from the Federal Government to help towards transport costs for the ship. He did not know whether *City of Adelaide* would be fixed to the deck of the heavy-lift ship or whether she would be placed inside it. People were beginning to fill up the space cordoned off for guests attending the Ceremony. Several people introduced themselves and made polite conversation. I singled out a striking woman wearing an outfit of tartan material. Rosemary McKay. We hugged each other and had our photo taken with our beloved ship in the background.

Suddenly there was some commotion. The Sunderland contingent had arrived with the replica rudder to make their protest at *City of Adelaide* going to Australia instead of to Sunderland. They were denied access to the area. A black car arrived. Bodyguards appeared and His Royal Highness The Duke of Edinburgh stepped out of the limousine. He was wearing his trademark beige raincoat, and looked none the worse for his recent illness. Several men dressed in dark suits, white shirts and dark ties surrounded him, their eyes darting all around. Dignitaries began to fill the seats on the rostrum. I recognised Peter Roberts and Peter Christopher. Soon the Ceremony began, with all members of CSCOAL present, and an honorary captain wearing a naval uniform from the era. He was introduced as Andrew Chapman, the son of one of the CSCOAL directors. His role was made clear as he began his speech: he was there to appease King Neptune and the four winds. He poured a glass of champagne and toasted the North wind before taking a sip and throwing the remains into the Thames; he poured a glass of champagne and toasted the East wind, took a sip and threw the remains into the Thames; he poured the third glass, filled it with champagne, toasted the South wind, took a sip and threw the rest into the Thames, before finally toasting the West wind, took a sip and threw the rest of the champagne into the Thames. By now the River must be tipsy! A breeze had got up. Andrew's next task was to purge the name *Carrick* from King Neptune's register. He said that usual practice was to have the ship's old wooden name plaque burned, but since there was no such thing, he had written it on a piece of paper he tore up and set fire to before placing the pieces in an ice bucket. The wind kept blowing out the flames, so Andrew resorted to throwing the shreds into the River Thames. The covers were removed from the name on *City of Adelaide*'s hull to great applause, and the Duke of Edinburgh unveiled a plaque commemorating the Renaming Ceremony. Everyone enjoyed the whole occasion before retreating to the Naval College's undercroft to join The Duke of Edinburgh in a cocktail reception and enjoy the famous South Australian Vili's pies, canapés and drinks to seal the ceremony. I mingled with interesting people and spoke with some of the CSCOAL group, including Rosemary. She told me she first found out about *City of Adelaide* when she read an article by Michael Foster in the *Adelaide Advertiser* on 29 August 1994. That gave birth to her passion for the ship. The words of Sir Robert Gordon Menzies, former Prime Minister of Australia, sprang to her mind,

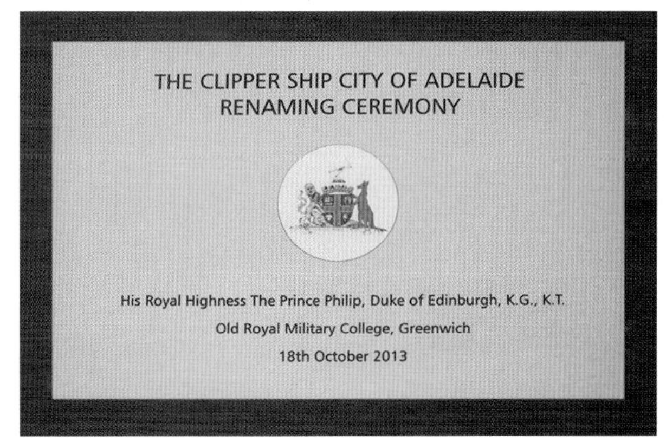

'I did but see her passing by, yet, I will love her till I die'.

Rosemary had read the headline *Raised from a Watery Grave – 'City of Adelaide' Bound for 21st Century Glory.* She never anticipated that the 'glory' would be in South Australia and not Irvine, Scotland. She was struck by the stark contrast of a picture of the ship in all her magnificence, splendid in full sail in her 19th century heyday that is housed in the State Library of South Australia, and what she saw in the article, a sorry state of just the hull of this, the oldest surviving composite clipper ship in the world. Rosemary was inspired to send a letter to the Lord Mayor of the City of Adelaide who was at the time Mr Henry Ninio. She suggested as a goodwill gesture he extend greetings to the Lord Provost of Glasgow and to Jim Tildesley, Director of the Scottish Maritime Museum to wish them well on the very exciting project of restoring the *grand old lady.* The Lord Mayor did indeed do this. Rosemary visited local schools when she was in Irvine for the departure of the ship in 2013, including one class who had penned letters to schoolchildren in South Australia that would be taken on the ship on her voyage home. Rosemary told me she wept unashamedly when she was amongst the crowd of hundreds of people waving *City of Adelaide* farewell on her long journey. After the ship was gone, she and the Directors of CSCOAL enjoyed haggis and champagne in The Ship Inn in Irvine.

I was so excited to meet Peter Roberts, who had been wonderfully instrumental in keeping me informed of what was happening with *City of Adelaide.* I felt I had known him for a long time, we had exchanged so many words over the last few years on our common passion. I was astonished to be invited to join in the evening celebration where I continued to meet new people, share in food and the delicious celebratory cake iced with the words *Clipper Ship City of Adelaide 18th Oct 2013.* I promised to send Adrian Chimes, a Master of the sailing ships of bygone days, a postcard from wherever I landed with *City of Adelaide*, if I was permitted by the shipping company to go with her to Adelaide.

With great reluctance, I tore myself away and headed for the bus back to my accommodation. I was euphoric, yet a pang of loneliness engulfed me.

SIGHTSEEING AND *CITY OF ADELAIDE* ON HER WAY

I DECIDED TO do some sightseeing the next day and took the Tube, then the DLR into central London. It would give me a chance to reflect on the amazing events of the last two days. I did the usual sights, and walked across Tower Bridge. I had booked a ticket for a book launch by poet Pascale Petit. I met a lady there who told me her father had been in the RNVR during WWII as a translator between the Russians and British Admirals at Archangel. Another lady who was fascinated by my voyage plan had a connection with Greenock. I went back to Greenwich and discovered the underpass beneath the River Thames. I decided to walk over to the other side. It was getting dark, so I returned more or less right away, trying not to notice areas of seepage on the walls. I had decamped from Hotel Angerstein before sightseeing and had got settled in to St Christopher's Hostel. This move kept my costs down as well as being more convenient for the next three nights in Greenwich. No more buses for me. I had a fairly restless night on the top bunk in a tiny, windowless room with five other women, worrying about whether I would need to visit the toilet during the night.

I arose at 5.45 am and left those women in various states of slumber. I walked back under the Thames and was greeted on the opposite side by a fox and a blackbird that made a feeble attempt to welcome the onset of sunrise as the moon began to slip on his day gown. It was almost 7 am, and a spiritual light bathed *City of Adelaide* and Greenwich College across the River Thames. I felt Sarah close to me. I closed my eyes and saw her image. Three crows cawed; several people came out of a boat house carrying a kayak; a wind got up. I wondered whether *City of Adelaide* would be able to leave today as planned. Tears filled my eyes. I fretted that now she was leaving British waters, the chances of me ever seeing her again were very slim. I still had no idea whether I would be permitted to accompany her to Australia. For now, she was only going to Rotterdam to be shrink-wrapped and fumigated to kill off any micro-organisms that might have jeopardised her acceptance into Australia due to their strict quarantine regulations. *7News* had asked me to take a video recorder with me. I have been warned about being physically prepared for the voyage as I would have to undergo training in fire-fighting, self-survival in a suit and all sorts of hoops I would have to jump through. Nothing would put me off this journey; if it was to be I would comply with anything. Alan had phoned me the previous night and said he had met someone whose mother worked in the RNVR Clubhouse in Glasgow. He seemed excited by this, the affection and esteem the ship is held in was evident, and I felt he was beginning to come onside. I took a batch of photographs as daylight broke of *City of Adelaide* from this side, showing the masts of *Cutty Sark* towering over the trees: the last two remaining composite-built clippers together in one capture, and the two domes of Greenwich College behind *City of Adelaide.* Then I headed back under the Thames to St Christopher's, grabbing a bakery for breakfast along the way. I almost got soaked by a sudden downpour, but I made a run for it. I had a shower, got dressed and began to get organised for *City of Adelaide*'s final farewell to Britain from her home port.

Cameras – video and still, fully charged spare batteries, plus phone, plus bottle of Scotch whisky. I bought a stack of shot glasses from a shop on the way back down to *City of Adelaide.* I placed myself as before, right in front of the ship and amongst the CSCOAL members who were present, and their respective wives and husbands. Rosemary was there. Peter Christopher was busy with media personnel. A good crowd of people was gathering. I stepped as far forward as I could and stood on stone steps used by people landing from their boats. I looked down and saw a cobalt blue jar that had washed up on the step below the one I was standing on. I bent down and picked it up, poured the water out of it, found silt pressed hard in the bottom. I took it as a message from *City of Adelaide.* Her presence was in this jar that had shared the same water and silt with her. I carefully stashed it into the bag containing the whisky, without washing away what lay in the bottom of it. Things started to happen on the water so I re-joined the others. Tug *Louise* and *Dutch Pioneer* were put into action. Several men on board the barge *Lastdrager 28* were busy with ropes and chains, securing the boats as before to the barge – *Dutch Pioneer* at the stern, *Louise* at the bow. John Riddell was animated. He disappeared, and came back with the news he had chartered one of the Thames Clipper River Buses for them to film from. They only had a short time, but it would be worth it to get close-up

shots from the water of preparations for departure. The piles fixed into the river bed were lifted. I could feel *City of Adelaide* bristle. She would soon be free again to ride the waves, not by her own sails because they and their masts were long gone, but continuing meantime as a passenger on board *Lastdrager 28*. The sky darkened. The swollen and now muddy-brown River Thames rose in the tide. Every now and then the blue and white of the Thames Clipper appeared from behind *City of Adelaide*. I poured whisky and passed it round. We toasted *City of Adelaide* and tossed shots down our throats and into the Thames. Then suddenly, just as swift and quiet as she had arrived, she began moving, towed by *Louise* and pushed by *Dutch Pioneer*. In no time at all she was rounding that bend in the river to the vanishing point of the Millennium Dome.

A terrible emptiness swamped me.

The river rose further and flooded the lower step beneath where we were standing. A solitary man leaned over the railings, his long, grey hair and dark overcoat flapped in the wind. I knew he was crying. Water lapped round his ankles. He willed it to wash him away. The River Thames began to boil. The sky opened up and let fall a deluge of heavy raindrops. My CSCOAL friends dashed to the Trafalgar Bar and shouted an invitation to me to join them in a champagne toast. I could not believe my luck…again! We sat cosy in the bar. I brought out the whisky for more toasts. We sang the sea shanty *Bound for South Australia*. We stared at the empty hole in the Thames where *City of Adelaide* had been not half an hour before. We wished her *Bon voyage*.

We later heard she was taken to safe haven until the rough weather subsided before she made to cross the North Sea for Rotterdam. After a few days I found this media item by Peter Roberts –

> *'Dordrecht Arrival – 24 October 2013*
> *The 'City of Adelaide' arrived at the Hook of Holland at 18:00 local time on 24 October 2013 where it entered the canal system. It arrived at a quay in Dordrecht, Netherlands, about 22:00.*
> *Gale force winds had delayed the crossing of the Channel for four days and the tow had to shelter at Sheerness.*
> *Final preparations for the voyage to South Australia will be undertaken at the quay in Dordrecht before the clipper is hoisted aboard the heavy-lift ship.'*

It was a pleasant surprise to see Brian Oglanby, whom I had met when Peter Maddison smuggled me on board *City of Adelaide*. He was adding to the documentary he had started. He asked me to meet him the next day for an interview. We all spent a few hours in the bar before discussing what to do about an evening meal. We sauntered away from the riverside in a large group, and found a bar where we enjoyed tapas, conversation and laughter. Wiebbe Bonsink, whose company *Hebo* had been engaged to transport *City of Adelaide* from Irvine to Adelaide, had joined us, his job so far carried out with excellence and to a layman's eye, perfection without hitch. I presented him with the remains of the whisky as he was unable to partake in the toasts since he would later be driving a car. After an enthralling day, I climbed into my top bunk to the sound of tongues clicking and irritated sighs. No one heard my smothered sobs, both of joy and grief that *City of Adelaide* was gone.

PERMISSION IS GRANTED

I TOOK TIME the following day to reflect on everything that had happened over the last few days. I spent time in the National Maritime Museum and explored more of the beautiful architecture and grounds of the Naval College. Later, I took the Tube to Canary Wharf where opulence and people dressed in expensive outfits with phones stuck to their ears contrasted with my imagining of what the area would have been like one hundred and fifty years before. I was to meet Brian Oglanby at the *Cutty Sark* for filming, but he was held up with interviewing Fiona Hyslop who had come from Scotland for the Renaming Ceremony, and it never happened.

I had one more thing to do before I went home. I wanted to meet up with a friend of my father, whom I had known since I was a small child. He was the last link I had to him. I had last seen him at my father's funeral in 2002. He had the diary and photograph album my father had kept after WWII at a Displaced Persons Camp for Ukrainians. I wanted them back. I phoned him, he sounded very frail, but he agreed for me to visit him the next morning before my train back to Scotland. I was lifted. The sight of the Emirates cable car that took customers from one side of the Thames to the other appealed to me, and I made my way towards it. As I approached, I noticed Peter Gabriel was performing in the Millennium Dome. I enquired about tickets and was stunned to find there were still some available; I bought one. I continued with my mission to ride in the cable car, and was back in plenty time for the concert. It was a mind–shattering end to my London experience.

Next morning I packed, checked out of St Christopher's, and made my way across London. I found the house I was looking for, and rang and rang the bell. I knocked. I waited. After about half an hour someone came out of the back door of the house and I approached him. He knocked on the same door I had. He tried several times. In the end he called someone on his mobile phone. The person on the other end would come over. My time was running out. I could not afford to miss my train. With a heavy heart and great reluctance I left, disappointed. My mission to regain ownership of my father's records was not accomplished.

I emailed Ruth Currie on 30 October 2013 recapping what had happened with *City of Adelaide* since she left the slipway at Irvine and how I thought that was her on her way to Australia. I told her I had read an extract from Sarah's diary to the crowd and about Hugh Loney filming the whole thing with the poem and tune. I told her how *City of Adelaide* had sat within yards of where *Cutty Sark* is, high and dry on land, and how it was wonderful to see the two clippers together, but the comparison between rags and riches was heart-wrenching. I told her how I had struggled to find allegiance between Sunderland and Australia, but that in my heart-of-hearts I knew that she belonged to South Australia. If she had not been commissioned to take migrants there, she would never have built. Ruth responded she had received an invitation to the Renaming Ceremony, but had decided not to go.

Another fundraiser was happening on the CSCOAL website, where people could pay various amounts of money for a passage on *City of Adelaide* to be virtual chickens, pigs, trunks, stowaways, crew, captain, cargo etc. I managed to buy the last *stowaway* ticket for Alan as his Christmas present in case I did get to go on the *real* voyage. This prompted Peter Roberts to contact me about the schedule for *City of Adelaide* arriving at Rotterdam after her shrink-wrapping at Dordrecht, Netherlands. If I had not bought that ticket, this might not have happened and I might have missed the boat, pardon the pun. He gave me news that the heavy-lift ship would depart from Dordrecht, Netherlands between 25 and 30 November. There was no information on what ship, or whether passengers would be permitted. I responded with great enthusiasm that things had reached this stage. I reiterated my dearest wish to escort the magnificent gem back to South Australia, with a footnote to say I was desperately trying not to reach for the soft holdall I had bought in anticipation of the voyage during the summer sales in Edinburgh. It was the perfect ship's luggage, and even coincidentally had the green and gold of Australian colours on it.

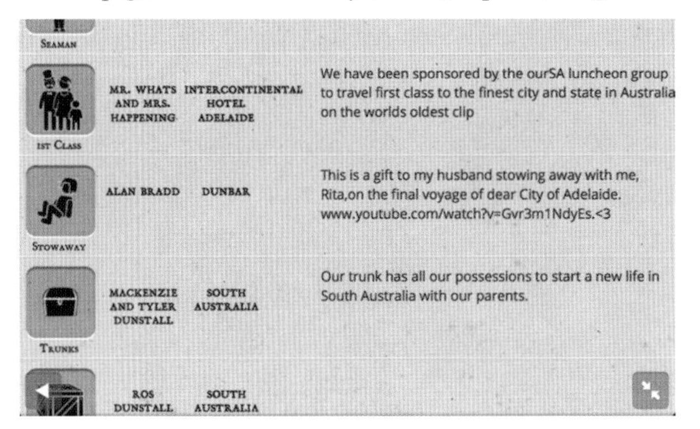

On my son's birthday, Friday 15 November, I had been to my doctor for a check-up for travel insurance just in case I was permitted to go. When I got home I opened my emails. Peter Roberts and I had heard nothing from the shipping agent Peters & May. Now here was Peter advising me to contact them *with gusto.* My heart sank, but I read on. He told me it was likely the heavy-lift ship would visit the United States of America and South Africa en route to Adelaide, South Australia. Again, no guarantee of me being allowed to go. I popped out for some groceries. When I got home it was 3 pm and I rushed to my laptop. My heart jumped and my hand shook over the touchpad. *Simon Judson* stared at me from the *From* column in my email. This was the moment I dreaded. This was the moment I yearned for. I clicked on his name...

PERMISSION IS GRANTED...PERMISSION IS GRANTED...
PERMISSION IS GRANTED...

My head spun. I collapsed to the floor and sobbed.

IT REALLY IS HAPPENING!

THAT NIGHT I booked the ferry to Ijmuiden, Amsterdam to leave on Monday evening to ensure I was on site in Rotterdam in case of any changes in *City of Adelaide*'s leaving dates. I was not going to miss this boat! I knew connection from Amsterdam to Rotterdam by rail was straightforward, and I booked two nights in a hotel beginning on the 19 November. I had a mad scramble over the weekend to gather things I would need for the voyage. I had no idea about visas for the United States or South Africa. I would cross those bridges when they loomed before me. I had received a very warm *Letter of Invitation* from Peter Christopher that would help me obtain a visa to visit Australia. Another email came in from Simon Judson that indicated a delay of the arrival of Motor Vessel *Palanpur* in Dordrecht, Rotterdam. At last I had the name of the heavy-lift cargo ship that had been chosen to carry *City of Adelaide* from Rotterdam to Adelaide that would become my home for however long, I did not know. I could now track her progress from Bremen on the Marine Traffic website. I cancelled one night in my hotel and changed my ferry booking for twenty-four hours later: an extra day at home; an extra day for things to go wrong. I received a further email from Simon with a link to the Mammoet website. He informed me Mammoet Terminal was where I would be joining *Palanpur*, and to have access to the dock where she would be berthed I had to pass a Health & Safety questionnaire. I opened the link to take the Mammoet Terminal Safety Test. This involved watching a video, then selecting an answer from multiple choice boxes. My hands were clammy and I kept getting up and walking around before selecting my answers. The moment I submitted the form I thought I had scuppered my chances, but no! Words of *congratulations* arrived from Mammoet.

Dear Rita Bradd,

You have successfully completed the safety instructions and associated test on the Mammoet Safety web site. You have therefore obtained your safety certificate! For security reasons we are not making this certificate available as a pdf on the web site, but are sending it to the email address given. You need the certificate, together with your identity papers, to enter the site and it is valid for one year.

Yours sincerely,

Mammoet.

On the morning of my departure for my hotel in Rotterdam, I checked blood results with my doctor, set up travel insurance and phoned Hugh Loney in Irvine to let him know I was off to Australia with *City of Adelaide*. He was so excited! I broke down and wept when he said, 'The ship chose you. *City of Adelaide* chose you.'

Clipper Ship 'City of Adelaide' Ltd.
ABN 65 134 550 388
PO Box 535
Kent Town
South Australia 5071
Tel: +61 (0)448 589 079
www.cityofadelaide.org.au

15 November 2013

Mrs Rita Bradd
Scotland

via email rita.bradd@btinternet.com

Dear Rita

Invitation to the city of Adelaide, Australia

Thank you for your ongoing interest in the 'City of Adelaide' and in particular your participation in recent activities in both Irvine, Scotland and Greenwich when the historic ship was moved.

Both your music and your poetry added to the cultural significance of what may otherwise been seen by some as only a massive engineering feat. Your participation added a very important human dimension, and one which I am aware the media covering the events appreciated.

The agreement between the Scottish Government and CSCOAL requires us to develop ongoing cultural links, and several programs to achieve this are underway, including as you are aware exchanges of letters between school children in Scotland and Australia.

In this context, I write to invite you to Australia, to participate in these cultural activities. A fascinating aspect of this whole project has been the interest in social history associated with the ship. Your presence in Adelaide would be appreciated, and I look forward to seeing you here.

Best wishes

Peter Christopher
Director

BRINGING HER HOME

PAGE 1 OF 1

Patron: His Excellency Rear Admiral Kevin Scarce AC CSC RANR Governor of South Australia

Part Four
ROTTERDAM

'This was it. I was stepping away from stability and the security of land into a world where I would be tossed around on the high seas and isolated from everything I knew for an unknown length of time.'

DEPARTURE: Home 19 November 2013
ARRIVAL: Rotterdam 20 November 2013

'CHRIST, WHAT HAVE I done?' A searing red-hot poker stabbed the words from my breast onto my tongue. They steamed out and overwhelmed our ears. I was saying goodbye to Alan at the ferry terminal at Newcastle. I did not know if or when I would be home and see my family again. I had not a clue what life on board a cargo ship would be like. Would I be slung up in a hammock with sixty guys in one huge area? What nationality would the crew be? What would the food be like? Would there be communal showers? Would I be the only female on board? None of this mattered. I looked back at my husband before I entered the gangway that would swallow me up and throw me on board the DFDS ferry to Ijmuiden. There was no going back. This chance would never happen again. This was absolutely unique. My stomach was tumbling into the complete unknown. What had started as an impossible, all-consuming dream was turning into reality. I was mad to be going. I would be mad not to go.

There were no wheels on my holdall. It was stuffed with my library of nautical books and notebooks, still and video cameras, two laptops, numerous packets of various herbal teas, a few items of clothing, toiletries and hair dye. I struggled with it till I hauled it into my cabin, where I took time for reflection. I pinched myself. If I had still been at home, I would have been addressing the theme *Navigate* at my writing group in two days' time. I went to the top deck to watch our departure from Newcastle with a sense of relief, excitement and dread. I watched the shores of Northumberland disappear in the wake and in the morning after a restless sleep and a breakfast of fruit gum sweets, saw a multitude of push bikes herded together on the shores of The Netherlands. The ship cleared of passengers, cars, trucks, lorries and I was soon on a coach taking me into Amsterdam City, where I boarded a train for Rotterdam. The countryside ambled past, I had got on the slow train in error, and arrived later than I had intended. It did not matter, I was not making any travel connections. I had one night to spend here. I had a quick bite to eat and a cappuccino before taking the tram to my hotel situated on the waterfront. I checked in and found my very basic room without en suite facilities, but free wifi. I spent a while searching for directions to Mammoet Terminal at Schiedam. I could get to Karel Doormanweg by Metro. It was dark and horrible outside but I went to check where the nearest station was. When I got back I found yet another email

from Simon Judson asking if I had the safety equipment I needed to access Mammoet Terminal. Panic set in. Here was a further hurdle. How many more would there be? I knew safety gear would be required. I had assumed I would be issued with it. I trawled for the rest of the evening on the painfully slow internet where I might get it. I now had to work out how to get to the supplier I found, across the water. I did not sleep well that night.

Next morning I had a shower, followed by breakfast of orange juice, cereal, croissant, Leerdamer and Brie cheese, salami, tomato and cappuccino to wash it all down. When I returned to my room there was another email from Simon telling me I needed a visa for the United States of America. What?! Peter Roberts had indicated it looked like we might call there but there was no time to organise such a thing. I was boarding *Palanpur* today! I spent a good hour filling out the Electronic System for Travel Authorization form on-line, but backed away from the *Proceed* button. Time was against me and I was unsure as to whether my application would be processed before we left, money was tight and I did not want to waste $74. *City of Adelaide* was to be loaded later this afternoon or the next day, and I needed to get final items. I looked at the instructions on how to get to the store for my safety equipment –

'Take Leuvehaven Metro (pink) to Vijfsluizen to Mammoet.

From Vijsluizen to Pernis then Taxi to Walhaven-suid.'

I needed –

Hard hat

Safety glasses

Safety boots S3 or S5

Body covering clothing with long sleeves

Life jacket

I decided to risk it. I decided not to bother and just to get to Mammoet Terminal. I would take things from there.

I checked out of the hotel, and headed into a future that promised me a very special, unique adventure.

CHAPTER NINETEEN

BOARDING MV *PALANPUR* at Mammoet Terminal, Schiedam 21 November 2013

It was rush hour when I headed for the Metro, and changed trains at Boeurs. I was a bit unsure of what platform to go to, but a young Muslim woman paused in her hurry and helped me out. I knew I had made her late, as she checked her watch and sprinted away without further interaction. I arrived, and found the bus terminal where I asked a driver for directions to Mammoet Terminal. He explained I could only get there by a bus from the other side of the very busy carriageway. All I had to do then was go straight. But when I recognised the Mammoet Terminal tower from the window of the bus I had boarded, I pressed the bell for it to stop, got up and dragged my library and tea supply off and struggled up some steps. The sun was strong, and I soon felt dishevelled and sweaty. Relief poured over me when I got to the Mammoet shop about twenty minutes later, but that soon dissipated when I was told I was far away from the security gate. I despaired, and asked them to order a taxi for me. While I waited I drank the cup of coffee they gave me with deep gratitude.

The taxi arrived and a couple of minutes later I was dropped off at the security gate.

Instructions

1. ISPS (www.imo.org/en)
2. Report to security at first barrier. Proceed to security lodge (red)
3. Show ID and complete registration form in duplicate. Present access instructions certificate. Give registration form back
4. Wear hard hat, safety glasses, safety boots (S3 or S5) and body covering clothing with long sleeves on entering Mammoet terminal. Must be worn at all times
5. Obey all instructions, luggage examined
6. Be safe, do not walk under loads, only pass vehicles when sure the driver has seen you
7. (Parking)
8. Walk on footpaths (yellow)
9. Muster points – green signs
10. No drink/drugs
11. Life belts for work between water and yellow lines
12. Life jackets on board pontoons ships
13. No photography

I filled out the necessary paperwork, and they arranged the loan of the necessary safety gear to get me to *Palanpur*. I felt diminished when I gave my shoe size. As they handed me over-large boots with steel toecaps, hard hat and hi-vis jacket they asked me if I was the Cook. 'No. I am not. I am writing a book.' I set out to find Motor Vessel *Palanpur*. It took about half an hour for me to get there. I knew from the site safety test I had to walk within yellow lines with walking men painted between them. I weaved through a maze of shipping containers of various colours with company names marked on them. Cranes loomed overhead. Everything seemed vast and surreal. I felt like I had walked through a gateway into another world. There was not another soul around that I could see as I manoeuvred my way through this metal city. My head was bursting with the unfamiliarity of everything – the surroundings, the sounds, smells. The sun beat down as I followed the painted yellow men, yet I was walking through a deep, muffled shadow. I felt very alone. I felt very excited. I had almost reached my goal. I could see water at the end of my street of steel containers. I was nearing the dockside.

I emerged from the darkness into bright light. Through squinting eyes, MV *Palanpur* loomed before me. I was smacked in my guts by a cannonball of butterflies. I had never seen anything so huge on water in my life. I felt like a fly in the shadow of a skyscraper. The world around me where sounds of steel hammering against steel echoed round the dockside, forklift trucks zoomed, and looming gantries wheeled along on rails carrying massive loads all stood still in my amazement. I felt deafened as I stepped off the pathway and pointed myself towards the gangway of *Palanpur*. I craned my neck to look above the dark blue steel hull, strained my eyes towards the white structure at the bow of the ship. *That must be the bridge*, I thought. Two bright yellow cranes towered high above *Palanpur*'s deck. I felt like Frodo must have when he saw the towers of Mordor, in J R R Tolkein's *Lord Of The Rings*. I seemed to walk for ages alongside the length of the ship before I spotted a crew member on Watch. He was wearing a hard hat and overalls. He scrutinised me when I said who I was. He expected me. I felt tiny as I scrambled up the gangplank behind him. I was so grateful he carried my luggage. He took out his radio communicator, said a few words in a language I recognised but did not understand, disconnected and spoke to me. 'Wait a few moments, an officer will be here to show you to your accommodation.'

'Thank you,' I replied, as I watched my feet shuffle inside my boots. Plenty room for my toes to curl. 'How many crew members are on board?'

'Seventeen.'

'What nationalities are they?' I heard myself ask.

'Fifteen Ukrainians and two Russians.'

I almost dropped to the ground, flabbergasted. Inside my luggage was my father's little teddy bear, the one I gave him the Christmas before he died in 2002. I brought it to have something of him along with me on the voyage. He had pinned a metal badge from L'viv Cathedral in Ukraine, his homeland, on its chest. I had never had a harmonic relationship with my exacting father, but I knew he was with me now. I knew he wanted me to know more about his country and culture through this crew. I tingled that at last I might be doing something that would have made him proud.

Within minutes a well-built man in overalls came from nowhere. This was it. I was stepping away from stability and the security of land into a world where I would be tossed around on the high seas and isolated from everything I knew for an unknown length of time. I looked into startling blue eyes shielded beneath safety goggles strapped round his hard hat. His face was covered in sweat. There was little in the way of greeting as he delivered me to the officers' mess and effortlessly disappeared with my luggage. A man dressed in chef's whites came in.

'Anatoliy,' he slapped the palm of his hand against his chest. 'I am Cook.' I held out my hand and joined it to his, and introduced myself.

'Rita.'

He took me to a corner in the mess where an electric soup tureen stood on a cupboard, and ladled some potato soup enhanced with slices of smoked sausage into a bowl for me. I sat in the space he indicated in the far side of the mess and scooped it up. I was famished. He brought me a plate of meatballs, pasta and salad with a cup of Lipton's Yellow Tea to wash it down. He said my cabin was being prepared, and disappeared. At least an hour later he returned, raised his eyebrows and said, 'No one has come for you?' I shook my head. He reached for the phone in the mess, spoke in a direct way in Ukrainian, then told me my cabin would be ready in five to ten minutes. I contemplated that by the end of this 'cruise' I might be able to speak the language my father had tried to teach me as a child. I thought of the email Simon Judson had sent where he said that Christmas would be 'quite an experience'. He would never know just what an experience I was already having.

City of Adelaide is being loaded tomorrow at 8 am. We are not leaving till Monday, so this allowed time for me to pick up last-minute essentials. I would hear from Simon over what visa to apply for for the stopover in the United States of America.

Now I was following Chief Officer Igor Boltov through a yellow-lined stairwell whose steep metal steps covered with blue linoleum took the breath from me. He was very chatty and obviously under pressure, as he wasted no time and no words to tell me it was *all hands on deck* for the crew members as they prepared for the loading of my precious cargo. I would have to wait a bit longer to know what my living space would be like, as he deposited me in his own very spacious accommodation: two rooms, one for sleeping and one for lounging, with some work space where there was a desk covered in papers, pens, photographs. He invited me to rest in the couch area of the lounge before he disappeared back to duties. I could not even sit down, I was so excited! I waited for what seemed like a couple of hours before someone came to take me to my cabin that turned out to be just along from where I was. I could see a young crew member through the doorway, placing spare sheets and towels on the bed he had just made up. As I stepped towards the threshold I looked up, saw an engraved metal sign above the door –

Blue linoleum. Pine laminate. One upright oblong window looking out to the deck. To the right as I stepped in was the ensuite shower room. Everything was seamless, sink, toilet and shower all moulded as one for easy sluicing down. Walking forward and partly recessed behind the ensuite wall was the wardrobe, a bedside cabinet and bed, fixed, slightly wider than a single, with two in-built drawers underneath. Above, two portholes, the same size and shape as the window. At the foot of the bed, a desk! A proper writing desk with drawers and a chair pushed into the kneehole. Shelving for all my books met the corner that led to the fridge '…for beer, if you wish'. Mmmm, yes please! Then there was a corner couch similar to that of the Chief Officer, and in the space squaring it off was a table fixed to the floor by stainless-steel legs, and two further chairs. I was astonished at the comfort and spaciousness. Phew! Not quite the sixty hammocks slung in a communal space I had expected then! There were even curtains! My bag was placed by the door beneath coat hooks for later unpacking, but for now it was meal time again. Igor took me back down to the officers' mess where pigs' liver in cream sauce (*yuck!*), mashed potato and salad awaited my fork and knife.

After supper I went to my cabin where I spent the entire evening at my window watching the deck covers being replaced over the middle, or 'tween deck that had cargo loaded already. There is a lot of repeat work for the crew – jumping onto and jumping down from the deck covers, hooking them on and off the crane. They fitted back the covers from Crane 2 forward. After that, huge metal supports like great big yellow drainpipes were craned onto the deck and strategically placed in the middle of it. My eyes danced with the blue flashes of light as metal plates were welded to the deck where *City of Adelaide*'s stern would be positioned. Ten minutes after midnight, all went quiet. I settled in to my first sleep on board MV *Palanpur*.

CHAPTER TWENTY

PALANPUR INDUCTION, INTRODUCTIONS, MORE HURDLES TO CLEAR

I AWOKE AT 7.10 am and peeped out of my cabin window. All quiet. A barge with a crane was moored alongside and I thought it might have something to do with *City of Adelaide*, but it moved off. I went down to the mess for water for my kettle to make a cup of tea. At 7.40 am a crew member named Stepan knocked on my door. He invited me to take a tour of the ship for a guide on Health & Safety on board, and to complete the indemnity form that would waive away various rights to make any claims against the shipping company in future. He asked if I had had breakfast. I replied I did not want any. We arranged he would come back for me at 8 am.

I put on the essential safety gear and we descended the external staircase to the weather deck where he pointed out the muster station and explained signals that would be blasted on a horn to denote various actions for crew to take. I began to make notes but he said these would be provided. He showed me the life boats and how they were operated. As Stepan and I proceeded across the weather deck, he explained we would be crossing the Atlantic to the United States of America. Here it was. Confirmed. We were to pick up further cargo, six locomotives from Norfolk, Virginia, for the iron ore mining industry at Port Hedland on the west coast of Australia. We were also licensed to carry potentially dangerous cargo. He explained about the waste system on board, any glass or plastic is stored in bins, the rest is incinerated. He showed me the fire points and how to set off the alarm, and mentioned the dry powder fire extinguisher outside my cabin. Stepan showed me the ropes, literally, and mooring gear. He showed me the lifeboat at the stern of *Palanpur*, a bright-orange pod shaped like a missile. I did not like the look of it. It seated 24 crew members. We were 18. I shuddered at the thought of being inside it, its nose pointed at the sea at a very sharp angle.

Stepan and I walked back to the bow and went up to the bridge, where he took his leave and someone immediately offered me a cup of tea. It was like walking into a party, a hive of activity, men everywhere, animated, talking excitedly, looking over the deck of *Palanpur*, drinking from mugs with *H&P* printed on them (for Harren & Partner). I was introduced to several of them. It was impossible to take it all in. I got into conversation with someone from Australia, an inspector, I think. I was hearing the names of the company owners and operators of *Palanpur*. I had seen *www.COMBI-LIFT.eu* sprawled in huge lettering on the side of *Palanpur*'s hull. *WWW.COMBI-LIFT.EU* logo was emblazoned on crew overalls, hard hats, and paperwork. The Combi-Lift colours of blue and green were evident on the Harren & Partner flag that was raised on the short pole at *Palanpur's* bow. I was amused my dressing gown had the same colours in it. I found that Combi-Lift is one of the world's leading specialists in ocean transportation with a global reach responding to enquiries and deliveries in the most safe, time-efficient, environmentally conscious, bespoke, all-year round service to clients. I heard that Harren & Partner commissioned the build of *Palanpur* that was launched in 2010, then leased her to Hyundai for two years, and she was re-named *Hyundai Phoenix* as part of their fleet. It seemed *City of Adelaide* had something in common with this leviathan. Both had had their names changed. I doubted that the change back to *Palanpur* in China after Hyundai's charter ended had involved a renaming ceremony like *City of Adelaide*'s! I was invited to come up to the bridge any time I wanted to.

The issue of me not having a visa to enter the United States raised its head again when reassurance was sought from me that I would not try to get off the ship when we docked in America. They were nevertheless still very keen for me to get the necessary visa. I felt very strongly that my purpose for being on board *Palanpur* was purely to escort *City of Adelaide* home to South Australia. I was not particularly interested in setting foot on American soil, and did not want to be detained for any reason if paperwork was not available or correct. It was explained that if I did go ashore and was detained, this would cause costly delays for the shipping company. I was compliant with all the requests, and signed necessary paperwork even though there was no time to read and inspect what it was I was signing. I spent a very pleasant morning chatting to the two inspectors for the insurance underwriters in Bremen. One told me he is very fond of sailing in Scotland and is very familiar with Oban. He had been on a boat ride over the second largest whirlpool in the world, the Corriefrechan. I could not help thinking what would happen if the engines failed! His enquiry as to whether I suffered from seasickness paled into insignificance at that thought. I had only twice felt seasick, once when I had overindulged in brandy on a crossing of the Firth of Forth helping crew a yacht for a friend, the other when I was cooking below decks for another friend, off the west coast of Scotland. I found on that occasion that as long as I could look out and see the horizon every few seconds, all was good. He went on to tell me a relative, his cousin if I recall correctly, owns the *Swan van Makum* and the newer-built *Swan*. I knew both these ships from my tall ships travels.

I met the ship's Master, German – pronounced with the hard 'G'. He was very attentive, making sure everything was all right, that I was comfortable, did I need a drink, was there anything I needed? It was hard for me to take in who everyone was, and what their role was, there were so many people and so much busy-ness. I was overwhelmed. German beckoned to me to come to the starboard side. He pointed to a white shape far below. It looked like something had been put into plaster, like you would a broken limb.

'There is your ship,' he smiled.

There she was, cocooned, wrapped and sealed beneath the white plastic she had carried on her top deck all the way from Irvine. I went weak at the knees. She was still on the barge *Last Drager 28* that had brought her from Irvine,

and had now been fumigated to meet Australian quarantine regulations to at last be loaded onto MV *Palanpur* for her last ever sea voyage. She would be leaving northern waters never to return. She was going home to South Australia to take up permanent berth in her namesake port, return once more to where she carried so many thousands of migrants between 1864 and 1887. I could not believe how small she looked from this great height. I was dancing inside, pinched myself to make sure I was not dreaming. I noticed the shipping agent *www.petersandmay* banner on her starboard bow, and her freshly-positioned rename of *City of Adelaide* snuggling beneath the white plastic. Loading would start shortly. Mark Gilbert introduced himself. He was the only Director of CSCOAL that I had not previously met, and Director of Aztec, experts in the field of heavy lift transportation. Their banner hung beside that of Peters and May. He introduced me to his friend David, whom he had invited to watch the loading of the ship. We chatted about architecture, the grid system Adelaide is built on, the events at Irvine when they had removed *City of Adelaide* off the slipway beyond the bridge. Mark too was concerned about the visa. He also said I would need to check out of The Netherlands and would need to get to border control to do this to avoid any complications further down the line. Another hurdle to clear. There was talk of Simon taking me there: I should go and discuss this with him. Simon? I did not know he was here! Mark pointed him out to me way down below and I braved it: I descended into *Palanpur*'s world of masculinity that washed over the weather deck to discuss this with him. I introduced myself. He said he was too immersed in preparations for loading *City of Adelaide* onto *Palanpur*, so someone else would need to take me. I returned to the bridge and found German had already made arrangements for someone to do this next day. Just as I had not wanted to miss anything with the loading of *City of Adelaide* earlier that morning with the tour of the ship, I was relieved that I would now not miss a thing because of having to deal with red tape.

I was excited when Wiebbe Bonsink, whom I had met at Greenwich, appeared on the bridge. His company was responsible for the entire safe shipping of *City of Adelaide* from Irvine to Adelaide. We shook hands and exchanged pleasantries. At last the wait was over. Loading of *City of Adelaide* was about to begin.

LOADING *CITY OF ADELAIDE*

22 November 2013

THE SWADDLED *City of Adelaide* sat cradled on the deck of *Last Drager 28* whose tug bobbed bow to bow with MV *Palanpur* in the shadow of the Mammoet Terminal control tower on a dull Dordrecht day. There was barely any blue in the stretch above reflecting into the River Maas that was like corrugated iron – steel grey and rippled. *City of Adelaide* bristled with anticipation, like all of us up in the bridge overlooking her. When she was moved to the port side of *Palanpur*, we all moved as one mass to the back of the bridge that overlooked the deck where action was underway. There were computer screens, two-way radios, men, men and more men talking, pointing, shouting orders. Chief Officer Igor was in charge of operations, in communication with *Palanpur*'s Master German Koltakov and the men on deck. Two of the yellow drainpipe things were on the deck. I was told these were *spreaders*. Beside them stood a couple of men in their orange overalls and white hard hats. At their feet lay two huge twisted steel loops I was told were *grommets*. Crane 1 swung into action. Its enormous double hook dangled above one of the long spreaders. Onto each side of the hook a grommet was snapped into a secure clip like that on a dog lead to keep them from jumping out. These were joined to longer grommets by massive shackles that were then shackled at the other end of the loop onto the spreader. At the underside of the spreader on each end two further shackles were fitted. A grommet was threaded through each shackle to give it double strength then two more massive shackles were fitted to keep the loops together. Crane 1 then lifted the whole system to dangle in the air. Crane 2 came into operation, and the whole procedure was repeated until two hoops hung at each end of the two spreaders, ready to take the 600 tons load of *City of Adelaide* between two cranes whose combined maximum load capacity was 2 x 450 tons = 900 tons.

On board *Last Drager 28* I saw two men each carrying a huge oval of what looked like iron in their hands. I do not know what their purpose was. Now the barge was facing the opposite direction, I could see Wiebbe's company banner on the barge, *Hebo*, in blue and red lettering on a bright yellow background. A bright yellow clamp was fitted to *City of Adelaide*'s cradle. Four clamps in all were bolted to the cradle, two on each side at front and back to balance the weight of the clipper ship on lifting her. Each of the four shackles dangling at each end of the double grommets was locked into one of the clamps on the cradle. I watched intrigued as the cranes began to move. *City of Adelaide* was fished into the air beneath a crochet of steel, iron and rope triangles. Not a breath could be heard on the bridge.

Now *City of Adelaide* was being gently angled to fit through the space between the two cranes. The precision of the crane operators was breath-taking. It seemed they were guiding the ship millimetre by millimetre through the limited gap that could barely take her width. Everything was in slow-motion as she was edged through the gap, stern first. Above, a drone captured proceedings through a birds eye view. With half the ship above *Palanpur*'s deck and half of it sticking out over *Last Drager 28*

I could not for the life of me fathom out how they were going to position *City of Adelaide* onto those steel plates at the stern that had been welded to the deck earlier.

Men were constantly checking her safe progress. On, on she came. Her stern was now hanging over the wharf, her bow further across *Palanpur*'s deck. Barges and other vessels passed by behind her. I panned my video camera round to the mammoth Mammoet crane that was helping build the secret project going on next to us and quickly panned back. On the wharf a forklift truck was unloading large oblongs of steel and stacking them alongside *Palanpur*. I noticed a few lay on her deck in front of *City of Adelaide*. Back on the water the barge *Last Drager 28*, now free of her load, was being pushed away up river by the tug that brought her. *City of Adelaide*'s buddy for the last month or so had done a magnificent job in bringing the clipper ship from Irvine to Rotterdam in one piece to get her ready for the voyage to the other side of the world that was looming. More and more from her stern forward was coming over *Palanpur* till all I could see as she passed behind Crane 1 was the forward-most part of the bow where the bowsprit would have been in her heyday. It was like the profile of a face. The cranes were twisting the ship round, bringing her more parallel with *Palanpur*, yet having to be very careful not to knock the 'face' against Crane 1. Dusk was taking hold of the day. Lights came on behind *City of Adelaide*, where Stepan had shown me the pod lifeboat. Tension was mounting. The delicate operation was taking hours. There could be no mistakes, no rushing, no risks.

More and more men gathered at the bow as it gently swung into position. A couple of seabirds made a fly-past as the ship came to hover over the metal plates. Men were checking, checking, bending over to watch for a perfect landing.

At last! She was down. Grommets and shackles crumpled as *City of Adelaide* came to rest where they wanted her. The bridge erupted with cheers and applause. Wide smiles looked into wide smiles. Backs were patted. Hands shook hands. You would have to be a stone to not feel the sense of enormous relief, pride and achievement that swelled the bridge in that moment.

CHAPTER TWENTY-TWO

ALL HANDS ON DECK

Securing *City of Adelaide* for the Voyage to South Australia

ALL WENT QUIET. I went to my cabin and lay down. I was completely overwhelmed that the last important, tricky, dangerous preparations for *City of Adelaide*'s final voyage were now complete. What could go wrong now? I sat up and bounced off my bed. I looked out of the window and saw the only view I would have for the indefinite future – *City of Adelaide*. I blew her a kiss. I turned to the corner of my cabin where Sarah Ann Bray's photo was. I took it to the window and showed her the ship she had sailed on one hundred and forty-nine years before. That shudder again. I squeezed myself and scrunched up my face in exhilaration. I still did not believe this was happening. Why me? Why was I taking this photograph and the spirit of Sarah on this leviathan cargo ship to the other side of the world? I lay down on my bed and was swallowed into another world.

I was wakened by the sound of hammering, that familiar sound of steel on steel. I jumped up and drew the curtain of the window that looked over the deck and saw *City of Adelaide*. She looked ghostly in her white shroud. She looked ethereal. I was mesmerised, could feel the anticipation emanating from her as men worked with oxy-acetylene torches to weld the legs of her cradle to secure her to *Palanpur*'s deck. The blue flames reflected against her plastic shroud, spread a spectacular sapphire-blue bow-wave right across her entire front. She looked like she was ploughing the ocean.

Men were busy on deck, illuminated by crane spotlights. I felt hunger pangs, so went to the mess where several officers and inspectors were having supper. The mood was jovial and inquisitive, but I did not join in. There was too much to watch on this unique adventure.

I stayed up as long as the men working on deck did. It was after midnight before they stopped. By that time my video camera, camera and phone SD cards were exhausted, as I was. I tried to sleep but was too excited. I tried to read, but could not concentrate. I put out the light and found myself staring into the dark. I landed into next morning and dived over to the window. Work was continuing on welding the ship's cradle to the deck. It was going to be a long haul. I still could not work out what the oblongs of steel were for. I took my time to go down for my first breakfast in the officers' mess. I could not have eaten a cooked breakfast along with the others at

7.30 am, nor face a mess of men at that unearthly time of the morning. It would be home-from-home for me to have one fennel and one liquorice Twinings tea bags infuse together in the ¾ pint black and white cow mug my youngest daughter had gifted me for Christmas a few years earlier. I would squeeze every last drop out and drink the brew to stimulate and refresh my system. I could not see any cereal bowls, so I helped myself to a cup and shook muesli from a jar into it, to about a third full. I removed and binned the dried fruit. Cook Anatoliy came in and we said *good morning*. I asked him where I could get a bowl and he showed me plate racks in the galley and the store for cutlery. I went back to my seat and transferred the muesli and milk into the bowl before I raided the fridge for a couple of slices of cheese to put on half a slice of brown rye bread, and brought over the honey jar to smear some onto the other half. I did not bother with a side plate, I just put them onto a paper napkin. My perfect breakfast.

After this I headed for the bridge. German told me he had discussed with Michel Vlieland last evening that there was no need for me to go to Rotterdam after all to find an internet café to fill out the ESTA application form required to visit the United States of America. There was internet access at the security gate, so I could do it there. At the same time I could return the boots and hard hat I had borrowed from there on arrival. German provided me with details of the ship to say when we would be arriving, how long we would be staying, ship's identification and so on, all information that prevented me completing the form two days earlier in my hotel. I returned to my cabin to put on my pink sparkly bed socks that filled the gap between the end of my toes and the end of my brand new boots. The laughter from the guys on the bridge yesterday echoed round my head when I told them I was foot size 38. They issued me with the smallest pair they had on board, 44. I packed up my beautifully embroidered red backpack crafted in Palestine with my passport, the details of *Palanpur*, my credit card to pay for the privilege of holding the ESTA form. I put on my coat and hard hat, tied the laces of the boots I had borrowed from Mammoet security into a bow and slung them over my shoulder, then hooked the webbing of their hard hat round my fingers. I decided not to retrace my steps of the previous day and ended up going too high on the site towards the Mammoet tower. I could not believe how close it was to the dock entrance. I saw now how much unnecessary extra walking I had given myself two days earlier. If I had ignored the tower and kept going straight down the carriageway and turned right as the bus driver had directed, I would have come to the dock entrance.

I found myself lost. A female security guard put me back on track. On the way I was baffled by the sight of a man with a long, flowing beard who was dressed in red robes. He was carrying a long staff and had a mitre on his head. If I had hands free, I would have rubbed my eyes. Santa Claus? On the 23 of November? I *had* to ask.

'What are you up to?'

'I'm Santa Claus.'

'I can see that. But…why?'

'Children are coming to see me on a boat.'

'Oh.'

When I got to the security hut, I handed over the Mammoet boots and hard hat. I was given back my Society of Authors Membership Card I had left the day before as identification and security against the borrowing of the safety gear. The guard said he knew nothing about me coming to use the computer. Nevertheless, he obliged, logged me on, and returned to his desk. Almost immediately he began swearing and flapping around. He made it obvious that today Santa was not his favourite character. He was late, and the children who had come to see him were getting restless. He was annoyed on their behalf. When he settled down he offered me a coffee. I relished its aroma as I completed the ESTA form. On the bigger screen I could see boxes I had been fretting over not having answers for were optional, not a requirement after all for the granting of a visa. I had struggled with my small netbook screen for the task of completing this form. Here, it was done in very few minutes, at a cost of US$14. I asked the guard to print it out. He muttered about not knowing whether the printer was connected. I was not going to risk my session timing out, so I pressed *Print* on the screen. The printer purring out my granted ESTA was music to my ears. I had read it could possibly take seventy-two hours, yet here it was in an instant.

As I walked back to *Palanpur*, I heard my name called. A maroon people-carrier slowed down. Inside were Mark and David, who said, 'Would you like a lift back to the ship?' I hopped through the side door behind the passenger seat and we were back at *Palanpur* within seconds. I went up the gangplank and headed for my cabin to take off my coat, safety boots and hat.

There was loads of activity again on the deck. I noticed a couple of men way up on the top deck of *City of Adelaide* and decided to film. I put my coat back on and headed for the roof above the bridge, known as the *monkey deck*. I filmed the men as they walked from stern to bow. One of them slipped on the plastic covering. My heart leapt into my mouth. He quickly recovered himself. They were fitting several lengths of heavy-duty webbing straps round *City of Adelaide* that were fixed on either side to *Palanpur*'s decks by colossal shackles to help hold her secure during transit to Adelaide. German's head popped up at the top of the ladder. He handed me his mobile phone. Michel was returning my call. We arranged for the taxi to pick me up at one o'clock to head for Rotterdam. He asked me if I would like to spend some time there to pick up some last minute shopping. I could not get over the generosity and thoughtfulness of everyone who is helping me get underway on this voyage of a lifetime. I said I would be happy to go straight there, do the business, and get back again.

He was kind enough to organise this final bit of red tape for me and I did not want to complicate things, even though he had asked the question. I finished up filming and went down the ladders to my cabin. I took off my coat, the safety shoes and hat and lay on the bed for a bit of rest and chill time. After about ten minutes I got up to see what was happening on deck. I am finding it impossible not to keep checking its status every few minutes. It is ever changing. As soon as the crane hummed, I was up there, like a dog trained to obey the whistle, ears cocked and eyes focussed. I drew the line at hanging out my tongue.

I popped down for lunch. The food Anatoliy prepares is excellent. After breakfast I passed the galley and he was sitting peeling piles of potatoes. It reminded me of my time on board the 1921 fishing smack *Excelsior*, during the cruise-in-company stage of the 2002 Tall Ships Race between La Coruna and Santander in Spain, after my father died. Today's lunch was potato and dill soup, savoury rice, salad coated in his own very special dressing, and the most succulent, mild, tenderly cooked fish I have ever tasted. I thought it was chicken at first. He had spooned some fishy sauce with peppers over it. I wondered if it was oyster sauce. If it was, it was my first taste, and I survived. I am not at all adventurous with shellfish.

I was down by the gangplank watching operations from the dockside when the taxi arrived at 1 pm. The driver was very pleasant and I sat in the front seat beside him. We chatted on the way to Rotterdam about various things, weighing up the pros of cons of me shopping for the few last minute things I had not managed to pick up in the hasty departure from Scotland. We even discussed rearranging with Michel so that I could spend that time in Rotterdam he had at first suggested. Twice I pulled my phone from my bag and twice I put it back. Our joint decision was to stick to the original plan. When we arrived at border control we went in through a revolving door. The taxi driver explained to the officer behind the desk what was needed. He seemed confused, so the taxi driver stepped aside and let me speak to him. I tried several ways to communicate with him, but he could not seem to grasp that I had come from Scotland via the DFDS Newcastle to Ijmuiden ferry, then taken the train to Rotterdam and joined *Palanpur* at Mammoet Terminal. It took a mature, sensible, female officer who came out from an adjoining room to explain it to him and sort it out. In the end I was rubber stamped, discharged from Netherlands soil. Another unexpected hurdle overcome. The two officers were very taken with what I was up to, and wished me *Bon Voyage*. They were interested to hear more, but I was conscious that the taxi driver had other orders, and we left them with the knowledge *Palanpur* would be sailing on Monday morning. We chatted again on the way back to Mammoet Terminal.
I wondered if the official was being pedantic, but the taxi driver told me that he really could not get his head around me travelling in this way. All he had ever known was people voyaging on cargo ships arrive by plane and join the ships, or they come off the ships and head for an airport. We discussed whether I should walk to Schiedam tomorrow or take the Metro to Rotterdam. I did not say I had arrived at Schiedam by Metro and again was surprised when he showed me where the bus terminal and Metro were, and how close they were to the Mammoet security gate. Happy days. We chatted less about Somalian pirates. I told him I had deliberately not gone to see *Captain Phillips* starring Tom Hanks during the ferry crossing from Newcastle to Amsterdam.

I do not want to see, hear or think about pirates.

Back in my cabin I tried to rest. After a couple of bobs off the bed to the window to see what the crane was humming about this time, I finally sunk into a pretty deep sleep, wakening about an hour before suppertime. A couple of seconds later it was suppertime. I went down to the officers' mess. There were a couple of guys I had not seen before. One of them asked me if I was bored yet. 'No way,' I said. He said he was. He asked me if I had a Kindle. 'Not at all, I like touchy-feely books,' I said. But I did have a thought about how much easier it would have been to have had a Kindle than lugging my selected personal library with me.

Two slices of pork edged with hot mustard, mashed potatoes and salad were wolfed down. I had a cup of coffee to follow. Brian Oglanby appeared. I thought I had seen him earlier in the day filming from the dockside. We blethered quite a bit, mainly about his documentary and the passion Peter Maddison had for *City of Adelaide*. Brian asked to interview me the next day. I got up and poured another coffee. We agreed it would be good to film with *City of Adelaide* in the background. I asked Brian about his colleague, Petr Strach, who had been inside *City of Adelaide* at Irvine when I had climbed aboard when Peter Maddison occupied the ship. He said he has a full-time job now. Brian talked about finance and I made him roar with laughter when I told him that my mother had given me her funeral fund for this trip. He said that was really quirky. 'That's me,' I said, and went back to my cabin to make a couple of phone calls. I noticed I had a phone message. It was from Alan with a pathetic voice, saying, 'It's only your poor, lonely husband phoning to see how you are.' When I spoke to him he sounded a bit too jolly for me to believe his message! He was going partying with friends and our eldest daughter.

I peeped out of my window and saw a cherry-picker on deck. The two new guys I had met earlier at lunch were operating it. Instead of taking impromptu video from my window and getting insect corpse smudges on it, I decided to go outside. By the time I got there the cherry-picker was folded up and the guys were walking towards the staircase. They passed me and we said goodnight. I went up to the monkey deck again and took some more photos of the deck below, then went to get a drink. I met German on the way. He got me some bottled water, said he would leave it outside my room and I went on down to get a hot chocolate and a cheese sandwich.

With curtains closed and all quiet on deck, I began to set out my story, beginning around 10.30 pm. It is now 1.33 am, 24 November 2013.

I decided to spend the day in Rotterdam where there was a greater choice of shops than at Schiedam. It would be my last chance to get a supply of contact lenses. I had a prescription for contact lenses, but found that no optician I approached in Rotterdam would supply them unless they had carried out the eye test; also they would have had to be ordered in as they did not hold stock. I went to buy a couple of lightweight long sleeve tops and was desperate to have my long hair cut to make it easier to manage. I knew brushing out tangles from wild winds at sea would annoy me. I found a hairdresser who had space, so I waited half an hour till she was free. Afterwards I went in search of a sketch pad and graphite, and some other odds and ends. I looked round the exhibits outside the Maritime Museum before going back to *Palanpur* secure and relaxed in the knowledge that the final clearance for me sailing with her was clinched.

'BOWLED OVER'

Why Me?

TODAY IS OUR final day before sailing tomorrow. I awoke at 7 am after having slept an unheard of, for me, eight hours. Hot chocolate had again worked its magic. I turned over, skipped breakfast and had a lie-in until 10 am. Later, Brian Oglanby took pictures of me for his documentary. This is the first time I have been documented and I found it fun. It was a bit twee, but he insisted I do the *Titanic* pose from *Palanpur*'s monkey deck, copying Leonardo di Caprio and Kate Winslet by stretching my arms out to the side. I was nowhere near as glamorous as her in my padded hooded coat and extra years. I went on deck and posed against *City of Adelaide*. It was so good to be touching her. I did not know when that would happen again, maybe not till we arrived in South Australia.

I was by no means alone in being transfixed by *City of Adelaide* and her wondrous presence. The following abridged transcription is from a DVD Hugh Loney sent me that paints an atmospheric, spiritual picture of his experience with the ship.

'I got a phone call to tell me "Carrick" had a protestor on board. That intrigued me, so I made my way down. I wasn't sure how to get access to the ship. I climbed over a six foot iron railing fence at Ayrshire Metals to get in. The closer I got to the ship the bigger it got, the smaller I got, and I was bowled over just standing next to it. I didn't hear anybody inside so I shouted up 'Hello, protestor!' because I didn't know his name. After two or three minutes a face came to the square porthole and I said, 'How are you doing? Can I get some video footage of you?' He asked if I was with the Press. I said, 'No, no, I just want to document you being here,' and said I was doing local history work, I'm a local artist. He said his name was Peter Maddison. He spoke into the camera for about ten minutes through the square porthole. I was intrigued by why he was there and what he was doing. He seemed to be on his own. It was a cold night the night before and I asked him how he'd got on. He said it was 'Okay, but water was a problem'.

A couple of days later I kept thinking about him sleeping on that ship, so I thought I'd take him some food and some water. I bought two bags of tinned food and two big bottles of water. I had to throw these over the fence. I shouted up, 'Hello, Peter,' and he came to the same porthole. I asked him to send down a rope to hoist up the bags of food and water. He said, 'Why don't you come on board, Shipmate?' I asked, 'How do I get on board?' He said, 'I'll put a ladder down and you come in through this porthole.' So he did that, and I took the bags up and handed them in first. Then I had to work out how to get through this small porthole. It was one leg first, hand outside, hand inside then the rest of me followed through. I became aware of all the noises going on around the harbour: the traffic; the trains going by; the seagulls, and the wind. Something changed for me when I went through that porthole. I don't know what it was. It was almost like a lull in time, time stopped within this vessel for me. I've never been a ship person, being inside this vessel was a whole new experience for me. I was staggered by the dryness of it, the silence, the calmness. It was church-like, cathedral-like, a special place.

I got film footage of Peter. He talked into the camera and gave me a tour of the ship. I knew absolutely nothing and I knew nothing about Peter and he was amazed I should come along and bring him two bags of food out the blue. He said next time I was round I was welcome on board. I can't remember how many times I've been on board but each time was almost the same, not quite the same impact as the first time but once I got in through the porthole I lowered my voice like you would do in a library, or a church. I filmed Peter when friends came from Sunderland to take him back down the road. I asked him if the ship made noises in the middle of the night. 'Oh, yes, a lot of small noises all through the night.' He said to me, 'I now know more about the ship and the ship knows more about me.' I was quite moved by that and I would love to have asked him what it is that the ship knows about him. But that was between him and the ship.

I think the porthole to me became a portal, like travelling from one time outside the ship to another time inside the ship. It was like a coming home for me.'

Hugh goes on to describe how we met. He was sheltering with friends inside their car, drinking hot coffee when they saw me take my harp out of the boot of my car on the day *City of Adelaide* left Irvine for Greenwich. *'I need to get this,'* he said, *'I don't know what's going on but I've got to find out.'* He approached me. His account continues. *'Are you going to play the harp,' and you said, 'Yes.' I said, 'Can I film you?' You said, 'Of course.'*

And the journey for me filming Peter Maddison and his protest is ongoing now with you. What I thought would just be a short 'Hiya, how are you doing?' is ongoing to this day. I'm now supporting you with a wee bit of encouragement like, 'You can do this, it's your journey'. Just before you were leaving you phoned me, you were a bit nervous about going to the ship, and I said to you, 'Maybe the ship's come to you, chosen you'. And I think that's the way life works sometimes, things come to you and you're meant to go with them for whatever reason, or work with them, and this is now your journey. I think it's passed from Peter Maddison, the Australians, and now it's you, and you're all part of the longer history of the ship right back to the people who chopped down the trees to get the timber to make the ship. So it's ongoing. The journey's ongoing.'

With Hugh's words ringing in my ears, my adventure into the unknown began.

City of Adelaide

DIARIES OF HER MAIDEN AND FINAL VOYAGES

SARAH ANN BRAY

(August – November 1864)

and

RITA BRADD

(November 2013 – February 2014)

DAY ONE

August 12, 1864 – Friday

A beautiful day. About 9.30 A.M. a footman came to tell us that the City of Adelaide was in sight. Tom and I took a walk and bought several little things. At 1 P.M. we took a Boat and sailed to the ship. Blanche and I wrote letters to the Patersons. Tom stayed on board for about two hours. We sailed at 4 P.M. We stayed on deck till after we had passed the Eddystone Lighthouse and then went down to bed but not to sleep. We were dreadfully seasick during the night.

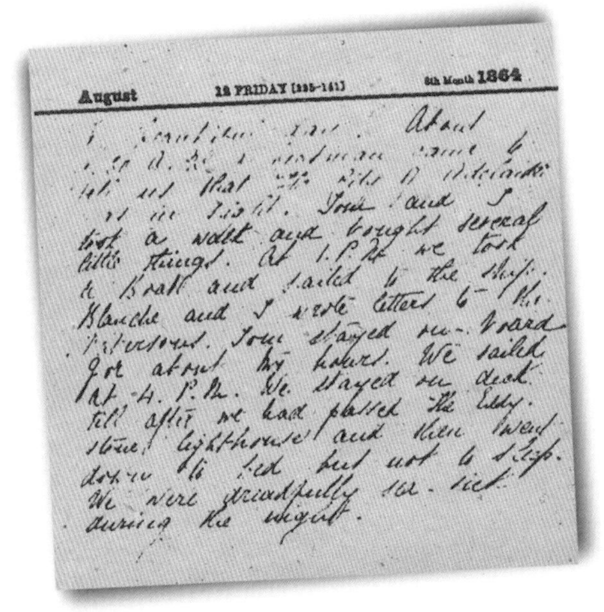

August 12 FRIDAY [225-141] 8th Month 1864

A beautiful day. About
9.30 A.M. a footman came to
tell us that the City of Adelaide
was in sight. Tom and I
took a walk and bought several
little things. At 1 P.M. we took
a Boat and sailed to the ship.
Blanche and I wrote letters to the
Patersons. Tom stayed on board
for about two hours. We sailed
at 4. P.M. We stayed on deck
till after we had passed the Eddystone lighthouse and then went
down to bed but not to sleep.
We were dreadfully sea-sick
during the night.

I have known City of Adelaide all of my life. As a child living in Helensburgh on the Clyde we would visit great aunts who lived in Greenock on the opposite shore in the house that they had been brought up in by their parents, Sarah Ann Bray and John Smith Kerr. The family were proud of the fact that my great grandmother had been born in Adelaide in the 1840s, daughter of an English emigrant who had 'made it'. Although I knew that Sarah had written a diary on the maiden voyage of City of Adelaide, travelling comfortably with her family in First Class, it was decades later I acquired a copy, thanks to the Scottish Maritime Museum. As I grew up I knew City of Adelaide as the RNVR clubhouse on the Clyde in Glasgow – and even was on board at a few parties. Then there were the sad years as the ship sank and despite the efforts of the Scottish Maritime Museum and others it looked like she would rot away and be doomed to an existence as a mere paper record. Then CSCOAL to the rescue! RUTH CURRIE

26 November 2013 – Tuesday – Rotterdam, Netherlands / North Sea

A grey day, 8 degrees centigrade.

City of Adelaide and I are nose to nose on board Motor Vessel *Palanpur*. She is cargo on the deck of this huge steel leviathan, a massive white parcel swaddled in plastic for a voyage that will take us to the other side of the world. I am looking straight out at her from my cabin. I am recalling what she looked like when I first saw her in March 2012, a derelict, languishing forlorn on a slipway at the Scottish Maritime Museum at Irvine.

Sarah Ann Bray is smiling. Her dreamy eyes are trained on the bow of clipper ship *City of Adelaide*. They are old friends that sailed together on *City of Adelaide*'s maiden voyage to Adelaide, South Australia, in 1864. She is looking out from the window of my cabin to where *City of Adelaide* is lashed down to the deck. We are on board MV *Palanpur* from the Harren & Partner fleet, en route from Rotterdam, The Netherlands to Port Adelaide, South Australia. This is *City of Adelaide*'s absolute final voyage, in her one hundred and fiftieth year, and I am going with her.

From the vantage point of the *Palanpur* bridge, I watched several crew members slow-dance with the gangway as it dangled from the hook of one of the twin Liebherr cranes and swung like a metronome. Smaller ladders were removed from the inner side of the ship, and the gangway was manoeuvred into that space. The ladders were taken elsewhere, and the gangway was secured into place with steel arms fixed to the side rails of the ship. The ropes that had steadied the gangway against the side of *Palanpur* were rolled up and stowed away. Below, in the River Maas, a tiny yellow craft resembling a rubber duck in comparison to the size of *Palanpur* sped up to our bow. The ship's Master, or Captain, German Koltakov turned to me, pointed at it and said, 'The pilot boat is coming.' I had expected a substantial tug, and thought he was joking. I saw the yellow duck speed away. Two men appeared on the bridge. It was not till later I realised they had come aboard us from that little yellow duck to guide *Palanpur* from the bridge and control her safe passage out of the River Maas to open sea. I watched the mooring lines be cast off one by one from the stern of *Palanpur*. Her stern swung away at an angle from the dockside, the bow still tethered, until at last she was set free to crab into the flow of the River Maas. A shiver ran up my spine, yet my stomach burned. There was no stopping it now.

It was 1400 hours when we cast off from the wet but calm Mammoet Terminal, Rotterdam. Sailing down the flat water of the Maas River was interesting and picturesque, with industrial landscape mixing with the modern architecture of high-rise flats clad in mosaic tiles, their glazed balconies affording magnificent views to the abundant and goliath river traffic. Chief Officer Igor Boltov remarked on the beauty of these buildings. The river widened to mudflats at the edges, here and there people fished or cycled along pathways. I was reminded of the story of the Little Dutch Boy holding back the tide with his thumb as we spilled out into the North Sea and there was a long stone dyke. As we left the lee of the land, the wind began to whip up. There was a great swell and splash from *Palanpur*'s bow. I thought *City of Adelaide* might be glad of her new raincoat, but really I knew she would rather be sailing under her own canvas with her keel firmly steeped in brine. The strong, broad webbing straps bracing her plastic cover down to the deck and onto the iron cradle supporting her hull began to thrash about in the wind. I watched *City of Adelaide*'s stern rise against The Netherlands background like a frisky foal kicking up its hind legs and dropping them to sprint, then gallop away from a standing start. A group of crew members huddled on the weather deck round the first strap that was in a wild flap. They brought a winch and worked it until the strap was once more taught. It was important that the tension was just right. Just tight enough to stop the flapping, but not so tight as to damage the plastic protective covering that had been shrink-wrapped around the *City of Adelaide* at Dordrecht a couple of weeks before. The crew members repeated the tensioning procedure until they were at last content that our precious cargo was safe.

The crew are nearly all Ukrainian. There are seventeen men plus me, the only woman, the only grandmother, on board. Eighteen in all. An extract from a document given to me by Ruth Currie, great-granddaughter of Sarah Ann Bray written by her great-nephew James Kerr reads:

> *'After a short stay in Blackheath they left London for Plymouth to catch the City of Adelaide on 12th August. There were 18 passengers in all. From the start they had a very rough passage with contrary winds all down the coast of Europe and the west.'*

The pilots who boarded *Palanpur* at the Mammoet Terminal had to disembark now we were in open seas. A boat, *Polaris*, was standing off awaiting instruction. Two-way radio contact brought it charging towards us. Engines idled while the two pilots descended from the bridge. *Polaris* launched a RIB (Rigid Inflatable Boat) that darted through the heavy swell to pull up alongside *Palanpur*. The first pilot dropped into the RIB with no effort and complete accuracy. The RIB adjusted its position against the side of *Palanpur* and soon the second pilot was safely on board the agitated craft. They sped off towards *Polaris* as our engines began to drive. We were on our way. *Polaris* remained in position as the bridge emptied of crew one by one. German turned to me and said it was time for coffee, tea or hot chocolate. A signal to relax. We had gone into auto-pilot.

I went to my cabin to gather my emotions. I placed a kiss on the face of each member of Sarah's family in the photograph Ruth Currie had given me. I lay on my bed with my arms folded behind my head. Soon *Palanpur* rocked me to a sound sleep. Then a noise from the next door cabin occupied by the Second Engineer woke me. I had slept for over an hour. It was not yet time for dinner. I began to write *'Day One : 26 November 2013'*. Sarah's equivalent Day One was 12 August 1864. This would become the format for our story.

When I went for dinner, a huge skewer of pork chunks with roast sliced potatoes and wedges of tomato and slivers of cucumber was presented to me on a large white plate, followed by a home-baked chocolate cupcake. I washed it down with a cup of milk, and finished the fennel tea I had made. I heard great laughter from the crew mess. Time to play after all that hard work.

I retreated to my cabin and continued to write.

DAY TWO

August 13, 1864 – Saturday – At Sea

A fine day. We cannot see land and are sailing along very well. Mama, Blanche and I have been sitting on deck all day scarcely able to move.

27 November 2013 – Wednesday – English Channel

Another grey day. There was quite a lot of thumping and shuddering going on in the night. There had been some wind and rain. There is no sign of land.

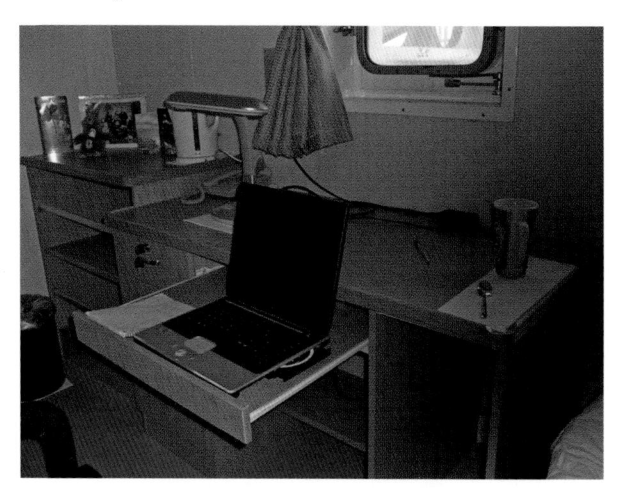

I cannot believe how well I am sleeping on board this massive cargo ship. It feels like being pushed around in a pram. The air conditioner hums away, the cabin is warm. My bed is comfortable and there is a square feather pillow I also use to support my back when sitting at the desk, an ordinary pillow, a duvet and a soft blanket.

I dived out of bed at quarter to ten with a phone call from German. He informed me there would be a safety drill at 10.20 am. I was out of the shower and dressed just in time for Igor's knock that brought me a brand new bright orange boiler suit and waterproof jacket I was told to wear for mustering on the deck. Size 48, the smallest they had. It fitted over my warm clothing. I put on safety boots and hard hat and reached for the life jacket and survival immersion suit stored in the labelled compartment above my wardrobe. I stood inside the outer door ready for the seven short hoots and one long one that would sound the emergency alarm. I clunked down the staircase and joined a few others already at the mustering point on the starboard. I chatted with Stepan about his family back home. He smelled of tobacco. Andriy Vyshnyakov, Second Officer with responsibility of Safety Officer, began to take the roll call. Most of us were dressed the same, but some had green body warmers as well. My father used to wear one of those. We had all brought the red bags that contained our immersion suits. We practised putting on and tying our life jackets, and made sure our torches and whistles were in working order. My equipment was brand new, and everything worked. After this was fire training. As a passenger I was not included in this, so sat in the mustering station. I watched one of the crew put on an asbestos suit he took from a storage bag. The trousers had yellow rubber boots at the end of the legs, all in one piece. He then put on the jacket and was assisted by another crew member who secured it round his middle with a bright orange belt. After this he donned a balaclava I presumed was made up of fireproofed material. He topped off his safety gear by covering his head with a fire helmet with face shield. His hands were protected with gloves. He looked like the *Tin Man* from the *Wizard of Oz*. Stepan brought breathing apparatus and everyone disappeared indoors. When they came out, we mustered again. We were to carry our survival suits in their bags to the stern where the lifeboat pod was fixed. To get to it we had to walk the full length of the deck, 115.14 metres, then climb two levels of stairs. I had seen the lifeboat station on my tour of the ship in Rotterdam. This time the capsule was open. We were all to go inside. I was horrified. Steep steps led down to twenty-four paint-thin iron seats that faced the only access door at the rear, six rows of two seats side-by-side on the left, and six rows of two seats side by side on the right. This seating arrangement meant that on impact with the ocean there would be minimum risk of whiplash or injury. Lifejackets are not worn in the capsule, but are put inside it before you enter and are stowed by a crewmember. We had to remove our hardhats to avoid the risk of head injuries on impact. I left mine outside and stepped into the capsule to take an inner seat around the middle of the pod. I struggled to find the safety belts with all the extra bulk and lying back like an astronaut. Igor helped me, but I realised in the event of a real life emergency I would have to be slick at this; others' lives would depend on how quickly each of us got settled into the cramped space. My knees were bent up tight. The Chief Officer advised me to press my back against the seats with touch points of lower back, shoulders and back of the head. I quelled an upsurge of panic and claustrophobia as the space filled with sixteen further

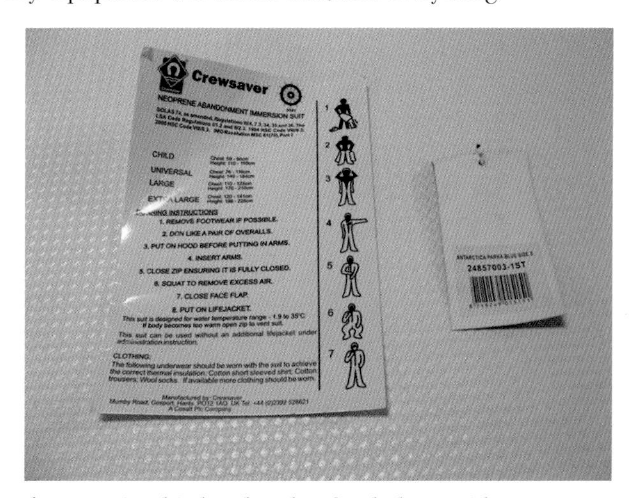

bodies and I anticipated a backwards launch into the sea. German remained on the bridge, directing operations via a two-way radio.

When everyone had been seated for a few minutes, to my great relief we were all to get out again to stand on the platform. Igor told me the next safety exercise – search for terror threat or bomb scare – was not relevant to me as a passenger, and he asked me to return to the bridge. He said he would bring my equipment, so I just took my hard hat. When he brought the equipment later, it was not the same. The lifejacket was not brand new, and its torch did not work. The Second Officer came round later to demonstrate putting on the immersion suit. He said he would attend to my lifejacket. He said it is essential to get into the survival suit within two minutes, so I should practise a lot. My heart sank. This was exhausting! I returned to the bridge where German reiterated I must ask for anything I need.

Igor brought me cleaning fluids, toilet cleaner, cloths for sink, toilet, floor and surfaces in my cabin that I had requested. I had done a basic clean when I first arrived. Now I had a plastic bowl and sponges in different sizes, some with an abrasive side. There was toilet roll and kitchen paper. I asked Igor to show me how to use the washing machine. He took me to the deck below the bridge and opened a door marked *Toilet.* There is a toilet in the corner, but before it is a silver Miele industrial washing machine not much bigger than a domestic one. Above it is a matching dryer. Igor demonstrated the dials and showed me where to put the powder and conditioner. The instructions appeared in Russian on the display. Igor changed this to English.

Lunch today consisted of trout, potatoes and salad, soup for starter as usual. It was similar to yesterday's traditional Ukrainian green borscht, made with spinach. I had a good chat with Igor in the mess. He told me about our journey to Australia. He told me how much he loves Canada and the United States of America. He said things in America are about a third of the price of those in Europe. He told me he was born in Siberia, and when he was eight years old his parents moved to Ukraine. He is married with one child. He works away from home for six months then has four months break. He loves the Great Lakes in Canada where he worked for some time. They remind him of Siberia where it is very open and there is a lot of nature. A section of highway separates a very populated United States of America from a Native American Reservation. His eyes shone at the memory of hearing a wolf howl. Igor spoke of the route we are taking. We load new cargo at Norfolk, Virginia, United States of America then call into Cape Town on the west coast of Africa before rounding the Cape of Good Hope to head for north-west Australia. With the scheduled stops, *Palanpur* would circumnavigate the entire Continent of Australia. I cannot contain my excitement. It just gets better and better.

At lunch German told me there is chocolate on board. And beer. Oh, how I wish he had not. Two weaknesses, and there I was thinking I would have a couple of months away from those to lose a bit of weight. Eating Anatoliy's fabulous meals twice a day is not going to help me with that cause, even though he serves first class healthy and balanced meals. Yesterday's chocolate fairy cake was the first sweet thing that has been served up. Usually there is a piece of fruit for each crewmember. Anatoliy took me into his store, an Aladdin's Cave full of teas: rosehip, fennel, Lipton's Yellow, camomile, peppermint, green. He got a plastic bag, chose a selection and added a bottle of runny honey. Third Officer Andriy Kostenko arrived and took me to another store called the *slop chest*. Here was chocolate, beer and other snacks. I chose a tin of pistachios, a box of Cheese and Onion Pringles, Saltzen sticks, a white chocolate Ritter bar, a milk chocolate Ritter bar with almonds, a box of hard-boiled fruit sweets, a Toblerone, and a tin of Dutch butter biscuits like the ones my father was very partial to, he always had a tin handy for my children when they were small. The tin has Beatrix Potter characters on the outside, and I told Andriy K that my youngest daughter has the full collection of stories from when she small. We added cartons of juice and UHT milk. Andriy insisted on carrying everything, including a case of German beer to my cabin. He said, 'I am very strong.' I feel like a princess. I went back to my cabin and set to cleaning, becoming Cinderella. Igor arrived. He covered the table in my lounge area with something called *elephant skin*. He explained this is an artificial material that grips onto slippery surfaces and things placed on it are stopped from sliding around in the ship's motion. He left the whole roll for me to use as I saw fit. I abandoned cleaning and was soon busy with scissors, fitting the fascinating covering to every surface I could find.

About three in the afternoon I went to the bridge to see what our position was. I found Andriy V working. He is the Health and Safety Officer from this morning. His watch shift is from noon till 4 pm then midnight to 4 am. He showed me our digital position, latitude 49°53.83'N, longitude 003°31.63'W. Our course was 259 degrees and we were travelling at an average speed of 13.5 knots. We were in the English Channel between England and France, approaching the North Atlantic. When we enter the North Atlantic we will proceed west and hold a course of 270°. The temperature outside is 11°C. Andriy showed me the barometer and said that it is checked each watch for a drop, as this indicates a change in the weather. Andriy informed me that we would be passing the Greenwich Meridian about 6 pm tonight, and we would put the clocks back at midnight. He had a glint in his eye and a smile when he said we would gain an extra hour of sleep. I told Andriy that *City of Adelaide* had been in Greenwich in October. I did not go into detail, but said I would make a slide show for the crew to learn a bit of *City of Adelaide*'s history and her continued varied and exciting life.

I returned to my cabin and began to write today's account before going down to supper. I think I may have eaten duck for the first time. It was a huge leg, more like the size of that of a chicken, bigger than any I have seen in the supermarkets in the United Kingdom. The meat was dark, stronger than chicken in flavour. There were also pasta spirals in butter sauce, and salad. Andriy V was speaking with Anatoliy and I scoffed my food, munched a few massive grapes with pips in before going back upstairs. I have switched off my cabin lights. It is 7.30 pm and I am staring out of my cabin window. I am sobbing. I cannot believe this impossible, crazy dream I have had for almost two years is actually happening.

DAY THREE

August 14, 1864 – Sunday – Bay of Biscay

A rough day. There was service in the cabin which only half the passengers were able to attend. In the night the weather was very squally so that we were unable to sleep.

28 November 2013 – Thursday – English Channel to Atlantic Ocean

A rough night with quite a swell. I struggled to get over to sleep, yet enjoyed the motion of *Palanpur*.

In the end I read, re-read and read again the preface of Gavin Francis's *Empire Antarctica*. I had met him at a book awards ceremony where he was the overall winner. I was intrigued he had travelled on a cargo ship to Antarctica, and we chatted about this. This is what he inscribed in the copy of his book I bought:

'For Rita,
an adventurer!
Gavin Francis
Some shipboard reading for you!
Lennoxlove 2013'

We chatted about his next planned book, and he told me he was jealous of my impending trip. I have to say I am jealous of myself. At that point not all was sealed with my journey. All I knew was my request to travel with the heavy-lift cargo ship was being considered.

Cleaning Stations

Today I continued to give my cabin a good clean though it was not that dirty. It was good to freshen it up to my comfort level. It had been prepared in haste, when so much was happening on the dockside and the decks. Someone had made up my bed. It was the floor that needed particular attention. It is amazing how much fluff reveals itself on a pale blue linoleum floor covering. Can someone please tell me just how a very dark, curly pubic hair got into the reading light above my bed? It matched several I found in the drawer under my bed on Day One when I was looking for somewhere to stash my black sandals and red shoes.

THAT FEELS A WHOLE LOT BETTER. I have been down on my hands and knees washing and rinsing the floor. It will never be perfect without some specialist cleaning fluid for the black scuff marks. And no, I do not have a cleaning obsessive compulsive disorder. When my mother and I went to Chelsea Flower Show in 2003, she bought me a beautiful picture of a pressed flower collage with the words *Dull women have immaculate homes* inscribed amongst those pretty squashed petals. Every now and again as I rinsed out my cloths I saw her fingers red raw with disinfectant as she washed down surfaces in our café when I was a child. All I could claim were prune fingers. I hate prune fingers. I gave them a chance to unwrinkle before starting afresh.

For only the third time since I boarded *Palanpur* a week ago, I went down for some breakfast. I fancied a bowl of muesli, but removed the dried fruit. At home it goes on the window ledge for the birds. Anatoliy was playing some rock music as he prepared lunch. When I took my plate through to the galley, I remarked on the music, appreciating it. He became animated, and when I told him I had seen Iron Maiden twice, my kudos went through the roof. He said he has all their albums on his laptop. The band he was listening to is the Russian equivalent to Iron Maiden, he told me. Lunchtime came round very quickly. I had not quite finished my self-inflicted chores, but wanted to get to the mess before 12.30 pm even though it was less than two hours since I had breakfast. There was no point in taking a shower till I had finished cleaning, so I changed my leggings as the knees were wet, wiped my face and combed my hair. The mirror reckoned I was shipshape. On board a cargo ship nothing is set in stone. The smooth, safe running of the ship is the priority. Breakfast is between 7.30 and 8.30 am, lunch 11.30 am to 12.30 pm and dinner between 6 and 6.30 pm. Anatoliy always leaves food out for those who do not make it during the allotted meal times. Delicious green soup with gherkins through it, followed by curry flavoured rice, a pork chop covered with mushrooms and onions topped with a slice of cheese, and salad with lots of shredded red cabbage went down well. Igor was once again my companion. Sometimes there is no one in the mess. On my second day on board I asked one of the crew if I could sit beside him. He replied in the positive, so I took a seat diagonally opposite him. In walked a great bear. 'That's my seat,' he said, in a tone similar to one my three year-old granddaughter would use. I thought of Goldilocks. Later, I saw him going into the cabin next to mine. Second Engineer. I tiptoe through the leaves in the forest very carefully.

Igor is very interesting. He is well-travelled and has a chest stuffed full of stories. Today he told me about China. He has travelled to many places, but the China coastline is never the same each time he returns, so much new building is going on. Food is very good there, and cheap. I thought of dogs. Housing is quite expensive, two thousand dollars per square metre, if I recall correctly. I do not always have my notebook with me. Igor said the Chinese are building roads right through Cambodia and Vietnam. There is no shortage of money. I remarked they are also doing a great deal of building of infrastructure in Africa. I worry for rhinos, tigers, elephants. Igor reiterated for me the procedure for disposing of waste. Glass and tin go in one bin, plastic in another. Paper and cardboard go in a third one for incineration. Each type of waste produces its own type of ash that is then disposed of in port. Food is the only type of waste it is permitted to throw overboard. This makes the fish very happy. We began to talk about plastic in the oceans and waterways. Igor told me that in the Malaka Straits the bottom is thick with plastic. There are many pipes and cables that trap carelessly discarded plastic. I asked him why it is not cleaned up. He said it is an imprisonible offence to even try to do this, because any attempt to clear it might inflict damage to pipes. I told him of the awful scenes I had seen in documentaries, even on the most beautiful, remote islands. There are no fish for parent birds to feed their young. All they find is plastic. Plastic from packs of beer cans, fishing nets, all manner of cartons. They feed this to their chicks and eat it themselves, then choke and die, and their ribcages become bone cradles for this scourge of the planet. Andriy K came in and asked me to bring my ESTA visa for America to German on the bridge.

I got back to my cabin, washed down the outer shower floor, the shower floor and took down the curtain. Each and every plastic hook fixing it to the rail snapped, they were so brittle. At the first one I thought, 'Oh shit,' but then I realised why there was a paperclip where once there had been a plastic hook. I had just finished my shower when there was a knock at my door. 'Hello,' I called. I was glad and I bet he was too that the door was locked, for he turned the handle when I called out. All I had on was a towel. I quickly threw on a pair of leggings and thick jumper and opened the door. Andriy V had come for the ESTA form. I apologised and explained I normally have my shower in the morning, but I had been cleaning. I seem to be making a big story about this cleaning. Hmmmmmmmm. Once I got dressed in fresh clothes, I went up to the bridge to see where we were and to get the readings for today. We are in the North Atlantic, west of Ireland, latitude 49°30.09'N, longitude 012°15.93'W to be precise, holding the course of 270°. Our speed is 12.5 knots. There is a small swell, 1.5 metres from the north-west. It is a treat to chat to Andriy V, for he sees I am interested in the charts and readings. He showed me *absolute zero* on the chart. He told me that we would be crossing the Equator, and that because I will be *crossing the line* for the first time, he will present me with a certificate to commemorate this, and I will be given a new name from the realms of Neptune. I can choose this myself. I spoke of *Ariel*, thinking of my granddaughter's favourite Disney character. But I thought it would be cool to have a name chosen for me. Andriy suggested *Adelaide* and also *Queen of the Sea*. I quite fancy a piratical name, for I have always been a bit of a rebel. I wished now I had brought one of the storytelling books from my library at home. At any rate, I shall be some form of princess. Andriy showed me Antarctica, the southern seas, and Cape Town. He spoke of a great cyclone there had been off the Gambian coast. We talked about the Northern Lights, and I told him of the time I had been so lucky to see them in their full glory when coming home from work one night. I had stopped the car at the top of the last hill before my house, and drunk in the sight of flickering curtains of greens, purples, reds and pinks.

The sea is bubbling away at the flanks of *Palanpur*. It is the colour of the washing powder my mother used when I was a child, spearmint. *Palanpur* is definitely in the middle of the wash cycle. *City of Adelaide* is well-harnessed down, steady in her stays as *Palanpur* rolls her spine from side to side, forwards and backwards and straight again. The twin Liebherr cranes are back to back like sentinels over *City of Adelaide*.

Their great hooks are secured to sturdy, fixed parts of the ship. I can see Number 1 crane hook right outside the window of my cabin. There is a stack of funnels sticking out from the top of the engine room at the stern of *City of Adelaide*. Each one is emitting some sort of exhausted heat, and I see black smoke, grey smoke, and a blurred horizon above another. Over to the port side there is a bright break above the horizon, the colour of buttermilk.
From the bridge window it looks like we are bobbing on a gunmetal blue circular plate.

I returned to my cabin, using the Ukrainian for *see you later* to Andriy that he wrote down for me the previous day – 'До Робачеия' – pronounced *Do Pobachinye*.
I took my first load of washing to the machine one floor up. I shut the door behind me, for the space is cramped, and followed Igor's instructions. It was good to take time to experiment with the dial, and having selected a *Delicates* programme I went back to my cabin and typed up some notes I had taken earlier on the bridge. When I went back up, I found the washing machine was hot, and I dreaded seeing the woollen polo neck jumper I had put in. I transferred the load to the dryer and set that also to a *Delicates* programme. I came down to my cabin again, gathered my bed linen and towels and threw them into the machine upstairs. I returned three times to the dryer for my clothes. The *Delicates* spin was 600 rpm, so they were taking longer than if I had used a 1000 rpm spin speed. There was no hurry. While I was working away at the machines, German and Igor came along the corridor. I asked them how they were today. German responded. 'I am all right, but you are not.' My stomach lurched. 'What is it?' I asked, expecting something devastating. That blooming ESTA visa for United States of America again. There had been further correspondence from Head Office.
It is not possible to use the ESTA form when arriving on a cargo ship.

No America for me. Am I bothered? No. I had already agreed I would not go ashore in Virginia. My purpose on board is to escort *City of Adelaide* back to Australia. I had shaken hands with the Harren & Partner representative/owner agreeing I would not leave the ship in the United States of America. Somewhere along the way after this I was advised it would be best to have a visa for America even if I was not going to leave the ship, and that is why I applied for the ESTA. At the time I wondered whether it was because it would provide me with a get-out if I found I could not hack the journey. It may well just have been a kind thought by well-meaning practised sailors, who suggested that it would be nice for me to have a break from being on board *Palanpur*, and go ashore for a trip. It might have been nice to give a surprise to my family by sending them some Christmas presents from America. I do not think there are any shops in the middle of the Atlantic Ocean: that is where I am told we will be on 25 December.

By the time suppertime came along, I had the clothes from the dryer in my room. I hung them up to air on the three hangers Igor had brought me. He had thought of everything. On arrival I had stored most of my clothes rolled up on the shelves in the wardrobe. The only dress I wanted to hang I had already hung, by lifting the rail in the wardrobe from its socket and slipping the straps of the dress along it, before fixing it back in place. The damp bed linen I decided to dry tomorrow, because I did not want to be wandering about disturbing people and encroaching on their deck level in the evening when they are relaxing. I took it to my room, folded it up and placed it on top of the elephant cloth covered table. I had washed the shower curtain, and folded it up, not having any hooks to hang it back up with. A knock at the door. Andriy V slips eight paperclips into the palm of my hand. 'You are an angel,' I say to him. I hope he does not think I am calling him an angle. When we were looking at the chart earlier in the afternoon, he had pronounced 'angle' as 'angel'. I will tell him the correct pronunciation in time. After supper of a delicious pork stew, I was feeling a bit lonely, so I took out Alan's sunglasses case. Inside, the perfect remedy. His wee MP3 player. I began listening to the Peter Rowan Quartet and *Dust Bowl Children*. I am at home now, with the guitar and banjo strumming in my ears, and the tears begin to flow at the line '*...but it don't pay too much to think of things you leave behind*'.

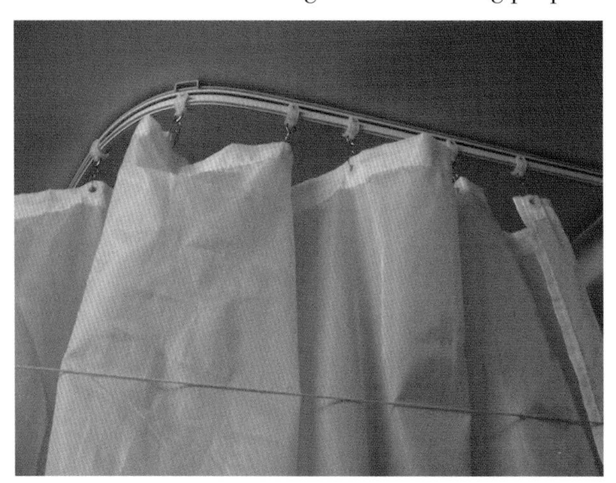

During the Night

It is 5.30 in the morning. The ship continues its sway. I kneel on my bed to look out to the port side. The sky is a sheet of coarse grain wet and dry sandpaper, tiny grains of glass glint in the light of the moon. *City of Adelaide* is having the pain of her years of neglect rubbed down with the rise and fall of the North Atlantic. Crane 1 is holding his arm out, shielding his eyes against the brightness of the moon. It breaks up the silvery beam the moon is projecting at a tangent from the port side of *Palanpur*. *City of Adelaide* poses with pride as her court of stars bows and curtsies at her majesty. Her robes tonight are almost diaphanous. I am frustrated to not be able to go out and take photographs, most of the crew are sleeping, and the heavy steel door to the outside is closed with a heavy bar. For me to open that door, I have to shove the bar from the two o'clock position upright to noon, put my backside against the door, grab a hold on the handrail on the wall on the right hand side, push against it and dunt the door open. I take good care when doing this. I do not want to hurt my back. I sketch the silhouette of *City of Adelaide.*

The sound of the sea caressing *Palanpur*'s hull is the same as the sound of the waves massaging pulverised rocks that make up the beaches of Belhaven and Dunbar. *Palanpur* is swaying from side to side like a dancer with seduction on her mind in her flamenco dress, skirts hoisted, flashing the delicate lace of her underskirts at the winking eye of the moon. Beneath her satin bodice, off-duty crew men and I rest our heads on her bosom and hear the beat of her heart drum out the rhythm of her dance. *Palanpur* is leaving footprints of spearmint bubbles as she traipses through the gentle, rolling waves of the North Atlantic. Everything is quiet and peaceful. The odd clank of metal against metal is the only sound, other than the sea shushing the world. Before I go back between the sheets, I go for a pee, turning on the tap to override the sound, for the cabin walls are thin and a bear sleeps next door.

DAY FOUR

August 15, 1864 – Monday

A fine day. Strong favorable breeze but we are all too sick to care for anything. The Captain is delighted with the distance we have come.

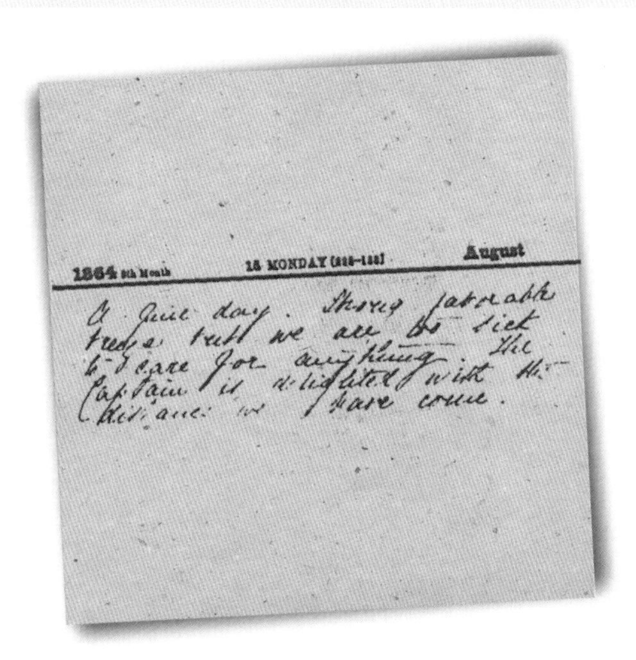

1864 8th Month 15 MONDAY [illegible] August

A fine day. Strong favorable
breeze but we are all too sick
to care for anything. The
Captain is delighted with the
distance we have come.

29 November 2013 – Friday – Atlantic Ocean

A fine, calm day, with bright sunshine off the port side. One of the crew members is suffering badly with seasickness. He has been unable to eat, and has drunk little since he boarded *Palanpur*.

I unwrapped the morning from its crinkly-lined curtains that are so efficient at keeping the daylight from sneaking in beneath my eyelids. The noise they make reminds me of opening Christmas presents. A thin sun spills towards *Palanpur* from the horizon. I dive out of bed and grab the paperclips Andriy had brought me the afternoon before. I sat and twisted them one-by-one, including the blue original one, into the nine eyelets of the shower curtain that I then hung from the rail in the shower room. The makeshift hooks worked perfectly with the runners. I turned the spray on and showered. I was looking forward to using the new dark blue towel Igor had given me a few days earlier. Yesterday I had felt something irritating me after I had towelled myself dry, and found something hard stuck to my upper arm skin. I peeled it off. It was a bogie. Yes, girls. A bogie, those horrible crusty things picked out of noses and eaten by some! I re-washed the area, giving myself a good scrub. I knew this would not happen with a brand new towel. I squeezed my hair dry, then rubbed my body. I looked down and saw I had developed a hairy chest. Then I saw it was not just my chest. My whole body was covered. I had turned into a dark blue teddy bear.

Note to self: Always wash brand new towels before use.

I made my way up to the bridge with my smartphone in hand to capture the image of the outstanding morning. A flag was slung over the window on the port side, shielding those on the bridge from the glaring sun. I asked what country it belonged to, and was told it was for Antigua, *Palanpur*'s port of registration. Third Officer Andriy was on the bridge, vacuuming the non-slip floor. As soon as he saw me he came over. He said he needed some descriptions of me for my shore pass. He looked at my hair. 'Brown,' he said. 'Bottle brown,' I corrected. 'Eyes? Blue.' He scribbled this into a notebook. German came over. He asked Andriy what he was doing. He told him he did not need to complete this information about me as I would not be going ashore in Norfolk, Virginia, United States of America.

City of Adelaide was having some adjustments made to her stays. She had slipped back a little during the night. A group of crew members were clustered around the foremost support. One was pounding at one of the legs of the tripod iron strut with a mal. He stopped. A large chunk of wood had been brought on deck, and a substantial wedge was formed from this by crew members. Igor was taking photographs, and I noticed German had made his way down to watch over proceedings. Before long everyone was satisfied the job was done and the deck was clear once again.

I asked German if there was a slide projector on board so that I could share some of my photos of *City of Adelaide* with the crew. He said there was not, but that if I put the photos onto a memory stick, he could upload them to the bridge computer and distribute them via the Local Area Network. I went outside to the front of the bridge to take in the view in the raw air and feel its fingers ripple through my hair. I noticed in front of me on the prow of *Palanpur* there was a ladder with iron rings round it at intervals, designed to keep safe any crewmember using it. I thought of Jack and the Beanstalk. At the top of it I could see three brass nozzles covered in verdigris. They were attached to the ends of some sort of hose, possibly fire hoses that would draw water from the sea if the need arose. I recalled spending a peaceful afternoon shining up similar nozzles on the deck of sail training ship *Stavros S Niarchos*, whilst crewing her round the Canary Islands over Hogmanay in 2005. I know what I will do if I do not get ashore in Norfolk. I shall get out the Brasso and present Jack with three golden goose eggs.

I went down to my cabin and spent the rest of the morning preparing the sequence of photos, right from Irvine to the ceremony at Greenwich. I added a folder I thought the crew might be interested in, of a car show. It contains great images of steam engines and vintage cars beneath a clear blue sky. The third folder had some random photos from the Tall Ships Race at Liverpool in 2008, mainly of *Mir* and things Beatle-ish, and one of *Mir* at Shetland in the Tall Ships Race of the summer of 2011. At 11.30 am I went down to the mess for lunch, well, breakfast for me, as I had not yet eaten. Tomato soup made with tinned tomatoes was served, followed by salad, a pork chop covered with mushrooms and onions and topped with a slice of cheese, and pasta spirals. Anatoliy told me that this calm weather is unheard of in the Atlantic. Normally it is pretty rough, or stormy. After lunch I went back up to check the photos on the memory stick, then took it to the bridge. German tried to copy them onto the computer but it did not work. The memory stick is temperamental. I pocketed it to try another day. I took my reading from the computer, latitude 49°29.79'N, longitude 020°27.46'W. Course 270° will be maintained for the duration of the voyage to Norfolk. After this I cracked open a beer, and began my entry for today. I had hoped all afternoon to put my damp linens into the drier, but it was busy each time I passed it. It was not until 7 pm I finally removed it from the drier, after a half hour cycle, and supper. During a supper of pork meatballs, salad and pasta, I had a good blether with Valeriy, the Chief Engineer. He is from Kiev, is married with two boys, one aged eighteen, the other six. 'Both with the same wife.' He must have read my mind processing the age gap between his children. We talked a bit about the ship. Once again a crewmember remarked on how he would have preferred the ship to be German built rather than made in China. I felt the same.

DAY FIVE

August 16, 1864 – Tuesday

Fine day. Contrary winds.

30 November 2013 – Saturday – Atlantic Ocean

A blue sky with pink-tinged clouds is emerging from the black of the night. We are going along steadily after a night of swell and quite a bit of rolling that forced me to bed to avoid falling over.

Two pees through the night. I have found a position where I can almost complete this bodily function in silence, depending on how the ship is rolling. I secured everything in my cabin last night, right down to the empty beer can that threatened to clank inside its plastic bag in the metal waste bin. I stashed it in my fridge along with the plastic litre bottle of water I had drunk.

This morning I awoke to thoughts of America and the red tape saga around the ESTA. My normal reaction to what has been happening would be to feel that I am a nuisance. It was a name I was frequently called by my father when I was a wee girl, and if someone tells you that often enough, you begin to believe it. It sticks, even though the tone he said it in was not always unkind. But today I am taking German's attitude. I wondered if there would be a guard posted at the end of the gangway, that rainbow leading to the pot of gold of Norfolk, Virginia, or would I be placed under cabin arrest? Will I be allowed ashore? Will I want to go on shore after this inflated experience? Where was the *special relationship* that is supposed to exist between the United States of America and the United Kingdom and the Celtic connection with Scotland? I am sure none of us expected my application would cause such a stir. There is a week to go before we near the shores of Norfolk. I am a tiny wren, flitting into and fleeing from the feathers of the Mighty Golden Eagle.

This morning I will tell German that I have a formal letter of invitation to Australia from the Directors of Clipper Ship City Of Adelaide Ltd. I will also tell him I have been in email correspondence with the Scottish Government Minister for Cultural and Foreign Affairs, Fiona Hyslop, over my journey to Australia with *City of Adelaide*. I had an acknowledgement to my email before I left Scotland, but I do not know if I have had a full reply, because I do not have internet access on board *Palanpur*. It exists, but I do not have access. I had sought advice from Ms Hyslop on what department I might apply to for some funding for my journey, for although I am self-financing it, I hope I will receive some support from the Scottish Government.

It would be nice to be able to give my mother her funeral fund back. I am treating her loan as an insurance policy that she will not be going anywhere while I am away! She will want to hear all about everything when I get back. There are several other potential sources to explore, such as Creative Scotland in my capacity as a writer; Historic Scotland, since that Department has been assisting with the return of *City of Adelaide* to Australia; Visit Scotland, not only because *City of Adelaide* has had a long involvement with Glasgow and Irvine in her life when she was known as *Carrick* and used by the Royal Naval Volunteer Reserve and others as a clubhouse in Princes Dock, Glasgow, but also because of the diaspora of Scots who are connected to *City of Adelaide*, particularly those whose forebears emigrated to Australia on her; and the Department of Culture and Foreign Affairs, who wish to strengthen cultural links with Australia.

I went to the bridge to say *good morning* and to see whether there is any progress with my visa. German told me he thought everything would be all right because I am from Scotland, and my ancestors went to America two hundred years ago. I beckoned him close and said *sotto voce*, 'My father was Ukrainian, I am a first generation Scot.' I thought this may cause further complications with the granting of a visa. I had no idea when I came aboard *Palanpur* that I would arrive in little Ukraine. Friends had suggested the crew might be Barbadians, or Filipinos, but no one considered Ukrainians. I squeeze his little teddy bear I brought with me. German's reaction to my paternal parentage was one of disbelief. I was not surprised. He walked away a few paces, then came back. 'It's true?' A brief smile flickered across his mouth. He told me about Ukraine. He spoke of his hometown that is about the same distance from Odessa as my home is from Edinburgh, about thirty miles. He spoke of where my father came from, near L'viv. It is almost one hundred per cent Ukrainian, whereas in other areas, particularly in the south, the population is diluted by all sorts of border nationalities, with inter-marriages with citizens of Belarus, Poland, Russia and so on. Kiev has a very good university. I am on a feeding frenzy for information about this culture that makes up fifty percent of my parentage. German spoke of currency. There are eight 'grybo' to one US dollar. People can exist on about five hundred dollars a month. This covers food, energy and so on. Education is expensive, and university education varies in cost depending on the university. German asked me if I had been to Ukraine. I said I had not, but that I would like to go sometime. I told him I thought not having the language was detrimental, but now I have learned English is taught in schools there, I am no longer daunted. When I was small my father encouraged me to learn Ukrainian. I would sit on his knee in the evenings and read from 'Bykbap', pronounced *Bookvar*. I learned how to say, 'Where is my Daddy?' 'There is my Daddy.' 'Where is my Mummy?' 'There is my Mummy.' I even spent time one summer at a Ukrainian Camp at Middleton Hall, near Edinburgh, with my older brother. I am excited to learn something of my father's homeland first hand, and now I might learn some of the language.

I went to lunch at 11.45 am. Today Anatoliy tells me the soup is Eintopf. Igor came in. We exchanged *bon appetites*. He told me Eintopf was soup, traditionally made in Germany at the weekend from all the leftovers gathered earlier in the week. Every scrap of food was vital to the impoverished population; nothing was thrown away. Traditionally Eintopf is made so thick with all the ingredients that you can stand the spoon you use to eat it with in it, so that it is at right angles to the bottom of the bowl you eat it from. Anatoliy's version is a thinner consistency to suit our more privileged situation, more like that of lentil soup. Good size chunks of potato and dissected slices of Wurst, or German sausage, float in it. I gathered a handful of croutons from a side bowl and scattered them over the surface of the soup. It made it perfect.

I made my way to my seat at the far end of the mess. Igor came back in, having taken his empty soup bowl to the galley, where he swapped it for a platter of carbohydrates and protein. As always, the greeting of *bon appetite* floats across the mess between whoever is seated and whoever is coming in. I asked Igor about the place he told me of a few days before, where he heard the wolf howling. It is at Lake Superior, South Alaska, and he reiterated the difference in landscape from the American side and the side of the Native American Reservation. He told me Little Red Riding Hood smuggles cigarettes and alcohol to the Native Americans, and that she must watch out for the Big Bad Wolf who would howl and eat her up if she got caught sneaking in her illegal basket of goodies, that most other people on the planet have the freedom to access.

Valeriy sat beside me in his place. He also told me the background to Eintopf. I did not let on Igor had already filled me in on this, or that I already knew about it before that. The bear came in. No greeting. His stay was brief. He took only Eintopf. I began to chat to Valeriy, reviving last night's conversation when he had asked me what my husband thought about me making this journey. I told him at first he was not happy about it. I said it is my passion and he knows I am headstrong. I said it has been my wish to make this journey with *City of Adelaide* for two years. I told him I felt a spiritual connection to the ship and how I had found out about her, and that I am writing this final voyage in tandem with Sarah Ann Bray's diary from the 1864 maiden voyage.

Back in my cabin I look out of the window and see *City of Adelaide*. I smile at her. I can see a squall rising behind us, and the wind is whipping up peaks of white alongside *Palanpur*. I reckon we are at a Force 7, I will check this when I go up to the bridge at around 3 pm. I wish I had thought to bring some of Alan's seafaring books with me so that I could accurately read the waves and determine wind speed, but no matter. I learn better on the hoof anyway, and I had brought so many books I would have struggled to bring more. It is getting to be quite rough, and I am feeling sleepy after lunch. I am not good at picking off meat from chicken wings and legs, but the salad and rice were tasty. I went to my laptop and found all of Day Four had been lost. I can only think I chose *No* to changes when it came to saving the document. I was annoyed and felt deflated about doing any more writing today. There is so much fresh information churning out each day it is hard to keep up without having to recall yesterday's events as well. I went up to the bridge and Andriy V was on watch. He seemed subdued today, so I did not linger. The clock has gone back another hour. That is two since we left Greenwich Meantime. We continue on latitude 49° give or take a few minutes and seconds. Our longitude reading is 028°30.66'W.

It is 12°C outside. Just before lunch I had seen a bird away over towards the horizon. There is one above the *Palanpur* now, hanging in the wind like a kite being pulled by strings from the deck of *City of Adelaide*. I see another, further in the distance. The waves are thrusting past our hull. They are gunmetal grey, mottled with Prussian blue. It is easy to mistake their white peaks for birds diving into the deep. The sun is pale off the port side. Pale, but so strong that to look at it is blinding. A palette of grey tones smudges the clouds, and here and there a selection of blues peep out from behind them. Within minutes the pale sun is covered by a donkey-grey rag, yet it manages to scribble a silver line along the horizon. The wind is whistling dolefully to the sound of the clashing cymbals of Neptune.

On my way to supper, I met the bear on the stair. He swept his arms for me to come down past him; I invited him to come up past me, but he persisted and I descended. I met him again later at supper and asked him his name. 'Vitaliy,' he replied, with a wide grin. He was not so grizzly after all. When I arrived at supper Valeriy was the only person in the mess. We exchanged *bon appetites* and I took up my place beside him. I told him about my father being Ukrainian. This brought forth some information that made me glow inside. I felt myself getting closer to my father. Valeriy said he lives in Kiev, where it is very beautiful. He asked where my father had come from, and I told him a village about eight miles from L'viv. I told him I had seen pictures in books my father brought back from visits to Ukraine when eventually he could return safely, but that it was wonderful to hear of the City first hand. He told me western Ukraine is very beautiful. We talked of the rich soil and the vast wheat fields. I spoke of my father's visits back home and of the few relatives I know of. Valeriy told me also that there is a great mix of bloods with neighbouring countries. Most people in Ukraine can speak Russian. It is taught in schools. At one time there was an attempt to eradicate the Ukrainian language, but it has endured. He told me his son is studying law, and hoped he would find work after qualifying. I said it would give him a sound grounding for any job if it did not work out. I asked if he was going to specialise in criminal or civil law, and he told me he does not have to decide on this until next year. I asked Valeriy about the housing situation in Ukraine. He told me most people buy their own houses; they are not individual houses but in the main, flats. I asked about conveyancing, thinking this would be an opportunity for a career based in law. He said things are changing, Ukraine is aligning itself to the European Union and he is not sure of the current situation. We talked about language, about my early learning of Ukrainian. He is very pleased to be able to practise the English language. He talked about differing pronunciations of English and Scots, and how it is hard sometimes to understand dialects. I said Scotland is a small country compared to Ukraine, with many dialects and sometimes even I have difficulty in understanding the very broad accents. And then there is Gaelic. I said this is being taught in schools mainly on the Hebridean Islands; not many people speak it, but this is changing.

I told him it is St Andrew's Day today, and that Scotland and Ukraine share this saint who visited Ukraine but not Scotland. He shrugged his shoulders, not knowing about this. He asked me if there were many celebrations, and I said most main towns would have some music and dance to mark the day. I told Valeriy about the town of

St Andrews, and said that it is famous for golf. 'Do people play golf in Ukraine?' I asked. He replied, 'No, only football.' He asked if we call football *football* in Scotland, or did we call it soccer. 'Football,' I said with emphasis. Valeriy told me the words for *good morning*, and *good evening*, but I have forgotten them. *Thank you*, I remember. I asked him if he would write them down with pronunciations, and how they would be written in Ukrainian. We are exchanging cultures and my root is growing arms and legs. Valeriy voiced a thought I myself have had since the first couple of days on board *Palanpur*. Why, out of a crew of fifteen Ukrainians and only two Russians does the crew speak Russian? Although there are similarities in the languages, some pronunciations in Ukrainian are very different. Valeriy left me mulling over my chats with German and him. It has indeed been interesting today as far as my Ukrainian heritage is concerned. I returned to my cabin, resolved to begin writing Day Four again. There is a definite jinx about. My laptop did a complete flip and ended up in portrait layout so that I had to twist my head to read it. I managed to get the cursor that had become unstable to point at the stages to *shut down*, and succeeded. Curious to see whether it had resumed normality, I switched the laptop back on. It came up in its usual landscape display. I decided to do a system restore to see whether I could clutch at straws and recover Day Four. No success. I ended up playing Pinball and Solitaire. Anatoliy had laughed at supper when I told him about the loss of the document and said I was going to have to miss playing Pinball until I had re-typed the work.

DAY SIX

August 17, 1864 – Wednesday

Showery day. We were obliged to take shelter several times in the Saloon which looked like a hospital with all the sick people lying about.

01 December 2013 – Sunday – Atlantic Ocean

A very windy day with a rough, swelling sea. Horizontal spray and rain is lashing the Liebherr crane outside my window. *City of Adelaide*'s raincoat is dripping. The sky and sea share fifty shades of grey.

I was awake till midnight plus twenty minutes, 10.20 pm Greenwich Meantime. A storm is raging. The ship is hurling through wind and waves. The constant knife-edge whistle, sometimes like a wolf's howl, cuts through the night's shroud and murders any thought of sleep. The ship is juddering and I am thinking of Cabin 503's lifejacket and immersion suit I saw outside the Chief Officer's cabin as I went down to the slop chest before 6 pm, and my supper. I checked the number on the equipment he had given me after drill on Wednesday. 305. They had got muddled up.

I put on the headphones of my husband's MP3 player to muzzle the howling wolf, and headed towards Antarctica with Shackleton on the safer vessel of the pages of a book, with Karine Polwart as my singing companion. I fell asleep with the light on and awoke at 5 am to deadened thudding as *Palanpur* slapped her way over one trough of waves to another. This is the wildest sea so far. We are rolling like a gimballed cooker. I feel for the poor lad below who has suffered seasickness from Day One. Yesterday German told me he has not eaten and has drunk little since we left Rotterdam nearly a week ago, but that he was a little better having managed to take seasickness pills. German says he may have to disembark at Norfolk to fly home if he does not overcome his condition. I am amazed at how things are not flying about, although just after midnight there was an almighty crash outside, on C Deck where my cabin is. Someone went to investigate, and I could hear some clashing and scraping as whatever it was was cleaned up. I do not have much stored on surfaces; this would amuse Alan, for he teases me about my *flat surface syndrome*; he thinks I cannot bear to see a surface without something on it. The elephant skin Igor gave me is holding steady the kettle and lamp, Teddy, and three cards from my girls back home between whose generations I am sandwiched.

If I was making love at this time, neither of us would need to move. I dozed off. *Kettles boiling*, I heard in the distance. I opened my eyes. It was just the frenzied song of the wind, its throat shrilling out a reveille on the instrument of my cabin porthole seals. I am reminded of a screaming banshee. It is a sound that could drive you insane, and I reached for the MP3 player. *Jeez*, I jumped out of my skin. A vintage motorcycle had crashed into my ear and splattered me on the ceiling. I had put on *Voice Recordings* instead of *Music* and found a day out Alan had had with Eric to a motorbike show. I turned the volume down from fifteen to eight and wondered why anyone would want to record seventeen minutes of passing motorbike engines. I admit it does give me a great thrill to hear and see them whenever swarms of motorbikes go past, like in Callander, during the Poetry Scotland Weekend in September, and in Rotterdam just the other day. When I get home I might just experiment with a sound sample of motorbike engines, and write a harp tune around it. Suddenly, silence. I am about to remove the earplugs when a horse whinnies in my ear. It is Ginny, my old mare I had for twenty-three years from when she was aged ten. It is the morning of the last day of her life. The birds are singing in the March bloom of spring. I have taken her out from her field to have some last special moments with her. She is munching along the verges on her favourite wild fennel, burdock, thick blades of grass and wild garlic. Her prehensile lips are adept at selecting exactly what she wants, and if a piece of root is still attached to it, she grinds her teeth with expertise until it falls to the ground. At last we must return to the house. Her hooves are clip-clopping against the tarmac road. She is walking the green mile. The vet is due at 1 pm to still the breath of this horse, my best friend who has shared all my joys and secrets and sadnesses. I rub my favourite place between her ears, under her forelock. It is soft as cotton wool. I find it unbearable that this beautiful creature is still so alert, intelligent and able, yet she is growing thinner and thinner each day despite increased feeding. She has had cancer for several years, melanomas have spread from the top of her neck to between her front legs. It is impossible to know what is going on inside her, but it is the ones under her tail that have sentenced her this day, for her muscles are not strong enough to expel her poos beyond the mass of lumps under her tail. The vet arrives, she administers a sedative to Ginny's neck and leaves the cannula in. All the way up the field my horse whinnies. We stop at the chosen spot. Her grave has already been dug by our farmer neighbour, with his JCB. The vet gives her yet another Polo mint. She attaches the syringe with the fatal dose to the cannula and presses the plunger. My best friend drops to the ground. Stone dead. I throw my arms around her. Her minty breath freezes against my cheek.

Exactly four weeks later, I lost Morgan, my second horse to organ failure. Cause? Suspected broken heart.

Liquorice and fennel tea went down exceptionally well this morning. I decided it was not safe to shower in the unsteady weather conditions. The shower curtain closed and opened itself with the roll of the ship. I headed to my bedside table for my notebook. Before I reached it a surge threw me backwards onto the bed so hard my legs went up in the air!

I am not sure Cheese and Onion Pringles are the thing for breakfast at 10.40 am in these near-gale force conditions, but I am giving them a try. I am amazed the elephant skin is keeping my cup steady and marvel that humans are so clever, yet despair that they are also destructive, and intolerant of each other's customs, beliefs and cultures. I thought I saw sunshine reflecting on *City of Adelaide*, but it is just the Liebherr crane. Chrome yellow is Alan's favourite colour for a car. We have had several sports and kit cars in the past clad in that colour. At least they saw us coming. A huge sideways wave clobbered the side of *Palanpur* and sent one of my cards from home flying off the bookcase. I tucked all the cards safely away into the top drawer of my desk along with the photograph of Sarah's family. I am thinking of the contrast of my living conditions on board *Palanpur* compared to theirs on board *City of Adelaide*. I have all mod-cons and comfort is home from home. I imagine Sarah would have had cold comfort beneath scratchy woollen blankets, damp from the sea spray, food of who knows what quality. Was there heating on board? There would have been paraffin lamps for light, and these would have radiated a measure of heat. Were there log burning stoves? Were there weevils in the flour? What practicalities did the women have to cope with menstruation? How did they dry their heavy clothing? Were there vermin sheltering in *City of Adelaide*'s secret cracks? She did, after all, carry cargo back to Britain from Australia, and wheat is tempting to any small creature.

I went up to the bridge. Andriy K is on watch during these four hours. Our wind speed is 6 to 7, about 28 to 33 mph, near-gale conditions with waves 4 to 5 metres high. Andriy said he needed some information from me for Customs in the United States of America. I had to give him a list of what electronic equipment I have with me. One laptop, one mobile phone, one MP3 player, one external hard-drive. Then I remembered my neighbour's old Mac laptop she had loaned me as a spare at the eleventh hour. Andriy told me Customs in South Africa can be pretty scary. They can come on board and search everything, even making sure you are not smuggling anything in your socks. That knocked on the head my brother's idea that I could stash some cash for an emergency return home in my socks. Andriy was very thorough today about showing me the ship's log. Every two hours entries are made relating to course, magnetic compass reading, wind speed, speed of *Palanpur*. Today we are going at 13 knots, that is, 15 metres per second. We are on course latitude 49°30'N, longitude 035°36.00'W. Temperature is 8°C. Magnetic compass heading is 285. This compass is located on the roof above the bridge. Andriy told me of monsoons and weathers en route to Singapore. He showed me the gyro compass locked in the computer station on the bridge. *Palanpur* undergoes three to five inspections in a year. Africa is very strict about ships having their inspection certificates up to date.

There were a few spaces at lunch today, only me and Vitaliy at first, then Valeriy arrived. There was not much chat. I took my plate back to the galley for Anatoliy. We laughed when I balanced it against the motion of the ship. 'I am dancing with my plate,' I jested. I met a second Igor, Igor Ivanov who was in the galley with Anatoliy. I introduced myself and we shook hands with a *Pleased to meet you.* Anatoliy and I had a good blether today. He told me he is having a career change. He never intended to be a Cook, but an Electrical Engineer. He works eleven hours in the galley, and then does his home study course. He prepares assignments whilst sailing on board, and sends them when he gets to a port. His log is then marked. In the afternoons after his duties in the galley are completed, he goes to the engine room for as much electrical instruction as can be given in that more motor mechanical environment. Anatoliy told me that there are only twelve people on his course, whereas there are sixty on courses to do with Navigation and so on. He became a cook because there are no longer cadet apprenticeship places with Harren & Partners. They stopped offering these in 2012, but in 2017 it is going to become compulsory that all ships carry an electrician on board. I said to Anatoliy that he will be in great demand and will be able to command his own level of salary. We laughed. I love Anatoliy's *Beyond The Nine Dots* thinking, or, lateral thinking. We had pork stew for lunch. I asked Vitaliy about the whistling from my porthole. He said it is not closed properly. Later, I screwed both the large porthole catches tight to the frame and silenced the banshee.

I did not go back up to the bridge at 3 pm, deciding instead to type up the technical notes from the morning, and the chat with Anatoliy at lunch-time. For supper I was presented with squid rings. Now I had a dilemma. I had never eaten squid, for I am not very adventurous with seafood, sticking to cod, haddock and the occasional pair of lemon soles. I do not eat prawns or any sort of shellfish. The squid was served with a tasty savoury mushroom bulgar rice. There was salad with little cubes of mild cheese through it. The first thing I put in my mouth was a squid ring. I bit through it, and was pleasantly surprised by the tender texture. I had heard that it can be very rubbery. The flavour was nowhere near as strong as I imagined, and I managed to eat three of the six rings on my plate. Anatoliy and Vitaliy, who was chatting to him in the kitchen, could not believe that I, a Scot, had never eaten squid before. Anatoliy obliged me by meeting my request for coffee and toothpicks after supper. I took my swag to my cabin and stashed it with glee.

I plugged myself into Pink Floyd. *Meddle* provides the perfect music for these sea and weather conditions. After my rest and relaxation, I worked until just after 1 am. The ship was very unstable due to the weather conditions. My cabin is cold. I got into my pyjamas, pulled up the cosy velour blanket Igor had given me over my duvet, and snuggled down. But sleep avoided me. I think the Sandman must suffer from seasickness. It is impossible for me to get comfortable with the roar of the sea and the roll of the ship. At some points I feel as though I am going to be ejected from my bed. A heavy thud breaks through the roar. And another. And another, and several more, until one of the crew on C Deck gets out of bed and secures the outer door that has somehow opened us all up to the elements. I try to sleep. I keep my light on. I peep out to port, and wish I had not, for I see a cauldron of boiling liquid racing along the hull of *Palanpur*, desperate to burn its acid through her steel skin. At 4 am I crack open a small can of German beer, my second in a week. I got a case of it from the slop chest when I got nuts, chocolate, fruit juices, boiled sweets, Pringles and so on the other day. I have found since my first visit there that there is also whisky, vodka and wine on board. This is because Andriy K gave me a picking list at lunch before my second visit to the store. It has my name at the top of it, and the first column has been filled out with the choices of goodies I made the other day. I have now replaced the Toblerone and Ritter Milk Chocolate with Almonds bar, and have bought a tin of cashew nuts to add to the as yet unopened can of pistachios. And I now have a bottle of J P Chenet Merlot, stashed in my wardrobe, so that it does not roll about and smash. What I do not have is a corkscrew.

My diary is becoming a twenty-four hour one. I was still awake at 4 am, but the wee beer was soporific. My last recollection of this night was of me wondering how the passengers coped in 1864 without the benefit of electric light, warmth, engines when they could not sleep.

DAY SEVEN

August 18, 1864 – Thursday

Almost a calm. We have scarcely advanced in the right direction. The Captain has been about the same latitude at the same season fifteen times and never experienced such unfavorable weather.

02 December 2013 – Monday – Atlantic Ocean

Much the same weather conditions as yesterday, the wind is perhaps a little less strong. There are patches of blue squeezing through the grey.

There are zeppelins on the horizon, throwing out thousands of ropes in an attempt to tether down. There is a definite opalescent wash beneath these clouds, and a single torch shines a beam from beneath the malachite onto the turbulent waves. The sky is a mess, an apple pie bed like the ones girls used to make at my boarding school just thirty miles from my childhood home. Hairbrushes, toilet bags, knickers, padded bras, toothbrushes, toothpaste, sanitary towels – anything the girls could lay their hands on to make a bed uncomfortable was chucked in. The bottom sheet at the foot end of the bed was then folded back and tucked in halfway up the bed, so that when the victim tried to get in, they ended up in the foetal position with their feet meeting a dead end full of prickly, cold horrors. Pale amber, freshwater pearls, bone, silver and mercury are all in the sky mix this morning. I see a shimmering angel hovering, his shadow illuminating a path towards *Palanpur* and *City of Adelaide*. Handkerchiefs that have mopped the sadness from Neptune's eyes are wrung out, his spent tears falling on our decks. He is sad, for he does not mean to get so wild. *Palanpur* tips them overboard, returning them till the next time.

I dreamed of receiving emails during my sleep, between 4 am and 9.50 am. They brought good news. Who knows when I will be able to log in to any of my communication networks. With my rapid departure, I was not able to send apologies for a number of commitments I had, and wanted to do this. My hair and skin were delighted when I said good morning to them today. They missed me yesterday, with me skipping my shower with the sea being so rough. I was glad there is a grab rail in the space, because the ship is still pitching from side to side at various degrees. After my shower I got out my handbag for the first time in a week, and looked for the little Beatrix Potter mirror that had been a gift to one of my daughters in the mid-1980s. I am glad I am not superstitious, for I cracked it by accident just before I left home.

I went up to the laundry and put the two guilty dark blue towels in for a shave. The fluff that came off the drier filter when I collected them later could have made a cat's blanket. I also did a general wash, so everything is up to date. I went up to the bridge to see if German was about. He was not. It is two days since I saw him. Andriy V was on watch. I asked him what the structure on the front of the boat was. 'It is the mast,' he said. I never gave it a thought that a mast could be so short, being more used to the tall masts of sailing ships. He talked me through the Navigational Rule Book and drew me a diagram about what lighting *Palanpur* must have. He drew in the angles. There is a claxon on the mast to warn other ships of our presence in the event of poor visibility, such as in fog. He outlined Rule 1 to 19 are the Basic Rules; 20 to 31 are Lights and Shapes; 32 to 37 are the rules for Sound; 38 is Exemptions and then there are loads and loads of Annexes and Additional Signals. He said it is the *seaman's bible*, and all sailors abide by these rules. He offered me to take the book away. I shall borrow it somewhere between the United States of America and South Australia. I asked Andriy about the brass fittings on the top of the mast. On closer inspection there was no way they were water hoses attached to the nozzles. Andriy said they were covers for the electrics for the lights on the mast. I could see it all now. I asked him about the ladder with the circular cage around it. I said a person would have to be quite thin to be able to climb it. He said this was not the case. So I said I wanted to polish the brasses if I could not get ashore at Norfolk, and he laughed. 'Rita,' he said, twinkling. 'That is not necessary.'

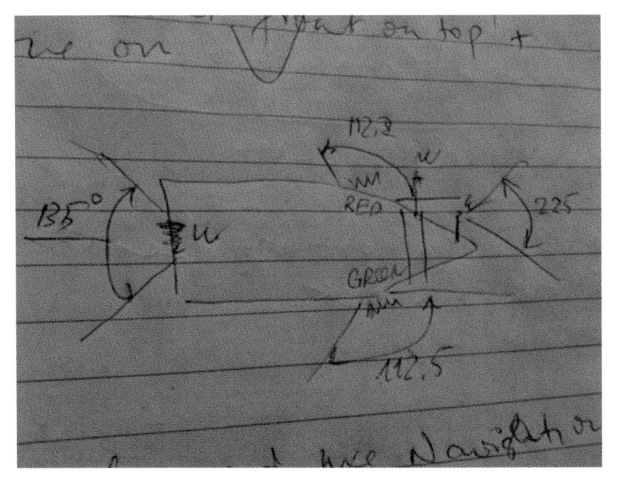

I thought we might have come about 1,500 miles since we left Rotterdam. Andriy checked the log. At noon today we had travelled 1,899. We still have 685 miles to go till we reach Norfolk. We are averaging about 300-350 miles maximum per day. We have changed our course today to 250. I saw this on the gimballed compass. We are at latitude 45°15.47'N, longitude 041°06.53'W today. We talked about crew quarters a bit. Officers have more than ample accommodation, with seating areas, en-suite showers and so on; apart from food and cooking facilities, everything you need is behind one lockable door. The crew have what I have deduced to be cubicles. 'The more space you have, the more you have to clean,' said Andriy. We laughed. I agreed with him.

I amused him by telling him about the *Dull women have immaculate homes* picture my mother bought for me at Chelsea Flower Show. Andriy knew about this annual event in London. I liked the sailors' philosophy he shared with me: *White Vessel, black life*, because it means a lot of cleaning. I asked how the young cadet was who was suffering seasickness. I was delighted to find he is much better. Andriy explained favourable positions to be in when the ship is rolling. The higher you are, the bigger the roll, the lower you are, the less. Andriy gave me a really good tip. 'If you are not sleeping because of the rolling, sleep on your corner couch at right-angles to the prow of the ship.' This makes sense, as it puts you in synch with the roll of *Palanpur*. I will definitely follow this welcome advice. It was during this conversation I gave Andriy the correct pronunciation of *angle*, and he was glad.

Andriy took me on a trip to where the North Atlantic Current is – where the Labrador Current and the Gulf Stream meet. The cold water of the former mixes with the warm water of the latter, and this creates unsettled waters. He also told me he has never had a problem with Customs in Cape Town. No visa is required, and he advised me to make a visit to Table Mountain if I can. When Andriy had a task to do I went down and sorted my washing, putting on the drier again. I also went to get the memory stick with the photos on it that had not copied over to the ship's computer the other day. This time it was successful, and he was interested to see the Haddington Car Show, but more interested to see just what lies beneath the *City of Adelaide*'s raincoat. He was really impressed by her beauty. I left Andriy to get on with his tasks. Cleaning out the filter coffee pot would be one of them. He apologised for the weak strength of what he had presented me with, and said he needed to replenish the bridge stock to make a decent cup.

Lunch today was chicken liver pancakes. I declined, and raided the fridge for a few slices of cheese and Polish pork sausage to have with the savoury rice and cucumbers instead. Valeriy came in and ate his lunch. He went for seconds, and I wished him *bon appetite*. An alarm sounded in the mess. Valeriy explained there is something in the engine room that needs attention. The alarm sounds on the bridge, in the cabin of the engineer who is on Watch, in the mess and in the engine room itself. It can go off during the night and must be answered. It is a long way from bow to stern on this ship, and my mind thinks of manoeuvering along that lonely deck in the dark, with waves crashing into the sides of *Palanpur*, the plastic iceberg of *City of Adelaide* towering above, and her raincoat belts fixed to the deck. The guardrails provide little in the way of protection if King Neptune sneezes at the wrong moment.

For supper there was sauerkraut with a little grated carrot through it, delicious mashed potato and three slices of beef with sauce over them. I have a tiny morsel stuck between my lower left pre-molar and molar. I have tried to dislodge it by brushing my teeth, using toothpicks and my tongue, to no avail. If I get ashore at Norfolk, I will get some dental floss. I spent all afternoon typing from my notes and am up-to-date. I can start to fill in the back story of why I am today sitting at a computer desk on board a cargo ship in the middle of the Atlantic Ocean at 10 pm, when my family is back in Scotland in the dead of winter, just sitting down in their own homes to their evening meal at 7 pm.

DAY EIGHT

August 19, 1864 – Friday

A fine day but very little wind. A week since we left Plymouth. It seems a much longer time. We are only just commencing to speak to the other passengers.

03 December 2013 – Tuesday – Atlantic Ocean

A bit fairer today. It is a week since we left Rotterdam. I agree with Sarah. A week at sea seems a lot longer. The clouds are not so disjointed. The sea is rolling gently compared to the day before yesterday, and the wind has dropped considerably. There is a hand stretched out in the sky catching argentum streaks streaming out of the firmament.

After my fennel and liquorice kick start to the day, I went to take my shower. There was no hot water. Up until now it has been constant. I knew the situation would be resolved, and would wait it out. In the meantime I decided to practice putting on my immersion suit. The emphasis that has been placed on that it should only take two minutes to put it on has been on my mind. I was pleased with progress, having followed the procedure of putting unshod feet in first, then pulling the whole suit up and putting the hood over my head, before putting in first one arm, then the other till my hands reached the rubber gloves at the end of the arms. Well, in a large suit, my hands only reached the cuffs of the sleeve, but no matter, there are straps with Velcro on them to make necessary adjustments. What could not be adjusted was the size of the hands of the rubber gloves. I am a size seven. My fingers barely reached the openings for them. I made to pull up the zip before making finer adjustments. I found it was stiff. I pulled, but only managed with cautious effort, to seal it up to about an inch and a half from the bottom. I stripped it off again and decided to go to the bridge to see if Igor was on watch. We exchanged *good mornings*. I told Igor about the zip issue, and also about the torch not working. German appeared. More greetings, like old friends. None of us had seen each other since Saturday. Igor explained the situation to German. Right away Igor and I went down to my cabin to see the problem. He too found the zip stiff, though he did manage to get it to close, and open, and close, and open, but it was not smooth running. He said it needed some paraffin to loosen it off. He would take it to his cabin and have it sorted. Meantime if I needed it I was to just go and take it from by the door. He looked at the life jacket. He said there must have been a mix up when he brought my equipment back from the drill last week, because his torch had not been working. He gave me back my original lifejacket, and took number 305. I said he must get his torch fixed. He said he had already arranged for a new bulb to be fitted. I found later my life jacket is marked

Owner. My final request was for some more loo paper. Sorted.

I went back to the bridge. I was standing looking out at sea – what else? – when German came over. He asked me what religion I followed, whether it was Roman Catholic or Greek Orthodox. I said I am spiritual. I fell out with God when my brother died when I was fifteen. He refined the issue with the question of what calendar I followed. Ukrainian Christmas is two weeks after the Christmas date of 25 December in the Julian Calendar. This is the calendar I follow, although when my father was alive we celebrated two Christmases, and I often went to Ukrainian Church in Dalmeny Street, Edinburgh with him on 7 January, Christmas in the Gregorian Calendar. The singing was out of this world, the best choir singing and harmonies I have ever heard. There is a photograph of my father in a group of Ukrainian singers dressed in traditional costume, with baggy Cossack pants and embroidered shirts in my mother's photograph album. He would always sing in the mornings when he was getting dressed, shaving or polishing his shoes. German asked me what my father's profession was. I told him he was training to be an actor at age nineteen when WWII broke out and he volunteered to fight for Ukraine's freedom. Because he fought alongside the German army against Stalin's Union of Soviet Socialist Republic (USSR) he was unable to return home after the war due to risk of punishment. He settled in Scotland along with many other Ukrainians. German told me of a relative's experience and imprisonment in Cuba. We agreed it is all very shocking, what people do to each other.

I went down to lunch. It is always pleasant to open the stairwell door and smell the aromas arising from the galley. I met Andriy V on the stairs on his way to duties beginning at noon. When I got to the ground floor the door to the outside was open. I noticed rags and towels around the floor from the outside door and all along between the galley and the mess.

'Has there been a flood?' I asked Anatoliy.

'Yes,' he replied. He showed against his leg the level it had been up to. Just below halfway up his calf.

'What happened?' I asked.

'A valve blew open, and needs to be replaced.'

'Is that why there is no hot water?' I asked.

'Yes. All the water drained from the tank.' There were again misgivings about the ship's build.

I tucked in to yummy savoury potatoes, chicken breast and salad. By using different dressings and varying the ingredients for his salads, Anatoliy keeps them interesting. I was feeling a little sick this morning, and it is persisting. I may take an indigestion tablet to try and settle it. The few chunks of chocolate I had after lunch have not had the desired effect. I rested for a couple of hours, listening to Pink Floyd, dozing and reading a little. About 3.30 pm I went up to the bridge to take my daily readings. We are at latitude 43°91'N, longitude 048°44'W. We are on course 247. The temperature, cooled by the wind is 11.5 C but on the outside thermometer it is 14°C. Andriy was working and I took in the vista. I had seen some sort of sea birds playing in the waves and thought I might get a photograph or two. The sun came out over the horizon and I took a couple of pictures. I had also taken some video of *City of Adelaide* on the way up to the bridge, and later took a shot of her with the sun casting a crane shadow over her hull, bathing her in gold.

German was on the bridge. He came over and we chatted more about Ukraine. He asked what religion my mother was. I told him she is German. Once again he was surprised. He asked why she had gone to Scotland. I said she had come to Scotland after the war along with nineteen other German girls to nurse tuberculosis patients at East Fortune Hospital, near North Berwick. Everything in Germany had been flattened, there was no work. My grandmother had been broken-hearted to lose her young daughter, only nineteen years old. She had already lost her youngest daughter, Renate, aged three-and-a-half, when travelling across Germany escaping from the Russians. She had contracted diphtheria whilst they were staying in some lodgings. I have tremendous respect for my mother for leaving home to work in a country that only a few years before had been Germany's enemy, and whose language she did not speak. She only intended spending a limited time in Scotland, but the Ukrainian Camp was situated across from the hospital on the opposite side of East Fortune Airfield. She met my father and they eventually married. There were many Ukrainian/German marriages. German wondered why my father and mother did not go and live in Germany. I said it was because my father had work in Scotland and had good opportunities to build up a business of his own. I told him I had been sent to boarding school just before my twelfth birthday.

German took me down to see the conference room that I found also gives a wonderful vista. He invited me to use it any time I wished, and said I am always welcome on the bridge. I began to draft out the section on *City of Adelaide* at Irvine. I have decided to begin right back in 2006 with correspondence with Jim Tildesley, retired Director of the Maritime Museum at Irvine, Scotland.

When I went for supper, risotto and salad, I spoke to Anatoliy. I told him German had told me his grandparents were from near L'viv. We shared stories and I was astonished to find his grandfather had also fought against the Soviet Union with the hope of gaining independence for Ukraine. Anatoliy spoke of how many languages his grandparents could speak. I said this explained why my father could speak seven languages, that L'viv was close to the borders of several countries. I am going to ask Anatoliy if we can do an interview about this history, so that I can record it for my children. I am feeling relief and joy at finding out something of my ancestry; my father and I did not speak much in my adult years.

I have cracked open a beer. For some reason it is tasting like cherry vodka.

DAY NINE

August 20, 1864 – Saturday

A fine calm day but rather warm. Still the wind is unfavorable. Somebody remarked this morning that we should be two years finishing our journey if we continue at this same slow pace.

04 December 2013 – Wednesday – Atlantic Ocean

A wild night. I looked out at *City of Adelaide* to check she was still there. Lights were trained on the deck and I could see her webbing stays flapping a bit, causing me concern. The waves are four metres high.

This morning there is blue sky, but the ship is rolling a lot. I slept on the couch, taking advice from at least two crew members not to be at odds with the rolling motion of *Palanpur*, and was much more comfortable. Neptune has been kicking at our hull all night long, but *Palanpur* is keeping her doors bolted. The mermaids are dying their long tresses aquamarine, and the waves are hi-fiving with palms greased

with silver. Outside, the iron stairs are dripping diamonds into Neptune's cupped hands, but the bribe is not working. His wrath persists. I slept little until I changed from lying on the bed to the couch.

I had a slow start to the morning. The first thing I did was to put on my boiler suit and then the immersion suit. The zip has been smeared with paraffin, improving its action. I took a look in the mirror and laughed. I was face-to-face with an orange Robbie The Robot from Space Family Robinson. Although today's weather conditions are if anything, worse than yesterday's, I needed a shower. The hot water was back to normal. I decided if I sat on the shower curtain on the toilet, and lowered the shower head, it would be safe enough. It worked a treat and I felt really refreshed. Andriy V came to my door. He had a clipboard with a form on it to do with my visa for the United States of America. A few more details were required, including my maiden name. After he left I went for lunch. I feel a wee bit queasy today, but I thought I would go down anyway. I also felt the waistband on my skin tight jeans was getting tight. When I said this to Anatoliy when he was dishing out my lunch, he said it is a problem for sailors: nowhere to exercise, much sleeping, and so on. I requested a small portion of carbohydrates. Soup was some kind of greens, probably spinach, followed by pasta, lemon sole and cucumber crudités.

Trying to walk is difficult, where you think your foot is going to land is in reality about twelve inches away. I imagine it is like walking on the moon. I had a wee lie down after lunch and dozed off. I looked out of my window when I came to, and saw a lot of spray with sunshine forming rainbows in it. I grabbed my camera and headed for the open door on the other side of the corridor. After this I went to the bridge for some shots of spray off the bow. Andriy V was there. We chatted about the meaning of my family name, about Christmas and New Year in Scotland, what my family would be doing, about Christmas and New Year in Ukraine. I took my daily readings and noted we had changed course. We are at latitude 40°39.53'N and longitude 052°42'W. There is a four metre swell and the temperature is 20°C. From Rotterdam to here we have travelled 2,476 miles as at 8 am today. From Norfolk direct to Adelaide, South Australia, we have 12,500 miles to go. We will be in Cape Town approximately three weeks and two days from now, to refuel. We have gone back four hours from Greenwich Meantime so far. By the time we reach Norfolk, that will become five.

German appeared. He told me he had been requested to send photographs that *City of Adelaide* is still secure on board. Someone has been watching the weather. We chatted a bit about dialects in Scotland and in general. I demonstrated my Glaswegian special. I told German I had slept on the couch last night, and had been more comfortable. He was taken with the word couch and I explained I thought it came from the French *coucher*, to lie down. He thought it was the same as *cushion* so I wrote down the spelling of the two words. He asked me if I speak French. I told him I had passed the secondary school exam a long time ago and had the opportunity to use it in 2011 when I visited France for the first time. It was very warm on the bridge. German switched off the radiator and pulled down a couple of shades. He said he had changed course to tame the action of the ship down to keep *City of Adelaide* safe, he had also reduced our speed. I remarked about the extra two weeks journey she had had to make because of having to go to the United States of America to pick up cargo. The cargo is six locomotives. Then she will have the same extra journey on the way back south, though of course we will not be going to Rotterdam, but straight to Cape Town, South Africa. I spent a bit of time on the bridge, going outside to take some photos of waves breaking over the bow of Palanpur. I enjoyed the wind ruffling my hair and lingered a while, reflecting. German said, 'До Робачеия'. I waved and went back to my cabin.

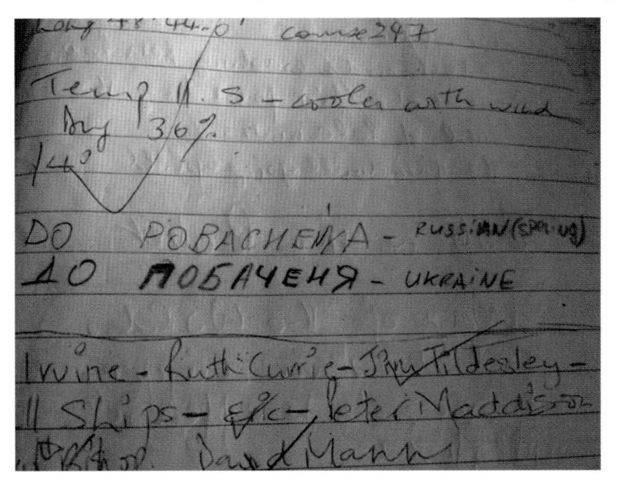

I managed to get the CD player working on my laptop and listened to the free Womex CD I had received somewhere over the summer. I was rather disappointed in it, finding the music quite basic and repetitive, knowing what fantastic music Scottish artists can churn out. Andriy V brought me a DVD *Personal Survival and Survival Craft*. I put it aside for later. He said if I cannot get it to play on my laptop, I could look at it in the mess. This would be interesting to see, as I hope to meet the crew one-by-one during the course of my voyage and gain their permission to include wee bits about them in this historical adventure. Andriy V picked up my copy of *Empire Antarctica*. I am finding it an interesting read, and am drawing several comparisons, particularly with reference to the joy of solitude and having the luxury of uninterrupted time to unscramble the white noise in my brain. I am beginning to feel myself unwinding with not having to think of the jumble I have to cope with in a normal day at home. It feels as though crumpled memories are being smoothed out, making way for fresh creases to form.

Supper was fairly plain, a pork chop, salad and chips for the second time since we sailed from Rotterdam. I ate quickly to get back to my cabin and continue typing the Irvine material. It is tedious sorting the emails that to-ed and fro-ed between me and Irvine, Australia and the International Sail Training Association into order, but I am relieved to be doing this. I turned in for sleep a good two hours earlier than on the last two nights, but then again I must remember that we have gone back four hours so far in total, so in fact it is about right. I feel like a pancake on Shrove Tuesday. I am being shoogled about, shaken loose, tossed up in the air, flipped and caught back in the pan.

It is 10.55 pm. Through the thin skin of the cabin wall, I hear the *beep-beep-beep* of a baby alarm. Vitaliy is on watch. I hear him leave to go and nurture his baby, *Palanpur*'s beating heart.

DAY TEN

August 21, 1864 – Sunday

A rough day. Strong but not quite favorable winds. The prayers were read in the saloon but Mama and I were too sick to attend. Several waves came over the Deck and our chairs rolled about so that they were obliged to be tied to the wall.

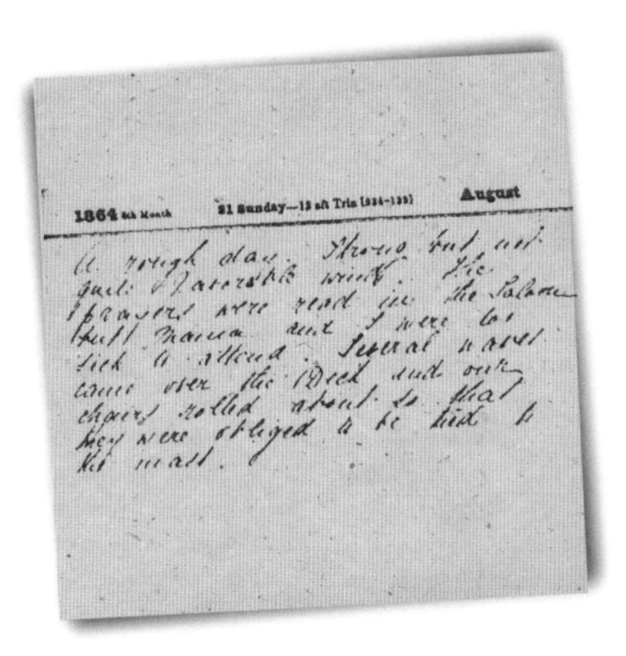
1864 8th Month 21 Sunday—13 aft Trin August

A rough day. Strong but not quite favorable winds. The prayers were read in the saloon but Mama and I were too sick to attend. Several waves came over the Deck and our chairs rolled about so that they were obliged to be tied to the wall.

05 December 2013 – Thursday – Atlantic Ocean

A much more calm night, with only just the odd thud and slap. I slept on the couch again, it is definitely the solution to minimising the discomfort caused by the rolling of *Palanpur*. Drawing back the curtains revealed a blue blanket tucking the stars and moon in for the day.

The large cup of drinking chocolate I had last night may have contributed to the fact that I slept very well, waking only once for a pee. I awoke in the morning, just after 9 am. I made a cup of fennel and liquorice tea, and followed that with one of the fruit teas. I felt a bit dried up inside, and thought I must be dehydrated. I added another bit of cabin maintenance to my previous triumphs. The first one was I found in a drawer the cosmetic cover of one of the wardrobe mirror screws. I twisted that back on. Then it was the turn of the window curtain gliders. The night before they had been scraping from side to side on the rail in rhythm with the rock and roll of *Palanpur* and disturbed my sleep. I sorted this by hooking the last curtain hook through the fixed end hooks on either side of the rail. Last night I put elephant skin on top of the fridge to make it easier to make hot drinks by giving me a closer, safe surface than on top of the bookcase beside the kettle. I had only put elephant skin under the kettle there, economising. I further cut eight smaller pieces of it to put under the feet of the two chairs in my cabin, to reduce any further scraping and sliding during the night horrors. Today it was the handle of the shower door. I noticed yesterday it was working itself loose. Girls, I went for my nail file. It was the perfect instrument to drive back the star-headed screw hard into its socket. The second screw was missing. I thought it was there yesterday: if it was and it is not there now, it must have worked its way down through the drain cover of the outer shower floor.

I had my shower, read a little, reflected a little, then went down for gherkin soup, curried rice, chicken leg and salad just after 11.30 am. Andriy V was having his lunch prior to doing his shift on the bridge from noon till 4 pm. He asked me if I had watched the safety video yet. I said I had not but would try and look at it when I got to my cabin after lunch. I teased him that he was starring in it, and we laughed. It is not the most glamorous roll to play, demonstrating the putting on and taking off of immersion suits. *Molto elegante*, I joked. This sparked off conversation about language, this time Italian and Spanish and Arabic. Andriy asked me if I spoke Italian. I told him my father had worked in Italy for a number of years after having got fed up with running the café he and my mother had established in the 1960s. By this time they had two ice cream vans, but eventually they gave up running around all over East Lothian in them, selling ice cream to people in villages, individual isolated homes, hamlets and popular beaches. They concentrated instead on serving customers, from bus parties of older people to young lads, some following the *teddy boy* fashion who wore drainpipe trousers and long coloured jackets mostly with black lapels and a certain slick-backed but long at the back hairstyle. Fish, chips and peas, milk shakes, ice cream floats were served, while chocolate boxes with pretty country cottage scenes, cigarettes, Fanta, Jungle Juice, sweets, chewing gum were sold while the juke box threw out any song on feeding it sixpence for one tune, or a shilling for three: *She Loves You; I Love You Because; I'll Follow The Sun; Sloop John B; He's In Town; As Tears Go By; Those Were The Days; Sorry; The Locomotion.* I had the best education in music, sitting in the café, watching the girls in their beehive hairdos and their full skirts swirling out, jiving and twisting to whatever carolled out from the Rowe Ami jukebox standing on green and beige floor tiles set out like a giant chessboard. Decades before, people had stood on those same floor tiles and bought their tickets to see films inside what was then The Empire Cinema. My Pinball skills were to die for. *Tommy* and I are in the same league, both wizards. On these nights on board *Palanpur* I practice my flipping skills, since my laptop came loaded up with the Pinball game seven years ago when I bought it. I had forgotten all about it till just before I left Scotland, when with great excitement I rediscovered it. I continued that my father had worked near

Verona in Italy for a while, running a turkey farm. We had several holidays there during which I picked up some of the ice cream smooth Italian language. Ruby red cherries, deep emerald green angelica and moss agate pistachios dripped from my tongue like melting Macedonia gelato. These happy days ended when my brother took his life in 1968.

I dreamed last night that when we arrived at Norfolk we were put into a rusting scrap yard of corrugated iron, old steel containers, bits of wood, cobwebs, dust. The town was just a walk away, and I could see a church spire, green grass, a stone bridge, pretty houses, just like the scene on one of the chocolate boxes in my parents' café. Some of us began walking towards the village, pizza on our minds. I had forgotten my money belt and went back for it. In the dream I met my last full-time employer in one of the sheds. She was one of the people who encouraged me to break off from formal employment to try and carve out a writing career. When I met a woman in a pub who needed her huge handwritten manuscript typed up, she hired me as a freelancer. This was the first stepping stone to a new life for me.

Andriy V and German were on the bridge when I went up at 3.10 pm. There was a lot of coming and going by crew I had not seen before. I looked round the 360° horizon. We are on course 215 , going 11 knots, and the wind speed is 31 kilometres per hour. It is latitude 39°46.06'N and longitude 057°14.98'W, wave height 2.5-3 metres. The clouds are a herd of big grey elephants all over the sky. I asked German what type of cloud they were. He loaned me *Mariners Handbook No. 9* that is full of delightful planetary spells. German told me we should arrive in Norfolk on Monday. He said that I should have a copy of my letter of invitation to Australia handy. They have been told that I am escorting *City of Adelaide* to Australia and am writing a book about her. There should not be any problem. German told me there is the wife of a Chief Officer travelling on one of the other ships in the Harren & Partner fleet who also requires a visa. Armed with the Mariners Handbook I returned to my cabin. It is quite chilly at 5 pm, and I have put on an extra jumper. I have managed to watch the safety DVD Andriy gave me. It is good to have the overall picture, and there are designated personnel who will activate all necessary rescue operations. Everyone should know what to do in case those personnel are not available in the event of an emergency.

There is no improvement in the welfare of the seasick cadet. He is to be flown home when we get to the United States of America. I wondered whether he would need to be hospitalised before this could happen, and what red tape would ravel itself around this young man's fate.

Supper was pork stew, salad and millet or Caska. Anatoliy amused me by telling me that it is called chicken porridge, because millet is fed to chickens. After I had eaten, I took my plate back and *puck puck puck puck puck puck pucked* at him. He laughed. I think he thinks I am quite mad. Valeriy was quiet at supper, but before he left, he told me that I can get news bulletins on the ship. German could set up for me to receive these in English, as they appear in Russian and Ukrainian. He also said I can send and receive text emails. My head lifted in disbelief. I grew several feet taller! Emotion swamped me. I felt giddy! I could contact my family and friends after all! It was strange not being in contact with them when we normally keep in touch on a daily basis. I was beginning to miss their voices, the hugs, hearing their news, seeing them on social media, speaking with my only grandchild, who had just turned three on her birthday. Valeriy said I could get an access card from the Captain. He spoke to Andriy V, who said this is so. I can get it set up and it would be working within twenty-four hours or less. This is great news, and I could not help wondering why I had not been told of this before. There is a crew computer on B Deck in the ship's office. Andriy said he is on duty on the bridge from 8 pm. I asked if I could come up after that to get the access card. He thought German would be there at that time.

It is fantastic and a relief to know I can be in touch with home. At the same time, I am relishing my isolation.

DAY ELEVEN

August 22, 1864 – Monday

A calm day. We had a bath, which is very refreshing, as the weather is becoming warm. Blanche and I read "I Promessi Sposi" after breakfast for about an hour.

06 December 2013 – Friday – Atlantic Ocean

A very brisk wind opened the day. I got up a good hour earlier than any day previous. I made my usual digestive system-loving brew, took my shower, changed my bed sheets and headed for the laundry.

I can safely say I have mastered the controls of the washing machine and drier now. I went up to the bridge to see about activating my email account. Andriy K was very helpful and got me started. I chose *ritalot* as part of my user name. German came over and said he had not realised I was unaware I could get email access. He said 'You did not say?' He was surprised, and I think a little embarrassed, as I was. He had thought I wanted complete isolation to get on with writing. I said I thought the email was reserved for business and for crew. Later, I met Valeriy on the stairs, and thanked him for getting the ball rolling. I explained I had picked up there was no wifi on board, and as it turns out, had wrongly understood on my introduction to the ship that I would not have email access. I later apologised to German for insulting his kindness, I felt bad that I had not asked him sooner about access to the email system. It seems a big issue. The time is right to be connected to the outside world. I have got the format of the book set up, and am about 20,000 words in now, so am relaxed about having the valuable distraction of contact with family and friends, and business contacts. It is becoming a day for sorting out and rationalising. First the emails, then the laundry, then I spent time cleaning my cabin; the floor is very fluffy again. I made up my bed with fresh sheets, watching the pale blue blot up a couple of dark patches that had fallen from my eyes. I was thinking of my inability to make requests, and be direct. I think of the word *nuisance* and I think of the strict nuns at my boarding school. Very few had special treatment under their austere, hawk-like gaze. I am thinking of the book I read not so long ago, entitled *Women Who Think Too Much*, and think, *I am at it again.*

Then I had a good giggle. It had become very warm. I had taken off my jumper, the one I bought in Rotterdam that is thinner than the two I had brought from home, for the warmer climate we are now in. I was just in my strappy top when I was combing my hair. I noticed my underarms. For someone who had the follicles killed off in their twenties by electrolysis, they were remarkably hairy. Dampened finger ends soon removed the fluff that had made itself comfortable in my pits. New towels have a lot to answer for. Before lunch I managed to do important file management in my *City of Adelaide* folder. I feel I can download photographs and videos since Rotterdam, now that I have opened folders for Irvine, Greenwich and Rotterdam. Then I went up to the bridge again. My email account is now active. When I went back to the bridge after lunch for my daily readings, I had a good blether with German about the split between the Russian Orthodox Church and the Ukrainian Orthodox Church. Same religion; two different churches. Igor joined in with us. I am learning more and more about my father as each day passes. We talked a bit about politics and that money is the root of all evil. I am amazed at the grasp the crew has of the English language. Everyday chat is easy, I help them with some pronunciations, but when German used the word rheumatism I marvelled at how deep he has absorbed the language. I went down to lunch and met German in the corridor. He eats breakfast and supper; we are all, it seems, weight conscious. He was munching a fish cake, and when I got stuck into mine, it was very tasty, served with tartare sauce, mashed potatoes and salad. I have cut down portions. Anatoliy and I swapped stories at suppertime about our weaknesses. He is mad for chocolate, can eat a whole bar at a time. We both drooled at the word *Toblerone*. I confessed to being more of a savoury girl, enjoying crisps, Pringles and nuts. I managed to scoff the best part of a tin of cashew nuts I had got from the slop chest the other day, just twenty minutes before suppertime. On my way down to supper, I passed three crew members on the stairs. I had met young Ihor on my first day, when he was on duty on the gangway; I had seen and greeted Sergiy when he was working but had not formally met him, so we shook hands. Next was Ivan, I had seen him a couple of times in the last few days. We shook hands. I told him my father was also *Ivan*, and he was Ukrainian. When I arrived at supper, Vitaliy was seated, toothpick wedged between his lips. Nikolay, Third Engineer left with a *bon appetite*, and Valeriy was just about finished clearing his plate. I thanked him again for helping me get on email. He told me there are three messages for me, I could pick them up either on B Deck that I have not explored yet other than to know that is where the bottled water is kept, also where the slop chest is. Vitaliy left with a cup of coffee or something he had heated in the microwave, then Valeriy left. Andriy K was finishing his supper. I asked him if he was going ashore in Norfolk. He said he would. He was hoping to buy some good shoes there, better and much cheaper than the ones he buys in Ukraine. He told me he had been to the United States of America before, near Mexico. Like Igor, he works for six months then takes three or four months off to relax at home. Home for him is a small village, not even a village, with only about two hundred people living there. It is about thirty miles from Odessa. I was touched by how free he was in sharing with me the depth of his feelings for his family and friends, nature, fishing, relaxing. He left me to finish two small slices of roast beef in horseradish sauce, pasta and red cabbage coleslaw. I was just leaving when Andriy V came in with his supper. We had a very interesting conversation about culture, and when I mentioned I had a poetry book by *Shevchenko* he almost choked. He says such a book would bring a lot of money at auction in Sotheby's. Sotheby's. He knew about Sotheby's. He told me I should not part with any of my father's books. It was too late; my father had willed them to his church in Edinburgh. Andriy V asked if my father had ever gone back to Ukraine. I said he had been back a few times in the 1990s. I told him he had travelled by bus for three days to get there. He was amused by this, and told me he had once travelled 1000 miles by bus to get from his home to pick up a ship he was going to work on. We laughed when he showed the distance it looked on the map, that of between his outstretched thumb to forefinger.

The computer keyboard reminds me of a box of chocolates in my parents' café. I lift its lid. I peel back the shiny, padded paper to reveal a delicious array of mixed centres. There are the soft, creamy fruits, smooth toffees, Brazil nuts, almonds and hazelnuts to tease the taste buds of my mind. I choose a chewy caramel to send a message home, and finish with a rose-scented Turkish Delight delivered straight from the Queen of Narnia, that she has first dipped in a churning bath of liquid cocoa, and blown a snowflake swirl onto the top. I address my email to the youngest of my three children. She is the most likely to open it sooner and will distribute it to the others. My email limit is 1000 characters, and I find it is just enough to let those back home know I am in my element. I also sent an email to Etta Dunn, a fellow writer who was an officer with the Sea Cadets who had been on board *City of Adelaide* when she was known as *Carrick* at Irvine. She knew of my aspirations and I had to let her know my dream has come true, that I am on board *Palanpur* with *City of Adelaide.*

The ship is nodding up and down and I am sitting at odds to the motion at my computer desk. I am feeling a bit queasy. It is very warm, the heating is on and we are riding on the Gulf Stream. Some of us are displaying a change in temperament. Vitaliy has had his music on loud twice today, and was singing along with it. At lunchtime he was singing *America, America*, in a tone I am not sure was celebratory. I remarked to Anatoliy about it, and we smiled. This afternoon the sun had been streaming in through a thrashing forty kilometres per hour wind that slammed *Palanpur* hard into the waves, though it felt like we had been thrown hard against the seabed. Everything shuddered like I have never felt it shudder before. German reduced our speed. At around 4.45 pm we were at latitude 38°51.46'N, longitude 063°21.91'W. Outside temperature is 22.5°C, reduced by wind chill, but I did not take this reading. Wind speed had dropped to thirty-six kilometres per hour, and all blinds had been pulled down to deflect the sun's embrace of the bridge. A peppermint elephant straddled our hull and was leaving giant footprints on Neptune's face. No wonder he is furious.

Ukrainian words learned today: Today = Segornia
Friday = Piatwitza (phonetic)

Last night something was clanking outside my cabin window, and woke me at 3 am. It is doing the same now, at 9.15 pm. I might just go out and strangle it.

DAY TWELVE

August 23, 1864 – Tuesday

A fine day. We are not making much progress. Two vessels were seen in the distance. I am reading Macaulay's Essays and I have finished "Milton", "Machiavelli", "Southey's Colloquial on Society", and "Pilgrim's Progress".

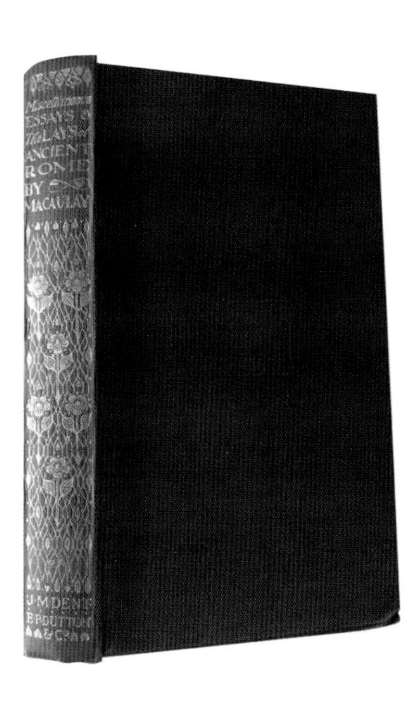

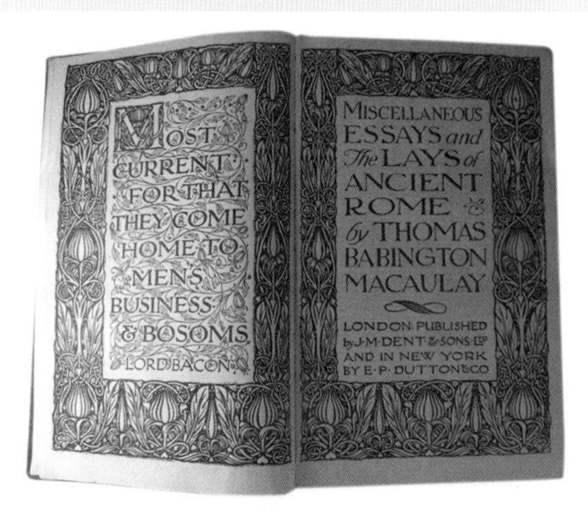

MOST CURRENT FOR THAT THEY COME HOME TO MEN'S BUSINESS & BOSOMS
LORD BACON

MISCELLANEOUS ESSAYS and The LAYS of ANCIENT ROME & by THOMAS BABINGTON MACAULAY

LONDON: PUBLISHED by J.M.DENT & SONS LTD
AND IN NEW YORK BY E.P.DUTTON & CO

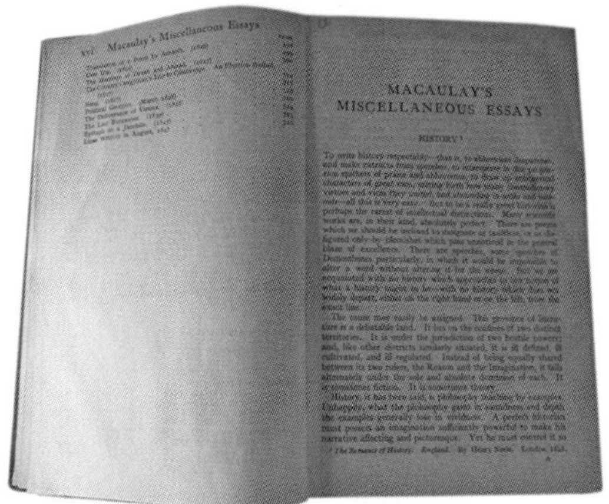

xvi Macaulay's Miscellaneous Essays

MACAULAY'S MISCELLANEOUS ESSAYS

HISTORY

07 December 2013 – Saturday – Atlantic Ocean

A grey sky slid out from behind my curtains. Within about half an hour, at around 8.40 am there was a lull, a pause just long enough for Neptune to fill his fists with iron to throw at *Palanpur*. The sky was already hurling steel lances at us. I was sure I saw a flash of pink quartz shatter across the granite canopy we were heading for.

I scratched for a good while last night before going to sleep. I was looking to see what was clanking in the drawer under my bed, when I spied a tiny splinter of a creepy-crawly on the linoleum. I squished it, but where there is one, there are bound to be more. At least it was not a cockroach. That would have had me running to hide beneath the protective covering of *City of Adelaide*. I could smell cigarette smoke, and ended up turning myself round in my bed so that my feet were at the headboard, taking me away from where it seemed to be coming from, trapped between my wardrobe and the port side wall. If I had not done this, I would never have slept as I have always been ultra-sensitive to cigarette smoke and would have psychologically asphyxiated. I awoke around 2.45 am. It was hot and sticky. This was the first night I had not put on pyjamas, and I was still hot. I got up, put the light on, cooled off, took a swig of water and settled back down to read for a while. I left the light on all night. The crane hook was still clanking now and again, but I had stopped keeping time with its metronome action. When the squall came just after 10 am I grabbed my camera and headed for the open door at the other side of the stairwell. I took some film of *City of Adelaide* shielding herself from the inclement weather. The spray was coming from both port and starboard sides and was dancing a melee in the middle of the *Palanpur* deck. I thought of the scene in Robert Burns' poem *Tam o' Shanter* when he witnessed the witches' sabbath in the Kirk at Alloway in Scotland. I went to the conference room and took more film, and a number of stills. The waves breaking over the bow were spectacular. One even broke so hard it spewed unbaked meringue against the window I was looking out of, and blinkered me. It melted away like ice cream on a hot summer day, and unveiled four metre waves billowing towards our hull, black with menace. Visibility to the horizon was obscured by Neptune's fume.

I fancied a cup of coffee and headed for the bridge. Andriy K was on deck for his usual shift from 8 am to noon. He had two Ukrainian passports on the computer station, with the national emblem stamped in gold on their covers. One was for the cadet who is still poorly. I told Andriy that my father had the Ukrainian emblem engraved on his headstone. He told me it is the symbol for Freedom. I made a comparison with Scotland and London, not England, but London, for that is where all the real money ends up, and that is why many people feel Scotland would benefit from independence: Ukraine had gained independence from the Union of Soviet Socialist Republic in August 1991. We talked about life on a cargo ship. I thought perhaps my son would enjoy this life, with a paid structure for six months of the year and four months off to do with whatever you pleased, until signing up again for a new contract. Cruise ships had been something he had spoken about on and off in the last six months or so. Andriy said that that is a good life, very sociable, meeting lots of people, and dressing in a smart uniform. I told Andriy that all my children had gone through the Sea Cadets on TS *Valiant*, at Dunbar, and had gained numerous certificates, including Watch Leader, and my son also had his Yachtmaster certificate. We talked about shifts on deck and the duties each member of the crew has to undertake. He showed me a schedule. With permission in due course, I will look at this and hope the crew members will give me the go-ahead to mention them in this book, for they are part of the history of *City of Adelaide* now.

I raised the topic of pirates. On the galley deck, there is a chart showing the locations of attempted attacks and actual attacks and possible attacks. Andriy has loaned me a manual on what should be done in the event of such attacks. German arrived and we bade each other *good morning*. The ship has been veered off course to minimise the effects of the adverse weather conditions on our precious cargo. We might have arrived in Norfolk on 6th December, however, various factors have now scheduled our arrival for the 10th. I feel for the sick cadet and his squashed ambition. We are at latitude 38°49.47'N, longitude 067°13.27'W. The wind speed is forty kilometres per hour and there are some belters of waves splatting against the ship, one so forceful that the whole ship cracked and shuddered. I am told this is nothing. Crew members are very considerate for my safety, young Ihor asked me to *please hold on to the rail.* I mentioned to German about the cash I had for emergency travel home that my wee brother had lent me before I left. He quipped that it would be no problem for United States of America border control, as long as it was not one million dollars. I said he was safe with that. I went to my cabin clutching the manual to look at later, and went down for lunch. Eintopf. It is Saturday. The main was savoury rice, salad and little patties (we are nearing the United States of America, after all) made of chicken and onions, dressed in egg and flour, just like the way my mother makes pork burgers at home. Very tasty. I said to Anatoliy that he would be missed as a Cook when he becomes an Electrical Engineer. 'No, this won't happen because I won't tell them I was a cook.' We laughed. He said, it seemed with some regret, that he will have to change company when he qualifies, as Harren & Partner are not employing such personnel at the moment. Anatoliy asked that if I am in the galley I do not put my hands on the stainless steel surfaces, as the fingerprints are a devil of a job to get off. There are some special chemicals that have to be used, not just any ordinary rag would do. I thanked him for saying this to me, because I do not want to cause anyone any extra work, and he thanked me for being so understanding.

I came back to my cabin feeling a bit bagged down. I am not sure if this is because of the rolling of the ship or whether I have overeaten, or what. I chose to lie down and read for while, but gave this up due to feeling a bit queasy. The weather had cleared for a couple of hours, but it is getting rough again. I have put on my shorts again, and taken off the checked shirt. I am quite comfortable in my strappy top. That was until I had a snooze and was awakened with a warning of a drill in ten minutes time. On with the sweater, the loose cotton trousers, the orange boilersuit, the hard hat, the safety boots, the life jacket. In hand, the red bag with the immersion suit I had slipped a two-litre bottle of water into that we were recommended to take; might as well have it ready, so it will stay there. Drill took about fifteen minutes for me, the rest of the crew had another hour of it. It is getting dark now and the crew were heading for a meeting on the bridge for a de-briefing when I was making my way back to my cabin with the day's readings. I checked my emails. Peter Roberts had obviously been watching our weather. He told me if I got seasick I should go and sit under a tree! Another, from Etta Dunn told me of a helicopter crashing into the Clutha Bar with terrible loss of life. I did not know this pub, but found it is located just beside where *City of Adelaide* was moored as *Carrick*, the RNVR clubhouse on the River Clyde in Glasgow. I shudder to think what might have happened to *City of Adelaide* had she still been berthed there.

What a laugh. I went down for my supper. Anatoliy spooned me out some buckwheat. He asked if we have this in the United Kingdom. I said I had seen it in the shops but had never used it. I said it looks a bit like Haggis, and explained that that is the heart, lungs, liver of a sheep mixed with barley and cooked in the stomach of a sheep, or a synthetic one. I told him we have the vegetarian option. He said buckwheat is fed to pigs in Ukraine, that during the WWII the Germans would not even eat it, no matter how starving they were. I said, 'So we had chicken food the other day, today we are having pig food. What next?'

'I don't know,' he said. More howls of laughter.

He said that pigs have rings in their noses. I bantered that when we get to Norfolk I will get a ring put through my nose. We laughed and laughed. He said, 'What will you say to the Customs?' I imitated a pig snort. We laughed and laughed again. I left with my dinner, saying I had my snout in the trough. When I went back with my empty plate, I told him about the expression *Happy as a pig in shit.* Then we went into the store to get me some more milk. He asked me what else I would like, 'Fresh meat?' I said then I would be like a wolf. I came away with an armful of muesli, a clear bowl, because Anatoliy likes to keep all the dishes the same, white Pyrex, a dessertspoon and my apple from the daily ration of fruit.

Saturday night is traditional wine drinking night in my home. I decided I would open the bottle of red J P Chenet Merlot I had bought the other day from the slop chest. Problem. No corkscrew. Girls, once again I reached for my manicure set. I took out the long-bladed scissors I use to shape my fringe now and again. I spread the blades apart and stuck one of them into the cork in the bottle, then removed it, closed the handles and stuck both blades in until they penetrated the cork. I then took those scissors out and got the nail scissors with the curved ends I use for trimming my fingernails. I wedged them between the neck of the bottle and the cork, and pressed. I stuck the points into the cork and levered the scissors against the neck of the bottle. The cork moved up a little. I tried to contain my excitement. This would be the first wine I would drink in over a fortnight. I removed the points of the scissors and inserted them a little further down the cork, repeating the process. I was glad the cork was not natural, made from the bark of those strange contorted trees that I have seen in southern Spain. The synthetic cork meant no little pieces would spoil the ruby red elixir. The bottle had a dimple in its belly, like an oversized navel. I had lain it on its side to see whether this was meant to keep it from rolling about, but it was ineffective. The neck of the bottle had a quirky lean to it, as if drunk on its own contents. I wondered what the reason for this was.

At last the cork sucked its teeth and I laid it to rest beside the bottle on the table. The trapped fermented grape juice breathed a sigh of relief and rose like Aladdin's genie to grant my wishes. I poured a glassful and it rubbed its fruity roundness around my mouth.

DAY THIRTEEN

August 24, 1864 – Wednesday

A fine day. Very favorable breeze. The first day I have felt at all well. In the morning we sighted land and about 4 P.M. were ten miles from Canaria. We distinctly saw villages and cultivated land and with the aid of a telescope were able to discern cattle grazing. A few hours later we had a good view of Tenerife (14,000 ft in height) which looked magnificent as the sun set behind it. A beautiful evening. We are sailing 11 knots an hour and the ship is much steadier than usual. During the night a squall. After we were in bed a wave came into our window and the water in the cabin was about 1ft deep. Papa baled it out but we got very little rest, for added to the noise of wind and waves outside there were continual cries in the Saloon of Steward! Captain etc.

08 December 2013 – Sunday – Atlantic Ocean

Another grey morning. The sky was full of sleeping seals lying in krill when I woke up at 7am. By the time I awoke again at 9.30 am they had become just one big blob with blurred outlines. The sea is calm compared to the lashing waves of yesterday.

It is lovely to read Sarah's diary entry for today. Her seasickness has subsided, she is feeling better, vitalised and excited about seeing land. How she maintained a steady hand to write is quite amazing, particularly as she is using pen and ink. I have been to Gran Canaria and Tenerife, and enjoyed reading her references to these two islands off the west coast of Africa. I am quite tickled that they had to bail out about a foot of water from their cabin, when the crew on *Palanpur* were doing just that five days ago. I am struck by the fact that the family are doing for themselves in baling out their cabin, and pick up a slight mocking of the people who were calling for assistance in the Saloon on board *City of Adelaide*.

City of Adelaide was making good speed, travelling at a couple of knots less than we are on board *Palanpur*. She had just the wind to power her, we have engines. The coast of the United States of America is in sight on the electronic chart. The waves today are much less awesome and there is little roll. I decided to change my sheets again, because the last couple of nights have been quite clammy. Tomorrow United States of America border control will board the ship and there is much preparation going on: hosing down of the ship's structure, mopping, people doing laundry. Most of these chores are done on a daily basis anyway, but I did get a wee surprise when I opened my stern-facing window curtain and got a cheeky jet of water sprayed at me. Thank goodness for the glass barrier! I had my shower and went to the bridge to give Andriy K my passport. He also needed my home address. I had taken my father's teddy bear to show German the badge he had pinned on it. I had brought the teddy bear from home at the last minute, scooping it up off the bedroom chair as I headed for the car and my journey to Newcastle for the ferry. German told me the badge is of a very famous cathedral in L'viv. It is a very beautiful monastery. He is encouraging me all the time to visit Ukraine, even saying that when my journey with *City of Adelaide* is over, I should make that my next mission. I am very tempted. He told me it is very cheap in Ukraine if you are discerning and not looking for luxury. We are both of the opinion that as long as you have clean, comfortable accommodation, you can do without the trappings of expensive, luxury accommodation. We began talking about sound therapy, since I had mentioned my eldest daughter had just qualified in this, and is planning on going to Chile. 'Why Chile?' German asked. 'Because there are many poor people there,' I said. 'There are many poor people in Ukraine too,' he replied. German told me he had once brought cargo from Chile that was the complete structure of a gold mine bought second-hand, to Egypt. I found this fascinating, even more so when he said that it all looked very dull and dirty, until the sun shone on it and you could see embedded gold dust sparkling in the sunshine. I joked about crew picking it off.

I went to lunch. It was duck. Anatoliy howled with laughter when I chose a tiny wee bit that had fallen away from the bone. 'You don't like duck?' he said. I said I thought I had eaten it last week. He said I had. I said I was not sure about eating it, because I liked ducks. Then I said I eat chicken, but I also like chickens. He said, 'And you don't like pigs?' It did seem ridiculous. I said I would come back for some duck if I changed my mind, but by the time I had layered rice and salad on top of the borscht soup made mainly from beetroot, I was full up. I said that next time there was duck I would take some. We then had a conversation about cherry vodka. He did not understand about the cherry part. He did not think cherry trees grew in Ukraine, and his wife's mother made liqueurs from the fruits she grew, such as strawberries, grapes, peaches. I said I thought the National Anthem was based on cherry trees. He said not. He said it is based on that Ukraine will always endure, go on. I made the mistake of raising this topic with the Chief Officer at lunch, forgetting that he is Russian born, although now he lives in Ukraine.

After lunch I did emails, finding the ship's office and using that computer for the first time as the bridge computer was in use. I also did some laundry before going to the bridge for the day's readings, latitude 37°34.63'N and longitude 072°57.51'W. Wind speed is sixteen kilometres per hour and outside temperature is 15°C. Land is in sight on the chart. We should arrive for the pilot boat at 5 am and reach the port at around 8 am. I sent an email to Ruth Currie to check the names of her family in the photograph she gave me. I wanted to find out the name of the youngest girl in the front row, and also to check whether it was Tom Bray who became Premier of South Australia in 1881.

I finished reading *Empire Antarctica* last night and decided to read some short stories. Soon it was suppertime. Anatoliy had found out the name of the berry for the vodka. Cranberry. The cherry thing is a mystery now. I will try to find a bottle when we get to Norfolk tomorrow, if I am allowed ashore. The weather has been changeable today, but no change to the greyness. There have been showers of various weights. The wind has been moody and the ship has echoed this. I feel quite tired tonight, having spent a while downloading my videos and photographs in readiness for tomorrow. I found my laptop is getting full, so I did some housekeeping with that. Supper was quiet. German was there for his meal for the first time since we left Dordrecht. I put my sheets back on the bed and hung up my second jumper that has been distorted by the washing machine. I noticed at dinner one of the crew had on a jumper that had had 'the treatment'. German had asked me if I was cold. He was teasing about the fact that I had on a thick jersey, when in fact the ship is pretty warm.

Vitaliy's music was loud. I found myself singing along to Pink Floyd's *We Don't Need No Education* and Snap's *Rhythm is a Dancer*.

DAY FOURTEEN

August 25, 1864 – Thursday

A very warm day. The breeze, though favorable, not very strong. We averaged about five knots. Nothing to be seen but flying fish. We went to bed shortly after 9 P.M. feeling very tired as we obtained so little rest the preceding night.

09 December 2013 – Monday – Atlantic Ocean/Norfolk, Virginia, USA

A very grey morning. Some orange lights flanking the river through the fog as we travelled up towards Norfolk, Virginia, United States of America. I saw rows and rows of naval ships, and the white hulk of a hospital ship. *City of Adelaide* had been a hospital ship isolating people with infectious diseases off the town and port of Southampton, England from 1893 to 1923. Small, duck-sized sea birds were flying in squadron formation.

I dozed for about an hour, then took my shower about 6.45 am in readiness for docking and passport control. It all happened very quickly. By 8.00 am the ship had been nuzzled into position by two tugs to starboard. Immigration was spilled on board on the port side from the pockets of the *apron*, the stretch of dockland between *Palanpur* and the walls of the massive shed we are moored alongside. I was astonished to see our cargo of six massive locomotives on rails already lined up on the apron. They looked like links of huge dark blue sausages in their plastic skins. There are kittiwakes and herring gulls on shed roofs and flying about our ship. I went on to the bridge and sneaked a few photos of the tugs pushing our hull. They are armed with some kind of weapon. I was glad they were covered up. This is the first time I have been on a vessel this size as it docks. I watched the lines full-stopped by monkey's fists knots being thrown to the stevedores, and then the massive, thick-girthed hemp ropes they were attached to being pulled to shore by them hauling on them from the apron. These were then

hitched over the bollards. The foremost bollard has three lines looped over it.

We were all summoned to the conference room for passport control. I arrived near the start and the Chief Officer pulled a chair out for me. Anatoliy waited behind me, his passport already stamped. Mr Immigration Control opened mine then drawled, 'I am sorry to tell you you are being refused entry to the United States. You do not have the correct visa.' I hesitated. So it was true. I would not be going ashore. Then he said, 'It's nice to meet you an' all, but you don't have to sit there all day.' I was unceremoniously dismissed. I felt humiliated and unwelcome. I came down the stairs feeling angry, but glad not to be going ashore if this was an example of American hospitality. I was bemused that fifteen Ukrainians and two Russians were being allowed to tread the soil of the United States of America, but that I was not. So much for the United Kingdom's *special relationship* with the USA.

I had a small list of things I wanted, sun cream in particular. I will ask one of the crew to help. No one is allowed to walk on the apron to get to the main gate even though we could practically spit at it from where *Palanpur* is moored; crew members have to arrange a taxi to come and take them to town and back. I am told this is quite costly. Ridiculous. I found it ironic that after the pilots had helped us moor up, one of them said there is a very good Mexican restaurant by the main gate. I checked this with binoculars and thought about border control.

As I was making my way to the bridge by the outside stairs I saw one of the distress flares beside the lifebelt got knocked from its holding. It tugged open and a mass of orange smoke belched out. The two Andriys took immediate action and tried to douse it in a bucket of water, with little effect due to its design to endure in aquatic conditions. I was embarrassed. It was an awkward few minutes. The orange smoke is a distress signal and we are docked in American waters. I expected us to be surrounded by helicopters and armed guards, but nothing like that happened. We just had to wait till the flare spent itself. I later found out that the flare must be replaced or we will not be allowed to leave the USA.

I watched a lot of animated gesticulation on the deck as our crew began to uplift the top deck covering. The six locomotives we are loading will be stored 'tween decks and on the lower deck. I tried to phone my mother and husband. Mother was engaged, no reply from husband. I prepared a text to my youngest daughter, but deferred sending it because I wanted to go to the bridge to see what was happening. This turned out to be a good choice, because I had just taken up position on the port side of the bridge when a young man came in. He began asking questions: when the ship arrived, what the loading plan was, how the locomotives were to be stored on the decks. The Chief Officer gave him answers to all his queries, including that chains would be used to avoid crane swing. The young man asked about the delayed arrival of the ship, the reasons were explained: sea conditions and weather, and the detour we had had to take to protect our sensitive cargo, *City of Adelaide.* The young man asked about the nationality of the crew. 'Two Russians and the rest Ukrainian and one UK.' He, German, and Igor looked over at me. I went across to introduce myself. His name is Rob Carbon and he had come from Australia to supervise loading of the six locomotives destined for the iron ore mining industry at Port Hedland. He told me each of the locomotives is worth around three to four million dollars. Their life in Australia will be to pull two to three kilometres of freight trucks from the mines to Port Hedland. Rob will be around until loading is complete. We talked a little about *City of Adelaide.* He told me he had looked up the Australian website and read up on her a bit. He knew about the quarter of a million Australians who had descended from people who had sailed out to Adelaide on her. We talked about my connection with her. I said to him he had a nice job. He agreed, though he said it is hard to travel and be away from his family. He has a young son, fifteen months old. 'Time to go home and make another,' he said to me, with a twinkle in his eye. He left with a request to German that he have access to coffee during his visits to the ship. I am sure they will also invite him to sample Anatoliy's culinary wizardry. Our crew is hospitable and polite. Fish for lunch today, with potatoes and red cabbage coleslaw. I took back the small ice cream dish I had taken to my room last night to eat the strawberry and vanilla blobs scooped into it. I like my ice cream to be a little warm, melted to a thick consistency. Anatoliy joked about it being my soup bowl; I joked about a thimble. He is not going ashore, no room and no money left from the previous visit to the USA, prior to *Palanpur* picking up steel at Bremen before Antwerp and Rotterdam where I joined her. German was at lunch for a change. We talked about traditional Ukrainian dishes, like *pirogi* and *varenyk*, dough parcels with various fillings. German talked about the different rules different states in the USA have about visa entry. He also told me about the port they are visiting after Adelaide, South Australia. It sounds like paradise.

I texted my youngest daughter asking her to phone me. It had hardly been sent when my phone vibrated. We spent a good twenty minutes talking, at 70p a minute. She talked about Christmas arrangements, the tree that is not up yet, her new carpet, the work that needed done on her partner's van after it failed its annual vehicle inspection. She told me of the tragic car accident of four young people from my hometown. I was shaking and upset to learn three of them had been killed when the car hit a wall. The whole town is in mourning.

Then I spoke to my mother for about half an hour. As I was winding up the call, we got cut off. So now, no visit ashore and no credit left in my phone. I went down to send some emails, one will ask Alan to top up credit in my phone. I received a text message from my brother, a man of few words. 'Landed then.' He is following *Palanpur* on the Live Marine Traffic site. I have scoffed an entire Ritter bar in about fifteen minutes, that will be the last chocolate until the slop chest opens again in at least a week's time, since folks will be buying goodies in Norfolk. Do you detect just a wee tinge of bitterness creeping in here? I feel it, now that I see crew head off to *terra firma.*

I saw a large, dark brown bird with a white head, about the size of a buzzard that looked like an eagle sitting on a light on the wall of a shed beside where the crew are storing sections of the deck they are removing one by one to open up the lower decks. I took a couple of photographs, wondering if it was a sea eagle. After some time it stretched its wings and took off. It was completely white underneath.

I received an email from Peter Christopher in response to mine of yesterday. He requested I send some photos. I said I could not send attachments to emails from the ship and would not have access to wifi as I could not go ashore. I said I had intended blogging on my website, and on my Facebook page but could not due to no access to wifi. He mentioned plans for celebrations on our arrival in Adelaide were underway, in February and again in May, when it is one hundred and fifty years since *City of Adelaide*'s launch, her birthday. When I was at the computer Stepan came in and mentioned Skype. I said, 'You can get Skype here?' He withdrew, saying he did not know. I will ask about this. When I got a phone signal this morning my mother had left a message asking whether I wanted her to get in touch with *The Scotsman* newspaper about this trip. She had had an epiphany through the night. I said it was a great idea, and had planned on contacting selected newspapers before I left, but because everything happened a few days earlier than anticipated, I had not managed to do this. I have my *Writers & Artists Yearbook 2013* with me, so have contact email addresses. Now that I have email access, I will progress this, and offer a weekly article to perhaps *The Herald* and maybe *The Sunday Times.*

I went up to the bridge to watch what was happening with the locomotives from *Palanpur*'s bow window. I looked back towards the stern at *City of Adelaide* and had a touch of vertigo as I looked down into the depths of the hold in front of her that had been opened to receive them. I could see people on the naval ship moored across from us but could not make out whether or not they were crew. I have been playing it safe with my camera and not used the flash, and I would not be lifting up binoculars to see what was going on on board that ship. I might find the deck gun trained on me. Andriy asked me if I had slept well last night. 'Yes,' I replied. 'Why, did you not?' I asked him. No. He told me he has been on duty since 8 pm yesterday evening, and will work till 6 pm tonight, when German and the Third Officer return from the town. Andriy said he had a present for me. He dug into a paper package and brought out a couple of calendars, first offering me one of young pin-up girls. 'You like?' I replied, 'Hmm, only now and again.' We laughed. 'It is better for crew he said,' and gave me one with scenes of America. Could be the only way I will ever see America. I quipped to Andriy that I wondered what the great conservationist John Muir would have said about American border control. He is considered the founding father of conservation in the United States of America. Guess what? He was born in my hometown of Dunbar. He left for America with his family when he was eleven years old and has become world famous for his love and conservation of nature, particularly Yosemite, and his friendship with President Theodore Roosevelt. Perhaps if I had mentioned this to the guard, I would have got special permission to cross the border. I do not think so somehow. My shopping list is ripped up. Andriy may be going ashore tomorrow. I have asked if he does go, that he gets me a couple of eight gigabyte SD cards for arrival in Australia, because by all accounts, that is going to be a momentus occasion. Andriy told me of previous celebrations by owners when cargo has arrived. I left him to get on with his work and met Nikolay in the corridor, all spruced up for his shore visit.

I overran supper by three-quarters of an hour. I was engrossed with working on the Irvine section of this book. When I went down, Anatoliy had laid out several dinners for those who had gone ashore. I apologised. We spoke about languages and on-line translations. I told him about my *The Three Craws* plays for radio, in particular *The Three Craws Gaun Tae Bayeux Wi The Battle O Prestonpans Tapestry*. We accompanied the tapestry on its visit to the Bayeux Museum in Normandy, France in September, staying in a chateau with all expenses paid. We discussed the French and German languages. He told me he will leave *Palanpur* in Cape Town as he has exams to do for his Electrical Engineering certificate. He has been away from home for six months.

I have been conscious of the crane working away, and the sound of metal on metal. The sounds appeared to come from the bow of *Palanpur*, but not so. I looked out of my window. Outside a great yellow caterpillar has appeared on the apron. Crew are working in the absolute pouring rain, standing on top of this caterpillar, manoeuvering the crane grabber. Tomorrow morning the locomotives will begin to be loaded. I am excited that I will watch this. It is chilly outside, very miserable. I take my hard hat off to these tough men who are working in the dark. Whether they will work through the night I do not know.

Flashing about on the water in the dark, a small blue insect is on patrol. We are being watched.

DAY FIFTEEN

August 26, 1864 – Friday

A fine day, but very warm. The wind is not very favorable.

10 December 2013 – Tuesday – Norfolk, Virginia, USA

A very cold, wet, grey day. There is little wind.

I was hungry when I awoke this morning. I made a double ordinary cup of tea in my mug, ate two pots of apricot yoghurt and a little muesli, picking out the raisins before I added milk. All went down well. Action was beginning on the apron. The caterpillar looked more like a preying mantis now that it was looking in at me through my cabin window, suspended in the air. I have not yet worked out what its purpose is. It just appeared from nowhere and I had not seen crew putting it together. There are about a dozen recruited workers standing in the mouth of the huge shed we are alongside, most in hi-vis jackets. The apron has become a global village of hardhats of various design conversing with each other in colours of white, black and day-glo green. Rain is pelting down. A wind has got up, it is changing the rain direction from southbound to westerly, forcing it to streak in sheets across *Palanpur*'s deck. A man driving a fork-lift truck emerged from the shed and disappeared into the side of *Palanpur* with a stack of something on the front carrier. The men are huddling. I went up to the bridge for a birds eye view. I asked German what the big yellow caterpillar was. He said it was lifting gear or a lifting traverse. The reason I had not seen it before is it is stored at the stern, behind Crane 2. There was much being discussed around the locomotives. The agent arrived on the bridge and voiced anxiety over the wooden spacers that are being placed between the grommets of the crane loops and the sides of the locomotives. He requested new spacers be made, with increased thickness to take the stress and avoid any damage to contact points with the locomotives during the lifting process

into the hold. Two men began tugging at pull cords to fire chainsaws into action. These were dull with the cold, wet weather and it took a few attempts before the air was filled with the sound of grinding, vicious teeth. Wooden plinths for the first locomotive were manufactured on site. They emerged from the huge shed on the prongs of the fork-lift truck from earlier. The agent asked for further strengthening, after they had been tried beneath the locomotive.

Andriy V was going into town in a taxi at 10 am. He asked me to give him a sample SD card. I gave him $30 from my emergency cash stash, and asked him to get me some sun protection cream. I received a text message saying my phone credit was topped up. There was a break for lunch and no locomotive had yet been loaded. I came down to my cabin and found it as Baltic as the sea that bears the name. I know this, because I ventured into that sea when I went to see the Tall Ships Race fleet when it visited Szczecin, Poland in 2007. My mother was born there in 1930, known then as *Stettin*, and part of Germany. We had often talked of going there. We made the trip that year, going by rail and sea for her to re-visit places from her early years. We took a day trip by train from Szczecin and travelled to the Baltic coast to visit Sinowitz, an island she remembered from childhood, and had managed to meet up with her uncle there some years before. This time it was a brief encounter. I just managed to submerse my body in the freezing waves before racing back to the comfort of warm sand and the return to the ships at Szczecin. I know my mother and I would never have done all this and more, if it had not been for my obsession with tall ships.

I received a phone call from Alan and my son. I was excited to hear their voices and news. After lunch the agent was now satisfied with the four strengthened wooden supports for the first locomotive. One was fitted beneath each side, front and back, parallel with the locomotive. One end of each grommet from the lifting gear was fixed to one end of each spreader, the other end was passed under the locomotive and attached at the opposite end of the spreaders, so forming slings. The locomotive was lifted with painstaking precision into the air, a man holding on to each line dangling from each corner of the locomotive to fine-tune manoeuvres, pulling this way and that to make sure the precious cargo did not touch any part of the hold whilst being lowered to the lowest deck level. The skill of these men fills me with awe. No problem is too big for them to solve.

I checked my emails. Two. One from the system saying they were unable to deliver an email from Rosemary McKay. I had been thinking last night that I must write to her, and here she was, writing to me. I added her to my address book. The system does not allow receipt of emails from people who are not listed in an individual's email address book, treating any that arrive that are not listed, as spam. I emailed her and asked her to re-send her message. Twa Scots lassies: one down-under and one on the brink of the United States of America. The second email was from Ruth Currie responding to mine requesting the dates of birth and death of Sarah. She was born in 1844 and died in 1906, making her sixty-two when she died. I am in my sixty-second year. Ruth also confirmed who the people are in the photograph she gave me last year. With the passage of time since I met her in 2012, and trying to link the subjects with the family document she had given me, I had got muddled. The photograph is of Sarah and her husband, John S Kerr and their five children: John, Charles, Ethel, Alice and Amy.

While German and I were watching the first locomotive being loaded, concern was brewing over the cadet who was being flown home today. There was no way he was going to conquer his seasickness. He had not wanted to walk on the apron to the waiting taxi, for he feared border control would apprehend him for walking on that area when we had been told we were not to walk on the dock. He wanted the taxi to come for him but the taxi was not permitted to drive on the apron. Stalemate. I did not see how the situation was ultimately resolved, but I heard the cadet made his flight. There was a lot of coming and going on the bridge, some crew coming for shore passes, others taking a birds-eye view of proceedings with the locomotive below. I was glad there was shelter in the huge shed for the men in between operations, because the rain was relentless, bucketing down. The men had protectors over the back of their necks that prevented the rain from pouring down their backs. I remarked to German that these were real men doing hard work, that many men do not know the meaning of the word, leading privileged lives and making decisions that affected the lives of these hard-working people without whose efforts there would be no economy and trade. Here I take an extract from the Bray family papers that shows one of the ideas from the new industrialists of the early 19th century. It is one example of the *tuppenny flyers* of philanthropist William Cobbett (1763-1835).

> *'Whatever the pride and rank, or riches or of scholarship may have induced some men to believe, the real strength and all the resources of a country, ever have sprung and ever must spring from the labour of its people.'*

German drew my attention to a train in the distance that was pulling a snake of fourteen locomotives. He also pointed to the next dock where there was another heavy-lift ship. It was flying the Netherlands flag, the Jumbo Company flag and the flag of the United States of America. They were loading locomotives as well. They were not destined for Australia, for they were covered in cloth rather than shrink-wrap like the six locomotives we were loading, and *City of Adelaide* that had had to meet the stringent Australian quarantine rules. We watched as the lower part of the first locomotive was power-washed by a hose linked to a generator, to ensure any seeds or bacteria or any form of contamination that might compromise the rude health of Australia, were banished. I had a phone call from my eldest daughter whilst on the bridge. All great news. She had been part of a concert in the Queen's Hall, Edinburgh, bringing her magic on her Paiste gongs to the Tinderbox event organised by a friend she had met in the Balkans earlier this year, whilst working with war traumatised children in music camp there. I was delighted to hear a DVD had been made of the event. I look forward to seeing this when I get home sometime in February 2014.

The first locomotive hovered over the yawning gap leading to the lower deck. Men manipulated each and every movement of the crane to ensure no contact was made of any part of the locomotive against any part of *Palanpur*. The men are minute against the Goliath locomotive, yet they coaxed it into place until it was swallowed into the belly of this great steel whale. I went down to my cabin, had a blue cheese spread sandwich on rye bread I had brought from the mess earlier. Rye bread is my favourite. It brings back memories of childhood when my parents would on a rare occasion bring a loaf back from Valvona and Crolla's in Leith Walk, Edinburgh, now of worldwide fame and much expanded in size. I remember it when it was just the front of the shop with a long counter with a range of salamis hanging down from hooks above it, and other meats and cheeses were displayed behind glass to tempt customers. The floorboards were bare. My nostrils are bathed with the memory of the aromas as I write.

A knock at my cabin door. Andriy V tells me he was unable to find a shop with SD cards. The sun cream was very expensive and he decided not to buy any. I was glad of this. $40 seemed a ridiculous amount to pay when I can get it in Scotland for a few pounds sterling. He bought dresses for his little girl. 'Princess dresses,' I said. 'Yes,' he grinned. He told me a couple of crew were going ashore at 4 pm. Did I want them to try to get the SD cards? I swapped the $30 I had given him earlier for $50, and said that would be terrific, but that they were not to take up their precious shore leave seeking SD cards for me, only to get them if they happened to be available in a shop they were visiting anyway. I think it is Stepan and Vitaliy who are going, for it was they who came to the bridge earlier for their passes. After this I had a nap and woke up at 5.45 pm, just in time for supper. I could have lain on. When I went down Anatoliy was quizzing me about my book. He is fascinated by it. He has a book about shipwrecks and he is amazed at how *City of Adelaide* has survived one hundred and fifty years. I told him about Sarah's diary and that in the entry for the other day she had written that her family were bailing out water just as they had been on *Palanpur* after the pipe bursting. He made a comparison with *Palanpur* and *City of Adelaide*: the people sailing on the wooden ship *City of Adelaide* were hard like steel, and the people who sail on the steel ship *Palanpur* are soft like wood. We laughed. I had been thinking a lot about rough blankets, heavy clothes getting wet and not being able to be dried, weevils in flour, cockroaches, rats, poor food, little or no heating. We have all the modern conveniences and are very comfortable. More detail of living conditions on board *City of Adelaide* will be unfolded as Sarah's voyage progresses. I ate my spicy beef, pasta and salad. When I went through with my plate Anatoliy wanted to know more about the book and mentioned the Renaming Ceremony at Greenwich, London. He asked me if I knew that *Palanpur* had also been renamed. I was surprised. He told me she had been renamed from *Hyundai Phoenix* to *Palanpur* on the 10 September 2012. I was struck right away by the name *Phoenix*. *City of Adelaide*, this former beauty with a glorious and far more prestigious and varied background than *Cutty Sark* had been left to rot. She is on her way for her pride to rise again, under the golden rays of South Australia. I wondered to myself whether peace had been made with Neptune and his Register of Ship's Names over this name change, like it had been when *City of Adelaide* reverted to her original name after having been known as *Carrick*.

I asked Anatoliy to write what he knew down for me to include it in my book. 'Co-writer,' he said. I laughed and said my youngest daughter had texted me my horoscope for today. It had made reference that a collaboration would bring fortune. I teased Anatoliy that I was not sure whether he would want to be mentioned in the book, that our conversations have been included in my daily logs. He raised his eyebrows. I joked that he had said a few days before he was not going to tell people that he had been a Cook when he becomes an Electrical Engineer. He assured me he was very happy to be included in the book. Many people know him as a cook. He talked about when I expected the book to be published. I said I did not have a publisher yet, but mentioned where I thought I would approach. I told him about the *Writers and Artists Yearbook*. He said he would try to write me what he could about *Palanpur*. He has been with Harren & Partner for nine years. He said in all this time he had not known of a passenger sailing on any of the cargo fleet of six ships, other than the wife of a captain. I said in all seriousness this was even better for my publishing prospects, because I am a lone woman, wife, mother and grandmother amongst seventeen men.

I came to my room with another slice of rye bread. I shall smear it with crotchets of honey and sing it for my supper, with accompaniment from a *vibrato* hot chocolate, the drone of the crane, the chimes of midnight, and all this harmonious humming in my head.

DAY SIXTEEN

August 27, 1864 – Saturday

A very calm day.

11 December 2013 – Wednesday – Norfolk, Virginia, USA

A clear, calm day with blue sky and sunshine. It is a bit chilly. *City of Adelaide* is slipping out of her pink negligee as the sun responds to the beckoning sky.

I looked out of my cabin window to see yellow has joined the global village of hard hats on the apron. The sun was rising just after 7 am and *City of Adelaide* was bathed in warm pink. I took a photo of her from my cabin window before the moment was lost. I threw my jumper over my pyjama top, took off the bottoms and pulled on my jeans. I headed for the open door on the other side of the corridor. With the sun's earnest quest to ride high in the sky, the bloom over *City of Adelaide* had halved, and I was glad of the earlier photograph.

As I was about to retreat to my cabin, Rob Carbon was coming down the outside staircase from the bridge. We bade each other good morning. He said he had some technical hitches the day before that meant we had not seen each other on the bridge. He told me he had brought me some newspapers from his hotel, *The Wall Street Journal* and *USA Today*. He said he knows what it is like to be isolated, and thought I might like to know a bit about what is going on in the world. I am very appreciative of his kindness. I will ask him to post my two postcards later, and have written a message on my last pictorial business card of me on the bowsprit of *Stavros S Niarchos* to him. I have only a few of my own postcards left now, but am happy I will keep my promise to Adrian Small, whom I met at the Reception after the Renaming Ceremony for *City of Adelaide* in Greenwich that I would send him a postcard from wherever we stopped. He is a retired master of sailing ships, and remembered Eric Newby who captured life aboard *Moshulu*, in his book *The Last Grain Race*. I am also sending one to my friend Hugh Loney in Irvine.

An American sailing ship came into view as I happened to look out of my window. Her hull was painted like *City of Adelaide*'s, in black and white. Her two masts were sloped back from bow to stern, like the *Baltimore* I saw in Europe somewhere along the way on my tall ships travels. I dived out of my cabin to the open doorway and took a couple of pictures of her. She looked magnificent, but she had no idea she was passing the wonderful 1864 composite clipper, *City of Adelaide.*

I showered and made my way up to the bridge. The third locomotive was being

loaded. It was already dangling in the air from the lifting gear and being manipulated into position by some men on deck and some inside the lower deck pulling on ropes attached to the locomotive. It was as though they were drawing down a great blue airship from the sky. Laughter rang out from some men two decks below *City of Adelaide*. I noticed yet another colour of helmet, orange, and got an instant craving for chewy sweets, seeing all the colours. Vitaliy arrived. With a broad grin he handed me a grey plastic bag. Inside was my change from the $50 dollars he had taken to try and get me the two SD cards. His mission was a success. I thanked him, and gave his arm a rub. I took my spoils down to my cabin and went to check emails in the ship office. Rosemary McKay had sent again the email from yesterday that had been rejected. It was a very warm message, asking when I planned on leaving Adelaide, what I would like to do when I got there. She was going to chauffeur me during some of my visit. She also said she wanted to interview me for Celtic and Scottish radio. What were my five favourite pieces of music? I am beginning to feel like a celebrity. I will send my response after I have thought this through. Meantime, I forwarded the email to Alan. I went up to the bridge again with Virginia Woolf's *To The Lighthouse* in my pocket, with the intention of taking in the sun from the roof of *Palanpur*. The small patrol boat is still buzzing about. There is a battleship sharing this dock with us that has a cannon that looked like a retracted bowsprit sitting right up on the foredeck, and lots of people, probably sailors and cadets, standing about at various points on the ship. Andriy and German told me Rob had left the two newspapers for me. I read Nelson Mandela had died a few days ago. I wondered if I was the only person in the world who did not know this. Last night at supper there had been mention of him on the television in the mess, and I did wonder, for there had been news before I left home that he was failing. The American newspapers are more manageable than the broadsheets of the United Kingdom, being of less width but equal height. I scanned the rest of the newspapers before going up to the roof, where I untied the plastic chair and moved it into the sun. It was exhilarating to feel its warmth on my face. It was very cold, there was ice on the puddles. German had told me there was frost earlier this morning on top of the locomotives that remain on the apron. I opened up my thin book and began reading the amazing language, descriptions and observations by Virginia Woolf of human behaviour. This charity shop find is my first encounter with her. Every now and again I took a look over the railings from the rooftop to see what was happening with the loading. The third locomotive was being put in its final spot on the lower deck. I took a video. German had told me the trade union had stopped the men from working any further because the first three locomotives needed to be welded to the floor, using lashings that looked like massive stays of a yacht attached to them. The plan had been to close the lower deck over the first three locomotives and weld whilst the next three locomotives were being loaded. The trade union would not allow this. I asked German if there would be extra shore leave then. 'Maybe,' he shrugged his shoulders. Me… I am anxious to be back at sea, and found I am not alone in this.

At lunch Valeriy told me *City of Adelaide* weighed about 600 tons including the cradle. The weight was spread over the two 450 ton cranes. *Palanpur* is very special, she has more lifting capability than many other twin-craned heavy-lift ships. I told him I would like to see the engines when we are at sea. 'This is possible,' he said. I ventured, 'Is it also possible to see inside a crane?' He grinned. 'This is also possible,' he said. We finished our pork chops in mushroom and cheese sauce, chips and salad and went to get on with our jobs. I took a banana for later and went to my cabin.

I was restless. Welding was going on all afternoon and continued into the night. I went up to the bridge for coffee. The Chief Officer had left himself logged on to the computer so I did not check my emails. I stood absorbing the sun through the bridge windows for a good while, even standing where the warm air rising from the radiators warmed the steel handrail running under the windows. It was very cold outside, the fluffy blue blanket sky was not yielding any warmth. Heated up, I went down to send a couple of emails from B Deck before going back to my cabin, and lying down to read. Soon I was asleep and awoke just in time to see a white cross on the blue background of sky. St Andrew's Cross, a Saltire. The Scottish flag, made from plane chemtrails, yes, but still a Saltire. I took a photograph, and a couple of the blood red horizon. It seemed no time since lunch, but I went for supper, neck of pork that Anatoliy had picked me leaner pieces of, salad and mashed potatoes. After supper Anatoliy and I spoke about music, he loves Pink Floyd, particularly the Division Bell. We talked about child rearing. German had been telling us about his teenage daughter and what she likes. I empathised with him, remembering how my own three children craved designer label clothing and electronic gadgets. Anatoliy said we had got him worried now, and we laughed.

I went up to my cabin and dozed for a while. I began deleting files from the laptop as I kept getting warnings that the memory was almost used up. It is nerve-racking deleting photographs, even though I had transferred them to an external hard drive. It was lovely to see pictures of my family, and it made me sad when I saw my two horses Ginny and Morgan, and our old Staffordshire Bull Terrier Marley, all of whom we lost to old age or sickness in the last couple of years. They are missed, but the happy times we shared are locked in my heart forever. I set the computer to defragment, finished the last of the red wine and drank three small cans of German beer. The last piece of the floor of the 'tween decks is in place. It is one in the morning. Karine Polwart is singing me to sleep.

DAY SEVENTEEN

August 28, 1864 – Sunday

A beautiful day. As the weather is so calm and warm, prayers were held on the Deck. There being no clergyman on board the Captain read the prayers and Mr Bruce the lessons. One of the sailors lead the singing. The service was very solemn. In the evening the Doctor played some hymn tunes and we sang for about an hour.

12 December 2013 – Thursday – Norfolk, Virginia, USA

Another clear, calm day with blue sky and sunshine. It is very cold, though the thermometer on the bridge says it is 15°C.

I awoke about 9.30 am, having been awake at 5 am and then not sleeping for about half-an-hour. I am missing cuddles.

The first locomotive on the 'tween deck has already been loaded. It looks promising that loading will complete today. I got up, showered, and worked on yesterday's diary entry before heading for the bridge. Up there I noticed a massive fresh landscape the battleship that had shared our dock to starboard had painted by its departure. To port, the twin cranes of lesser capacity than ours that had been growing at the end of the roof of the huge shed between us had been scythed down, leaving a clear view down river where those yellow stems had stood. I did not stay long in the control room; there was a lot of directing going on for loading the next two locomotives. The fifth one was brought forward on the rail tracks and preparations began for loading it. The wooden protectors and supports were put in place and fixed on. The power washer was brought out from the huge shed again. The locomotive was lifted off the ground by *Palanpur*'s crane for it to be sprayed underneath and scrubbed. When it was done, the operator whipped back the snaking black cable that powered the washer from inside of the shed. It writhed its way back into that dark hole.

After the fifth one was loaded I returned to the bridge to watch the last locomotive being slotted into the tight space, and marvelled how it fitted between the other two with their lashings stretching into its space. Everything had been calculated and checked several times, so there was no doubt all three would snuggle together comfortably. I noticed a sketch of the loops of the steel ropes, or grommets, supporting the locomotives. German's artwork. I went to the computer and found an email from someone who was helping me with my new website before I left home.

He was offering to load information up for me if I send it to him. I responded to Rosemary's email of yesterday. I said I would work on the list of five favourite tunes. It would be difficult to choose from my broad taste in music, and choices that reflect my immediate mood. I offered her an MP4 of *The Three Craws And The Bairn In A Manger* in the run up to Christmas, forgetting about the limits of the on-board system.

I met Igor in the corridor and confessed I needed more loo paper. I said it was not an emergency, and we laughed. He went off and brought me a couple of rolls, then asked me to return the roll of elephant skin, some of the crew needed it. I went out to photograph the men at work. Some of the American crew began to wave; I waved back. Rob was with them, checking this and that. I took my book outside to sit on the steel gangway below, where it is broad and there is space to sit without obstructing a doorway. A smell wafted from somewhere wood was being cut. The aroma was like tobacco. German passed me on the way to the bridge and said to get a chair to sit on. He was right. Sitting on cold steel is not clever. I fetched the duck down cushion from my cabin and sat on it. Rob came up the stairs, heading for the bridge. Igor had passed on my request for him to post my postcards for me. Not a problem. We went to my cabin to get the postcards. He was taken by the label above the door: 503 Owner, and was surprised at the speciousness of the cabin. He said he had seen some pretty awful conditions on board some cargo vessels. He homed in on the corner on top of the bookcase, where greeting cards from my wee family stand with the copy of the photograph of the Bray family. He spotted their little pug dog right away, tucked in at the folds of Sarah's taffeta dress. We remarked that these little dogs had not changed much in the one hundred or so years since the photograph was taken, other than perhaps their legs are shorter now. Rob was smitten with the fine, handsome Sarah, and how erect her posture is. Rob also saw the SCARF card with Peter Maddison flying the red ensign from the top deck of *City of Adelaide.* I told him of Sunderland's failed bid to recover the ship to the town where she was built, and that in March 2012 I had met Peter Maddison and sneaked on board her at dusk, when he occupied the ship at the Scottish Maritime Museum at Irvine for that entire month in protest. Rob was on the way to a meeting on the bridge. I took a photograph of him with three of the locomotives behind him, I will send it to him when I have the facilities to do so. He took the grey plastic bag my SD cards had been delivered in. In it were the two postcards, my card, and some dollars for postage. He refused the money, but I insisted, saying that if there was any left over he should have a wee dram on me.

I dozed on the couch and thought it was 2.30 pm when I awoke. the clock said

4.45 pm and not long till supper. My hunger was keen, having had a limit put on its demands. Sundown was blushing my window. I looked out and saw a blood orange trickling its juice along the gash that severed day from night. I grabbed my camera and took some shots from C Deck before heading for the roof. On the way I met one of the American crew coming down from the bridge, a lady carrying a clipboard. We greeted each other, and I said, 'Good job,' in best Mickey Mouse Clubhouse style. 'Thank you,' she said. Up on the roof the view was expansive. Cranes from the docks merged with the silhouettes of tall buildings floating in the juice. The American flag was limping on the flagpole, tangled. It liberated itself to give me some good shots of it flapping over the deck of *City of Adelaide*. I went back to my cabin for a hot cup of tea before heading for supper, gherkin wrapped in minced pork, salad and rice, and a wee sponge cake, the second cake since my arrival on board three weeks tomorrow. This sparked off conversation with German about cooking and baking.

There was a demob happy air in the mess. German anticipates departure before midnight, the right side of 13 December 2013. When I looked out from my cabin window at about 8 pm I thought there was no chance of this happening. The deck coverings were still lying on the apron along with the spreaders. It is now about 10.30 pm and I feel the heartbeat of *Palanpur* beneath my feet. I noticed I had missed a couple of calls from home that had come in during suppertime when my phone was in the cabin. My eyes welled up as I listened to messages from my husband looking for a chat before we went out of range of a phone signal. It was 2.30 am in Scotland but I dialled home. I left a farewell message on the answering machine.

I went up to the bridge after 10.30 pm. All was still in the darkness. The only light was the red one that glowed on the stairwell leading from the main stairs. Computer screens glowed our co-ordinates, the chart of the river, our position on it, us, a black dart stitching its way along pins pricking a seam towards open sea. Digital readings of wind speed, compass, temperature and so on joined the display of stars in the clear dark sky. Two pilots had boarded, the same two that had guided us into Norfolk. They were giving steering instructions to the Ukrainian on the wheel. The wheel is nothing like the large, spoked wooden helms of sailing ships. Rather, it is like a racing car wheel, compact, leather-bound, disproportionate to the massive vessel it commands direction to. Against our starboard hull outside, two tug boats had leached themselves onto our steel like black sea anemones. Their thrust against our hull restricted *Palanpur*'s bid for the high seas like police authorities apprehending a suspect, pushing them against a wall to stop them escaping. The three mooring lines at

Palanpur's bow were lifted off the bollard one by one by two stevedores responding to directions crackling into their ears through the chilled air. They were lonely figures bathed in artificial light, casting off *Palanpur*'s apron strings and setting us free.

Our stern waltzed from the dockside, partnered by the pilot boat in its pretty garnet and diamond jewellery. The second boat separated and soon we were out in the open waters of the river following a pilot boat along a liquid runway flanked with intermittent buoys marked on the starboard with red lights and on the port, green. The older pilot left *Palanpur* in the charge of the younger one, Captain Kevin Hartz. His voice carried through the silent confidence of the bridge. He remarked on how pretty *Palanpur* is, her front end being more like a cruise ship. He chatted with German in between calling steering adjustments to the helmsman. German brought me to the Kevin's attention and we began chatting about *City of Adelaide*. He had looked at the website and was struck by her history. We talked about my connection with her. He asked if I had been ashore. I told him the tale of the visa. He remarked it was a pity I had not been able to see how pretty it is, the parkland, the trees. He spoke of the army base and the stretch of beach that is used for practising manoeuvres. He showed me on his laptop where his house sits. He talked of spectacular Christmas lights to look out for when heading out to sea. He talked of his twins, a boy and a girl, due at the end of January who would augment his current family of a little girl of six. He talked of his yacht. I talked of John Muir, whom he knew of. He gave me his card. I noticed later from the logo on it that the Virginia Pilot Association is one year younger than *City of Adelaide*. He told me how mixed his blood is. I borrow Hugo Hamilton's book title, *The Speckled People*, and think of how many of us with mixed blood there are in the world, and what is true nationality, why is there so much prejudice, why do some people wear their blood in a cloak of shame whereas others shake those droplets off their coat of many colours and wear it with pride and confidence. Kevin also told me he and his wife had been to Adelaide and loved it. They have Scottish friends there whom he is going to email that we are arriving with *City of Adelaide*. He talked of the wine growing region. He told us an amusing story that he had hired a car to visit Kangaroo Island. Kevin was then told there is no insurance cover for driving after dark. That is when the kangaroos come out. The ones on their namesake island are different from the Western Greys of the main land, they are grey, smaller and stocky. Little tough guys I could picture wearing boxing gloves. Driving to his destination took about three times longer than it should have trying to avoid these hairy jumpers lining the roads, eyeballing their headlights. I remembered reading *City of Adelaide* had lost her rudder off Kangaroo Island at some point.

I went to my cabin to get my last card for Kevin. I would be sorry to see this personable young man so proud of his home territory leave the ship when his job was done. He had guided us beyond the seventeen miles long Chesapeake Bay Bridge-Tunnel that was once the eighth wonder of the world. The two halves of the bridge transform in the centre into a tunnel and connect Virginia Bay to Delmarva. It was so constructed to thwart any intentions by enemies to blow the bridge up. Bombed bridges are notorious for their debris falling in to the water below and blocking access up and downstream of rivers.

Kevin took his leave of our bridge, shaking hands with us all. He told us to watch out for the meteor shower that was forecast for this evening. I watched him emerge onto the tiny pilot boat from an open access in the hull of *Palanpur* and motor away up the glistening, cobbled path to the moon we had been looking at earlier. It was back to base for him and the end of duties for the night. Time to seal himself in to a blanket full of snuggles and baby kicks with his wife and unborn twins.

I saw those meteors he talked about, and made some wishes.

DAY EIGHTEEN

August 29, 1864 – Monday

A fine day. We are sailing along very well. In the morning we sighted a vessel going in the same direction and it was nearly dark when we passed her, distant only about half a mile. In the evening we walked about looking at the stars and the phosphorous. About midnight the wind changed and the sea became very rough. We passed a very unquiet night.

13 December 2013 – Friday – Norfolk, Virginia, USA/Atlantic Ocean

A beautiful, clear morning. *Palanpur* is dancing through the waves with a gentle sway of her hips. We are both happy to be free of concrete, clay, city lights and clamour.

I awoke at 9.30 am and again at 10.45 am when I forced myself out of bed for my shower before heading straight for lunch. I remembered last night's meteor shower, arrows of love piercing the black heart of the universe. They make me think of flying fish flirting with the air as they leap from their natural, liquid environment. German and Valeriy were seated at the table. German suggested I try Mexican relish with my soup. I knocked back the invitation because the soup was already tasty. Anatoliy was playing *Careful With That Axe Eugene* by Pink Floyd, when I went to get my main course. He has tweaked one of the crew member's 110V stereo system he had bought in Norfolk, Virginia, the man not thinking he needed 220V to be able to use it. 'You are a hero,' I said to Anatoliy. 'Maybe a small one,' he smiled. I took my lunch to my place and stuck my fork prongs into the jar of relish and put some on the side of my plate. I licked the residue off the fork. German and Valeriy laughed at my gurning; it was very hot, but very good. I smeared it on the fish and potatoes, spicing them up. I painstakingly picked out bones from the trout as we talked about food, particularly Mexican food – tortillas and jalapeno peppers, salsa, avocados and guacamole. After German and Valeriy left I found peeling back the backbone of the fish made things easier.

I spent most of the afternoon in my cabin reading, sleeping, writing, scrutinising the *Writers & Artists Yearbook*. I chose several newspapers to approach about articles, and drafted out an invitation for them to consider the worth of the story of this unique journey. I went to the bridge to use the computer there and began loading in the addresses for the chosen newspapers. I found there is a limit to the number of addresses that can be stored in the email system, so I had to delete some earlier ones I had not used. The message exceeded the permitted one thousand characters, and had run over into a second email, fracturing the whole. I wonder if my story will capture their imagination. Our reading for this afternoon is latitude 35°90.34'N, longitude 071°51.37'W. We are travelling at 15 knots per hour.

It is quarter past midnight. The clock started ticking loudly. The sea is getting rough. I was glad my supper was digested. The clock spun forward one hour. No dark forces at work then, near the Bermuda Triangle, just a passing through a line of longitude, losing an hour's sleep. It is payback time for the extra hours we all had on our way west across the Atlantic.

I was browsing some files on my computer containing things in the past that have caught my interest but have not had time to absorb. The poem below is for a wife and mother permanently gone, but it struck a chord with me in my current situation. The first home Alan and I bought was The Lodge at Bowerhouse, Dunbar, East Lothian in the late 1970s.

Palanpur is rattling round a bit. It feels like when you hit turbulence on a flight on an airplane. From my window I see a crystal clear star yo-yoing from the finger of some great force concealed in the dark mass of night. One of these nights I will leave my cabin and curl up beneath that wondrous blanket that shakes that sparkling dust over us at the end of day, and tucks into its folds La Luna, mistress of the sky, who beams her benevolence down on us.

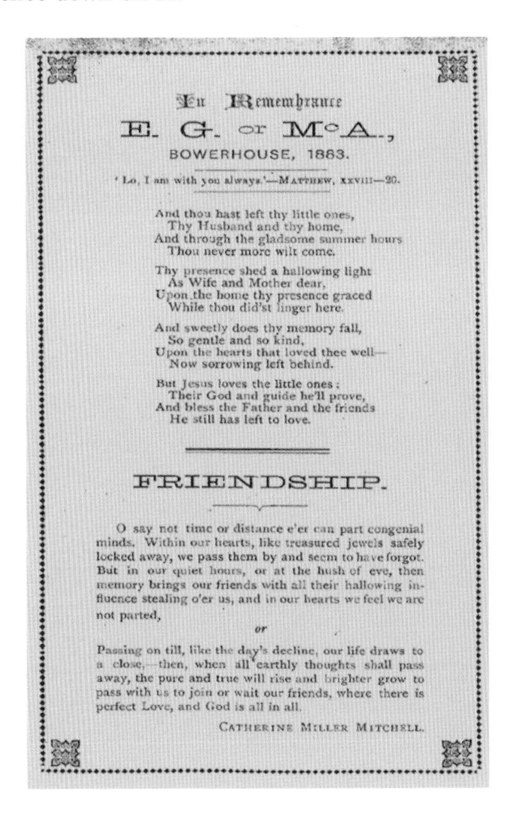

In Remembrance

E. G. or McA.,

BOWERHOUSE, 1883.

'Lo, I am with you always.'—MATTHEW, XXVIII—20.

And thou hast left thy little ones,
Thy Husband and thy home,
And through the gladsome summer hours
Thou never more wilt come.

Thy presence shed a hallowing light
As Wife and Mother dear,
Upon the home thy presence graced
While thou did'st linger here.

And sweetly does thy memory fall,
So gentle and so kind,
Upon the hearts that loved thee well—
Now sorrowing left behind.

But Jesus loves the little ones;
Their God and guide he'll prove,
And bless the Father and the friends
He still has left to love.

FRIENDSHIP.

O say not time or distance e'er can part congenial minds. Within our hearts, like treasured jewels safely locked away, we pass them by and seem to have forgot. But in our quiet hours, or at the hush of eve, then memory brings our friends with all their hallowing influence stealing o'er us, and in our hearts we feel we are not parted,

or

Passing on till, like the day's decline, our life draws to a close,—then, when all earthly thoughts shall pass away, the pure and true will rise and brighter grow to pass with us to join or wait our friends, where there is perfect Love, and God is all in all.

CATHERINE MILLER MITCHELL.

DAY NINETEEN

August 30, 1864 – Tuesday

A very rough day. The waves continually came over the deck, the hen coops gave way, the rain came down in torrents and nearly all the passengers were sick. We were lying near all day in the Saloon which resembled a hospital. There was scarcely any fresh air as both windows and shutters were closed. The Captain has never before experienced such a gale in the tropics. The storm abated about midnight.

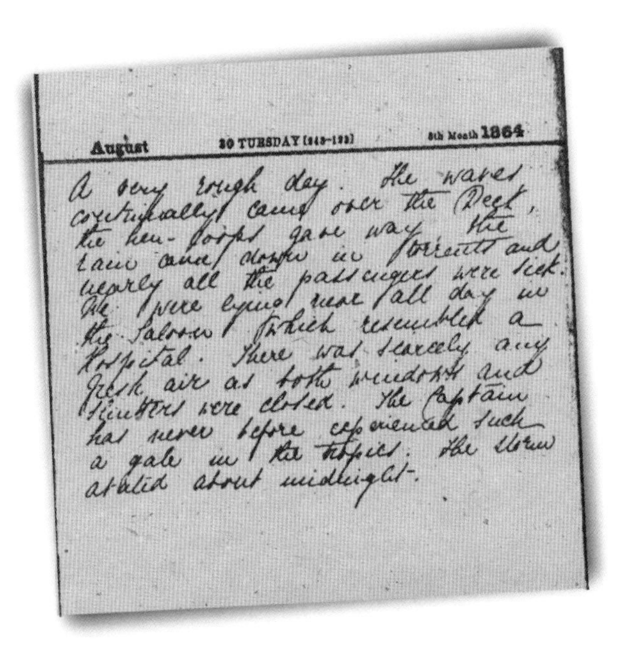

August 30 TUESDAY (243-122) 8th Month 1864

A very rough day. The waves
continually came over the Deck,
the hen-coops gave way, the
rain came down in torrents and
nearly all the passengers were sick.
We were lying near all day in
the Saloon which resembled a
hospital. There was scarcely any
fresh air as both windows and
shutters were closed. The Captain
has never before experienced such
a gale in the tropics. The storm
abated about midnight.

14 December 2013 – Saturday – Atlantic Ocean

Another beautiful, clear morning. *Palanpur* is gliding along with a gentle roll. Most of the crew are in fine fettle, being at sea and it being a morning of leisure.

Neptune is breathing with deliberate calm this morning. His skin is wrinkled, like boiled milk when it is allowed to stand. I see some more brown flotsam that yesterday I thought might have been *Palanpur* excreting our excreta. It is kelp, come loose and taking a tan in this Atlantic December sun. We are heading for Bermuda, and I am hoping the sharp edges of the triangle will not point at us. Last night I said to the Captain we must stop there. He and Andriy V roared with laughter at my suggestion. I have a friend, Christine Franklin, my 'big sister' from boarding school. We have kept in touch all these years, over forty-five now. In the Millennium year 2000 the tall ships raced to Bermuda across the Atlantic Ocean and I went to see them. It was wonderful to wrap my arms around Christine all those years later. If it had not been for her generosity of giving me a pillow to rest my head on, I would never have been able to visit her paradise home. Fulfilling my ambition to see her island ever since she bewitched me with its name, to feel its pink sand between my toes, and spend time with her as well as my beloved tall ships in one delicious package, was mind-blowing.

Great. A big, thick curly pubic hair, a coiled spring of virility comes out with my washing. It sure is not mine. I suppose you cannot expect less, with all these guys on board. Ah well, at least it was clean. I removed it gingerly with the edge of a hand-towel hanging on a hook by the door.

Anatoliy said if I bring down my rubbish after 4 pm he will put it with his kitchen waste and take it to the stern of *Palanpur* where the big bins are kept. He is so kind. I have three bags now, each containing separate types of waste as required. He also told me he has prepared the information on *Palanpur* for me, about her being renamed.

It is slop chest day. Hmmmm. No red wine. Can it be true? Am I bothered? No. I did think about a bottle of gin and some tonic, but thought I would wait for this till the last slop chest before Christmas. I am finding it very easy to go without alcohol. It would be nice if my weight would respond to this absence. I ordered a Ritter bar and two tins of Nivea cream as a substitute to sunscreen. I found them later outside my cabin door. I checked emails this morning. Two from Alan. He is sounding a bit lonely, but has band practice tomorrow afternoon, and a gig coming up at the end of January in a local pub. He told me they are desperate for photographs of *City of Adelaide* on this journey. It is really frustrating to have all these superb images and not to be able to share them with the world, particularly on *City of Adelaide*'s Australian website. There was an email from Newsquest. I had not approached them, and the system rejected it because it was not on my white list. I deleted an address and added Newsquest. I asked them to re-send their message. We are at latitude 32°37.67'N, longitude 066°33.58'W, wind speed 13 knots. I went up to the roof with my book and notebook and watched the sun being dabbed by cotton wool. I did not stay long as sun, wind and sea working as a pack can give a vicious bite. On the weather deck, a lone jogger worked off his lunch. My stomach rumbled. Eintopf, chicken breasts, rice and salad soon sorted that. I am amused that Sarah's diary entry for today mentions hens. Anatoliy said to bring down a memory stick for the *Palanpur* information he had prepared. He said if I bring an SD card later he would put music on it for me. I looked forward to being introduced to new sounds. By the time supper was over he had loaded up the SD card. I returned to my cabin full of anticipation.

German and Vitaliy were at supper. Everyone had been given a white plastic bag with red lettering. *Norfolk Seamen's House, Norfolk, VA USA* printed on one side, and their name scrawled on the other. 'A Christmas present,' German said. I said, 'Can I look? But it may spoil the surprise for the others.' Shoulders shrugged. Inside: a brown woollen hat and scarf and a men's speed stick deodorant. The smell of it reminded me of my teenage years when I used this brand instead of those for women. German suggested I could give this to my husband. Two plastic razors, six orange hard-boiled sweeties, two strawberry toffee sweeties, three sweeties wrapped in scarlet red cellophane that turn out to taste like the *Armies and Navies* back home in Scotland, three miscellaneous hard-boiled sweeties, a tube of toothpaste, a toothbrush marked *Soft* to clean your teeth after their sugar bath, a pen, a pencil, unsharpened with an eraser at the end, and a twin pack of playing cards. A wee comfort bag to return to sea with. I thought of the kindness of strangers who cared for the well-being of seafarers.

Back in my cabin, I snoozed for a couple of hours, read a while and played Pinball and Solitaire on my laptop. I finished reading *To The Lighthouse*. Virginia Woolf has an insight into and a sensitivity about human behaviour that is celestial in my humble opinion. Her observations about Mrs Ramsay resonate with my reasons, in part, for undertaking this voyage, aside from my obsession with *City of Adelaide*. If Rosemary McKay asks me during her planned radio interview why I am making this journey I will say it is my obsession that began with tall ships that has polarised on *City of Adelaide*. I am kicking against grey hair and retirement. I am filling a gap where once there were the vessels of my three children to steer. In making this journey I have removed myself from the hub of my family home. In doing so we are all growing. None of us will be the same when I get back. Virginia Woolf imparts acutely Mrs Ramsay's frustration with being caught up constantly with her eight children, despite the presence of a nanny. She has no time or facilities to carve out her own character beyond the realms of domesticity. Her duties as a wife and mother running a household disallow any opportunity for self-development, and her lamentation of this is obvious. Modern women have education and career opportunities with salaries that give them independence; gadgets; access to child care; can have a home, a partner, a family with time left over for a vast choice of interests and activities that help define them. I am living these weeks in a man's world as a grandmother, dealing with my inhibitions, wearing shorts and vest tops for comfort in the increasing heat trying to ignore the rasping voice on my shoulder that I am overweight, and that the company is all male. Today I wear a cardigan over my vest top. Tomorrow I will not.

DAY TWENTY

August 31, 1864 – Wednesday

A bright day. The sea is still rough. We were not able to go in the Saloon for meals and were delighted to spend the day in the fresh air. I have done scarcely anything but sleep being quite exhausted from yesterday.

15 December 2013 – Sunday – Atlantic Ocean

A clear blue sky gave way to cloud. It is humid. We are going along steadily through the Atlantic spray. I slept surprisingly well through the night, having fallen asleep after supper yesterday evening. The crew will be happy it is Sunday. With not so much to do they will be able to catch up on the hour lost during our travelling back east.

I awoke at 8 am, feeling refreshed. I connected with the MP3 earplugs, danced and did a little exercise, using the motion of *Palanpur* as an uphill and downhill treadmill. It felt good to be doing something physical, other than going up stairs to the bridge or down to the mess. I washed my cabin and shower-room floors, wondering again where all that fluff comes from, wiped surfaces, cleaned the loo, the sink and finally me. I detected a slight paling of the skin where yesterday's top had shielded the sun from me. It had only taken a few a minutes.

I opened the SD card Anatoliy had put some of his music onto. *Karunesh* makes gentle, meditating music that put me in mind of being massaged. Neptune is noisy this morning, but he is in a good mood, singing along with the tunes flowing from my laptop. I looked for the information Anatoliy had put on my memory stick. I could not see it. When I went to lunch Anatoliy asked me if I had read the information. I said I could not open it then realised I had been looking at the wrong drive. We checked it on the office computer after lunch. Sure enough it was there.

At lunch Valeriy told me the sea is 28°C. I said, 'We can go for a swim.' I asked if we had passed Bermuda yet. He asked Andriy K about this. He replied we had passed it during the night. I had eaten Anatoliy's best borscht yet. When I remarked on it he said that the previous batches had been made with a non-natural tomato paste. I am thinking of GM, genetically modified products. He explained the difference is that he used fresh beetroot and tomato paste made with real tomatoes. Main course today: duck. I decided to try it properly, along with pasta and red cabbage salad. Very tasty. When Valeriy joined me at our table I told him I had never knowingly eaten duck and told him why.

About forty years ago my husband Alan had been out helping his father control rabbits in his valley where he kept sheep. They had gone with shotguns. Three times Alan pointed his gun at rabbits, pulled the trigger and nothing had happened, just the dull clack of steel on steel. When a pair of resident ducks took off from the burn, or stream, flowing through the valley, Alan pointed his gun at them and pulled the trigger. BANG! One duck fell stone dead to the ground. It is very difficult to shoot duck, their feathers being close bound. To shoot one in flight with a shotgun is a claim to fame. He, however, was gutted at this unfortunate, unintentional taking of the life of one of a breeding pair of ducks that had made their nest in this quiet valley. Rather than waste this poor, unfortunate creature's robbed life, Alan decided to bring the duck home and prepare it for our supper. Feathers were plucked. He went to great lengths to ensure all the shot was removed from flesh, the vegetables he peeled were *al dente* and the mash was perfectly smooth. He served it up by candlelight reflected in the polished cutlery on the pristine, starched tablecloth. We looked at each other through the flickering candle flame. We picked up our forks and knives. Neither of us made the first move. Neither of us had an appetite for it. Neither of us ate it. One German Shepherd dog was very happy that night.

I moved the washing I had put in the machine prior to lunch into the dryer and headed for the roof for a seat in the sun. It was way too windy up there so I came down. A couple of days ago when German had seen me sitting on the steel deck, he had told me to use the chair on the deck outside his cabin. There is also a table there. The laundry leads out onto this level, D Deck. It was very convenient just to take that chair down from where it was jammed between the grab rail and one of the windows of German's cabin, and get some loo paper from the laundry to wipe it down with because it was grubby with Neptune's spit.

It was energising to turn my face into the sun. Some big rolling clouds acted as a shield against the powerful rays pouring down on *Palanpur* and *City of Adelaide*. I dropped the straps from today's top that were a bit wider than the ribbon straps of yesterday. I offered up my bare legs for tanning. I am wearing shorts in public. It is too hot to be shy. Shy at sixty-one. Who would have thought it? I saw some small fish leap out from the spray and dive back into the sea a few metres from where they had leapt out. There was a small piece of plastic floating nearby to where one landed. I wondered if it would have a go at windsurfing. I cannot see any other good use of plastic out here on this vast ocean. The first time I saw a flying fish was when I visited Bermuda. Six days ago Sarah reported seeing flying fish off Gran Canaria. They are the meteors of the sea, arrowing above the waves, fading into the burst of their element.

From where I was sitting, each little section of the rail became a little photo frame filled with mercury, or dark blue, or dark blue with mid blue stripes. Not a fleck of white interrupted the stretch from *Palanpur*'s bow to where Neptune's waistband merged with the pale blue tie-dyed t-shirt he had borrowed from Apollo. At the stern, socks of lilac-grey crumpled round his ankles. I looked up. A herd of sea horses had uncoiled themselves from their sub-aquatic tethers. They had made a flying leap into the thermals above. Their necks were stretched. They were racing their reflections, chasing mares' tails that vapourised before they could catch up with them.

I re-set the drier and went to my cabin to work. Half an hour or less in this sun is sufficient. Just after 3 pm I went to the bridge. It is 22°C. From every window a different shade of blue smeared our eyes: steel, gun-metal, bruises, everywhere.

Neptune had been busy. The waves were elipses, resembling Brazil nuts, their navy shells browning in the lick of the sun. Neptune had hurled his ribcage into the sky. He will have to wait for it to be drizzled back to him. We are at latitude 30°00.9'N, longitude 061°48.15'W. Andriy V and German were there. German and I chatted a lot about the housing situation in our countries, whether people bought their houses or rented them. People tended to rent in Ukraine, it gives them the freedom to move around to find work. If they ended up somewhere they were sure of a long-term steady job, then they would perhaps buy. I told him how difficult it is for first-time buyers in my country, how things had got more difficult in the last few years; that local authority social housing was hard to obtain since the implementation of the right-to-buy policy. Private landlord rents were high, and if someone had sessional work, only working and being paid during the educational calendar, they might not be considered for a mortgage due to irregular income. We talked of the good points and not so good points of property ownership.

We talked about further education and university entrance criteria. I explained about the university clearance system in the United Kingdom. He said at home a certain number of points have to be obtained to be considered for university. I asked whether there is career guidance in schools. His wife takes care of these matters as she is at home, whereas he is at sea much of the time.

At supper there was only Igor, Andriy V and me. Igor gave me some Ukrainian mustard. It nipped my sinuses. I reckon it would cure the worst cold. It was so good, though. There was a sweetness to it. 'Sweet?' said Andriy, in a tone of disbelief. Igor said it keeps the bugs away. He said about twenty years ago there were only three ingredients in this mustard, but since then all sorts of additives have been crept in, E numbers and so on. I told the two of them that I had been chatting to German this afternoon, describing what a *ceilidh* is. This is a Gaelic word. A ceilidh is when a group of people get together for a party. Each person brings to the company a song, a dance, a story, a tune – something that will entertain those present. Or it can be just Scottish country dancing. Igor said there is something similar at home, done voluntarily. I said it is the same, if you do not want to do anything, no one will be forced. The good thing is though, that if someone shy is in the company, they are often inspired to leave their inhibitions behind and contribute to the enjoyment. I suggested we do this at the Christmas barbecue. It went down like a lead balloon. I soon found myself alone.

I asked German earlier whether there was a facility to send photographs by email, that the Australians are keen to see some. He said that although there is a system for compressing photos for sending, no social media sites could be accessed. I am to put photographs on a memory stick and he will take it forward.

I finished reading Donald McKinney's short story anthology, *Why We Howl At The Moon.*

DAY TWENTY-ONE

September 1, 1864 – Thursday

A fine, quiet day. We were able to read and work as usual. I read some German songs which were headed 'Wo man singt da lass dich ruhig – nieder böse Menschen haben keine Lieder'. We also read some of The Ingoldsby Legends. I practised for about an hour. We saw a great many flying fish.

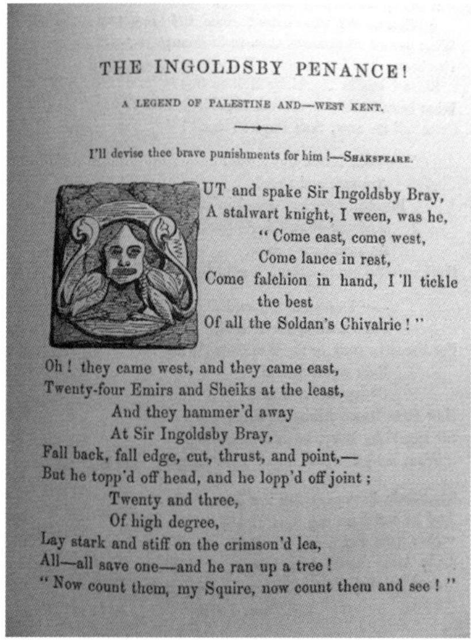

THE INGOLDSBY PENANCE!

A LEGEND OF PALESTINE AND—WEST KENT.

I'll devise thee brave punishments for him!—SHAKSPEARE.

BUT and spake Sir Ingoldsby Bray,
A stalwart knight, I ween, was he,
"Come east, come west,
Come lance in rest,
Come falchion in hand, I'll tickle the best
Of all the Soldan's Chivalrie!"

Oh! they came west, and they came east,
Twenty-four Emirs and Sheiks at the least,
And they hammer'd away
At Sir Ingoldsby Bray,
Fall back, fall edge, cut, thrust, and point,—
But he topp'd off head, and he lopp'd off joint;
Twenty and three,
Of high degree,
Lay stark and stiff on the crimson'd lea,
All—all save one—and he ran up a tree!
"Now count them, my Squire, now count them and see!"

16 December 2013 – Monday – Atlantic Ocean

A clear blue sky. It is humid. I saw a ship on the horizon. It looked like a clog in the distance. Nearer to us I could see it is a red and black cargo ship. There are many flying fish today. With great difficulty, I managed to capture a few on camera. I could watch the sea all day, it is an ever changing canvas.

I worked on the two days previous diary entries until lunchtime. I was up at 8 am. At lunch, chicken fillets dressed in breadcrumbs covered in pineapple and cheese, salad and chicken feed millet. I mentioned the flying fish to Andriy K. He said sometimes they land on the deck. He left and Igor came in. He was in a talkative mood. We covered everything from climates, sub-tropical, tropical, African immigrants to Italy, weapons, economies that evolve round the manufacture of weapons and private wealth, Honolulu, the nuclear industry. We talked about Fukushima, Japan and the differences between that disaster and Chernobyl, Ukraine, non-containment and containment of radiation, French nuclear power stations on British soil, windmills on the land, windmills at sea. It was a very good discussion. He told me about Cape Town. All the crew so far sing the praises of this South African City.

I went to my cabin and spent some of the afternoon reading, working and watching the sea. I went up for the readings. Andriy V told me he wanted to show me something. 'These flying fish,' he said. They looked far more splendid from up on the bridge than from my porthole. We are at latitude 26°58.61'N, longitude 056°53.67'W, wind speed 15 knots. The temperature outside is a very pleasant 24°C.

I put four photographs of *City of Adelaide* onto the memory stick to be emailed to Peter Roberts. When German appeared he took the stick and inserted it into the small machine above his computer and converted the files to .pdf. They are still clearer as .jpg. The Australians are keen for their general public to see images of *City of Adelaide* in transit. People are interested, and the more interest that can be generated, the better. He said he would send the images to head office for them to decide whether to release them to Peter Roberts, the Director whose email address I had given German, since he is the lead person for loading information onto the *City of Adelaide* website. I went to check my emails. Still nothing from any of the Press I contacted the other day in relation to an article.

I took a little more sun as it began its slide towards the horizon, then went for my camera. At the other side of the bridge, the moon was playing peek-a-boo, but I still managed to catch her on video. I felt quite tired by the time I went to supper. That soon changed. Anatoliy and I were discussing Christmas and the barbecue that was being planned. He told me there would be spit-roasting of a pig. I had been given this information earlier in the day from German. I told him where I thought the expression *spit-roasting* had come from. I said I believed it is because when the fat of the pig explodes, this is it spitting. Of course, the name of the turning machinery the pig is skewered on to is the spit. I prefer my theory. Us both being Pink Floyd fans I then told him about the ceilidh idea, that he should spread the word to the crew and ask if they are willing, to prepare some sort of entertainment for the Christmas Day barbecue. I suggested he could turn the handle of the spit in the best barrel-organ style, whilst singing the track *Pigs On The Wing*. We roared with laughter. I told Anatoliy that my second cousin made his living travelling through Germany with a barrel-organ until several years ago.

I came up to my cabin and drank three half-pint cans of German beer and read a while. The next book I will read is *The Great Days of Sail* by Captain Andrew Shewan. I bought it from King's Bookshop in Callander, when I was there in September 2013.

DAY TWENTY-TWO

September 2, 1864 – Friday

A calm day. We are sailing very slowly. The Doctor played Chess with me from lunch till dinner. I lost three games. The Captain assisted me with the first two.

17 December 2013 – Tuesday – Atlantic Ocean

A blue sky with clouds full of their own self-importance. I got up late, showered, and went straight down to lunch. After lunch I sunbathed for about fifteen minutes front and back, then went for a snooze.

A lazy start to the day. I slept for about eight hours last night from just after 11 pm to 7 am. I dozed and re-awoke at 10 am. We have lost three hours since leaving Norfolk. Some crew were washing down the steelwork of *Palanpur* near my cabin. We are rolling gently in a small sea. We are almost beyond the North Atlantic now, and I heard we have left behind eleven metre waves. I count our blessings that we were not subjected to those. Mushroom soup for lunch, then chicken legs and wings, salad and rice; fresh watermelon or ice cream to finish.

Andriy V was at lunch, as well as Igor. German came in and began a conversation with him. Brian Oglanby who is making a documentary about *City of Adelaide*, whom I met at Irvine, Greenwich and Rotterdam has requested to come on board *Palanpur* at Port Hedland. There is no accommodation available and so this request will be denied. Brian had told me at Rotterdam his original idea was to come on board there and travel with us to Australia. I said to German this would have been a waste of his time and money, since all he would be filming was *City of Adelaide* on the back of *Palanpur* with a changing sea and sky all around. Sensitivities over the filming of crew abound, just as they do in relation to me sending photographs or articles about life on board *Palanpur*. I felt German was re-emphasising this position in having this conversation with Igor in my presence. I got the picture, if you pardon the pun, and respect the reasoning. German invited me to have his water melon, he took ice cream from the mess freezer, and left with Igor.

I went to my cabin and rested before going up to the bridge. Andriy V was on duty. He was looking at charts. We looked at Cape St Blaize to Port St Johns. Chart comment: '***Abnormal waves.*** *Abnormal waves, preceded by deep troughs, may be encountered anywhere in the main stream of the Agulhas Current*'. This is the Cape of Good Hope. I was glad my fresh suntan disguised my blanching at this information. I knew from geography at school that this is an unpredictable area. *Palanpur* has a 7.5 metre draught. We are heading towards the level of the north coast of South America, approaching the line of Brazil, and in line with the Canary Islands, but two thousand miles away from them. We are going along at 11 knots, at latitude 24°24.08'N, longitude 053°08.37'W.

Andriy asked if I had seen my email. I had picked it up after lunch. It was from Alan. He had given me all good news about our family about musical performances by the oldest two; that his band practice was going well, including introducing some harmony singing; that he is going to our youngest daughter for Christmas, going overnight on Christmas Eve and taking our wee dog, Zac along. I hope he is not sick on her new carpet, as he has been having some problems with his aged stomach. We reckon Zac is about fourteen years old, a Staffordshire Bull Terrier we took on after Alan's father died exactly four years ago today. I began my reply to Alan with the comment that everything was so positive with the family that I would have to leave home more often. I wonder what his response will be.

Andriy asked me how long I was planning on staying in Australia. I said I wanted to see *City of Adelaide* into her new home, that there would be celebrations and another celebration in May to mark her one hundred and fiftieth birthday. I said I would probably leave Australia in February and return in May, even if I have to sell a musical instrument in order to achieve this. He laughed. At lunch German, Igor and I had speculated about how *City of Adelaide* would be received in her new home. In previous conversation with him I had told him there were celebrations planned, and there would be a huge crowd to welcome *City of Adelaide* to her namesake town. I have thought now that this might not happen with *Palanpur* because *City of Adelaide* will be offloaded in a dock away from the public gaze, as had been the case so far. We thought that she would be placed on a barge similar to the one provided by Hebo and towed to her new residence. This would make more sense than if she were to be loaded onto a road trailer and trucked to the new site, although German said the Australian roads could take this precious load.

I saw some flashes of welding going on at the port side near the stern of *City of Adelaide*'s iron support. Checks are made daily by crew that she remains secure. *City of Adelaide* may well be enjoying the feel of salt water spraying on her skin through the rent in her raincoat. The opaque plastic shrink-wrap covering is tearing on the starboard at her main deck. It is not something that can be tackled at sea, being far too dangerous to send anyone up in these rolling waves on to that slippery surface. German had come up to the bridge. He thought the tear would not cause a problem for entry to Australia as the ship had already been fumigated. I hope this proves to be the case.

Supper was roast beef in horseradish sauce, salad and mashed potato. Valeriy and I chatted a bit about horses. This had sprung from me comparing the sound of *Palanpur* landing in the water from being lifted on the crest of a wave and slammed down, to the sound of a horse kicking against a stable door. He asked if I had stables. I said not. I told him a bit about my life with horses, how I have been around them since I was about eleven years old, how my mother-in-law had a pony I helped exercise. We had a discussion of what defined a pony. I explained the measure of *hands* was the stretch of four inches from the point of the thumb to the heel of the hand with fingers pressed together, and that upwards of 14.3hh, *hands high*, defined the animal as a horse; below this it was a pony. He was surprised, as German had been, that horses are kept as pets. I told him how I used to gallop through the waves at Belhaven Beach on Ginny. I had told him earlier about how Ginny had been lead horse when my children were small; how from my position on Ginny's back I had led them on their pony by rope clipped to a head collar that had been placed on top of the pony's bridle, allowing the child to still have reins to hold on to, to learn how to control the pony's speed and direction before they were on their own.

Valeriy told me that his fifteen year-old son had been to Scotland twice with a group of young Ukrainians. He had walked the West Highland Way. He said how much his son loved Scotland. I asked him if he would visit there himself one day. It is difficult to get a visa from Ukraine. I thought: these visas are such a restriction on people. Why should someone not be able to go on holiday to a country they are interested in, especially someone who travels as their profession? Why should someone not be able to visit a country in a special relationship with their own, and see a bit of the United States of America? Why should my father's cousin's daughter be given a visa for only one weekend, arrival on a Friday and departure on the following Monday, in order to attend my father's funeral? It would have been interesting for us all to get to know each other for a few days before she had had to return. She had even brought some Ukrainian soil to sprinkle on my father's coffin before he was sealed into the vault of Mother Nature.

I told Valeriy of the Edinburgh International Festival, the Book Festival, Harp Festival, all the street theatre and events that go on in the fringes. We had a laugh over the great Scottish midge, that tiny vicious blood-sucking insect, exchanging stories he had heard from his son, and mine on the last camping adventure I had been on, with my son. We had wondered why people were wandering about the campsite with towels on their heads when we arrived on the island of Skye. We thought ourselves lucky at finding the last flat piece of ground by the almost dried up burn, or stream at the far end of the campsite. By morning we were sucked dry. We bundled the tent into the boot of the car and drove about five miles before stopping. We opened up the boot lid, dragged out the tent and shook a cloud of midges from our lives.

I was still restless after supper. The reason I give for this is the full moon. She was streaming in through my cabin window. I decided to go up to the bridge and take some photos. It was only just after 7 pm. Igor and German were on the bridge, chatting. I had put on my coat and a thick jumper expecting it to be chilly outside. It was 24°C. I took three photos, two were hazy and the first could only be described as moondrop. It was just a downward squiggle in the middle of nothingness. German offered me to use the camera they had been given in Rotterdam to record any issues with cargo. He showed me the controls and I took a couple of good shots of the moon in her splendour. The low battery warning came on so I gave it back to him to put on charge. He and Igor searched everywhere for the charger. It had disappeared into thin air. It was a complete mystery that not even the magnifying glass was going to help solve.

I came back to my cabin thinking about Cape Town that everyone so far has described to me as beautiful, with Table Mountain sheltering the city. When we get there for bunkering, that is, taking on fuel and supplies, we may only be a few hours in port. We do not need to take on water as *Palanpur* has a desalination system on board. This projected short stay means it will not be possible to take a taxi as Andriy V had suggested, and see Table Mountain up close. German suggested a trip to the Cape Town version of Edinburgh's Deep Sea World. It is reputed to be the second best in the world. He has not seen it and if there is time we shall go together. This will put Alan's mind at rest about me going alone to the City.

I played some Pinball before the rough sea advised me to put away the computer for the night to pre-empt anything happening to it in the slam, judder and shoogle *Palanpur* was receiving from Neptune. At times it felt like being shaken in a sieve, where the fine soil is separated from weed and stones.

I began to read my book. I am finding it hard to pull myself away from it, it being about Shewan's reminiscences of ships and shipbuilding in the mid-nineteenth century. Many of the ships he mentions were contemporaries of *City of Adelaide* built in the same City as her, Sunderland: *Chanticleer, Malabar, Thunderer, Lammermuir, Wynaud.* He writes *Wynaud* was built for the opium trade, and belonged to Jardine that I had seen a documentary about. *Wynaud,* he said, 'was designed partly as a pirate catcher and partly as a carrier of the precious drug. She was armed with six nine-pounder guns – a larger armament than that of most tea-clippers of the fifties.

In his book there is mention of young lads *squeezing up the crinoline hoops of the ladies in 1863.* I looked at the photograph of Sarah. The way she is sitting on the chair and the folds in her taffeta dress looks like she has pushed hoops behind her in order to sit down. There are also several references to *City of Adelaide*'s younger cousin, *Cutty Sark.* The *Cutty Sark* was ordered to be built by John Willis, son of John Willis who was born in Eyemouth. I have seen their family home and have known of this connection for years, Eyemouth being roughly twenty-four miles from my home town, Dunbar. Shewan also describes the differences in parting between sailors and their families and the emigrants, the former knowing they will be coming home and so made a less fussy farewell, the latter made prolonged, miserable, final partings, going off to make new homes in foreign lands, and more than likely never seeing the loved ones they left behind again.

Sometime after one o'clock in the morning I tried to get to sleep. The rush of being horizontal and surging along on the crest of waves is similar to being dizzy, or going up in a lift. I find it really relaxing, but I still could not sleep. In the end I blocked out peripheral noise with earplugs and fell to slumber with Pink Floyd.

DAY TWENTY-THREE

September 3, 1864 – Saturday

Mama's birthday. A lovely day but so calm that we are scarcely moving. In the morning we saw a large Steamer which sailed across the front of our ship but too far off to signalise. In the evening the Sailors played and we danced.

18 December 2013 – Wednesday – Atlantic Ocean

Tall waves gave us a noisy, roller-coaster night. The ship gave a loud bang as it landed back from the lift of the sea. The sound of metal banging against metal persisted throughout the night. The morning blue sky with large clouds gave way to grey. Arcs of rainbows where sunlight played through droplets of spray bridged the main deck. It is the birthday of one of the Able Seamen.

I was not able to sleep last night due to the business of the ship playing in the water. Often *Palanpur* thudded down from a lifting swell, shuddering as she landed. The clanking of metal against metal was more pronounced than it has been so far, something outside my cabin is not lashed down hard. I thought the first time I heard this it was Number One crane in its cradle, but dismissed this as it did not sound like heavy metal. Heavy metal. Iron Maiden. I think of Anatoliy in the kitchen. He told me yesterday he is going home from Cape Town to do exams for his electrical engineering certificate. He will be home for Ukrainian Christmas, something for him, his wife and his little girl to look forward to. He teased at lunchtime, saying we were having my favourite dish. 'Liver,' he said, with a mischievous grin. I baulked and said I would raid the fridge of cheese and salami. He offered me a piece of pizza left over from breakfast. Pizza for breakfast. I said I thought this only happened in our house. It is the perfect thing on the morning after a heavy night. He heated it up for me then put some salad on the plate, with some of that pig food, maize. We snorted at each other and I went to eat. Andriy V was checking crew about the missing camera charger. He asked me to check my cabin. I said I could not understand why it would be there. The first I knew about the camera was last night, when I had been given it to use for the lunar pictures. A thorough search had been made of all the cupboards and surfaces on the bridge, but it was nowhere to be found.

After lunch I went to the bridge, took readings for today, latitude 22°00.59'N, longitude 050°04.74'W. Temperature is 25°C, wind speed 30 knots. We are passing from the North Atlantic Ocean to the North Equatorial Current. The computer was in use, Andriy V is engrossed in work. I went to my cabin, having found the computer in the ship's office not logging on. I read a little then dozed till nearly suppertime. We had pork kebabs, *Shishi*, as German told me they were called in Ukrainian. The apple pie, he said, was in honour of the birthday of a crew member. I took it to my room for later, being full up from all the meat, salad and baked potatoes.

For some reason after supper the loneliness of being aged twelve at boarding school came gushing at me. I had a vivid picture of me in my billowing pale blue uniform summer dress belted at the waste with white plastic, white ankle socks, brown t-bar sandals, short hair with my fringe swept to the side. Then another came of me with my older brother, he in his scout uniform and crew cut hair, me similar as before, but in a tartan checked dress with white collar. I wondered if the loneliness was triggered by the isolation of not being able to check emails from family. Before I had access to emails I could accept not having contact with home, but now I know I can be in touch via email, it has hit hard that it is not available, even though I know this is only temporary. It is a month now since I arrived at Rotterdam.

I have been reading more of Shewan's book. He mentions *the first composite vessel, a schooner, was built in the following year.* His allusion to a particular year at the end of the previous chapter was 1863. Since *City of Adelaide* is one of the earliest composite built ships, that is, iron ribs with wooden cladding, in 1864, I wonder whether it is not she he is alluding to, and that he has placed her as a schooner instead of a three-masted clipper. A point for further investigation.

On 28 October 2013 Peter Christopher sent me an extract from a book he had written, *Australian Shipwrecks A Pictorial History.* When he found out when I met him in Greenwich at the Renaming Ceremony that I was from Dunbar, he told me about the wreck of the *Dunbar* he had written about in his book. Peter has included a scroll in his illustrations –

'*A narrative of the melancholy wreck of the Dunbar*, James Fryer, Sydney, 1857'.
It reads:

'The shore is literally white with candles,
and the rocks covered or so deep with
articles of every kind – boots, panama
hats and bonnets are here in abundance.
Drums of figs, hams, pork, raisins
drapery, boots and pieces of timber are piled
in heaps along with the keel of the Dunbar,'

Said the Sydney Morning Herald on 23 August 1857.

'The rumours as to the fact of a dreadful shipwreck having just occurred soon assumed distinct shape and certainty. At length it generally became known in Sydney that numerous dead and mutilated bodies of men, women and children were to be seen floating in the heavy surf at the Gap thrown by immense waves at a great height; and dashed pitilessly against the rugged cliffs, the returning water sweeping them from the agonised sight of the horrified spectators ...'

The *Dunbar* had been built in Sunderland in 1854, ten years before *City of Adelaide*, for passengers and cargo. The order given to the shipbuilders James Laing & Sons had come from Duncan Dunbar to meet the demands of the Australian gold rush. She was 1167 tons, almost twice the tonnage of *City of Adelaide*, and was the largest ship to be built in Sunderland's shipyards up to that date. There were fifty-nine crew and sixty-three passengers on board on 20 August 1857. *Dunbar*'s Master was Captain Green, who had made this voyage seven times before. Heavy rain, high seas and darkness caused confusion between the North and South Heads at the entrance to Sydney Harbour. Instead of turning into the clearing that would take them to the safety of the harbour, she was turned into the rocks to the south of the entrance, and smashed. Her cargo included furniture, machinery, food, alcohol and cutlery, as well as ink dye for the colony's first postage stamps. There was only one survivor, a young crewmember, James Johnson, who was rescued two mornings after the disaster. Ironically, in 1866 James Johnson was instrumental in rescuing the only survivor of the shipwreck of the paddle steamer Cawarra off Newcastle, Australia where he had become keeper of the lighthouse. Twenty thousand people turned out in Sydney on 24 August 1857 for the funeral procession for the deceased, and flags flew at half mast. A plaque and Dunbar's anchor mark the location of her wreck on the cliffs above the site. The Australian National Maritime Museum houses items salvaged from the wreckage. This tragedy and the further loss of twenty-one lives two months later from the barque *Catherine Adamson*, caused the construction of the Hornby Lighthouse on South Head.

I have included the above with permission from Peter Christopher, in tribute to all those who had perished in the awful shipwreck.

I began reading the background to Sarah's diary that had been given to me by her great-granddaughter in March 2012. The information had come from James Kerr, grandson of John S Kerr and Sarah Ann Bray. I found that in the same year as that shipwreck tragedy, Sarah was beginning school in Boulogne, Italy, before the family began their Grand Tour. They spent time from 1857 in their home at Blackheath and at Boulogne until the *City of Adelaide* trip in 1864. They had visited *City of Adelaide* in London Docks on 21 June 1864. This may be when they booked passage on her to Adelaide, South Australia. Amongst the papers I found a photocopy of a letter to a Dr Platt from James Kerr sent from 24 Sydney Buildings, Bath on 24 October 1990. In it he thanks him for his interest in Sarah Ann Bray's diary and invites him to come and see the original at his home. A bell rang in the depths of my memory. I searched back to the first email I had from Jim Tildesley, retired Director of the Scottish Maritime Museum on 31 October 2006. In it he mentions his 'very good friend Dr Alan Platt, living in Scotland, who has prepared the bulk of two volumes of the history of *Cutty Sark* in conjunction with Bob Sexton in South Australia'.

I went to bed, exhilarated, and with a shiver tingling down my spine.

DAY TWENTY-FOUR

September 4, 1864 – Sunday

A showery day. In the morning we sighted a Ship which saluted us and asked our name to which we replied but the wind blew the flag in such a direction that it could not be distinguished. We saw a great number of dolphin. Prayers were read on deck. In the evening it rained almost incessantly so we stayed in the Saloon and had music and singing.

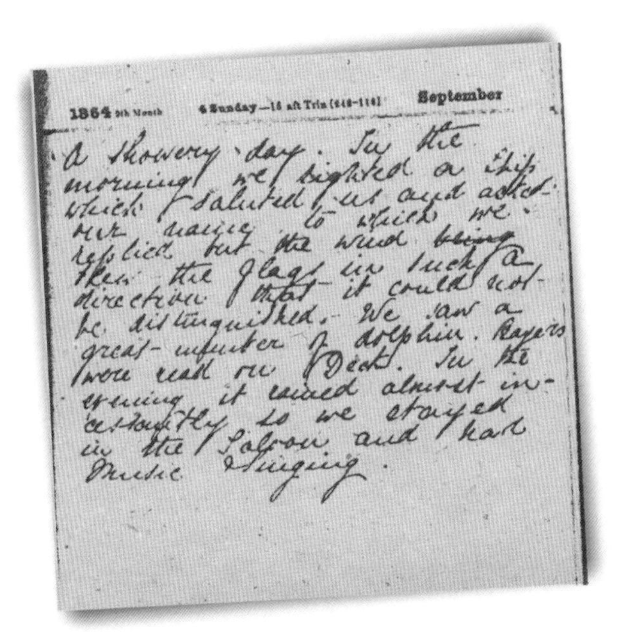

1864 9th Month 4 Sunday—14 aft Trin (248-118) September

A showery day. In the morning we sighted a Ship which saluted us and asked our name to which we replied but the wind ~~being~~ blew the flag in such a direction that it could not be distinguished. We saw a great number of dolphin. Prayers were read on Deck. In the evening it rained almost incessantly so we stayed in the Saloon and had music & singing.

19 December 2013 – Thursday – Atlantic Ocean

Patches of blue beneath huge rolling clouds. The moon was still high in the sky at 7 am. I got up to take a photograph of her smiling down on *City of Adelaide*. It has been a noisy night, I did not sleep until after 3 am, but this could be because of the long nap I had yesterday. We have lost another hour, passing west through another line of longitude.

I made my way to the bridge just after 7 am to take a photograph. Igor was doing morning exercises, stretching his legs against the rail overlooking the deck and *City of Adelaide*. It was reminiscent of a scene from Karate Kid. He was glowing with the exhilarating air of the new day and looked very handsome. He says he likes to keep himself fit, and does about fifteen minutes exercise each morning. I thought I should take a leaf out of his book. I took a few photos of him before getting a shot that was not too dark. He took one of me, billowing in the wind with *City of Adelaide* in the background. I left him to continue his regime and went back to the cabin where I had a cup of tea, read some of *The Great Days of Sail* and went horizontal on the bed for a while. I fell asleep and woke about 10 am, had some breakfast for a change, a cup of ordinary tea and then took my shower. I went to sit in the sun in my usual spot below the bridge for a while. Everything was covered in wet salt. It looked as though there has been a hailstone storm. Little crusty grits covered the handrails, making them slippery. The deck looked as though it was covered in puddles of slush. It was not long before I noticed darkness looming ahead and made my way up to the bridge, arriving there just before the squall hit. Andriy V had the oversized window wipers going to keep visibility clear. I checked my emails. Nothing. From memory, I added Jim Tildesley's address to my list and sent him a message. German came over. He asked if I was receiving emails all right. I said I was, but that I had none. I will get round to mentioning that I have heard nothing from any of the newspapers I wrote to the other day. I wonder whether there is a quota that I may have overused, or whether they were stopped by the system manager because of the need for discretion on board these cargo ships.

I went back down for a short sit in the sun before going down for lunch: spinach soup, rice, fish in tomato sauce and red cabbage salad. After lunch, two squares of wholenut Ritter. I am keeping to my self-imposed ration of two squares a day. This is a huge improvement on a couple of weeks ago when I scoffed a whole bar in an afternoon. Igor was at lunch. We had a conversation about what he will do when he goes home from Cape Town. He said in the past he has gone to Egypt, but that is not an option now it is closed due to civil war. He said he enjoys spending time with his wife and nine year-old son, going swimming, to the gym, just spending precious time together. He was glowing again, in anticipation of this family reunion.

I was inspired today to write poems for the first time since the one I wrote about border control at Norfolk, Virginia, United States of America. I ended up writing five, on varying topics. I went to sit in the sun again after 3 pm. On the way down the staircase one of the webbing straps stretched over *City of Adelaide* from one side of *Palanpur*'s deck to the other snapped with an almighty crash. I went back up the stairs to tell German and Andriy V who were working in the chartroom. German said the purpose of the straps is to reduce flapping of *City of Adelaide*'s raincoat. He pointed out it was not the first to snap, and one near the stern is also half-severed. He and Andriy were pleased to learn the word *frayed* to add to their stock of English vocabulary. I resumed my date with the sun. When I had had enough I checked emails on the way back to my cabin. One, from the system saying Jim Tildesley's email address had been added. I composed a message to him, asking after Dr Platt, and to see whether a meeting could be arranged with him on my return to Scotland. I took a note of readings, latitude 18°51.86'N, longitude 046°41.81'W, wind speed 28 knots. We have passed the North Equatorial Current and are heading for the Mid-Atlantic Ridge, on a level with Cuba and West Africa. It is about 1600 kilometres to the Equator. We should be there in about seven days. Andriy invited me to use fresh computer copy paper as well as scrap sheets with one side already used, for printing out my drafts. He is going to try and get me a notebook, having asked how I was placed for supplies and having seen what I was working with. We had a chat about his plans to further his career beyond Second Officer. He is studying and sat exams a few months ago. I left the bridge and went down to rinse off the sea salt from my skin before going down for supper, feeling refreshed and content.

At last I have arranged to visit the engine room. At supper, pork burgers, salad and mashed potato, German and Valeriy teased me about the filth in the engine room, and that they expected me to shovel coal into the boilers. I said I had had plenty of practice at shovelling, having shifted tons of horse manure over the years, and they laughed. I told them about the taxi in Italy where the driver had taken us to our destination and insisted we look under the bonnet of his car. Inside was a tiny vase with a fresh rose in it. There was not a drop of oil to be seen on the engine, and not a drop of water had been spilled from the vase during the journey. I mentioned to Valeriy about the photos on the main computer on the bridge, the ones of Haddington Car Show. He had not seen them. German remarked on how much he had enjoyed seeing these, in particular the vintage cars, and the marvellous condition they were in.

The clock is chugging another hour forward. The long hand is ticking through a whole hour, each stroke must signify twelve minutes. It has stopped at 1.05 am and the loud ticking it was making during this process has returned to normal, just sounding on the minute. I have a date in the morning at 9 am with the Chief Engineer. Time for bed.

DAY TWENTY-FIVE

September 5, 1864 – Monday

A showery day. The rain came on very suddenly. We were down in the Saloon the greater part of the day. We spent the evening on Deck.

20 December 2013 – Friday – Atlantic Ocean

A hazy grey sky. Neptune has shaken out his blue patchwork quilt with lace trimming. I got up at 8 am and headed for the mess. I greeted Anatoliy who is preparing lunch with his Russian rock music band bolstering him. He would rather be wearing what I am wearing than his chef's whites.

No girls, not a dress. A day-glo orange boiler suit with go-faster reflective stripes at the cuffs and ankles. I am heading for the engine room and I cannot contain my excitement. I meet Valeriy as appointed, 9 am in the officers' mess. I finish my coffee and off we go.

Our path took us alongside the three locomotives in the 'tween deck. I realised now that the crew did not need to walk the top deck to reach the engine room and be exposed to the danger of weather and rough seas. All along there were thick pipes, boxes, silver insulation. I noticed a sign saying *Keep clear for pilots.* This would be the entrance/exit that Kevin Hartz used when we negotiated the river at Norfolk, Virginia, United States of America. Valeriy signalled for me to step into the control room. It is a gingerbread house full of screens, gauges, knobs, dials giving the same readings, but in much greater quantity as those on the bridge: rate of speed, governed to 200 rpm although we have a capacity for 500 rpm; rudder direction; alarms for fire, CO_2, alerts to call out the engineer on watch during the night; a fuse box; a range of communication telephones, including the old-fashioned winding-handle style. He explained that to communicate with a particular area of the ship, the dial is set to the number on the list that relates to that area. For example, say the bridge area is 6. The dial would be pointed to 6, the handle would be wound round and round causing a whistling sound at both ends. A crewmember would pick up at the other end, completing the connection. Computer screens show various information regarding status of fuel, ballast and so on of *Palanpur.* The engine is 1000 hp.

Next we hit the workshop. Give me a workshop any day over a perfume counter or a beauty parlour. Great spanners were slapped methodically on boards on walls, the missing ones that were in use outlined like a dead body in a crime scene thriller; there were hacksaws; towering boxes like skyscrapers with drawers containing screws and other components; there were welding machines; there was a huge lathe, with a drill set up ready for action, assisting in manufacturing spare parts where possible; there is a soldering bay, where Anatoliy wears his other hat and perfects his soldering technique for his future career as an electrical engineer; there is a vice for gripping things in place while you work on them; there is a spare cylinder for the main engine stashed on a top shelf. A deep, grungy sink bore witness to the all-important cleaning of filters. Vitaliy was in the workshop. We said good morning through his ear defenders.

There is something really sexy about boiler suits. Inside them, in the norm, there is a hard-working guy, using his muscles to keep the masters of their universe well-oiled and primed to optimum performance. I love the smell of oil and grease. One of my favourite memories of Alan in the early days that lingers right through to the present when he is capped with silver hair is the sight of him in a dark blue boiler suit with his long brown hair flowing. He still wears one when maintaining our cars, gathering logs, or carrying out roof repairs. I have given him a wee surprise on occasions by standing behind him and slipping my hands into the bottomless pockets at the sides in search of a spanner or some nuts and bolts.

Valeriy and I stepped into the engine room. Spacious. Noisy. The disposable ear-defenders he had given me were very much necessary and appreciated. Everything was painted in pale green. There are six cylinders, housed in heavy-duty steel casings with water-cooling systems protected by perforated steel covers. A huge cylindrical extractor carries away heat to the exhaust stack above. It is lined with special material, but on the outside it is painted as stainless steel. There are two auxiliary engines for use in port. *Palanpur* uses about 75 tonnes of fuel each day. We went downstairs to where the propeller housing is located. Valeriy shone a torch for me to see the propeller turning. There are at least two access points, for maintenance, repair and greasing. He showed me the same dials as those on the bridge, one is for rudder direction. The rudder is constantly adjusting to the onslaught of the waves and currents to hold Palanpur on a steady course. Again, there is a selection of telephone communication systems with the bridge. The fire control system is also in this area. Valeriy pointed out the desalination plant that has an intake of 22 tonnes of salt water. I think I heard him say approximately 80% of fresh water is produced from this. The sewerage plant proved me wrong in thinking we discharged effluent into the sea. This plant is packed with tiny microbes that break down the sewerage until it is almost pure water before discharge. I am impressed with the environmental considerations on board *Palanpur*. The waste disposal management, as I said before, is managed in three separate categories: plastic, household, and glass and metal. Valeriy wondered how the old tea clippers had to manage their fresh water supply. He remarked on how our water is stored in steel containers, whereas during the great days of sail it would have been stored in wooden barrels and dispensed via a ladle, or cup. I added that there would not have been the luxury of drinking two litres per day then, that their H_2O intake would be rationed.

When we began our tour, Valeriy had asked me if I had brought my camera. I said I had not, because I wanted just to absorb the information and write about it on this visit. I hoped to make a further visit when I could take photos. We returned to the workshop where Igor was busy snipping some sort of metal. Valeriy had asked me if I had been inside the crane yet. We arranged with Igor that he would take me up there sometime next week. I am truly spoiled. I said, 'До Робачеия', to Vitaliy and Igor. On the path back to accommodation, Valeriy pointed out the fuel pipes. He had shown me at the start of my tour where the connectors for taking on fuel are located. These will be put into use in Cape Town, for bunkering. By the time I got back to the accommodation block, sweat was pouring down my back. I felt like I had been in a sauna.

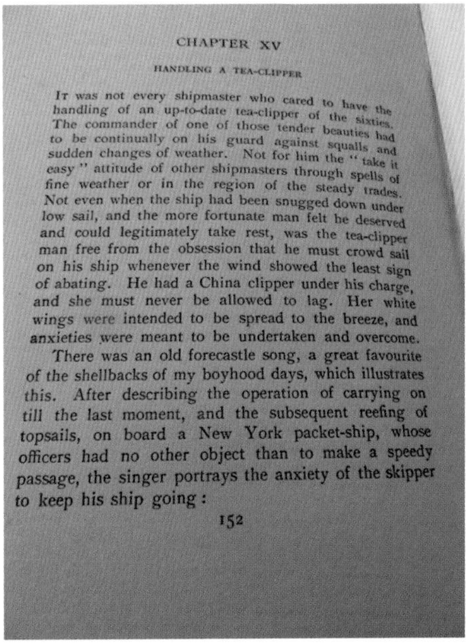

When the men come in for meals, they do not wear their boiler suits in the messes. There is a locker room between the officers' mess and the mess for the ordinary crew. I was chatting to Anatoliy after supper of pork with aubergines and courgettes, salad and maize, or chicken porridge if you remember. I had brought down *The Great Days of Sail* for him to look at. He is interested in old books. I had told him about the thickness of the pages. He had homed in on the figurehead of the *Chaa-Sze* as one of the illustrations in the book. He had worked out with another crewmember how this had appeared on photographic paper in the book, and thought there must have been a process of photographing the original sketch or some similar image. Anatoliy and I had quite a blether about various topics after supper, from charitable donations, aspects of religion, China, theories of evolution, Darwin, DNA, the weather in Scotland, the weather in Ukraine, solar panels, piracy around China in the days of the tea clippers, *City of Adelaide*'s era, piracy of today, particularly in the Suez/Aden area, what happens when we die. All this in about half an hour.

CHAPTER XV

HANDLING A TEA-CLIPPER

It was not every shipmaster who cared to have the handling of an up-to-date tea-clipper of the sixties. The commander of one of those tender beauties had to be continually on his guard against squalls and sudden changes of weather. Not for him the "take it easy" attitude of other shipmasters through spells of fine weather or in the region of the steady trades. Not even when the ship had been snugged down under low sail, and the more fortunate man felt he deserved and could legitimately take rest, was the tea-clipper man free from the obsession that he must crowd sail on his ship whenever the wind showed the least sign of abating. He had a China clipper under his charge, and she must never be allowed to lag. Her white wings were intended to be spread to the breeze, and anxieties were meant to be undertaken and overcome.

There was an old forecastle song, a great favourite of the shellbacks of my boyhood days, which illustrates this. After describing the operation of carrying on till the last moment, and the subsequent reefing of topsails, on board a New York packet-ship, whose officers had no other object than to make a speedy passage, the singer portrays the anxiety of the skipper to keep his ship going:

152

It has been quite a day. I have had a few naps to absorb each stage of information, and discussions. This was not all. I have not told you about the afternoon yet.

After lunch of chicken leg, pasta and salad, I checked emails. One from Alan. He said he sees we are approaching the Equator. Meanwhile he has installed the new plastic oil tank at home in the freezing, wet and windy cold, so bad the mortar fixer blew out. He was expecting an oil delivery on the next Monday, so had no option but to tackle this job on the weekend. I also had a response from Peter Christopher with information I had requested on what will happen with *City of Adelaide* when we arrive in Adelaide, South Australia. She is to be lifted onto a barge in the outer harbour and towed to the inner harbour. Crowds will be able to see her, but have restricted access.

The tear in *City of Adelaide*'s raincoat is getting worse. There is a grey under-layer that is now ripping too, and it looks with my naked eye a small rent is appearing on the bow wrapping. There is a chance we may have repairs done to it in Cape Town;

that would incur a longer stay there, maybe a day and a night or longer. I will make the trip to Table Mountain if this is the case. Otherwise if we are just bunkering, it will take from four to eight hours. I am really looking forward to speaking with my family when we arrive there, estimated time of arrival is 5 January 2014. As for shopping, there are apparently loads of outlets near the port along the shoreline. I cannot think of anything I really need other than sunscreen. The limited clothing I packed seems to have been a good choice, though I am bored of rotating the same things. The heavy jumpers are relegated to the bottom drawer for now. Today's temperature is 27°C. I decided yesterday I would give my skin a rest and not sit out in the sun today.

I popped straight up to the washing machine after checking emails and put in a dark wash. When I went back to put it into the drier I could not get the machine to unlock, the technique I talked about before did not work. I put the load to spin and hung about. The same problem happened again, so I set it to spin once more and went down for a rest. The machine is not in constant use. I have had to wait on occasions for someone to go and remove their washing at the end of a cycle before being able to use it. This can take hours. About forty minutes later I went back up to find my load had been moved to the drier. I felt indignant that someone had messed with my personal clothing. Usually I wash my knickers in the sink by hand and hang them on the expanding washing line in my en suite shower, but I had chucked two pairs from yesterday in with the load I had accumulated, knowing I would be washing it today. I was not sure how to handle this situation. At the end of the day the most 'he' might have found out was that I do not wear a g-string! It may be he thought he was doing me a favour by speeding up the drying process. It may be he wanted his clothes washed in a hurry. Who knows? I swallowed my initial reaction and took my clothes down to my cabin to air off. I discovered later who the 'culprit' was when I heard him flapping out the two items he had washed. He had hung them to dry on the handrails along the corridor from my cabin. Neither of them were knickers.

There had been a hooting noise, like a fog horn, blasting just before I had dealt with my laundry. After I had hung it up to air I went to the bridge, curious about what it was. I could see no fog. Andriy V figured out that tests were being carried out to make sure the horn is in good order. This is different to the fog horn; it is used to sound a series of specific signals to indicate our intentions to other vessels nearby. For example, five short blasts on it would signal that we were in doubt as to the intentions of the other vessel. I had noticed a hatch open on the fo'c'sle earlier when I looked out of the conference room window whilst waiting for the spin cycle to finish on the washing machine. Andriy told me this is where the horn is located. He was in a chatty mood. I took my chart readings, latitude 16.05°33'N, longitude 043°32.30'W, wind speed 30 knots. We are travelling at 13 knots. Andriy told me some container ships travel at twice this speed. He explained the electronic equipment on the bridge. We talked about the AIS system that tracks ships at sea. This is what I used to follow *Palanpur*'s progress to keep one step ahead with my aspirations to join her. I had seen her cross from the United States of America to Bremen, where she sat for a few days before sailing to Rotterdam. I had also used the live marine traffic site to track the tall ships race when they were passing the Scottish Maritime Museum at Irvine in 2011.

The AIS ship tracking system can be switched off whenever German feels this is necessary for the safety of the ship. There are two of everything on the bridge to cope with possible equipment failure, including printers. Andriy explained the magnetic compass and showed me how adjustments have to be made to course direction that are given on charts at specific points of latitude and longitude. In all the visits I have made to the bridge I had not registered a black scope fitted to the ceiling of the bridge above the helm. It reminded me of a periscope housing in a submarine, but there were no handles to it. Andriy tried to show me that this is how the magnetic compass located in a hatch on the roof of *Palanpur* is read. There are two mirrors that reflect the reading, one trained on the compass above, the other at eye level that can be swivelled to give the projected reading to suit the height of the person viewing it. Andriy let me try to read it. I could not see a thing. I think he is at least six feet tall, so it was easy for him. He went to get a chair for me to climb up and stand on. Voilà. All was clear. We looked at the gyrocompass. Then he showed me the sextant that is kept in a wooden box in a cupboard in the chartroom. This is a device that can be used to take compass bearings in the event of equipment failure. He said it can take half an hour to set it up. There are a series of lenses and about five darkened ones that can be put over the eyepiece to protect the eye from the sun. The stronger the sun, the more lenses used. There are measures of distance and height that can be set by twisting an adjuster similar to that on a camera or a pair of binoculars. There was more to learn, but Andriy took a call and had to respond to instructions. I took my leave, my brain on system overload and went to my cabin to absorb all this information in a position parallel with the horizon.

It is four weeks today since I boarded *Palanpur*. I have absolutely no regrets at making this journey. There is still a long way to go, another month at least, but I am sure I will stay the course and remain in great spirits.

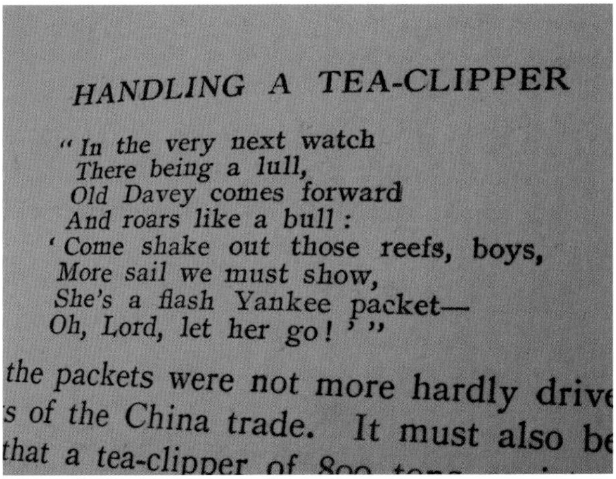

HANDLING A TEA-CLIPPER

"In the very next watch
There being a lull,
Old Davey comes forward
And roars like a bull:
'Come shake out those reefs, boys,
More sail we must show,
She's a flash Yankee packet—
Oh, Lord, let her go!'"

the packets were not more hardly driv
s of the China trade. It must also b
that a tea-clipper of

DAY TWENTY-SIX

September 6, 1864 – Tuesday

A showery day.

21 December 2013 – Saturday – Atlantic Ocean

A hazy grey sky that gave way to blue, with sunshine and big white clouds.

I wrote until about 2 am and then could not sleep. There seemed to be a great light outside the windows. I could not see whether it was the moon. There was a dark shape, a big black tongue licking the ceiling of my cabin. I felt afraid. I got up and peeped out through the curtains. Nothing there. Not long after this, I fell asleep.

It is Winter Solstice, the shortest day. I awoke at 9.50 am. It looked a bit grey outside. I recalled there had been a heavy shower of rain during the night before I fell asleep. This greyness soon passed and I decided to get on. I had finished reading *The Great Days of Sail* last night. I am not ready to begin another book till I have digested that one. I went to lunch for Eintopf, Anatoliy's best yet. I had an extra half ladle before the pork burger, salad and pasta he dished up for me. I put my order in for the slop chest, hoping the juice would arrive as grape. I got apple. The Ritter Bar was wholenut, I had hoped for almond. Had Andriy K still been at lunch I would have been specific, but he was gone. Oh well. Anatoliy asked Vitaliy to give me the only pen in the crew mess he was using to fill out my sheet. I was happy to wait my turn but he passed it over so the others had to wait while I ticked my choices. There is no facility on the sheet to make specific requests. Juice is juice. Ritter is Ritter. After lunch I went to sunbathe. It was glorious outside, an occasional gentle spray spritzing my skin. I can see a definite tan coming along. I had ordered another two tubs of Nivea cream from the slop chest. I will need to keep my skin nourished as we go on. I did not order any alcohol, we will have some on Christmas Day and I still have rakes of beer left from three weeks ago. After sunbathing I stood in the strong wind on the port side and got a really good pummelling. It was good and cool on my skin, but my hair was a nest by the end of it. I saw a few flying fish.

I have not spent much time chatting today. After my sunbathing session, Andriy V was talking to one of the ordinary crewmen. I wanted to chill out anyway. I ended up writing a children's story, *Gypsy Dragon Of The Ocean Moon*. It was inspired by what I hope will be my new name when we cross the Equator. I think there is one ordinary crew member on board who is also passing the Equator for the first time. I wonder what name he will choose, or be given. I am excited about this maritime tradition.

Yesterday I told Anatoliy I would make a copy of a few figureheads from tall ships for him to look at. As I was searching for the images, I spotted a folder on the external hard drive I had totally forgotten about. It contains two newsletters from the Scottish Ukrainian Community. I had got in touch with them in 2010 after I had seen an article in the Evening News about a Robert Burns-Shevchenko event. I thought this might be of interest to Valeriy, since his son has been to Scotland twice. I found in one of the newsletters that there is also a small chapel in Lockerbie that was built by prisoners of war. It is twenty-five years since Pan Am flight 103 crashed at Lockerbie.

After supper of pork, unusually tough, salad and pasta I went to the bridge for late readings: latitude 12°37.20'N, longitude 039°34.37'W, windspeed 35 knots. Our course is 125°. Igor and German were chatting. I did not chat long to let them get on with it. I sent emails to everyone at home, responding to one my eldest daughter had sent me earlier, and one to Rosemary McKay with my choice of songs for the radio show she invited me onto after I arrive in Adelaide. I also sent one to East Coast FM to wish them a Happy Christmas and to say feel free to play *Three Craws And The Bairn In A Manger* in the few days left before Christmas. I am feeling a bit overdone with meat. Tomorrow I may just have a sandwich, for a break.

Back in my cabin I played computer games for a good while, being a bit bored, but it was pretty boring in itself. I had a go at Minesweeper for the first time. What a pointless game. The clock started that loud ticking again. Another hour forward.

Much mention was made in *The Great Days of Sail* of pirates around the waters of China. It was deadly for a sailing ship to become becalmed, or run aground. Pirates, thinly disguised as fishermen, would storm the ships and totally ransack them, kill the crew and burn the ships. I have had a few discussions on board this ship about pirates, particularly off the West Coast of Africa or in the Suez/Aden area. I have read that pirates carry out attacks from skiffs – very small craft – that can be supported by or launched from a mothership, or towed by an open whaler carrying large quantities of fuel. Their speed can be up to 25 knots, power provided by two outboard engines or a single 60 HP engine. Motherships are the spoils of pirates with their crew on board as hostages. They can operate over a much larger area and are less hampered by weather conditions than the traditional methods mentioned above. Pirates are known to camouflage attack skiffs they carry on board motherships, to avoid detection by naval or military forces patrolling high risk areas, mainly that bounded by Suez and Straits of Hormuz. Their method of attack is to use small arms fire and rocket propelled grenades, focusing fire on the bridge and accommodation areas to try to intimidate the ship's master to cut speed. This enables them to board the ship. They use a variety of boarding techniques, including knotted ropes attached to a long hooked pole to climb on board. Generally speaking, attacks do not take place at night, unless there is a clear, bright moon. For obvious reasons, information on deterring or minimising these attacks will not appear within the pages of this book.

What defines piracy is contained in the 1982 United Nations Convention on the Law of the Sea (UNCLOS) (Article 101). However further guidelines exist to help in assessing what constitutes an attack of piracy as opposed to what is considered suspicious activity. Descriptions are provided as guidance, however, ships' masters may have personal experiences of attacks of piracy or they may have heard of other situations of attack or suspicious activity through the maritime community that will enhance their awareness of how to identify intended acts of piracy. Pirates are also known to have hijacked vessels. I am told there are various methods of dealing with captured pirates by the different nations patrolling the main area of piracy; some of these can be viewed on the internet. There is also special advice for fishermen and private yacht owners, including *do not go there.*

I go to sleep, grateful that we are not voyaging via the Suez Canal.

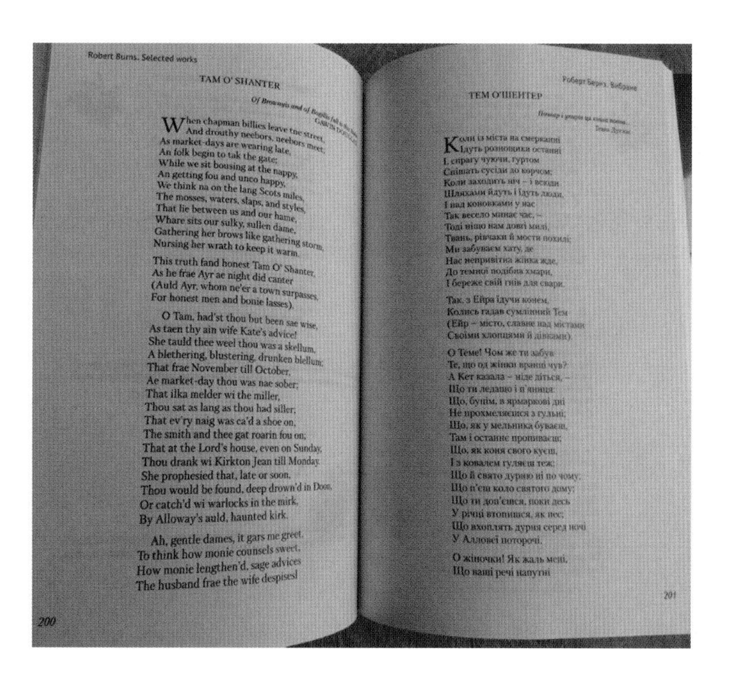

Robert Burns. Selected works

TAM O' SHANTER

When chapman billies leave the street,
And drouthy neebors, neebors meet;
As market-days are wearing late,
An folk begin to tak the gate;
While we sit bousing at the nappy,
An getting fou and unco happy,
We think na on the lang Scots miles,
The mosses, waters, slaps, and styles,
That lie between us and our hame,
Whare sits our sulky, sullen dame,
Gathering her brows like gathering storm,
Nursing her wrath to keep it warm.

This truth fand honest Tam O' Shanter,
As he frae Ayr ae night did canter
(Auld Ayr, whom ne'er a town surpasses,
For honest men and bonie lasses).

O Tam, had'st thou but been sae wise,
As taen thy ain wife Kate's advice!
She tauld thee weel thou was a skellum,
A blethering, blustering, drunken blellum;
That frae November till October,
Ae market-day thou was nae sober;
That ilka melder wi the miller,
Thou sat as lang as thou had siller;
That ev'ry naig was ca'd a shoe on,
The smith and thee gat roarin fou on;
That at the Lord's house, even on Sunday,
Thou drank wi Kirkton Jean till Monday.
She prophesied that, late or soon,
Thou would be found, deep drown'd in Doon,
Or catch'd wi warlocks in the mirk,
By Alloway's auld, haunted kirk.

Ah, gentle dames, it gars me greet,
To think how monie counsels sweet,
How monie lengthen'd, sage advices
The husband frae the wife despises!

200

Роберт Бернс. Вибране

ТЕМ О'ШЕНТЕР

Коли із міста на смерканні
Ідуть рознощики останні
І, спрагу чуючи, гуртом
Спішать сусіди до корчом;
Коли заходить ніч – і всюди
Шляхами йдуть і їдуть люди,
І над коновками у нас
Так весело минає час, –
Тоді ніщо нам довгі милі,
Твань, рівчаки й мости похилі;
Ми забуваєм хату, де
Нас непривітна жінка жде,
До темної подібна хмари,
І береже свій гнів для свари.

Так, з Ейра їдучи конем,
Колись гадав сумлінний Тем
(Ейр – місто, славне над містами
Своїми хлопцями й дівками).

О Теме! Чом же ти забув
Те, що од жінки вранці чув?
А Кет казала – ніде діться, –
Що ти ледащо і п'яниця;
Що, буцім, в ярмаркові дні
Не прохмеляєшся з гульні;
Що, як у мельника буваєш,
Там і останнє пропиваєш;
Що, як коня свого куєш,
І з ковалем гуляєш теж;
Що й свято дурню ні по чому,
Що п'єш коло святого дому;
Що ти доп'єшся, поки десь
У річці втопишся, як пес;
Що вхоплять дурня серед ночі
У Алловеї поторочі.

О жіночки! Як жаль мені,
Що ваші речі напутні

201

DAY TWENTY-SEVEN

September 7, 1864 – Wednesday

A calm day. No breeze and making no progress.
We saw several "portuguese men of war".

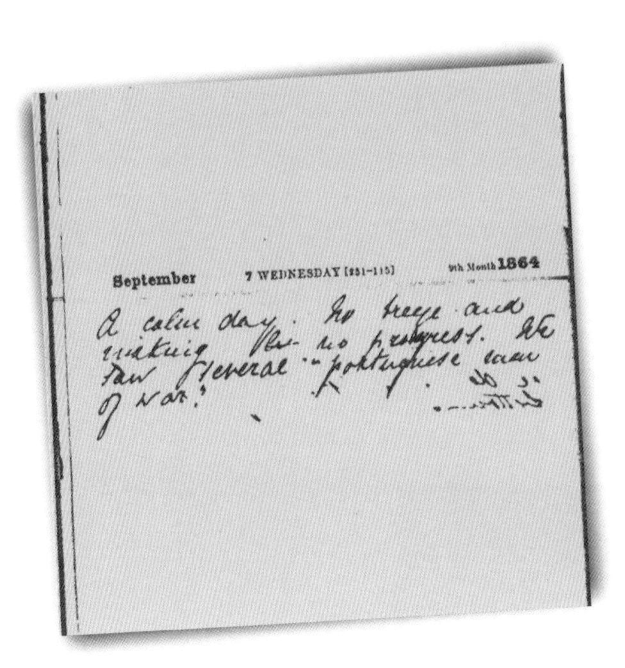

September 7 WEDNESDAY [251-115] 9th Month 1864

A calm day. No breeze and making no progress. We saw several "portuguese men of war".

22 December 2013 – Sunday – Atlantic Ocean

A hazy grey sky. The wind has dropped and we are lumbering along on gentle waves.

I slept through till 11.10 am, please bear in mind we lost an hour so it was only a little longer than my usual getting up time. I had a quick shower and went to lunch. Borscht soup was all I took today. I have been feeling bloated and know I am eating too much meat. Vitaliy was playing music and singing.

Andriy K asked me at lunch whether I had had a Yellow Fever injection. I said not. I explained I had not known that we were calling in to ports in other countries en route to Australia. My general practitioner and I had discussed the need for immunisations, and we decided these would not be necessary for a direct trip to Australia. Looks like I will not be going in to Cape Town after all, with not having been immunised against Yellow Fever. I just have to remain philosophical about all this, and keep in mind my mission, and I am happy that it is going well. It may be there will not be time to visit Table Mountain anyway. German was talking about a visit to the sea life centre, but if I cannot see this I am not bothered. The crew have sold Cape Town to me so hard that there is no doubt I am disappointed in this latest development. I can add it to my to see list for the future.

I have been advised to have my camera ready for the approach, it is by all accounts, spectacular.

I asked Anatoliy what he was making for Christmas breakfast. I told him about what we used to have – *mish-mash*, my mother called it. You fry onions, add smoked sausage, pancetti, tomatoes, mushrooms, cook till ready and then put whisked eggs through it and scramble it all together. I couldn't eat it nowadays. He is keeping it simple. No wonder. He is the one who has to cook for eighteen people three times a day seven days a week. I am tempted to offer to help, but do not want to impose. I need to keep resisting this womanly urge to have an input into the celebrations. There has been talk of fancy dress. I thought of what I could wear – a white gypsy-style blouse and a royal blue and gold reversible wraparound skirt I bought a couple of years ago, or my red velvet and black bodice dress I got last year. Thinking about it, the red would be more in keeping with Santa Claus and Christmas, and the blue and yellow for Ukrainian New Year, since they are their National colours.

I went up for today's readings. Temperature is 28°C, though it is hazy, the sun is struggling to make an appearance through the film. Wind speed is 31 knots. We are at latitude 10°0.02'N, longitude 036°21.78'W, still on the North Equatorial Current and nothing on the radar. I asked German whether they would be filing reports early due to the holiday. He said not, they would be at the end of the month as usual.

Andriy V was working on the computer. I went outside and walked round the bridge. The air is lovely, and being pummelled by the wind is refreshing in these humid airs. I saw two flying fish erupt from the sea in unison, then fly across the waves until they both landed back in the sea in unison. It was like synchronised flying...or swimming. They are so sweet and pretty to watch, the closest things to birdlife out here on the big wide ocean. When I went back inside, the computer was free. Three emails, one from the server, saying it has added East Coast FM to my address book, one from my son and one from my youngest daughter who outlined Christmas arrangements. She is being the little mother, with her big sister, Alan, and Zac the dog going to her house for Christmas Eve and staying over. I left instructions as to where I had left Alan's *stowaway* ticket, and she is going to buy virtual *chickens* from the CSCOAL website to give on my behalf to everyone as Christmas presents, thus bringing them along with me on the rest of this voyage. My little chickens. Feeling sentimental about them. It is lovely to think of them seeing my little granddaughter opening her presents at her three and a half years of age, and all the excitement that goes with that. I think of the crew, none of whom will see their children at this time, or on Ukrainian Christmas in two weeks' time, except for Anatoliy and Chief Officer Igor, who are going home from Cape Town on leave for a few months. My youngest daughter is on holiday from work now for a couple of weeks. My granddaughter will love having extra time with her. She also told me my mother is going to my brother and sister-in-law for Christmas.

Squid rings for supper. I had two, and a fair wee pile of chips and salad. I had taken down a flash drive with a few photos on it to Anatoliy. It also had on it my illustrated poem about the death of John Lennon and one I had written following a discussion we had had a couple of nights ago in relation to what happens when we die. It is my take on reincarnation. After my meal he handed me back the flash drive he had loaded up some of his photographs onto, of various ships and sea scenes. German and Valeriy were still at dinner but left, leaving me with Vitaliy. He left and Andriy K arrived. I mentioned the Yellow Fever immunisation, asking whether not having it would debar me from going ashore in Cape Town. He said not. We have immunisation on board but I for one would not want to administer it, even to myself, with a rolling sea. They have medication for the treatment of it. Andriy also told me not many of the crew would go ashore since they will need to watch for people trying to get on board as stowaways. Other crew would be involved in bunkering.

I went to my cabin and opened the flash drive. Anatoliy's photos are amazing. I will copy some images onto the flash drive of animals painted on hands, for his wee girl. I feel in a much better frame of mind than I did this morning about my prospects of being allowed to visit Cape Town. Not being immunised against Yellow Fever seems to no longer be an issue. I will weigh up whether it is worth the risk when the time comes, but the chance of going ashore might be just too much of a temptation.

DAY TWENTY-EIGHT

September 8, 1864 – Thursday

A fine day. We had dancing in the evening. I have finished "What will he do with it?" by Bulwer Lytton.

23 December 2013 – Monday – Atlantic Ocean

A lovely blue sky with puffy clouds. The night wind has calmed. We are sailing along fairly steadily with the odd roll.

I slept through till 11.00 am again, the only excuse this time being I did not go to bed until 2 am and it was a while before I fell asleep. I turned topsy-turvey with my head at the foot end of the bed. I was claustrophopic. Sometimes I am okay, but not last night. It was also very humid.

I cleaned the en-suite and washed the floors. I could get used to doing all the housework that needs done within the space of about twenty minutes. Lunch was mushroom soup. I resisted the fish course, and made a sandwich with rye bread, Wiejska and salami, with a slice of cheese to top it off. Tasty. Anatoliy and I discussed my poem *Waiting in the Wings*. I explained it was all metaphor about dying and being reincarnated. It is a good way to explore language. We also talked about his photos, he explaining the circumstances that brought about loss of cargo and how a square rigged tall ship can be loaded onto a cargo ship.

Last night I had a brainstorm about the cultural exchange between Scotland and Australia. I remembered about poetry workshops with primary ones to fours a couple of years ago. I have images and poems from those workshops on my external hard drive. They are to do with *My Home, My Street, My Town, My County, My Scotland* as part of the Curriculum for Excellence. It would be cool too, if *The Three Craws Gaun Tae Rabbie Burns Birthday Pairty* were to be performed by older children for Robert Burns' birthday on 25 January. It quite tickles me, a Ukrainian/German born in Edinburgh taking a little Scottish culture to South Australia.

I put some washing into the machine and read for a bit. I have begun *Master and Commander*, by Patrick O'Brian. I have seen the film a few times, having it on DVD. The book is second-hand from King's Bookshop where I bought *The Great Days of Sail*. It is a gift from someone who came with me to Callander Poetry Festival for her first time this year. It was she who told me my ship was leaving for Australia, when *City of Adelaide* was being removed from the slipway at Irvine. Inside she has inscribed *For Rita, Ahoy Matey! Finola Scott.*

I kept an eye on my washing, and went for a sunbathe. Andriy V was on the bridge, he was absorbed in work. I sloped off down the staircase and lay on a bed of salt that stuck to my coating of Nivea cream, turning me out like a snowman. It really feels like being on holiday. Ten minutes on each side was enough, as the sun is strong. I am shielded by the film of clouds that is hanging about. The sun would be unbearable today, I think, were it not for the clouds. The holiday mood continued when I got back to my cabin, and I cracked first one, then a second, small can of beer. When I collected my washing from the drier, I felt a wee bit tipsy. I did a bit of reading of Sarah's diary, typed a bit, then read until time for supper, beef stir fry, pasta and salad.

At supper I gave Valeriy my memory stick with a few photos. There were a few of North Berwick Law and the artificial whale jaw bone that crowns its summit, replacing the original whale jaw bone that deteriorated to such a degree it was deemed unsafe. He told me there is also a whalebone arch at Odessa when he came to my cabin later to return my memory stick. He was not my only visitor this evening. Anatoliy and I often discuss language. When I told him about the visit to Bayeux in September of *The Three Craws* to highlight the visit of the Prestonpans Tapestry to the Bayeux Museum, and that I had translated some of the script into French, he told me of an excellent dictionary programme he has. He had offered to install this into my laptop. When he arrived I offered him a beer. He was taken with *The Three Craws* screensaver. We talked about the plays quite a bit. He reckons I should have it on Russian television, they would be a huge hit. He asked if we had costumes. I said at the moment we just have t-shirts but said I was looking at taking *The Three Craws* to Edinburgh Fringe at some point. I took great pleasure from his interest and encouragement in this.

Anatoliy had brought a different dictionary from the one he had intended, one that Vitaliy had given him. He said it is a better programme than his. I love it when he used the word 'cracked', pronounced by him as 'crack-it'. We talked again about the tall ship in his photos that had been loaded onto a cargo ship. I wondered how it could have been lifted with a crane on board, like *City of Adelaide* had been onto *Palanpur*. He said it had not been lifted by a crane. These cargo ships are semi-submersible, and instead of it being lifted on board, it had been floated on. I continue to be amazed at how clever human beings are. Anatoliy spoke of massive container ships, that *Palanpur* is small compared to many. I said to Anatoliy that he should write a book about all these incidents he has seen on his travels.

At lunchtime when I was talking to Anatoliy in the galley about his photos and about language, one of the crew came in for his food. *Barabashkar*, he said to him, laughing. I said, 'What does that mean? I like the sound of this word. I would like to write a poem about it.' He said it was a house spirit, a good one. He was poking fun at a fish, looking in all its glory like old shoe leather. He agreed to look up the word and give it to me later at supper. Sure enough, he pulled out a slip of paper from a drawer in the galley with the Russian, Ukrainian, written in Cyrillic, and English translation of the word 'brownie': *housespirit*; *poltergeist*. He had also painstakingly written out the word of that town on the Isle of Anglesey:

Llanfairpwllgwyngyllgogerychwyrndrobwllllantysiliogogogoch.

Fifty-seven letters long. He thought this town was in Scotland, but it is in Wales. I showed Anatoliy the photograph of the Bray family. After some time, he succeeded in installing the full electronic dictionary. He left about 8.30 pm. I lay down for a nap and awoke at 10.30 pm and went for a pee. I tried to get back to sleep. During the night there was a bit of a storm.

I awoke at 4 am. The lights were on on the deck, a sight that always worries me.

DAY TWENTY-NINE

September 9, 1864 – Friday

A rough showery day. We spent most of the time in the Saloon and scarcely knowing what to do, danced the quadrilles. In the evening the weather cleared and we went on Deck but as the ship rolled very much we were obliged to keep seated.

24 December 2013 – Tuesday – Atlantic Ocean

An early fog gave way to shades of grey clouds smeared on a pale grey canvas to port side, broken on the starboard with cracks of blue. We are ploughing through the gentle waves fairly steadily with the odd roll.

The sound of a cow bellowing for her calf woke me this morning. Fog: in the distance, but still necessitating the use of the horn to warn off ships that may be on the radar. That would be an unusual occurrence. I have seen only two ships since we left Norfolk, Virginia, United States of America. The sun is determined to make a full appearance. We will reach the Equator tomorrow. A double celebration for Christmas Day. The crew are in fine fettle. The Christmas tree might appear today.

I fell asleep last night after Anatoliy had installed the dictionary onto my laptop. I awoke to see *City of Adelaide* being battered by wind and rain. It is the first time in a few weeks I have been worried about her. I thought of a tooth coming loose from diseased gums, but her lashings hold her firm. Anatoliy has seen first-hand experience of a yacht that came away from her lashings and was lost at sea, but he has no fear of that happening with *City of Adelaide*. Her lashings are good and strong, and are monitored on a daily basis. I have seen flashes of welding on occasions to her supports, some strengthening going on. All to the good, her lashings are holding strong, but her white raincoat is shredding more and more each day. She is feeling the heat of the Equator and wants rid of it. Last night it had to endure wind speeds of up to 40 knots, near gale force. I wish the crew would pull it off and let her breathe. Speaking of this, breathing at this latitude can be a little laboured at times with its close humidity. A good way of getting a blast of air is to lean into the crack of one of the doors out to the stairway and let the cool breeze glide across the skin. I had cereal for the first time in days this morning. Muesli, raisins removed as usual. I popped my sheets into the washing machine. They are now airing over the table and chairs in my cabin. I have a spare set, but I will just put these ones back on. Lunch was soup, gherkin and potato. I did not chat to Anatoliy as he was already doing so with Vitaliy, and he was gone when I put my bowl in to be washed. After lunch I decided to pull Days 1-28 together, managing the diaries in four-week chunks. I will read it through before I go on further with Patrick O'Brian's *Master and Commander*. Time is running short, with only four weeks approximately to go. I will not have enough time at sea to equal the time Sarah was at sea: her voyage began on 12 August 1864 and ended on 7 November 1864, a total of eighty-seven days. We left Rotterdam on 26 November 2013 and will arrive in Adelaide, South Australia in the last week of January 2014, making our voyage something in excess of sixty days. I will be spending some time in Adelaide, but I doubt I can stretch my time away for an extra month.

The sound of the foghorn abated, but gave way to the power hose being used to wash down the ship, smartening her up for tomorrow, I supposed. The noise of it meant I could not concentrate on reading over the first twenty-eight days of this book, so I took my notebook and went up to the bridge for today's readings. We had rain after a while, that cleared the air. Did I say we had only seen two ships since leaving Norfolk, Virginia, United States of America? Well, now make that three. Andriy V handed me the binoculars. On the horizon, a blur of white smudged the lenses. On the AIS tracking system, we could see the name of the ship is *Orange Sun*. She is a refrigerated cargo ship, used to carry fresh fruit for supermarkets in Europe and so on. She was about fifty miles from us. We looked at her position on the radar. It looked like we were on a collision course. I paled, but held back from rushing for my immersion suit. We are moving at 15 knots per hour. *Palanpur*'s maximum speed is 16 knots, but with a strong current behind her, for example in the English Channel, this can give her 4 extra knots. Andriy reassured me that *Orange Sun* would change course a few degrees to starboard to avoid us. She, being on our port side, would give way; it is the rule of the sea. Passing would be port-to-port, red light-to-red light. Sure enough, *Orange Sun* passed and crossed our stern. I noticed she was lying high in the water, the bulb at her front was only half submerged, ploughing through the waves. I wondered as to the fuel efficiency of this. Speaking to Anatoliy later, he said she was high in the water because she would not be carrying any cargo. Once she picks up fruit she will carry back east what is in season at the moment in South America – perhaps avocados, bananas, mangoes. Andriy told me he had a friend who had worked on one such a ship for ten years. When they were out for dinner one time, Andriy asked his friend if he would like a piece of fruit. He scrunched up his face in a definite *No*.

We are at latitude 03°40.12'N, longitude 029°03.38'W, the temperature is 27°C. I had my video camera with me. I wanted to record the sway of *Palanpur* and *City of Adelaide* in the heavy swell. Standing at the side of the ship exaggerated the movement. I tried to capture an image of a flock of flying fish, but failed. I call them a flock because they are above water. If they were under the waves, they would be a shoal. They are enigmatic little fish. Little. Andriy K told me at lunch they are not so little, they are more than a foot long. I had watched some skiff over the waves, belly-flapping against them to flit to the next one until they dived in before their gills would explode.

I sent an email with Christmas greetings to the family at my youngest daughter's house, then came back to my room with a handful of A4 paper, a pencil and eraser.

I just cannot help myself. After supper of beef stew, salad and maize I popped up to the bridge to ask for more toilet paper and 2-litre bottles of water as I do not want to bother them tomorrow for this. German sent Igor, teasing that he wants to lose a couple of kilograms anyway. I said next time I would ask for two lots of 2-litres of water to give him extra exercise. We chatted about what my family were doing this evening. I said they were all going to my youngest daughter's except for my son who was going to his girlfriend's, and my mother who would be going to my brother's tomorrow morning. We talked about tomorrow, that the men would have a day off, spending most of it relaxing and snoozing. They can only have one day off, as the ship requires constant attention and maintenance. We talked a bit about language, too. They were interested in London, asking if it would be a good place to live. I said I find it too busy, it is good for a visit, and has a complex transport system. This took us on to talk about Cockney rhyming slang. I told them that a *north and south* is a mouth, they howled with laughter that the slang for wife is your *trouble and strife*.

I took a walk round the outside of the bridge and let the wind blow through my hair as I watched another orange sun, a real blood red, juicy beauty, flirt with the clouds on the horizon. As it retired, it sent out a few beams for the clouds to catch hold of. They obliged by coiling themselves gently round the rays until they lowered the sun from sight, tucking it in for the night. I bade the boys *goodnight*, and went to my cabin. Left outside it, at last! No toilet paper rations. Three whole packs of four rolls each! Christmas had surely arrived. And water too. A six-pack! What more does a body need? I opened my door. There the stash of A4 paper, pencil and eraser waited in silent patience. I began the self-inflicted task of drawing seventeen greeting cards, one for each of the crew. I first folded the A4 sheet into half, then half again. Then, using the side of the pencil I began to sketch. First a big, fat snowman holding a banner. Then a whale, this one for Andriy V since he told me his Equatorial name is *Whale*. His season's greeting is speech-bubbled in the whale's spout. Andriy K told me his is *Barracuda*, so I drew him a blunt-nosed fish. There was a shivering bird, a matchstick man hauling a tree, another standing in front of a tree he had chopped with an axe while three crows escape from the

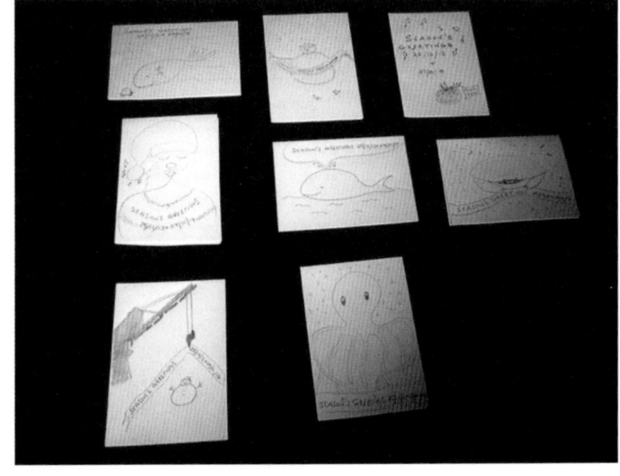

branches. There is a crane for young Ihor who operates No. 1 450-ton crane. There is a deer watching a mouse make a mouse snowman, the last piece being the second ear being rolled along; some are sea creatures holding banners. It was a good diversion and took about three hours. I wrote each man's name on the back from the list of crew members Andriy V had given me.

Today has been pretty full on. It is 12.15 am. *Merry Christmas everyone.*

DAY THIRTY

September 10, 1864 – Saturday

A bright day but rather rough. We had several showers and even when able to go on Deck, there was too much motion to walk about.

Footnote: Sarah's Diary Entry from *"The Murray"*, March 19th 1866

We crossed the Equator at 8 P.M. We are all anxious for cooler weather. The thermometer has been 88° in the Saloon. We have had heavy falls of rain which make the atmosphere very close and damp. I have been ill for three days with English Cholera. Mama Papa and the Doctor were up with me part of the nights. I feel quite strong again to-day.

25 December 2013 – Wednesday – Atlantic Ocean

A fine, blowy day with blue sky and cumulus nimbus. The air is full of holiday. I am full of anticipation. Today I will be given a new name for crossing the Equator. Anatoliy is very busy in the kitchen. I popped down with the cards for all the crew, putting them in the place for each officer in their mess, and gave Anatoliy his one and left the ones for the boys in crew mess for him to put in their places. It is Andriy K's birthday as well. He is 25 years old. He appreciated both his cards. I popped my wee Christmas tree earrings in and went to lunch just after 12 noon. There was the expected soup, but apple pie as well was a surprise considering Anatoliy is up to his elbows in spit roasting a pig, and other specialities that will be revealed as the evening arrives.

A packet of Saltzen was outside my door when I was going up to the bridge. A small gift to each crewmember, German confirmed. I had a brainstorm about the paper cases from the biscuit tin I have been stashing. I marked five of the paper cases with the words of the verse for the 1st Craw, five with the words for the 2nd Craw and five with the words for the 3rd Craw, and the remaining three were for the Craw that *wisnae there at aa.* I have folded them into little florets and put them in the big tin I had fetched from the bridge. German asked what I was doing. I said it was a surprise. He said about it being a drum, and it will be good for this once the lads, if they agree to this game, have picked out a floret that will reveal which crow they are to be. I hope they will enjoy this wee bit of fun.

What touched me most was the surprise of a bottle of wine and huge packet of

Quality Street, presented to me as a gift from the crew by Andriy K on the bridge. I was moved to a wee tear. He took the wine to my cabin for me. I jested with him that it was a surprise on two counts: one, the gift of it; the other that the slop chest is supposed to have no wine in stock. It is crossed off the list. We laughed about this. He said there are a few bottles. I expect it is being held in reserve for occasions like this. I feel very special and honoured. We passed Igor, standing in his Speedos and goggles outside his cabin. That was another surprise. He looked as though he was about to swim the channel. I wonder if this is his fancy dress. I suspect not.

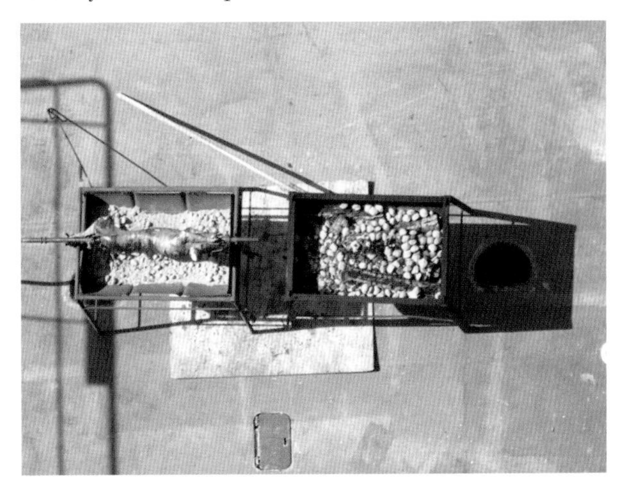

There is the aroma of wood smoke and cloves in the air. I do not want to see the pig whilst it is cooking. Two lads were busy fixing up the barbecue this morning, with a gentle tap-tap drumming to the roll of the sea. I went for a sunbathe. It is the most beautiful day so far. We have picked up a couple of hitchhikers, a booby (*sula sula*) and her chick. They have taken up position on the foremast. The chick's beak is a lovely salmon-pink colour with violet shades through it. It has dark feathers. It can fly, otherwise how would it have got here? Its mother is testing herself against the 30 knots wind, flying into it, side-somersaulting like a stunt plane, hanging like a kite, gliding and skimming over the waves at great speed in the hunt for a flying fish. She catches one. It gets free. She pursues it. It has taken such fright it disappears never to be seen again. I cannot see it escaping such an attack without some damage. The booby disappeared for a while after this, then came back to our bow, searching, searching, for some unfortunate innocent little flying fish. They eject from the ocean as if someone had been holding them down and suddenly let them go, like a plastic ball in the swimming pool. They flutter their fins into overdrive so fast you cannot see them move. They spin like the clockwork of a silver time machine across the waves then plunge. Gone! Gone from the beady eye of Mrs Booby and the gullet of her baby. It amuses me that a fish can outfly a bird.

I see the preparations going on below and head for my camera. Click. It will not be long till supper. *City of Adelaide* is watching all this unusual activity with great interest. She is following us like the great white whale, Moby Dick.

In the end I wore neither the red dress nor the blue and gold skirt. I popped my swimsuit on and tied a sarong with a fish pattern on it round my waist. I topped all this with a wine-coloured shrug with sequins. I put on some makeup for the crossing of the Equator, green eye shadow of course, and put my hair up. I felt comfortable and was pleased with the combination. I watched progress from my cabin window, and went down to the main deck around 5.20 pm. A few of the young lads had assembled, looking very bronzed and perhaps even a wee bit sunburned. They were in a jovial mood. German directed me to the deck above, where I found a long table laid out like a banquet. I was astonished. I feasted my eyes on several bowls filled with chopped vegetables before me. They had egg through, so I would not be sampling them. There were prawns, more the size of crayfish, snuggled under a silver foil blanket. There were platters covered with a variety of sausages, sliced up Wiejska, salami, Kabanos, and others I cannot name. There were olives, black and green, the green ones possibly stuffed with anchovies as they were very salty. There were gherkins and all sorts of sauces. Rye bread sliced into baskets was dotted around at intervals all the way along the long table covered with the same blue gingham pattern washable tablecloth material that is in the messes. There was bench seating to make up the shortfall of dining chairs borrowed from the messes.

The roast pig was served person-by-person, each choosing a piece. I picked a smaller bit that turned out to be neck. It was delicious, permeated with wood smoke and minimum spices. Meat just kept on coming. Chops that had been marinated and cooked over the coals arrived. Succulent and tasty, I tucked into mine. I went for a second smaller helping covered in crackling. I had just sat down with this when we were offered kebabs, large chunks of pig and large pieces of onion impaled onto steel skewers. Sometime around here we crossed the Equator. At 6.29 pm, precisely.

Stepan came over and pulled out a chair for me to sit down. He told me he is a pensioner but takes contracts from the agency whenever they call him up. He showed me a picture of his wife, Vitalyia that he has on his phone. He has two daughters, each have a son, making Stepan a *Jeda* – grandfather. He is very proud of his family and, as with all the men, time away is hard but necessary in order to make a living. Sergii takes this separation from his wife and son, who is not yet two, very hard. He told me he is a very good billiards player, and ran a club in his town. He got work at sea, encouraged by his father-in-law. Sergii grew up without a father and he knows what it is like to not have the input of two parents in growing up. I said this is a double-whammy for him, wanting to be there as the little boy's daddy, yet having to be at sea to make a decent living for his family, while remembering the gap in his own life that his father should have occupied.

Enter Kostya and the whisky. Grants and Grouse. There was a limit on how much alcohol would be consumed, for safety reasons. Kostya challenged me to down my dram in a one-er. At first I refused. 'I will be flat on my back.' Laughter erupted all around. Kostya persisted. Persuasion pervaded the walls of sensibility and down went the whisky to a round of cheers. I was not going to let him away with it. 'Dai,' I said in

Ukrainian. 'Go.' Down it went. Another round of cheers. The bottle was passed down, our glasses refilled. He gestured for me to drink. 'Half,' I said. The pourer was generous. 'Okay,' he said. Down it went. 'You now,' said I. And so it went. Most of the lads had a few whiskies. Each time we stood up and clashed glasses together, celebrating Christmas, celebrating Andriy's birthday and any other excuse to get up and clink glass against tin, or glass against glass or glass against beer bottle.

I went up to my cabin to pee. It had got cooler so I changed into my red dress. It is such a comfortable dress. I went back down. 'Dadaaaa.' Approving glances. I sat down. A contest was going on in regard to music. On Vitaliy's window ledge above, his CD player disgorged a selection of Ukrainian folk music, opera and general music that drowned out the younger crew's hip-hop. Andrei Bocceli came on. *O Sole Mio.* Vitaliy began singing and I…I joined him. At the end of our duet, he planted a brief kiss on my mouth and we bumped foreheads in musical camaraderie. Whisky brings surprises!

Tidying up began. There was an army of helpers so I stayed seated, not wanting to be in the way. I have no idea when the party wound up, but it wound up without the renaming ceremony happening. I was disappointed, but perhaps the excitement of Christmas and the feast had blurred remembrance. Tomorrow is another day. I went to my cabin, then up to the bridge. I wanted to see the stars. I went on the outer walkway in front of the bridge and lay down on my back. The night was pristine, its soft air caressed my face and kissed my eyelids closed. I was lost in the vastness of the ocean, gone *Elsewhere.* Footsteps interrupted my escape. German had come out to see if I was okay. 'Just admiring the stars,' I said, and pointed out Orion's Belt facing the wrong way. 'It seems so small compared to how it is in Scotland.' He went back inside and put off the lights that polluted the scene. I was mesmerised by the black sky of the night, hypnotised by the stars swaying above me as *Palanpur* strode through the waves. I felt the arms of Morpheus wrap themselves around me as I lay beneath the Southern Cross.

ESO/José Francisco (josefrancisco.org)

DAY THIRTY-ONE

September 11, 1864 – Sunday

A fine day but the waves rather high. We had prayers on Deck but were obliged to sit down all the time. In the evening we went to the Sailors' Service. Harry, one of the Sailors read a Sermon and then made a very earnest prayer. It was full of nautical expressions. The evening hymn was then sung. I have been reading some very interesting sermons by Revd. Guthrie of Edinburgh. Margaret Guthrie, his daughter was at school with us at Boulogne, 1857.

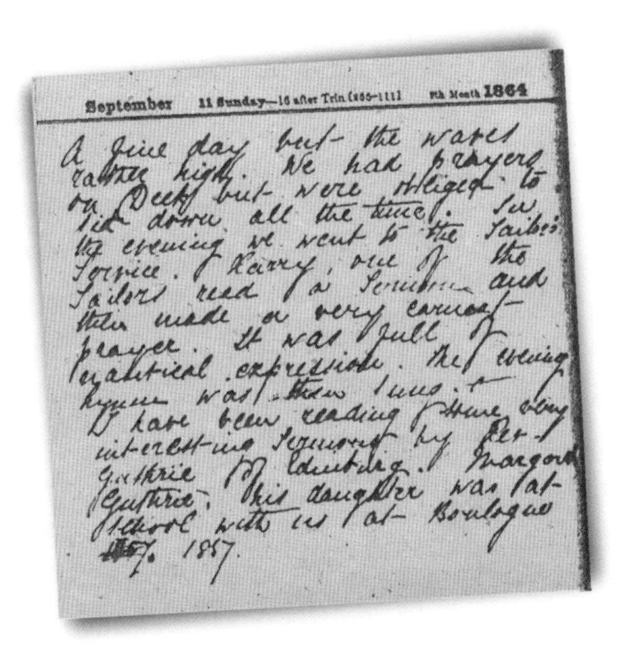

September 11 Sunday—16 after Trin (255-111) 9th Month 1864

A fine day but the waves
rather high. We had prayers
on Deck but were obliged to
sit down all the time. In
the evening we went to the Sailors'
Service. Harry, one of the
Sailors read a Sermon and
then made a very earnest
prayer. It was full of
nautical expressions. The evening
hymn was then sung.
I have been reading some very
interesting sermons by Rev.
Guthrie of Edinburgh. Margaret
Guthrie, his daughter was at
school with us at Boulogne
1857.

26 December 2013 – Thursday – Atlantic Ocean

A blue sky, but I kept the curtains drawn till the afternoon.

I am not sure how long I lay beneath the stars before getting to my cabin or what time it had been. It was like a dream.

I awoke around 11.10 am and decided lunch was not on the cards for me today. I could not be bothered getting ready. It had nothing to do with the slight headache I had. I drank a fair bit of water, had a couple of biscuits and a slab of chocolate with a drink of milk, then went back to sleep. I woke again about 12.50 pm and made myself a fennel and liquorice tea. It went down well. I had another couple of biscuits and a couple of Ibuprofen and lay down to listen to some music. I dozed off again and awoke at 4.45 pm. It is so good to have no pressures, it allows for total relaxation, an absolute luxury for body and soul. I got up and had a shower, washed a few smalls and went down to the galley. Anatoliy's time investment of yesterday paid him some dividends towards a more relaxed day today. He had laid out chopped up left over pork, kebabs, and those delicious chops. I chose a chop and a piece of pork, with loads of crackling that I did not eat. I gave a miss to the salads and made my way to the mess. German was there, and Andriy V. Valeriy came in next and then Andriy K, who was pretty chilled out from yesterday, and looked very happy. Slop chest today. I chose a Ritter Bar, a litre of peach and a litre of mango juices. German asked Andriy K to bring some beer. He had invited me to join him. I thought he was going to have one too but he said he does not drink alcohol, and sipped his cola. He said he did not expect to see me today. I said, 'You are going home from Adelaide?' 'Looks like it,' he said. He said he might have gone from Port Hedland but explained there is limited and very expensive accommodation there, and also flights are not so regular, so Adelaide it is. I am glad he will be with Palanpur for the rest of my journey. I met Stepan outside the galley. We had a hug. I apologised for standing on his toe.

I got a small plate from Anatoliy. He was asking about the drawings on the cards I made for the crew. He said he would not be able to draw a guitar, even though he plays one. I said my house is full of them. He said he had looked at each card as he placed them in the places of crew in their mess. He wondered if I had copied them from somewhere. I said not. German appeared. He asked if I was disappointed the crew had not sung my song. I said it was fine, just a bit of fun. I said if they were up for it on Hogmanay, then I would bring the tin then. The question of where the tin had got to arose. I had seen the Bosun go into his cabin with it last night – not unless it was a proper tin of biscuits he had. I asked Anatoliy if he could see if he could find out what had happened to the tin so we could retrieve it for a singsong. I could make them all over again. He hoped it was not in the garbage. This is the word that is used on board for rubbish. I took my plate and raided the fridge – a slice of rye bread, some of the selection of sausages, some black olives and a couple of slices of cheese. Tasty. There were pears too, so I took one for later. I finished the wee Dutch beer German had given me and popped my plate in the dishwasher, as instructed by Anatoliy. I was going to hand wash it and the beer glass. There are two industrial dishwashers that operate at a very high temperature and complete the cycle in two minutes. I opened the first machine, it was hot, and had clean dishes and bowls in it, so I put my two items in the empty second machine.

I decided to have a day off from taking readings today. We are south of the Equator now, as mentioned earlier. Not much has changed in regard to ship speed. The wind may be slightly lighter today. The air is much fresher than it was a couple of days ago. I opened a porthole and enjoyed the fresh breeze revitalising my cabin.

I am sleepy now.

DAY THIRTY-TWO

September 12, 1864 – Monday

A beautiful day and a fair breeze. I played at Chess with the Doctor and lost each time. In the evening we danced.

27 December 2013 – Friday – Atlantic Ocean

I woke at 8 am, got up, had liquorice and fennel tea and set straight to reading and editing Days One to Twenty-Eight, the first part of this book pulled together.

I worked till 11.30 am then went for a brief sunbathe before lunch. A crew member, Vadym, was making repairs to a rope ladder with wooden slat steps beside the life-raft station to starboard. These are additional boats to the lifeboat pod stored at the stern of the ship. I was not that hungry, having had some muesli for breakfast. I ate a little soup, a small portion of chicken curry, rice and salad. Anatoliy told me there was not good news about the tin. The lid had blown off and the contents scattered away across the deck and into the sea. The crew, he said, were not up for singing the song, he said they were *shame*, which we discussed, and found he meant *shy*. I laughed and said I know the feeling of being shy, and had stared it in the face and stood up to it over the last couple of years. We laughed at the thought of King Neptune and his entourage singing the ditty.

Andriy K came in. He told me there has been stormy weather with nine metre high waves off the Bay of Biscay. We are glad to have missed this. After lunch two emails had come for me, from each of my girls, wishing me a Happy Christmas. They have had a lovely time by all accounts, and even little Zac was on best behaviour and enjoyed his wee holiday. I am concerned to hear my son is not well.

Up on the bridge Ihor was working at the small computer, watching a training video. He is an apprentice, supervised by Andriy V. They have a good relationship, there is laughter and banter. Ihor called him over when I was taking my readings. Andriy called over that he was busy. I jotted down what I needed. Latitude changes now, as we are south of the Equator as of 6.29 pm on Christmas Day, so it is 06°21.82'S, longitude 018°40.60'W, wind speed 34.5 knots, course 136, *Palanpur* is travelling at 12 knots per hour. It is 28°C. I went outside to see if the boobies were still there. They are gone. I expected this, as they are making a terrible mess. I asked no questions. In my cabin I continued working as before. I sunbathed for a further half hour or so before supper, gherkin wrapped in ground pork and topped with a slice of cheese, mashed potatoes and salad. Just before supper Andriy V had phoned me to ask what size of notebook I needed. There was no A5 so I asked for A4. He presented this to me at supper, a very smart blue hardback book with gold motif.

It has been another quiet day. I dozed after supper then awoke to read *Master and Commander* for a while. I read a few more entries from Sarah's and my diaries till after 2 am, played some Pinball then tried to sleep after 3 am. I peeped out at *City of Adelaide*, the deck was a little wet but *Palanpur* is moving along in a very steady way, with few waves breaking against her sides. Sometimes it feels like being in a glider, when she sits on top of the current and just flows with it. It is a lovely, ethereal feeling, as if being propelled along into an unknown time zone.

DAY THIRTY-THREE

September 13, 1864 – Tuesday

A fine day and sailing along well. The Captain has had some rope quoits made for the ladies, so in the afternoon we had a game.

28 December 2013 – Saturday – Atlantic Ocean

I awoke at about 9.30 am to voices in the corridor. Chief Officer Igor and Vitaliy, Second Engineer were having a heated discussion. I got up, made my usual cup of liquorice and fennel tea and went for my shower while it cooled.

I went up to the bridge, thinking I would do some emails, but Igor was at the desk, so I took readings, latitude 09°22.07'S, longitude 015°29.42'W. We are going at 12.6 knots, wind speed is 30.8 and the outside temperature is a cool 25°.

I was surprised to see Eintopf in the soup tureen today. I questioned Anatoliy, saying, 'Why Eintopf today? It is not Saturday.' 'It is,' he replied. I went up the stairs satisfied with the soup, a slice of German rye bread, a couple of slices of salami and the same of cheese, but pondering over the days. Sure enough. Saturday. It is so easy to lose track of time, especially when a lot of sleep is happening. I popped into the ship's office to check emails. The system went down as I began deleting some of the older ones.

I was told my first on-board joke today:

> 'A man buys a cow at the market. He does not have a way to get it home. He asks a few people if they can take the cow home for him. Finally, he gets lucky.
> A man says he will lash the cow to the back of his car and drive slowly to the first man's house. They tie the cow to the back of the car and get in. Much vodka is consumed. The owner of the cow falls asleep. The driver is motoring along at 20 mph. He sees the cow in the rear view mirror. It is going along fine. He decides to increase the speed to 40 mph. The cow is running, it looks okay so he increases the speed to 60 mph, then 80 mph. At 100 mph he sees the cow has its tongue hanging out. He wakes its owner. In a drunken slur he says,
> 'What is it?'
> The driver says, 'Your cow has its tongue hanging out. What should I do?'
> 'What side is it hanging out on?'
> 'The right.'
> 'Oh, don't worry then. He is just overtaking.' '

I forced a polite laugh.

Vadym told me this joke whilst he was repairing the rope ladders mentioned earlier. I asked him if it was all right to pop down and watch him. As I did so, I thought of the quoits Captain Bruce had had made for the ladies that Sarah mentioned at this point in her voyage. The hemp ropes at the bottom of the ladder that have hooped ends were fraying. Vadym's task was to make them good. He trimmed off the frayed hemp and got some cord, laid a loop the length of the distance of the repair he wanted to make, and began winding from the middle of the cord that he had pre-wound onto a cylindrical piece of wood from a drum of cord. He wound and wound the cord round the thickness of the hemp, keeping the cord taught and each wind so close to its neighbour that a hair would not breach the gap, until he reached the end. He made a knot then pulled the length of cord in the middle of the repair and the end, making it tight, then cut off the ends of the cord. He repeated this process on the other side, trimming off the frayed hemp as before, but on this side he first added an extra strengthening beside the loop using coir or some other natural thin rope, before using the same winding process over the whole, covering the coir repair with cord as well. Vadym joked about it being a hospital, with the winding of bandages. That was how I first felt about *City of Adelaide* when I saw her covered in the white plastic wrapping in Rotterdam. It was as though she had a plaster cast on to set her old bones to strength again. Vadym told me he has a daughter who recently got married. He spends most of his time at sea, where he has spent the last 27 years of his life. I asked if it is he who operates Crane 2. He said, 'Yes.' He has asked for a change to Crane 1 when the opportunity arises. When we first began our chat this afternoon, Vadym had been apologetic about his language. I wish I could tell a joke in a second language. I could see no reason for him to apologise, I had no problem understanding him and he was happy to practise pronunciations and English with all its rules, in general. A few crew passed by as I was chatting with Vadym. We all greeted each other and commented on the Christmas party. We are looking forward to Hogmanay. The accommodation block is busy this afternoon, with some painting going on and other tasks there is never a shortage of, on this super-sized vessel. Andriy V was supervising proceedings all around. I told him I had read ahead in Sarah's diary, and that in a couple of days' time she would be passing the Equator. It is fascinating that she records sailors performing a ceremony to Neptune on this crossing. He said not a word about my renaming non-event.

I dozed off until suppertime, pork escalopes, like chicken Kiev, with garlic butter inside. With chips. I thought I smelled chips on the way down. Andriy K was at his table, and German and Valeriy were at mine. We spoke about chicken and pork. I asked about sheep in Ukraine. There are not so many, more perhaps to the west in the Carpathian mountains. My father has spoken of these mountains with great affection. Igor came in and said the temperatures in St Petersburg have gone crazy in the last couple of years, the seasons jumping straight from winter to summer, with perhaps a week of spring. I remarked that this must have an effect on bird life, if the natural pairing and mating season for birds is disappearing. They will adapt, but it is a thought. At the moment the temperature there is about 13°C higher than the normal winter temperature. German asked if I would like a beer, and he fetched a small Dutch lager from the fridge, opening it with the blunt end of a fork. They left and I took my plate to Anatoliy who was busy blethering with one of the crew. I bade him *goodnight*, and took my wee beer up to the landing on C Deck. I watched the sky. The clouds are so solid. They are the blue of Cinderella's dress and the sky is tinged with the pink of her underskirt. If I could step off *Palanpur*'s deck I could walk on water all the way to Namibia on the west coast of Africa. When Igor passed on his way back up to the bridge he said we had passed Ascension Island this afternoon. I asked if he had seen it. He said we were too far from it for that. I have heard of this island and seen it on the map, but could not place it. I went up to the bridge. German and Igor were talking, so seeing the computer was free, I sat down. There is still a connection problem. German came over and said they had had to restart the system because it had hung up. It was a good opportunity to ask him about the emails I had sent to newspapers a couple of weeks ago, and had not received a reply to a single one of them. He asked what they were about. I told him they were offering articles for the Sunday magazines. He said he did not know. I also said that perhaps because they were split into two because they had exceeded the 1000 character limit, I may have gone over some credit limit. I am sure he will come up with answer to these queries. We then talked about the structure of Harren & Partner, the relationship to Combi-Lift and the maritime employment agency Marlow. The three of us then went to look at the chart for this area. Igor pointed out Ascension Island. He told us he had been there ten years ago with a military delivery. He pointed out that we are between Ascension Island and St Helena where Napoleon is buried. These islands are volcanic eruptions, and there are several more in a line that are just beneath the face of Neptune bursting forth like teenage acne on the skin of a pubescent boy.

On the way back down I stopped off at my sunbathing spot and contemplated the waves. They were navy blue, a beautiful deep, solid shade, until the bow of *Palanpur* decimated them into shards of aquamarine. Every now and then Neptune would chuck a bucket of water over the smoky billow beneath our steel hull. The waves were frolicking like a gang of foals, the ones at the rear slamming into the ones in front in a stampede of unbridled power. I noticed the rope and wood ladder had been neatly stowed away beneath a tarpaulin. Everything was ship-shape and safe again. The sun was reducing its height in the sky, heading to dip beneath the horizon like a round biscuit into a cup of tea. It is so pretty and the air so clear. This is the perfect climate, and I think of those at home, shivering in the dead of winter. If I could sleep out on deck, I would. I went for my camera to take some pictures of *City of Adelaide* in the doze of the day and caught some glorious images of Apollo submitting to Neptune, but not before he trained a laser beam on the bow of *City of Adelaide*, pointing her out to the stars so they will look out for her.

I spent some time this evening looking at earlier entries in Sarah's diary and notes by James Kerr, who made up the background family documents for his family. He is Ruth Currie's great-uncle. I studied the family likenesses in depth and found Blanche, Sarah's sister, used spectacles that dangled round her wrist and were folded. There are no legs on them, so they would have sat on her nose, as pince-nez. I extracted headshot images of John S Kerr and Sarah Ann Bray as a young couple, then superimposed them onto their extracted images from the family group photo as a mature couple in a new document. They are indeed a very handsome pair. I can see Sarah dancing on *City of Adelaide*. She looks a very spirited young woman, and precocious. She never seems daunted by anything that comes her way and strikes me as being someone who enjoys excitement.

Top row: John, Ethel and John senior; Front row: Charles, Amy, Alice and Sarah

DAY THIRTY-FOUR

September 14, 1864 – Wednesday

A beautiful day. We crossed the Equator about 1.30 P.M.
In the evening the sailors marched (in costume) on the Deck. One represented Neptune – he had a long white beard and carried something like a trident.
We danced till 10 P.M.

29 December 2013 – Sunday – Atlantic Ocean

A film of smoke obscured the blue canopy this morning. It feels a little humid, despite there being a brisk breeze blowing. The sea is sapphire and diamonds, but the gold band to complete the ring of perfection has yet to be minted.

I had another late start to the day, having written long into the new day's conception. The hands of the clock quick-marched passed the dozen numbers on the clock at midnight, parading us forward through another line of longitude, causing the troops to lose the skirmish of a full night's sleep. Despite having had some muesli mid-morning I remembered it was borscht for lunch, so I showered and went down to the galley. I took a couple of expired wee beer bottles gathered over the last few days and a depleted carton of milk for the rubbish. This brought me into conversation with Anatoliy. I asked him how he was today. He responded with the rating of seven or eight today. He said he had had a blockage in the pipes that run beneath perforated drain covers that go round the galley, following the lines of the island cooking station in the middle. This is where he serves food from. He has low-sided oblong stainless steel oven pans for meat, huge pots for rice, millet, pasta, and potatoes depending on the dish of the day, then bowls for salad. They are all laid out in a row above where the oven is. He explained grease gathers in the drainpipes now and again. A blockage had occurred that caused an overflow all over the kitchen floor that he had to clean up, emphasising the use of bleach. He was angry about this at first but was not too miffed in the end, as he had planned a major clean up anyway before we get to Cape Town in a few days. His annoyance came from having it foisted upon him on one of the more leisurely days, a Sunday, especially when he had been robbed of an hour of sleep.

We spoke about the garbage system. I asked if analysis of the ash was carried out when ships came to ports to check whether they were conforming to regulations. He said I would be better to ask the Chief Officer, who came in at that point. I would ask him another time. Anatoliy said that the previous practice was to incinerate plastic and then scatter the ashes at sea, but even this has been stopped. Only food waste is permitted to be presented to Neptune for his larder. We went on to have a discussion about rubbish disposal in each of our countries. He said in Ukraine there is no segregation of rubbish, it is all put in one bin and each individual has to take it to a central point where it is then taken to a rubbish tip outside the cities, is bulldozed into a pit and set fire to. These areas are fenced off, birds and poor people rake them, there is no system for recycling. He feels this is a waste, as there is money in recycling materials, and to not do it is bad for the environment. I told him about the plant in East Lothian that currently processes rubbish from Edinburgh. It has recently received permission to take rubbish from the whole of Scotland. They bury the garbage then cover it over with soil. A pipe to the outside burns off methane gas. They provide some power to the nearby cement factory that burns shredded tyres for fuel. A nuclear power station completes the trio of industrial plant in this area. There is also a recycling plant at the other end of the county. Each week we put our bins out: one week it is the red coloured one for plastic and glass and the blue for paper and cardboard; nine days later we put out the green bin that contains general household rubbish; twelve days later it is back to the red and blue, and so on. Lids must be able to be closed, and the bin men lift lids to check there is nothing inside that should not be in that particular bin, for example car batteries, radiators or bed springs in the household rubbish bin. There is also a local council recycling depot in my town, where most sorts of rubbish can be taken and dumped into huge skips that are then removed and replaced with empty ones. There is another more major recycling centre half way between my town and Edinburgh where everything imaginable can be disposed of. Next to it is a furniture recycling place where people can give away their unwanted household goods, such as couches, dining tables and chairs, bookshelves, even electrical items that must be tested for safety. These are priced up and sold, the money going to the charity that runs the system, to cover costs. It helps people get a start when they have not much money to buy the basic items to help set up a first home, or replace damaged or worn out goods. Goodness me, what a conversation at lunchtime. I nevertheless ate my soup with relish, and discovered a very nice wholemeal bread, sweet and soft. I had a slice with my soup and raided two more to take up to have with honey later this afternoon. I totally forgot to take my ice cream and will go down for that shortly. It looked from the bowl the Bosun was carrying as he made to go up the stairs with this booty, that there was jelly with it.

Anatoliy and I had also had a conversation about the roads in Scotland and Ukraine. He was surprised to find that we had a road, never mind one that was full of potholes. In Ukraine country roads are mostly dirt tracks. We talked about sleeping policemen. I was surprised to learn they exist in Ukraine as well, around schools and medical centres in particular, to slow traffic down. I said the sleeping policemen combined with the potholes play havoc with our cars. My husband had got another car last year, a second-hand one that had been well looked-after, that had to have its springs replaced within two months, and he is a careful driver. I said a better use of the tar would be to take if from the sleeping policemen and fill the potholes with it. We laughed. He says there is a very good mayor in his town now, who is spending money on services and facilities and making big improvements for people. I told Anatoliy that at last the road running from the nearby village past our house to the next junction had been re-made since I left for this voyage.

I went to look at my emails on my way for a dose of sunshine and found the ConnectCrew server had been down and all my emails in both the *inbox* and *sent* folders were lost. I could cope with that but my address book was jumbled up, the corresponding email address against each name had all slipped down one line. I spent a tedious half hour taking a note of the names and email addresses and sorting it out before I continued on my way to my usual spot to sunbathe. It was in the shade so I took to the roof for a brief toasting. I stood in the embrace of the wind for a few minutes to cool down and enjoyed the feeling of freedom and privilege. Within half-an-hour I was taking the readings for today, latitude 13°24.32'S, longitude 011°04.23'W, wind speed 27.3 knots, course 133 and 27°C, before going back to my cabin, sufficiently dozed by the sun for the day.

I went to supper but declined, the ice cream mid-afternoon having melted away any pangs of emptiness I might have had. Anatoliy and I had another prolonged conversation. Gestures. He showed me that if a person pings their middle finger off their thumb against the neck at the end of the jaw line, this means he is saying someone is drunk. The same meaning is given to tapping a forefinger on its opposite side of the body on the neck, again just below the end of the jaw line. He added a superstition that when drinking in company the person who starts off pouring the drink must continue to be the pourer for the whole evening, or it will bring bad luck. If another drink is wanted, a mouse-like squeak sound is made by keeping lips tight and forcing air between them with blown up cheeks, whilst at the same time the three middle fingers from one hand are drummed on the sternum. Alternative to this, thumb and pinkie finger are spread out wide from the other three fingers that are folded down. The hand in this position is then swivelled at the wrist. In the same position, it can also be directed to the mouth, thumb first, and swayed backwards and forwards like a ship riding through peaks and troughs of a storm.

I told Anatoliy I was going into a crane in the morning with Igor. His face was drawn and not a twitch of a smile could be detected when he told me to be very careful. He advised there was a lot of oil about inside the cranes, making the soles of boots very slippery. He described the access, a series of upright ladders and the space was tight. I thought of when I climbed the ladder to slide into *City of Adelaide*'s belly at Irvine. On the topic of safety and the crane ladder system, he showed me the staircase to the crew laundry. It is extremely steep with metal treads at the 90° angle of the drop to the next step. There is only one handrail. This limits steadying oneself in the event of the ship pitching, particularly when carrying a load of washing. There are two machines below, one for dirty, oily overalls and one for ordinary clothing of the crew. Anatoliy told me he had helped install the washing machine in the officers' accommodation area. We went into the larder where he gave me a fresh carton of milk and another tin of Beatrix Potter's Peter Rabbit assorted butter cookies. I promised to put some more photographs on my memory stick for him tomorrow. He had been asking about images of *The Three Craws* a week or so ago.

'Come with me,' Anatoliy said. He opened the crew mess door. There were a few men eating their meal but immediately my eye was drawn to the corner on the

opposite side of the room from them. There, in full glory on a table top, stood a princess of a Christmas tree, bedecked in rubies, diamonds, emeralds, sapphires and amber. Damn this liquid salt. Where do these tears come from? To see the pleasure in the face of someone giving pleasure and to see the pleasure in the faces witnessing the pleasure that is given and received is to be sure, pleasurable.

I went to the mess to get a couple of slices of bread. I did not feel like eating duck. I almost collided with German who stepped out of the doorway just as I was stepping in. He had on a pair of beige shorts. It looked like there were little red, white and blue sailing yachts floating along on the hems. I bent down in front of him for a closer look. My sides ached later on when I realised why the officers all around were laughing.

Last night I had a deep sense of Sarah Ann Bray. It is the click I was waiting for. *City of Adelaide* is the link between us. I am getting to know what her life was like from her 1864 diary, and reading about the Grand Tour she, her sister Blanche, her mother and father were on before they sailed on the maiden voyage of *City of Adelaide*; what she looked like as a young woman and as the mature mother of five children; her hobbies and lifestyle. There is real comfort in feeling her close. A wash of completeness is permeating my bones. *City of Adelaide* has pervaded my life over the last few years, swamping my mind, sending me in a spin, panic and cold sweat until this year she spilled into my everyday life and everything domestic fell by the wayside. I abandoned day-to-day chores, cooked at will or not at all, kept friends and family in her wake. I cannot reason why I am on this leviathan cargo ship with the oldest surviving composite clipper ship in the world staring back at me as I look out from my cabin window.

DAY THIRTY-FIVE

September 15, 1864 – Thursday

A beautiful day and a favorable wind. The Doctor played Chess with me and won three games. I wished to practise but the Piano was engaged nearly all day. In the afternoon we played quoits. A most lovely evening – the moon full – we could read by it. We danced till nearly 10 P.M.

Later footnote to this diary entry: Arthur Le Mesurier Bray, born 15 Sept 1868.

30 December 2013 – Monday – Atlantic Ocean

A grey day all day until it began to break away just after 5 pm. It is windy, the waves are small, yet *Palanpur* is lumbering from side to side like a pregnant cow.

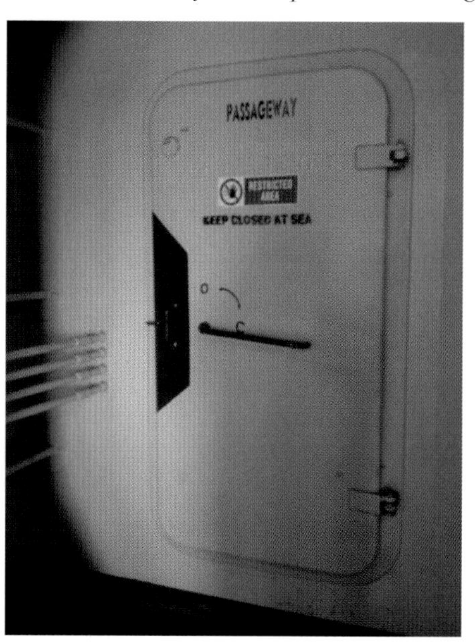

Glossy blobs broke out on my upper lip and hairline when the telephone trumpeted details of the rendezvous for my climb into the crane. My stomach felt like the chicken porridge Anatoliy serves up in the galley. I gulped a cocktail of air served up by the four winds. I met the knight who had promised to take me there. ***Restricted Area*** barred our way. The knight battled against its heavy steel armour till he released the waiting passage that shimmered with black hoses. He entered the mouth that would swallow us up, and beckoned for me to follow. I was Rapunzel as I entered the tower just after 9 am. A ladder was fixed to the wall. We would have to climb this to reach the first level. He led the way. I followed, aware the soles of my boots had become coated in a slippery substance. 'Take care,' he called. Hand passed over hand and foot passed over foot as I scaled the ladder up to the unknown. The knight waited with patience at my laboured ascent. I spilled out onto the platform. There was a much shorter ladder to the next level. He scaled it with ease and looked down at me. I had paused to take extra breath.

'It is not that I am out of breath,' I called, 'I am collecting myself for being in this small space.'

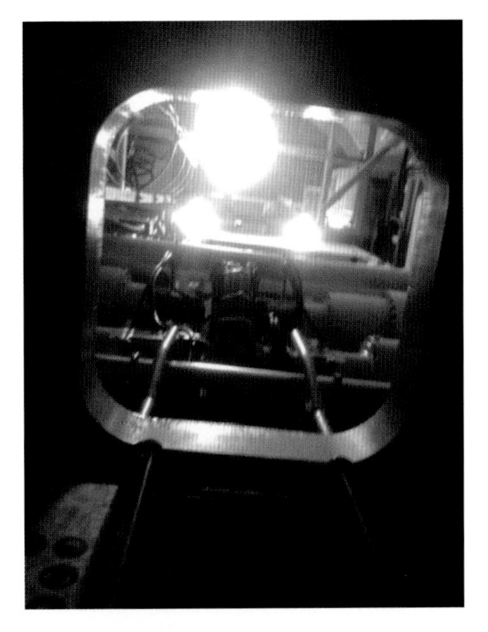

He understood, said, 'Keep looking up.'

I placed my boot on the lowest rung of the next ladder.

'Be careful of your head,' he called before I set my next boot to the task. I began to climb as before. Clonk. The knight could have spared the warning. I was glad my crown was protected by a white hardhat.

'Reach here,' he patted the grab rail I would hoist myself by to join him on the platform. He hauled me by the arm to assist me off the ladder.

Another ladder, longer again, would take us to the top of the tower. I looked up. I knew now I would make it. I quelled the thought of having to reverse the climb, a voice in my ear whispering, 'One step at a time. One step at a time.'

I burst onto the third platform where the treasure lay. My knight beckoned for me to sit down on a seat hinged in two places he unfolded from a wall. I sat down and feasted my eyes. To the left a panel with buttons that commanded the crane to switch to using the small hook or the big hook. In front of this a stubby gear stick protruded at thigh level, bafflingly disproportionate to its gigantic purpose. A computer monitor was just above eye-level to the left. In front, the giant, bright yellow crane arm stretched away into the distance. The view to the deck and across the ocean was vast. I surveyed the land, but there was none to see. Only water. Water, water everywhere, and this floating steel island, *Palanpur*. It was a pity I could not see *City of Adelaide*. The thick steel cables covered in grease, cogs, wheels, winding gear, access ladders, electrical wiring, fixed steel casings and everything it took to operate this mammoth 450 ton crane was fitted at the back of the operator and sealed in a roundhouse against daylight. The knight Igor showed me where my cut off (Rapunzel) hair was kept in case of emergency. It was slung in a bag hanging up to the left side of the cabin. In case of fire, the operator could open a window, hook the line of the harness to the crane tower, put the harness on, clip himself into it and abseil down my hair to safety. I thought of when my son abseiled off the Finnieston Crane at Glasgow to raise funds for Raleigh International in 2000 for his trip to Namibia in 2001. He was a tiny spider dangling from a thin strand of gossamer. We made our descent the conventional way, turning towards the ladder, holding the grab rails before placing the first boot with great caution onto the top rung. Then the rhythm of foot over foot, hand over hand began. Igor was practised at this; I however, took my time and placed two feet on each rung until I felt confident enough to speed up to one at a time. My hands were posed like a monkey's, clenching each horizontal rung so that if my foot did slip I could dangle by my hands until I re-found my footing. All this had been explained to me on the way up by Igor, and he had done a risk assessment prior to our setting out on the path, that we had both signed. I got some photographs of the greased up cables, the hydraulics and ladders, one of Igor and he took a few of me for the family album. I do not look so bad in orange overalls. Before we left, I could see three of the locomotives that had been loaded at Norfolk, Virginia, United States of America. They looked huge, confident in the 'tween decks, and very snug. They will be offloaded at Port Hedland, Western Australia. Igor showed me the huge grommets or loops that are used to lift cargo with the crane. There were massive octagonal nuts fitted to some kind of cylinder, and I asked if there was an equally massive spanner to remove them. 'No,' he said. 'Look.' And he proceeded with two hands to shift the nut until he unscrewed it completely from its male counterpart.

I left Igor there and made my way up some steps to the weather deck, so called because it is where the weather falls; it is open to the elements. I took a walk over to the side rails to absorb what had just happened and to look up at the crane arm in all its vastness. It stretched away towards the accommodation block and beyond, and its great hooks were fastened safely to a cradle set in the steel of the deck below my port side cabin porthole. I had seen crew members all around actively engaged in some task on the walk to the access door to Crane 1. I often wondered what the lads get up to during the day, and all has been revealed. Below the weather deck all sorts of jobs were being undertaken, grinding, welding and so on. Above in the fresh air, one crewmember was cleaning up the heavy-duty D rings that are used to fix sections of the deck onto the crane hook before being hoisted away and off from *Palanpur* to lie on the dockside till the time came to close the deck up again.

All this took less than half-an-hour. I had some cereal and a cup of tea when I got back to my cabin. I was fired up, restless and sweaty. I felt like I had been in a sauna, and the exercise on the ladders had stimulated my blood flow. I went up to the laundry for some washing powder and expended some energy by washing the clothes I had worn on this adventure. All traces of the scent of oil and grease were gone. I say scent, because I love the smells of these lubricants. I noted my boiler suit had been christened with some black grease, a tribal smearing from this early morning adventure I will wear with pride. I stepped into the shower and was reborn.

At lunch I had soup with mushrooms, potatoes and small bits of beef in. I told Anatoliy about the visit to the crane. I gave him the memory stick with the photos on that I had promised him. He asked if he could return it at suppertime. I went to check emails but someone was at the computer in the ship's office so I went to my cabin and read some more of *Master and Commander*. I did not bother going up to the bridge this afternoon for readings, and it was overcast so there would be no sunbathing today. I began typing up about this morning's visit to the crane. I fell asleep and awoke about an hour from suppertime. I wrote a little more and edited yesterday's entry. At supper, meatloaf, chicken porridge and salad, Anatoliy was very chatty. He gave me back my memory stick loaded with some music. He says he also has some Ukrainian folk songs, particularly wedding ones. Would I like these? Yes please! He spoke of the house he and his wife and daughter will move to when it is finished. At the moment it is just a shell, all the finishings need to be done, such as plastering the walls, putting in kitchen units, furnishings and so on. All there is at the moment is the concrete walls and floor, and points for connecting to services, though the natural gas pipes for heating and so on are already fitted. It is a two-storey flat. He talked about how he became a cook, how he had wanted to become an electrician but there were no courses available at the time he joined the employment agency. He had studied four years to gain the certificates to become a cook but had had to do a further six months practical work in setting menus in a company refectory. Now he has exams looming to get him towards the final stages of becoming an electrical engineer, but he will have to shadow someone for a period after he has qualified before he is able to work on his own. The practical side of his distance learning course is signed off by Chief Engineer Valeriy, on board *Palanpur*. Anatoliy remarked on the photos I had given him, particularly the hand-paintings and the one of me doing a firewalk to raise funds for a local charity. He said some of his friends do crazy things, but for a woman my age it is unheard of. We talked of some of the other extreme activities that exist. I began to laugh. I related to him the Spheremania experience with my brother when we were harnessed inside a giant double-skinned ball and bounced down a hill. We laughed about this till our sides split. He talked of one where people go inside a ball and get pushed around on water without wearing harness. He suggested I do a bungee jump next. We shall see.

We had spent an hour blethering. I came upstairs feeling a bit unwell, perhaps standing such a long time was not a good idea. I checked emails on the way up, one from my husband with an update of family, festivities and weather. There have been terrible storms and over a thousand homes in England have been without electricity for days. Everyone is going to be at my house for Old Year's Night tomorrow, excluding my eldest daughter who has other plans, but including my mother, so I am very happy. I went for a snooze and woke three hours later at 11.30 pm. I had an aching head, it felt like I had used my eyes too much, and I felt bloated and sick, so paced about a bit before taking an indigestion tablet, having a cup of water and putting the light back off, to seek sleep. It did not come, so I read some poetry and wrote some. I listened to Pink Floyd and had a thought.

I have not yet told Anatoliy about the simulated skydiving experience I had in Gran Canaria some years ago.

DAY THIRTY-SIX

September 16, 1864 – Friday

A beautiful day. We worked and read all this morning. I have commenced "Two Years Ago" by Charles Kingsley. We danced all this evening.

31 December 2013 – Tuesday – Atlantic Ocean

A beautiful blue sky, with a grey wall banked at the horizon to the port side. We sailed towards its shadow after I had my breakfast cereal. There is a run on the sea, quite choppy and I am glad I am not in a small sailing yacht. To starboard is another wall of cloud. We are sailing beneath a corridor of blue. I opened my porthole for some fresh air, and it soon felt chilly. I believe it will be much warmer outside.

I awoke about 8 am and rose to have my usual cuppa. My stomach was uncomfortable last night, I had had some meatloaf that I found was quite heavy. The digestion tablet had eased things a little, but the murmur of a headache persisted. I drew open the drawer beneath my bed, found the tin of hard-boiled sweets, removed the lid and took one out to pop into my mouth. It relieved the bloating enough for me to put headphones in my ears and fall asleep. I did not air the cabin yesterday and wonder if that had something to do with my feeling unwell. This morning the boys are washing the ship down again with a power-washer. It is noisy and not aiding my recovery. It does sound like a continuous foghorn. I typed out two poems I had penned last night, *Christmas Tree* and *Neptune's Girls.* I did not go to lunch in order to rest my stomach that had divulged its secret of an excess of bile. I am greatly relieved, but still not 100%. By suppertime I was ready to eat and went down to the galley, having been surprised to find from German that there was going to be a meal. I thought Anatoliy would be too busy preparing for the Hogmanay feast to prepare another meal. His galley was spotless, shining like new fallen snow with sun gleaming on it. He is very proud of his work. He said there was no dinner, we would be eating at 10 pm. I said I would take some bread and have a sandwich, with cheese in mind for the filling as I had missed lunch. I mentioned my tummy upset. He was crestfallen, immediately worried there was some problem with the food. I waggled my finger at him – the one that is distorted with arthritis – and said he was not to think like this. If there had been a problem everyone would be feeling the same. I mentioned the sore head and said it could be down to no fresh air in my cabin with not opening my porthole yesterday, but his face was disbelieving. I emphasised it is purely down to metabolism. He said he needs to know of these things in case there is some problem with the food.

Before I had gone down to the galley I had spent some time on the bridge computer sending New Year greetings to my family. We were at latitude 20°12'S, longitude 003°W, wind speed 34.5, were going at 12 knots and the thermometer read 25°. There were two new emails. One was from Rosemary McKay, the Scottish lassie down-under, who was sending me warmest greetings from the Gold Coast where she is staying with her daughter and granddaughter. I was overwhelmed when she told me one of the Peters was inviting me to stay with him when we arrive in Adelaide. I blotted my salt water eyes. I had no idea when we would arrive in Adelaide and how long the voyage would take, so had not been able to make any arrangements for accommodation on arrival. I wrote I should perhaps change the choice of Karine Polwart tune for the radio programme she has invited me onto from *Follow the Heron Home* to *The Kindness of Strangers*. She also said she lives not far from Peter and is looking forward to chauffeuring me about. Following on from her earlier email when she asked me what I would like to see and do when I am in Adelaide, I suggested a primary school visit or two.

The second email was from Jim Tildesley, retired Director of the Scottish Maritime Museum. I had written to him concerning Dr Platt. He told me the two-volume collection on *Cutty Sark* is now with his co-researcher, Bob Sexton, who lives in Adelaide. Jim asked me if I would send any significant updates to him now and then of what was happening on board *Palanpur* so that he could forward these to the Education Officer at the Scottish Maritime Museum. He told me there were letters from school groups on board *City of Adelaide* for when she arrives in Adelaide. I replied my thanks to Jim, and that I will be delighted to keep the school children informed. I will send the first note when they return to school next week.

German came onto the bridge. He spoke about whisky and the food tonight. I said I would be having none of it. I would just be drinking water, pulling his leg. He said that water is banned. It is bad for your stomach. As soon as it hits it, it turns it rusty. Whisky is mandatory. Anatoliy told me when I got my sandwich that vodka is always on the table at mealtimes at home. It kills off any bacteria that may be present from food served up. Sounds like a great excuse to me. He also told me that when he had to do practical exams, the judges had to go along a line of about thirty cooks to sample their food. They sloshed down vodka in between each sampling. Anatoliy said to be the last student judged was prime position. Good marks were sure to follow.

I sent an email to Peter Christopher with New Year greetings and received a reply before I went back to my cabin. I sent a few other greetings to friends who had no idea what I was up to.

I see today Sarah danced all evening on her voyage. I wonder if we will do the same. It would be really special to see some traditional Cossack dancing in the middle of the mid-Atlantic Ocean.

Everyone gathered on the weather deck for a photo call I had requested. One person, Andriy K, was on the bridge. I tried to get *City of Adelaide* in the background, but as it was so dark only one photo actually came out with just a ghosting of her. We will try again, maybe on Ukrainian Christmas, 7 January 2014.

We went inside to crew mess. The little tree was sparkling with pride. Sergiy had stuck strands of red and silver lametta onto the ceiling, creating a lovely effect.

There were also snowflakes made from paper plates one of these burly men had cut shapes into, as we did when we were small. I was struck by the sentimentality of these seventeen men and felt something move in my chest. A great bustling began. The big oven pan was brought piled with shishlaki. That is what I call them. They are metal skewers with great chunks of pork and onion spiked onto them: kebabs, or souvlaki as they are called in Greece, where they are very popular. The tables covered with the wipeable blue and white gingham cloths had already been set with a feast of dishes. There was an igloo of cheese blended with garlic and salt, a traditional dish accessible to all because of the basic ingredients being widely available in quantity and by pocket, as is Russian salad, that concoction of chopped vegetables, peas, carrots, egg, potato, gherkins – anything available, that is bound together with mayonnaise. I can eat mayonnaise, but I cannot eat eggs for some strange reason. The cheese and garlic, however, was very tasty and I enjoyed combining a spread of this with slices of succulent smoked salmon. The men were heartily tucking in to huge bowlfuls of large prawns eyeballing the scene. They cracked open the shells, peeled off their coral-coloured crustacean armour and devoured with relish the pale, curved, soft flesh approximately twelve centimetres long and the thickness of my middle finger. On the tables: whisky, vodka and gin. I was glad to see the gin, and there was even tonic! This became my tipple for the evening, after the starter of a Dutch stubby beer. There was a lot of *guid craik*, as we say in Scotland, good chat and laughter. Everyone was in great spirits and I was told, once again, that this was just a practise for Ukrainian Christmas and New Year. I shared a table with German to my right, Igor to my left and at his other side, Andriy V. I had been given the special honour of being head of the table. Before the meal began, there was an announcement by German, and I was presented with a greeting.On the back, each and every crew member had their name and rank printed out. Each had signed their name against their printed one. A round of toasts followed, and I thanked the crew. 'This is more treasure than gold,' I said.

Another round of toasts for the two crew members that were progressing up the ranks. Vitaliy would rise from Second Engineer to Chief Engineer.

Toasting was as before at Christmas, though we were more spread out in the crew mess. Many reasons came up for us to be once again on our feet and clinking glasses. We would move from our own table to the centre of the space, and clink glasses with the crew members from the other tables. By the end of the night I was fair worn out with all the exercise. German and Igor left the table around midnight. Andriy V went to take over duties on the bridge from Andriy K. Before he left for the evening, German asked me, 'Why do you not phone home?' 'What?' I said. Up went my eyebrows. I was not sure I had heard him correctly.

I spluttered, 'Phone home?'

'You mean nobody told you about this?' he asked.

'What?' I said again.

'About the satellite telephone. You can make phone calls.'

Igor interjected that you can buy credits with a phone card and make calls home. I was in a state of disbelief. German continued and told me the card cost $20 US for thirty minutes. 'It is worth it to speak to family,' I said. German told me to speak with Andriy V who had gone on duty. He would organise it, record the sale of a card for me and give me an access code. At this time it was around midnight, and we were two hours ahead of Greenwich Mean Time. I was desperate to phone right away, but decided to wait until I was sure everyone was gathered at my house. German took me over to the table across the room where there was a spare seat. I found myself beside Sergii whom I had sat beside at the Christmas banquet. Andriy K sat opposite. We had many conversations about religious beliefs, families, conditions and traditions in our countries, and we had laughs too. The best of these was when the shishlaki came round again. Andriy was highly amused at my word for these kebabs – *souvlaki.* He corrected me. *Shish.* Later, when we were talking about relationships and marriage, co-habiting and so on, he spoke of 'welding'. 'Welding?' I asked, eyebrows raised. 'Yes, welding,' he said. The penny dropped. 'Wedding!' I said. The staccato high pitch of amusement thrummed round the room.

At 3 am I went to the bridge. Andriy had company. A couple of crew members were blethering with him and having a laugh. He opened a ledger and wrote my name in it, then issued me with a number and instructions on how to use the phone on a small, white, square piece of paper. 'Thank you,' I said, feeling a lurch in my stomach. I could not wait to hear the reaction to my phoning my family to wish them *Happy New Year.* Andriy offered to dial for me, and I accepted. We got connected, but the voice at the end of the phone was a stranger, a woman with an English accent. As soon as I heard her, I apologised and said I had the wrong number. I wished her *Happy New Year* anyway, and she returned the greeting. After that both Andriy and I tried to connect to my home, without success. I was told to use the full telephone number for my house. I had wondered about the inclusion of the zero, as with connecting with phone numbers abroad the zero is dropped and an international dialling code for each country is substituted. For the United Kingdom it is +44. But this was a satellite system and an unusual situation. After a wait of half an hour to give time for lines at home to free up from the frantic New Year greetings of friends and relatives across the fibre optics, I tried two more times.

I gave up and went to bed, somewhat deflated.

DAY THIRTY-SEVEN

September 17, 1864 – Saturday

A rough day. The wind is favorable and we are going along well. I was not able to practise having burnt my finger with a match. In the evening we were unable to dance on account of the rolling.

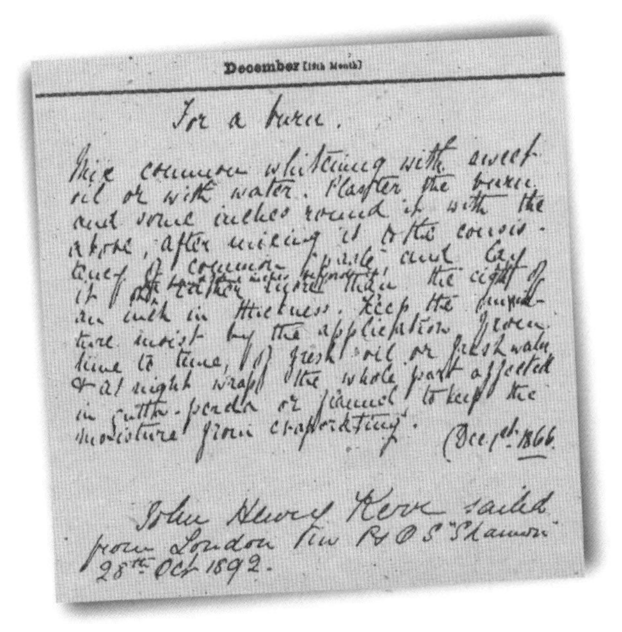

December (12th Month)

For a burn.

Mix common whitening with sweet oil or with water. Plaster the burn and some inches round it with the above, after mixing it to the consistency of common paste and lay it on rather more than the eighth of an inch in thickness. Keep the mixture moist by the application from time to time, of fresh oil or fresh water & at night wrap the whole part affected in gutta-percha or flannel to keep the moisture from evaporating. (Dec 1st 1866

John Henry Kerr sailed from London in R M S "Shannon" 28th Oct 1892.

Extract from Sarah Ann Bray's 1864 Diary – 'Dec 1st 1866

Cure for Burns

Mix common whitening with sweet oil or with water. Plaster the burn and some inches round it with the above, after mixing it to the consistency of common paste, and lay it on the hand and some inches beyond it rather more than the eighth of an inch in thickness. Keep the mixture moist by the application from time to time of fresh oil or fresh water & at night wrap the whole part affected in gutta-percha* or flannel to keep the moisture from evaporating.'

I wonder if this cure was used for her finger that she burnt with a match two-and-a-bit years previous.

**gutta-percha is made from the gum of a tree found in Malaysia (www.bbc.co.uk/news/magazine-30043875)*

1 January 2014 – Wednesday – Atlantic Ocean

A beautiful day. We are pitching and rolling a bit. There is a light breeze.

At the time Anatoliy and I were chatting two nights ago when he told me I was the only passenger in the nine years of working for Harren & Partner he had known of, apart from officers' wives, we passed St Helena at 7 pm. This is the island off the west coast of Africa where Napoleon was exiled and is buried. This is an extract from Sarah's diary, *Diary Notes from March 1866* from her voyage back to Britain on *The Murray*, for 19th March 1866. It was during this voyage Sarah got engaged to John S Kerr. She has used her same *Letts* diary to make entries from other years before and after 1864, as with her *Cure for Burns.*

> *"We arrived yesterday at St. Helena about 2 P.M. Papa and most of the gentlemen passengers went on shore and returned with a poor account of James Town. We anchored about half a mile from the town. This morning at 10.30 we left the ship and after about half an hour's row in a boat we landed at St. Helena, where horses and carriages were waiting for us. Blanche, Mr. Kerr, Mr. Henniker, Mr. Skelton and I went on horseback, Mama, Papa and some of the other passengers in carriages. We went direct to Longwood and (Napoleon's residence on the island) about five miles from James Town and nearly all the way up hill. It is a most peculiar barren looking island, only nine miles across, so at almost every turn in the road you have a view of the sea. There are several fine Summer residences of the Emperor Bonaparte and these have beautiful gardens with all kinds of tropical plants and shrubs. There are numbers of banana and palm trees with great bunches of fruit hanging from them.*
> *At Longwood we saw the rooms which Napoleon occupied, all comfortable looking and in good repair. In the one in which he died there is a beautiful marble bust, the cast of which was taken after his death. There is a large garden round the house. We afterwards rode to the Town about a mile and a half distant. This is one of the most beautiful spots on the island with cypress trees and geraniums growing in abundance. We returned by another road which took us all round the island. We then finished our ride with going up the principal street in James Town. There are only a few respectable buildings, the Church, Hospital & Post Office and two or three shops. Most of the houses are very poor and dirty. The people are of all colors from black to white though not many of the latter. Children and pigs were running about all over the place. Seven black-headed woolly little fellows accompanied us all the time (19 miles) though they cut off all the corners and jumped down the rocks which shortened the distance – they ran as fast as the horses cantered sometimes clinging on to their tails and always shouting and laughing. When we told them we did not want them with us they always answered "Masta lose im way". Blanchie and I had very quiet horses the only two on the island to be hired that would carry ladies. We returned to the 'Murray' about 6 P.M. quite delighted with our day on shore – Capt. Richards of the 'Nannon' dined with us and we had several visitors in the evening.*

March 23rd 1866
We sighted a ship this morning 'Edward Alfred' from London to Nova Scotia. We came close to her, saw the people on board and spoke with trumpets.

March 31st 1866
My birthday. We had Champagne for Dinner. The Captain proposed my health."

We passed Greenwich Meridian, so we have now changed longitude to East. Today's readings are latitude 23°19.23'S and longitude 001°05.48'E, wind speed 28.6 kph, speeding along at 12.9 knots on course 128, the temperature remains a steady 25°. German said he did not expect to see me today after last night's party. It was a quiet day due to the holiday, but I still want to keep my records. Lunch was left over pork from dinner last night, and prawns for those that wanted them. There was the same at suppertime, a massive cluster of prawns, with the addition of mountains of smoked salmon I had three generous slices of. I took a further three to my cabin to have for supper with the rye bread I have in the fridge from the other day. Whilst I was chatting to Anatoliy, Vitaliy passed by with a bottle of vodka on his way to the crew mess. The television was on and most, if not all, the crew were sitting watching something that was amusing them. Vitaliy invited me for a drink. I declined, but then thought it was not such a bad idea. I went through to the TV lounge and was ushered to sit beside young Ihor. They were watching *Shrek*. To hear *Shrek* in Russian is something else. One tune I heard was a Russian folk song. It was a Shrek film I have not seen, but I could follow what was left of it. The facial expressions and gestures or these inanimate characters are testament to the genius of artists and model-makers. Vitaliy offered me another vodka. I declined again, then reneged again. The young lads all said, 'Three,' with three fingers stuck up. This means it is tradition to have three drinks before stopping. Vitaliy respected the measure I indicated, and poured about a third of the small glass. He fetched a packet of dog chews. Ooops! Pork jerky. He almost begged me to try a piece, proffering a fairly small bit compared to those that were being chewed around the room. I took it between my thumb and forefinger, sniffed it and said, 'No thank you,' as politely as I could. Not long after this I went up to my cabin and had a beer, a snooze, then played Pinball, Solitaire and that infernal Minesweeper until taking to bed to read some more of *Master and Commander* before falling asleep.

Footnote On this day three years later in 1867, Sarah wrote in her diary of her brother's marriage:
On New Years Day at S. Paul's, Bedford by the Rev. M.F. Sadler, Vicar, assisted by the Rev. F. Pott, Rector of Northill, Beds, the Rev. T.W. Bray, Curate of Tapworth S. Agnes , Kent to Rachel, fourth daughter of the Rev. Henry Le Mesurier of Bedford.'

...and here she became an aunt –
Arthur Le Mesurier Bray, born 15th Sept 1868.

DAY THIRTY-EIGHT

September 18, 1864 – Sunday

A fine day but the sea very rough. I was quite sick in the morning. We had prayers on Deck. In the evening we sang and had a little music.

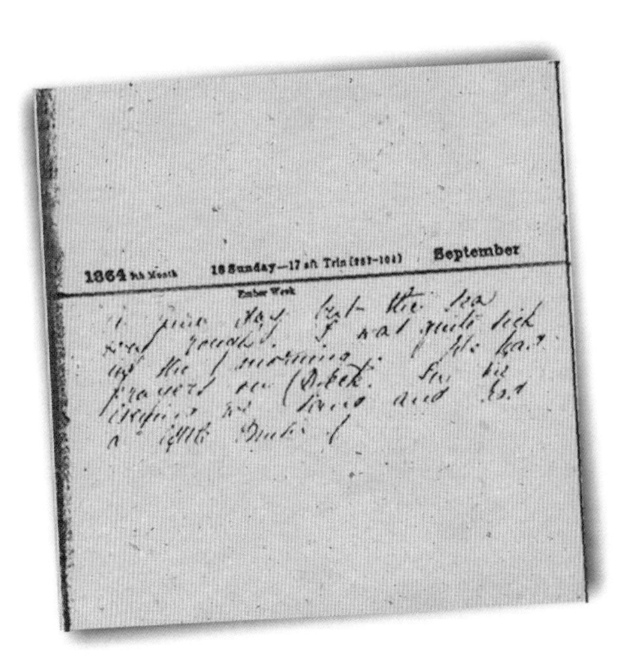

1864   18 Sunday—17 aft Trin   September

Ember Week

2 January 2014 – Thursday – Atlantic Ocean

A wild, wet start to the day, but by the time I got up the blue sky was dotted with puffy white clouds, and smears of pearl grey played with the sunlight.

Last night I felt a little pin prick on my big toe as I sat on the couch reading *Master and Commander*. I looked down and saw nothing, but became suspicious. On closer inspection of the blue linoleum, there was another of those tiny wee splinter-sized black beasts like the one I found a few weeks ago on the floor near my bed. I *knew* there would be more than just one. I squished it, just like I had its compadre. In case of my illness, you will find its squished DNA on a torn-off corner of a sheet of kitchen roll inserted between pages 264 and 265 of *Master and Commander* for identification. I made a brief reconnoitre of the battlefield and found no more adversaries. I decided to wash my bed-sheets, wash the floor, and do a general clean up.

The day began with the clanking that has been a regular feature of days recently. Now that the men have worked their way forward from the bow of *Palanpur* to the main deck, I can see what they are doing. Young apprentice Serhii was continuing to de-rust the D rings that the crane hooks link into, as described before. He was using a small grinder attached to an electrical drill and has a cute little four-legged stool to sit on. Bosun Anatolii was chipping away at loose yellow paint at the grooves where the opening hatch covers rest into the sides of the main deck. The men are certainly making up for their day of rest. They are wearing head covers similar to the bandannas pirates wore: a square scarf folded into a triangle by matching two opposite corners to each other. The smooth, long fold is spread across the forehead hairline and each end is led to the nape of the neck, where it is tied, with the triangulated point of the scarf held firm under the knot. This stops it from flapping in the breeze. The material is black, patterned with white skulls and crossbones and splashes of blood red.

I was not particularly hungry but decided to go for lunch in case I skip tea. I need to catch up on typing I did not do yesterday. I have written a few more poems to add to the collection that needs typed and edited. I have the Greenwich section to begin. I also need to press on with reading the rest of the first twenty-nine daily entries of this story. Ideally I would like to transcribe Sarah's diary in full, but for the now I am prioritising her voyage on *City of Adelaide*. Soup was served as usual, followed by those delicious specialties of Anatoliy's, chicken patties. He had made a tasty tomato sauce to accompany the pasta, and there was salad, less lettuce, more peppers. Valeriy was taking lunch, as was Andriy K. There was not much talk. I returned upstairs and tended the drying of the two loads of washing I had done earlier. It would take all afternoon to get the sheets dry. I have a spare set I will put on, but I need my one and only mattress cover to be dry. I popped up to the bridge for the readings: latitude 26°18.9'S, longitude 003°68'E. Temperature 25°. Our course continues around 130, at a speed of 12.4 knots with wind speed of 26 kph.

I cannot believe it. I was looking at some notes Sarah made in her *Letts Diary* 1864, page 2 and page 3, during her Grand Tour. There is a list of visits from 1863 at the beginning of this diary. This is what excited me:

June 5, 1863. I had my carta-de-visite taken at Deltonu's Avenue de l'Imperatuee. Went in the Jardin d'Accluisatation – in the Bois de Boulogne –, in the Aquarium –, we saw a sea-horse.

Sea-horse. The Equitorial name I hoped to be given, a short-form of *Gypsy Dragon of the Ocean Moon*.

Still no certificate from Andriy V, but I hope to visit the Aquarium in Cape Town.

I spent a good part of the day delving into Sarah's diary. I had a glass of wine after lunch and began typing up entries I found from her visit to Scotland. I was astonished to find she was at Greenock, where I first found out about *City of Adelaide*, then known as *Carrick*, in 1999; and Rosneath from where I sailed across the Clyde to see the ships taking part in that International Sail Training Association Tall Ships Race from water level. I was unknowingly following her.

In the end I did go for supper and was glad. Anatoliy had made salad, pork fillet dressed in breadcrumbs with mashed potatoes. Hooray! I had been craving mashed potatoes all day. We had a chat and he was saying how much he hates being a cook. He has been doing this job for nine years. Can you imagine? Nine years of cooking for goodness knows how many crew three times a day, and having to clear up afterwards, never mind all the preparation. I struggle to do this for my family when they all come visiting together, although I must say they tend to take over and I end up with just being in the way. Anatoliy told me he has written up his record book for signing off by the Chief Engineer. He works very hard and deserves to get on. He does not yet have flight details, only that he will be relieved on Sunday by another cook. If he is half as much fun and of interest as Anatoliy, he will be okay.

Apart from looking into Sarah's diary, I looked at the list of donors who have given funds towards *City of Adelaide*'s return to Adelaide, Australia. I was glad I had downloaded this from the website as, as you know, there is no internet access on board. The CSCOAL website has generated a good deal of money as will the latest fundraising campaign where donors can go along on this voyage in the virtual sense. I was impressed by the number of people who had donated to this round of fundraising: Jim Welsh saw *City of Adelaide* at Irvine, he will be in Adelaide when she arrives as he lives there now; John Bell from Paisley wished a safe voyage; Klaas Gaastra, Captain of the Barque *Europa* from Netherlands that I have seen many times on visits to the International Sail Training Association Tall Ships Race and on calendars I have been given as presents, said he would visit *City of Adelaide* in Adelaide in 2013. With the slippage in the original schedule for *City of Adelaide*'s arrival, this would not happen. I am sure they will return; Peter Morrison commented that his father had been Master of *Carrick* when she moved from Glasgow to Princes Dock. He still has the Pilotage Planning Papers and video of this occasion. I shall try to get in touch with him to see if I can see these papers for the next book.

The clock fast-forwarded again. Time for bed.

DAY THIRTY-NINE

September 19, 1864 – Monday

Bright day but the sea still rough. We are going about 10 knots an hour but rather too much to the westward. We saw 3 ships – one homeward bound, the other two we passed. One was so close that we saw some sailors in the rigging -. In the evening we danced and enjoyed ourselves very much. The sunset was magnificent. We saw the Southern Cross. It was nearly dark so we should have been unable to distinguish the signals and therefore had no intercourse with them. I played draughts with Mr. Sims and lost four games out of five.

3 January 2014 – Friday – Atlantic Ocean

The sea was a bolt of midnight blue velvet scattered with stardust this morning, graduating towards the horizon in shades of pewter. It has continued like this all day. My eyes and mind have been dazzled by the sparkles of sunlight flicking the peaks and troughs of the undulating mass of brine. The air is so pure and clear everything seems exaggerated in my eyes.

The men have been busy on the deck again today, a thankless task keeping the scabs from the scrapes with salt water at bay, picking them off to find smooth flesh beneath that can be anointed for a while against further scarring. The deck is covered in patches of paint, like little sticking plasters where rust has been removed and the area touched up. Off the main deck, at the sides that are painted dark blue, there are more patches that make the surrounding paintwork look tired. The noise from drills and tapping, and even hard banging against metal began in the early morning and went on for the full eight hours of the working day, until 5 pm. The men have a break for lunch at noon for an hour, and two twenty-minute coffee breaks, one at 10 am, the other at 3 pm. The outer doors have been closed to keep out noise. I kept my porthole open till late afternoon regardless: the air is delicious. Sometimes when I look at the sea, I think the choice of colour for these side walkways of *Palanpur* could not be improved upon. They lead the eye away beyond the rails towards the sea, and blend into it.

I went up to the bridge around 11.30 am to ask German if I could approach crew

members to sign an agreement for me to mention their names and any conversations we have had in the pages of this book, and also to publish group photos. I do not know if this is necessary, but I thought it would save a lot of running around in the future, if I find it is required by a publisher. I printed off copies. Master German Koltakov and 2nd Officer Andriy Vyshnyakov signed without hesitation. I took the rest of the forms down at suppertime and distributed them. Readings for today, latitude 28°56'S, longitude 009°27.06'E, wind speed 16.5 knots, going on course 125 at 13 knots per hour, with 25°C. I checked my emails and found one from Richard Smith, one of the CSCOAL Directors. He will be at Port Hedland, and will board *Palanpur* at that time to accompany *City of Adelaide* into Adelaide, South Australia.
It will be good to see him. We met at Greenwich for the *City of Adelaide* Renaming Ceremony from *Carrick*. He suggested I be ready to investigate some of the outback. I jokingly asked if there would be horses available for this. After lunch, gherkin soup, meatballs, pasta and salad, I re-checked the photo of my my e-visa on my phone. All okay. I am a bit paranoid about visas now. Happily, I will not need one to go ashore at Cape Town if I decide to do this. My legs might be too wobbly to cope with a brief land visit. We are only stopping for about eight hours to refuel. Valeriy said we would be taking on 650 tonnes of fuel. The tank holds 1000 tonnes. When Andriy V came in for his supper, beef risotto and salad, he asked what would happen if any crew member did not wish to sign the agreement. I said they would have to be excluded from the story, and their face cropped out of any photos. He said something about losers if they did not agree. We laughed.

Anatoliy is getting ready to pack this evening. He has his flight details now. I gave him an SD card I found after all these weeks at sea that has music from my son's collection recorded on to it, for him to download. I cannot work out how to get the music off the internal memory of my MP3 player to give him that as well. He will come up to my cabin tomorrow after lunch to see if he can work it out. I will also ask him if he can see why my camera will not let me format the microSD Vitaliy got me in Norfolk, Virginia, United States of America that came with an adapter converting it to ordinary SD size. We had a conversation about what we call meal times. I said I call it supper when we eat on *Palanpur* at 5 pm. At home this would be known as teatime. He says they call it *dinner*. I said we usually call a meal *dinner* when it is from 7.30 pm onwards, or when we go out for a meal to a restaurant, as in, *Would you like to go out for dinner?* After lunch I went for a very brief sunbathe on the roof. Andriy V said to keep to the middle. I wondered what he meant. He showed me the radio on the bridge and said he would put it off. I did not understand. He said it is safe, but there is radiation up there and extra care should be taken. I said I had already sunbathed up there a few times, and that I would be glowing in the dark. He also advised no more than half-an-hour in the sun. I was only intending going for ten minutes each side as the sun is very fierce. When I got to the roof I saw the radio mast amps at either end of the bridge. I had clocked them before, but never thought of the radiation aspect.

Not much else to report for today, other than another glorious sunset, with just a goose-feather of a moon floating in the azure sky, above a horizon radiant with the glow from the crucible of molten steel dipping below the blue.

DAY FORTY

September 20, 1864 – Tuesday

A lovely day. The sea is much smoother and we are going about six knots. I practised and read in the morning. For the first time all the passengers (24 in number) dined together in the Saloon.

On this date in 2013 I went to Irvine to see 'City of Adelaide' leave by being towed on a barge to Greenwich, London. I took this extract from Sarah Ann Bray's diary and read it out to the crowds in front of 'City of Adelaide'. You will have read about this in the Irvine section of this book.

4 January 2014 – Saturday – Atlantic Ocean

A beautiful day but a big swell on the sea. We are pitching and rolling a lot.

I almost bumped my head against the corner of the shower. I gave the cabin a major clean up, washing the floors, dusting everywhere, and wiping down the couch that had some Nivea smears on it from where I had been sitting after sunbathing. I hand-washed a few garments and took some others up to the washing machine that I later put into the drier. I went up to the bridge to photocopy the signed agreements from the Chief Officer and Anatoliy to give them a copy, but neither of them wanted one. Igor has his flight details through. He is travelling on 7 January via Paris Charles de Gaulle airport. He would have preferred to go via Frankfurt or Heathrow. He and Anatoliy will be staying in Cape Town in a hotel till then. This means they could visit Table Mountain and the Aquarium. German had suggested a week or so ago that it might be possible for him and I to visit this in shore time that might be available whilst bunkering happened. Igor put two pictures of the group photograph of the crew from Old Year's Night onto the bridge computer to be shared. I spoke to Andriy V about Cape Town, mentioning the marina and waterfront one of the crew had told me about. 'It was me,' he said, and reiterated how fine it is. I had a look at the logbook to check a longitude line I had missed recording the other day. I could just have looked in this every day instead of taking readings myself. I have stopped taking readings at more or less set times. Today we are at latitude 32°28'S, longitude 014°30'E, wind speed 13.3 kph. We have changed course to 181 to compensate for the swell, as the ship was rolling around quite violently. It still is. Several chairs scraped across the bridge floor. I was thrown off my footing and went bowling out of control across the bridge at a tangent. I just managed to save myself from slamming into the walls by hooking my arm round a pillar and clinging to it. Andriy altered course because if the ship rolls at an angle of 60°, this puts stress on the lashings holding the cargo down on the decks and risks its loss. We are travelling at 13-14 knots and temperature 25°. German arrived to see what was happening. I went down to lunch, Eintopf. I did not bother with the fish as I was full up. After lunch Anatoliy checked about coming up to help with the technical headaches I have been having with these new SD cards. I said he had enough to do with packing and so on, but he said this was okay. He brought some Ukrainian folk music for me and uploaded that. He formatted the SD cards at my request, as my old Kodak camera had been giving the message that this needed done. I think old technology is not meeting new technology here and the need for me to upgrade my old equipment is becoming imperative. I really like my camera though, it takes great pictures, and you might have picked up that I hang on to things that I am familiar with. It took about fifty minutes to get through all this nonsense. Anatoliy saw the picture of my family on my desktop and remarked at how strong my mother looked. This gave me great pleasure. He reckons I will also make it to the grand old stage of being an octogenarian, and I was grateful. I complimented him on the energy he has for taking on so much extra work whilst holding down cooking three times a day for the whole crew, studying for a change in career to become an electrician, being good with computers and working on finishing his new apartment when he is at home.

I had an email from Alan giving me bits of news on the home front. He told me Michael Schumacher is in a coma following an accident whilst skiing, suffering major head injuries. It is ironic that after all these years of being a champion Formula One racing driver, he has fallen foul of snow. I mentioned this to German and Igor. They had heard this news on the ship's system. Bad news came from German's mouth. No one is having shore leave tomorrow. There are no passes. I felt a rush of blood to my head. This subsided a little when he said we could go ashore to the seamen's refuge, where there is internet access. He made a joke about us being prisoners on this ship whilst ships like *City of Adelaide* took prisoners to Australia. I corrected him. *City of Adelaide* was specifically built to take migrants to South Australia, not prisoners. They are very proud that the State of South Australia was not built on the backs of people transported for misdemeanours. There is a waterfront of shops just outside the boundaries of the port. This is really frustrating. 'They sell diamonds there,' German said. I joked. 'I have no need for more diamonds, I have more than enough to cope with already.' I told them my son had spent three months in Namibia, and that during the environmental contingent of the work with Raleigh International in the Spergebeit diamond fields that have been closed for over a hundred years, he had discovered three ostrich eggs San Bushmen had blown out, filled with water and then stuffed the holes with dried grass. They then stashed them as water reserves for use when trekking the desert. He had looked over a ledge and there they were, in a little nest, or maybe not so little, given the size of the eggs. An archaelogist had been very excited about this find. He had been searching for ten years to find one such intact egg, and here were three. One of them had even been etched. I told Igor and German the story had made the local papers, and even back to Scotland where he was interviewed for the local Press who had then fed the story to the nationals.

I asked German if we could take another photo of the crew this evening so that *City of Adelaide* would be seen in the background, before Igor and Anatoliy leave tomorrow. He was happy to do this and suggested tomorrow morning might be a better time. He later changed it to 7 pm this evening with another possible photo call in the morning. We talked about this as I thought the men would be busy with bunkering, and border control would be on board. I said I had cleaned my cabin ready for the big search. He said 'What do you mean?' I said they will be looking for drugs and so on. He said not, they would be using sniffer dogs to search for illegal native Africans on board. I was thinking about how impolitically correct Sarah's remarks about the little children on St Helena were by today's standards.

A few more of my forms were returned to me. The youngsters are not so forthcoming with their signatures. Perhaps I will explain more about what it is all about in case reading my language is obstructive, or maybe they are just tired. They were working hard this morning in the hot sun, continuing the deck's facelift. Supper time soon came round with all this afternoon's messing about with photographs and technology. I was hungry and had a cup of coffee and a few of my replenished supply of tinned biscuits to keep me going. I have not drunk coffee for over a week. I lost the appetite for it, but really enjoyed that cuppa.

I took my camera down to supper. I tried to take some photos of Anatoliy but the camera would not switch on. I had put the new micro SD card into an adapter that upsized it to normal SD card size to make it fit into the camera. I went back to my cabin and got a different SD card. This turned out to be full, with the music Anatoliy had given me. So I went back up again. This is the most exercise I have had for weeks. I ended up using my phone. We cracked a few jokes whilst taking the photos. He said it was like being photographed for *Playboy* magazine. I said the circumstances would have to be a bit different for that. *Laughter*. I asked him to smile some more. He said if he did he would tear his face. I got some great shots of him serving up food, and more of him grasping his ticket and passport for his going home. I managed somehow to save the photos to the hard drive. Since the phone is reluctant to give up images stored there, this is a nuisance that I can only fix when I get home, I think. After this I ate the pasta and stir-fried beef, but left the salad based on red cabbage, just picking out a few strands of green and yellow peppers. I went up to my cabin, cleared the full SD card, changed the battery in the Kodak camera in readiness. I went down to the deck where several crew members were assembled, all having good chats in the beautiful evening sunshine. It felt like a holiday. They obligingly took up position with *City of Adelaide* in the background. A large white cloud made it look like she was coming out from the ether. It looked really effective and appropriate for this ghost ship from one hundred and fifty years ago. I took several shots, others took photos too, and then some were taken of me with the crew. I appreciated this immensely.

German asked me to come to the bridge with him and Igor after this to look at the photos. Andriy K was on watch. Igor showed me a photo he had been looking for earlier that he had taken on Old Year's Night. He had accidentally put the setting onto cartoon. We had a great laugh at the image. I joked if any of the crew do not sign the agreement, I will make them into cartoons. We all ended up having a great blether about Ukraine, the differences between the east and west, where L'viv is. My father used to speak of the Carpathian mountains and was very much endeared to that land, permanently homesick for it. We talked about how my father got his ice cream van and how he built up a business to end up owning a café. He met much kindness and encouragement from Scottish people, in particular a garage owner and a butcher in my hometown who helped him get on in life. German told me about a summer school scheme his daughter takes part in. He thought this might be of interest to my children to give them an opportunity to go to Ukraine as tutors for evening activities once the day's teaching of English was over. He is going to obtain the website from his daughter to pass on to me. Igor told me about the wonderful forests and a reservoir that creates hydro-electric power, and described the varying levels and widths of the water. We talked a lot about language, fathers, boarding school and how important horses had been to me when I was there.

I went back to my cabin and cracked open a beer, one of two that I had taken from a case that had been given to the crew in both messes after supper. I have improved on the common technique used by crew members to open a bottle. They prise the bottle tops off in one fell swoop with the end of a dessert spoon handle, causing a cascade of froth to spew forth from the mouth of the brown bottle that has to be slurped till the actual beer is reached. A bottle top has been known to fly across the room if not capped by the thumb of the other hand. My method is to first ease the end of a teaspoon under the edge of a bottle top, then work it round under each fluted edge that effects a slow release of gas, before transferring to use a dessertspoon when the gap is big enough. Thus the top is removed in a controlled way and a fountain of bubbles is quashed. *Cheers!*

DAY FORTY-ONE

September 21, 1864 – Wednesday – St Matthew. Ember Day.

A fine day. The ship scarcely moving. In the morning about 10 we saw a Shark. The sailors succeeding in catching it just before noon, with a large iron hook and a piece of salt pork as bait. There were a great many pilot fish swimming about with it. They are very pretty, with alternate blue and black stripes across them. In the evening we had dancing and singing on Deck. The Captain joined us in 'Auld Lang Syne' which we had in the true Scotch fashion – all taking hold of hands at the last verse.

5 January 2014 – Sunday – Atlantic Ocean and Cape Town!

A rough, heavy swell, wet night gave way as we approached Cape Town port for arrival between 8 and 9 am.

I hopped out of bed and went for a shower at 7.45 am, then went straight to the bridge to watch the docking action. Andriy K's eyes widened. He tapped his watch and said, 'Wow.' 'Cheeky,' I said, eyes glinting. Two tugs, one near at the bow, the other at the stern, the far end of *Palanpur*'s hull, each fixing on like two wee twins suckling their mother's breast. They gently nudged her towards the rubber tyres that protected her hull from scraping against the dockside wall. Stevedores received the lines thrown ashore with the monkey's fist knots adding weight for their sure arrival.

Ordinary Seaman Sergiy Fomin had this duty and his aim was true. Each massive twisted hemp rope was dragged from the hawse holes through the water by these lines before being looped over the bollard on the dockside before the bow. The stern was far off and I could not watch this operation without binoculars. A gentleman wearing an English accent, white shirt and naval trousers was directing mooring operations with the use of two-way radio, an old sea salt by the look of him. He was interested in *City of Adelaide* and German invited me to give him some information. 'If I'd known I would have brought my camera,' he said. I told him about the *City of Adelaide* website and encouraged him to look at it. Someone was calling him away on his mobile phone, but he was having his cup of coffee. German showed him photographs I had given him for the *Palanpur* local network, in particular the cake from the Renaming Ceremony. He noticed the image of the Duke of Edinburgh and the captain who was with him. 'Who is that?' he asked. 'An honorary captain of *City of Adelaide*,' I replied. 'A very smart uniform,' he said. There was no time to tell him of the event at Greenwich in October. He left, and I poured myself a cup of coffee.

Andriy K summoned me to the seating area on the bridge where German was with the border control officer. German asked him about facilities within the port. He responded that there was a Seamen's Mission and that was all. The agent, Peter Whitmore pointed out the seafront shopping area and Aquarium that were within eyeshot. He pointed out a reddish crane and the mini version of the London Eye as landmarks. German asked him if it was possible for me to go ashore for the day. What? My heart jerked so hard it almost broke out from my chest. Too calm, he said, 'Not a problem.' My head exploded. I barely heard him say that he would take me to Immigration and then on to the shopping complex. Never in my wildest dreams did I think I would be here in South Africa. Was this a dream? No. This was real. There was the mass of Table Mountain overlooking Cape Town, with her head in the clouds bumping against mine. Land. Land after six weeks! I wondered if I would be able to cope with a steady horizon and *terra firma*. I would need my passport that German held. I said to Peter I would need a few minutes to get things from my cabin. I took an allowance of dollars and my credit card, pulled out my backpack that I use as a hand-bag. I had not seen it for weeks. I stuffed my netbook and its cable in for internet access along with my phone that was not fully charged, then headed for the weather deck where we had arranged to meet. Peter had taken in hand the arrangements. He did not know if and when the Seamen's Mission opened on a Sunday. He suggested he take me to Immigration just beside the Seamen's Mission, and we could find out opening times then.

He did not notice the gangway bounce with the spring in my step as I crossed over the spread of *no man's land* between ship and shore. I swung into the passenger seat of his car as he held the door open. I clicked myself beneath the seat belt as he clicked on the engine. Everything felt strange. The ground was as the sea; unstill. We murmured our way to the Seamen's Mission. It turned out it opened between 3.30 pm and 10.00 pm on Sundays, so the decision to go into Cape Town first was clinched. Internet access would have to wait. He would take me to town and drop me off. We exchanged phone numbers to make contact for a pick-up time later in the day if he was available. He had another ship to deal with and other duties that would involve him going back to his office. He told me that if he was not able to come back for me, I should get a taxi from the waterfront, making sure it was authorised for access to within the Port boundaries, then clear myself for departure from Cape Town with Immigration. He emphasised that it was imperative I do this because it would cause tremendous problems if I did not. He said I could hold the taxi whilst I checked out, or later, if I went to use the internet, I should ask the Seamen's Mission minibus driver to take me to Landing Wall One. I wrote all this down with beads of sweat forming on my forehead and heat coursing through my body. So many instructions. What if I got lost, got it wrong? I had done quite a bit of travelling on my own, but this was different. I had a whole ship to consider, her schedule, her crew, my day's visa limitations, additional costs and inconvenience to the shipping company. The last thing I wanted was to upset anything. The last thing I wanted was to be stranded. The last thing I wanted was to end up in jail in this foreign land for being an illegal immigrant.

Peter had administrative duties to carry out at Immigration: Arrival Passenger List, Arrival Crew List, Letter Written By Agent – a pro forma requesting a visa for me, arrival time of *Palanpur* at Cape Town, given as 9 am. Peter is a laid back, organised man with a very methodical, logical line of thinking. He has a mild manner and I wondered if anything ever fazed him. A couple of stamps in my passport from a local female border control officer and we were on our way to Cape Town city. We chatted on the way. We passed the pink and white façade of the Cape Brace Hotel where, he pointed out, celebrities and royalty stay. There were colonnades, windows with shutters on the inside, and huge concrete champagne-like buckets with massive red ribbons tied around them. Certainly not litter bins for Mr Ordinary Joe. I take a guess and say they light up inside with bulbs, and are fitted with cloth made to flutter in a jet of air to make them look as though they are huge flaming torches at night time. Peter dropped me off at the entrance to where the Aquarium is. I asked if he had ever been there. He hesitated and said, 'A long time ago.' I thanked him and made my way casually along the harbour edge, photographing trimarans, luxury motor yachts and an assortment of sailing yachts all moored up with their masts standing to attention like a battalion of soldiers with fixed bayonets. I noticed a seal rescue advertising board. It had graphic images of seals who had got their heads stuck in bait box bands, fishing line, raffia cord and rope. As the seals grew, their necks became strangulated by these horrible nooses, causing serious injury and death, if they were not cut through in time. I looked at an adult and young seal basking in the sun on the deck they had made just for this purpose. I often wondered what happened to Peter Sarstedt. When I was a teenager he was one of my idols. My first concert was when I went to see him in Edinburgh at the peak of his fame when *Where Do You Go To My Lovely* and *I'll Buy You One More Frozen Orange Juice* were big hits we had in our café jukebox. There he was. Right on the Sappi poster. He had played at the Two Oceans Aquarium on 30 September 2010 to raise funds for a platform, where seal teams of the Two Oceans Aquarium and Oceans and Coast snorkel together to cut nooses off the seals and to tag them. They swim under the platforms and snip the nooses off the basking seals from below. You can find out more on www.sappi.com. I was glad to see my idol was still performing and delighted he was raising money for such a worthy cause. I noted some water attractions advertised on another board, and made my way to the Two Oceans Aquarium, that is reputedly the second-best in the world. I could not see where the entrance was. There was a series of windows and a door, but not an entrance. I asked at the café next door; it turned out to be the way to gain access. After a short wait in a queue, I was inside. The first attraction was a water-filled cylinder about three-to-four feet across. It was dazzling with swimming jewels of all sizes, colours and shapes: triangles, elongated, spotty, stripy, crazy paving; black, vibrant blue, yellow, gold, white, indigo. A tiny shadow of a woman passed, dressed in black from head to foot. All that was exposed were her sun-filled eyes peering out from a slit in her headgear. The next cylinder was filled with clown fish. There was a tunnel to duck through that led children and even some adults, no more than two at a time, inside the double-skinned tube to stand or crouch so that the fish were swimming around their heads. It must have been mesmeric, and at least it gave the fish a change of scenery. They were probably just as amused by these faces as the faces were by them.

I went into the *Atlantic* section since that is where I have spent nearly the last six weeks of my life. There was a wave tank filled with convicts in striped uniform that were regularly doused with artificial waves. Starfish sucking onto the glass and lying in sand at the bottom of the tank made this whole scene one for the United States of America, with its stars and stripes. The next tank had visitors a bit puzzled. A lady asked me what was going on in it. I would not have known if I had not just glanced at the label above the tank saying it housed a worm. A tube winding round in the tank had been sliced open to form a burrow for the worm, the open side presenting it to visitors. I pointed it out to her, saying 'boring.' I wondered if it ever moved. In the next tank were the tiniest Strawberry Anemones in Barbie pink and a cute little crab stroking its tendrils. *Hello, Dolly*. It is not known whether this next creature whose fingers filter food is plant or animal. Black starfish shared this tank, looking like fat, blown-up rubber gloves with skinny, wiry fingers. Then there were cuttle fish, said to have the largest brain to body size of all invertebrates. We used to give the skeletons of these to our canary, Rico, when I was a wee girl, to keep his beak in trim. Hideous hagfish were next and just to compare beast with beauty, the next tank was delectable.

Small, transparent jellyfish pulsated through the water, winking like mares in season, propelling themselves around the tank, looking like little atomic explosions or mushrooms, or dandelion seeds parachuting upwards, their fine fronds trailing behind them. 'Completely beautiful,' said a little girl behind me who looked about ten years old. She hit it on the nail. Someone else remarked that they bet these tiny, delicate beauties had a nasty sting. Museum staff had placed lamps in one of the tanks that made it look like they were changing colour like chameleons, only in day-glo colours. A tank full of Pinocchios with long pointed noses was labelled *Cryptic Fish.* Other labels in this area made up parts of the body: Sole, Tongue-Fish and Roving Eye. Massive starfish clung to an artificial tree root beyond the glass. The ones that clung to the glass had their faces wiped with a polishing cloth by a member of staff.

Knys Hippocampus carpensis were next. These ponderous sea horses are green to brown in colour and grow to about 12 centimetres in length. They are under threat. They must gallop away from human disturbance and pollution. They looked so at peace with themselves, bowing, nodding, fanning their tails and gills, linking tails in a loving caress. In the next tank Puffer fish blown up with their own self-importance pouted around beneath soft white clouds on a dark grey sky and silver seas. Ragged tooth sharks glided past, glinting us a cheesy grin. Rock lobster and South-West Lobster share a tank. The Rock Lobster's appetite for Sea Urchins was held responsible for their decline in 1994. This had a detrimental effect on Abalone as the spines of the Sea Urchins provided a nursery with protection for their youngsters. You can see how ecology is finely balanced. The Giant Spider Crab looked to me like King Neptune might, with its haughty expression and a simulated long bushy beard. In a large tall tank were housed the rays, or skate. They fluttered past saying, *I am the butterfly of the sea.* They landed in the sand like metal detectors or hoovers, blowing and sucking kisses of life, their upright tails like handles. Some were stuck to the glass, smiling out at their audience with pleasant little faces that said, *Look at me.* They reminded me of *Weed* from the *Bill & Ben The Flower Pot Men* television series in the 1950s. I came to the touch pool where fingers met fingers, but not mine. Then came mole snakes and dour-faced silver-striped fish glinting amongst the forests of kelp. The mesmeric motion of this tank reminded me of being on board *Palanpur.* Some fish looked as though they would happily head-bang each other with their big square foreheads, but somehow they never did. I came across a sign that read, *If people are the problem, then people are also the solution.* A child was running along beside a medium-sized shark in the next large tank. It looked as though they were holding hands. I passed the Yellowtail and Rock Cod on the way to the exit, wondering if they ever got dizzy. I bought several postcards and stamps at the merchandising shop, a couple of knitted hats for my girls with *Cape Town* embroidered on them, and a pink frilled-at-the-edges t-shirt for my granddaughter with *Someone who l♥ves me bought me this t-shirt at the Two Oceans Aquarium* printed on it.

I stepped outside and noticed the city bus tour. These tours are an excellent way of having a synopsis of a city in a short time and for not a great deal of money. The board enticed the reader to take the red route or the blue route. The red route went through the city, then up to Table Mountain and on to four beaches as part of a coastal route. The duration of this was two hours and would be all I could afford in time. There was also the option to take an aquatic sightseeing tour for an extra seven rand, approximately fifty pence. This would have been nice, but I was on restricted time. I bought my red route ticket, a bottle of water, some packets of sweets for the crew for the next gathering when we would all be together bar one, who had to mind the bridge, and a chocolate bar with toffee and peanuts through it. I joined a queue, presented my ticket and hopped on the bus. I made my way to the open part of the top deck for the best view, stuck the headphones over my ears and made sure the language setting was *English.* Some African music sang in my ears till it paused for each new description relevant to whatever attraction we passed. We were told that Cape Town harbour has been expanded through land reclamation. We were told of the three sections of Table Mountain: legend has it that Jan van Hunks, an early 18th century pirate retired from the sea to live on the slopes of Devil's Peak that flanks Table Mountain on the east side. He entered a pipe smoking contest with a stranger that lasted several days. Clouds built up from their smoke, these were blown by a strong wind towards the town. Van Hunks won the competition and the stranger revealed himself as the Devil, giving the name to the Peak. The two disappeared in a puff of smoke and the cloud of smoke left behind became Table Mountain's tablecloth that spills over the mountain when summer south-easterlies blow. Lion's Head is between Table Mountain and Signal Hill that forms the Lion's Tail, together making a crouching lion, or a sphinx.

When the bus stopped I could feel the heat of the sun. We passed Cape Town International Convention Centre that helped put the city on the world stage. We were told that the cable car up Table Mountain is the third most popular attraction in Africa. We were told that in 1488 Vasquez claimed the Cape for Portugal, and this influence is reflected by the food that is available locally. There was an attempt to have a penal colony set up at Cape Town but there was such strong resistance to this that the ship was forced on to Australia. I saw a sign for *Sleeping Beauty on Ice.* We then passed the railway station. I would love to have hopped off the bus to see the steam locomotive imported from Scotland on display here. I could have then hopped on to the next City tour bus that came along, as there is a fleet of them that leave within several minutes of each other to allow tourists to stagger their tour in order to visit attractions along the way. I did not risk the time I would lose. We passed Woolworth's, long demised in Scotland. Strand Street is so called because it used to be a beach. We were told that the City centre is good for arts and crafts, but there was a warning to be careful after dark and not go off the beaten track.

In 1696 Green Market Square used to sell vegetables and fruit. Now it is a place of entertainment where street theatre can be seen, such as jugglers. I saw a spire with a weather vane, very much in the Scottish style. Cape Jazz sounded a must-see, but not for me this time round. It is a mecca for musicians and I longed to hear the flavour. There is a museum that documents the slave trade. We passed Mandela Rhodes Place where residential apartments are helping regenerate the area. A song about Nelson Mandela rang in my ears. We passed the oldest garden in Cape Town, The Company Garden, established by the Dutch East India Company using water from Table

Mountain, that was also used to supply ships with fresh drinking water. We passed the Planetarium and Museum, where there is stuffed Guagga, a zebra-type animal that is now extinct, but was not at the time Sarah made her voyage. This last mare died in 1883, and can be seen in the Naturalis Museum in Leiden, Holland. We passed the University of Cape Town and the Pink Lady and Mount Nelson Hotels. I believe I heard the man in my ear say the (United Kingdom) *Sunday Times* holds that the best afternoon tea in the world can be had here. Next was the other entrance to The Company Garden and two Jewish exhibition centres that show first class footage from the life of Nelson Mandela. The Chief Rabi is quoted as saying he is the best role model for any human being. These may not be the exact words, for I was scribbling as fast as I could but the bus would not wait for me to finish before the next attraction was aiming at my ears.

Outside the Parliament building there is a statue of Louis Botha Boer, 1862-1919, who was the first prime minister, *Krysman, Staatsman.* I ponder as I type that he is a contemporary of Sarah, and had *City of Adelaide* called in to Cape Town, they might have met. District 6 came next. This is an area originally named in 1867 as the *Sixth Municipal District of Cape Town* that grew after slaves were freed in 1833 and was razed to the ground in 1901 after an outbreak of bubonic plague. From those ashes grew a community made up of former slaves, artisans, merchants and immigrants that thrived until apartheid became prevalent. New plans were made, mostly non-white residents were moved out, houses demolished, and the socio-economics changed overnight. 85% of the area is now wasteland. There was no stomach for demolishing the churches and mosque that still exist. In 1994 new flats were built and the first twenty-four families were housed. That had not been expanded on, but new houses are being built now. I looked about and saw Table Mountain. Its sheer drop from the top reminded me of The Crags in Queen's Park in Edinburgh.

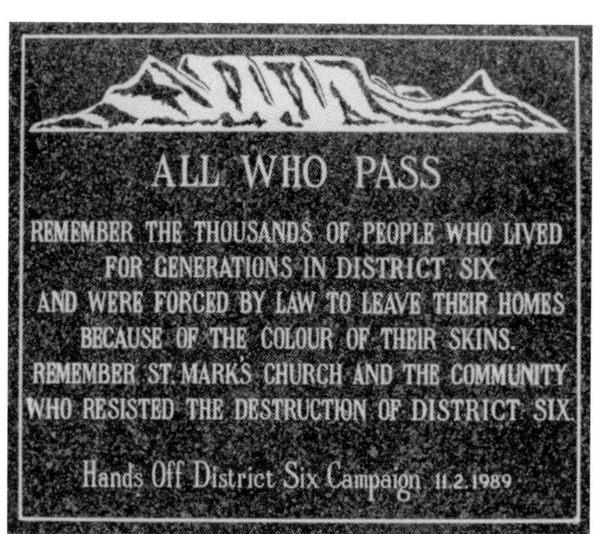

By the time we got to Woodstock we learned that this is the oldest residential area now, and it is undergoing regeneration. With reduced rates, the film-making and media industries are growing here. There is a great market selling fresh produce, but our guide advised to get there before 10 am because all the good stuff would be sold by then. We passed the Castle of Good Hope, the oldest standing building in South Africa. It was built between 1666 and 1679 as a monument to Willem, Prince of Orange by the Dutch East India Company in a 5-point star shape, each one representing his five main titles. There is a ghost that rings the castle bell, announcing the museum. Nearby is a large football stadium where FIFA World Cup took place in 2010. Peter Sarstedt and the World Cup all in one year! At the Clock Tower built in 1905 Nelson Mandela, or *Madiba* as he is called with affection by many, spoke here to around 2000 people on 11 February 1990 on his release from prison. He is quoted as saying, 'I greet you all in the name of peace, democracy and freedom for all' on the tape. I looked out to see a man on the street carrying a placard saying, *Cash for Gold.* The man in my ear continued. Flower sellers used to be strawberry sellers and this business is handed down from generation to generation. Horses and carriages used to go by in their hundreds. The advent of cars brought comments that they would be a whim, a passing phase because they were always breaking down and being unreliable.

Another stop I would have liked to see was the Gold of Africa Museum that is, surprisingly, filled with gold. If you go in you can receive a glass of wine with a fine dusting of gold leaf floating on top. The South Africa Diamond Factory is a place where you can browse through thousands of diamonds. We heard that local people like to pack a picnic in the evenings when there is a full moon and climb Table Mountain to watch it in its magnificence. Hang gliders swoop off the mountain in flocks of coloured kites. There is an area that is the most bio-diverse in the world where 8,600 species, some unique, thrive. Our guide drew our attention to the *salt, pepper and mustard* tower blocks whose architect had found a loophole in legislation that buildings could only be built to a certain height. This had enabled him to construct apartment blocks that towered up towards Table Mountain, well above any other building. It is known that some people call this *architectural terrorism.* It is not the first time I have heard this term. Our Scottish Parliament wears a similar badge in some people's eyes. On the way down our eyes were directed to two guns that were positioned to deter the British. I have had a taste of gun battles that took place between the marauding British against the Spanish, French and other nationalities in *Master & Commander*, and these guns looked insignificant for the job they were expected to do, though their vantage point would be of some help in defending their City.

We had stopped a little before this for people to step off the bus for a comfort break and to spend money at the tourist shop, or for a journey in the cable car to a greater height on Table Mountain. I am not sure whether it went right to the top. Again, I was itching to experience this, but in a way was glad I would not have to fight off butterflies swarming in my belly at the thought of dangling so high in the air suspended by steel. For now the adrenalin rushes I am having on board *Palanpur* with *City of Adelaide* are sufficient. I zoomed in with my phone camera from the giddy heights we were at and could just make out *Palanpur* and her two golden towers of strength guarding *City of*

Adelaide in the afternoon sun. We headed down to Camps Bay and were told of the Twelve Apostles that channel the wind down to the sea and keep the air of Cape Town clean. There are four Clifton beaches, each providing a different feature and so attracting different groups of people according to their desires, such as strength of waves for surfers, accessibility for young families and older people, those who want to play volleyball. We were told Leonardo di Caprio, other celebrities and royalty spend time at the beaches and photo-shoots take place, especially at 4th Beach. For me the closest I got to surfing was being pelted by raindrops the size of marbles, them bursting, lashing my cheeks and soaking me through within a couple of minutes. I might just as well have dived into those breakers on the beach. I waited for the rain to stop. It did not. I was forced to take cover inside. No room under the short roof at the top of the bus. I had to go downstairs where a kind Muslim woman took her not-so-small child on to her lap and made space for me to sit. Someone plugged my earphones into the system provided for *standing room only* passengers, and I was back on the tour. More mention was made of the Twelve Apostles, and the granite boulders that made this beach wind-free. Cobblers' Bay was founded in 1890, again within Sarah's lifetime. This was named after a cobbler who deserted from the Dutch East India Company and lived in the caves here. He made shoes for farmers passing on their way to market. He ended up being sent to the castle. We learned of corrugated huts that provided emergency housing for WWI soldiers, and expensive private houses built into rock, with a funicular access. In the sea there are Kelp forests, our guide extolling the virtues of these dark brown wavy fronds, also known as Sea Bamboo. We passed the Marine Institute before we were told of unscrupulous housing sales agents who tried to sell property in this area as being in the wind-free zone. 'Take a look at the trees,' he invited, and we saw their distortion by the wind. I saw a Staffordshire Bull Terrier on a lead and a tear sprang into my eye at the thought of my dogs at home, Mister Marley and Zac.

You can have a great Jazz Breakfast at Winchester Mansions Hotel. Not sure I could cope at that time of day, though no doubt it would zing you up. I saw a sign for Norfolk but did not try to get ashore. How the names of towns from Great Britain travelled. Robben Island is where Madiba was held for nineteen years. It also imprisoned people from the Cape and political prisoners from the East Indies. It was a maximum security prison until 1991. It was also a pit stop for ships. The Lighthouse at Green Point is known as *Moaning Minnie.* Approximately 2,700 vessels have been lost here with it being the most dangerous leeward anchorage in the world. At Fort Wyngard we see the guns outside the Stadium. There is the former Groote Schuur Hospital that is now a museum, where Dr Christiaan Barnard performed the first heart transplant operation in the world. We could see the landmark wheel that Peter Whitmore had pointed out in the morning, where the 450 shops and 85 eateries and the working harbour all sit in harmony. We passed the Red Time Ball that falls at 1 pm for ships' captains to reset their chronometers while at sea. I have seen this same feature at Greenwich Naval College, London, and watched it fall and rise. In Edinburgh the cannon *Mons Meg* is fired from the Castle Walls at 1 pm for people to set their chronometers by at the same time that the Time Ball that was installed in

1852 on Nelson's Monument on Calton Hill, built in 1807, drops. This visual and audible signal enabled captains to calculate longitude, so they could find the most efficient route at sea.

I got off the bus back down at the terminus and sat at a picnic table to continue writing the postcards I had bought in the Aquarium. The comfort break on Table Mountain is where I began to write them. Now I had a limited time to complete and post them to Adrian Small, Hugh Loney and family and a couple of friends. I put them in the bag beside the things I had bought in the Aquarium and hit the shops. And what shops. I saw ostrich eggs carved right through with lovely shapes and scenes and lit from inside to make them into lamps. I lingered to look at some jewellery and walked past a whole area dedicated to children's clothing. There were numerous cafés packed with people clouded with chatter. I exchanged some dollars at a Bureau de Change and went to the loo for a freshen up. When I came out I went straight to Woolworths where my phone rang. It was Peter Whitmore, asking when I expected to be back at Immigration. Before I could give a time we were cut off. My phone credit report came in. 60p left. I managed to send Peter a text and arranged 6.30 pm. My battery was critically low with all the photographs and videos I had taken. It was a double whammy. If I topped up my phone with credit, it was going to die anyway, with no battery. Had the phone not cut out there would have been time for negotiation. As it was I went to another shop where I got sun cream for Australia, 50 and 40 strength to start me off, two packets of rusks with seeds through them, another SD card, the last one on the stand that would suit my video camera, and a couple of mixed nut and seed bars. I stood in a long queue, spent nearly 400 Rand and made for the taxi rank.

There was an obese African man directing people to taxis. 'Where do you want to go?' he said in broken English. 'I need a taxi that has permission to access the Port,' I replied. He looked around, then walked away. A taxi driver nearby came over. 'Where do you want to go?' 'Landing Wall One in the Port,' I replied. 'I can take you there,' he said. We chatted on the way. He had spent four years in England, I cannot remember the name of the town, I had never heard of it. We went through the security gate to Immigration. He asked me if I wanted him to wait and I said, 'Thank you, no. I want to try to get internet access in the Seamen's Mission.' I gave him a reasonable tip, reserving some cash to pay for the internet, and thanked him with good wishes.

I went into Immigration. The man at the door was half-asleep in a chair. I asked what door would get me to the office. He pointed the way with a drowsy finger. Inside, the same staff as this morning. Peter and I had been there around 10.30 am. It was now 5.45 pm. I was early. The lady from the morning asked me if I wanted to terminate my shore leave. I answered in the affirmative. She took my passport, stamped it with *Cape Town Departure* with the date and handed it back to me. I said I would wait for the agent. She nodded acknowledgement. I waited some ten minutes then decided, as I still had more than half-an-hour to wait for the time I had sent Peter, I would go over to suss out the Seamen's Mission. I had also noticed a letterbox outside it where I could post my cards. I hoped the post would be picked up on Monday at 11 am as the sign promised. Inside the building, a few dark brown eyeballs followed the equally round football on the television. There were three staff behind the counter, two seated at the café area, none in the chapel, and a number in the poolroom shooting balls into pockets. I asked the lady on the till about internet access. 'No,' she said. 'No vouchers left.' What? I could not believe it. 'You must go to City, there is internet access there.'

'I have just come from the City,' I replied in a high-pitched tone.

'I have no vouchers. You must have a voucher for access.'

'I have not seen my emails for over six weeks, I really want to have internet access. Is there no way you can get me this?'

'Do you have a laptop?'

'Yes, I do,' I said, a gleam filling my eyes and a glow rising in my lower sternum.

She reached below the counter. 'I have this,' she said, passing over a crumpled ticket with a number on it. 'I do not know if it will work,' she said. 'It was lying about and may not be good. If it works, then you can pay.'

I practically snatched the white scrap of paper from her and set up my netbook without hesitation. I searched for the wifi connection. *Seamen's Mission* or similar spread out from a cone in radar lines. Yes. Password? *&£$!** dadeedah. I felt a surge that spread up my ribs to my thyroid. Nothing. Niente. Nada.

I took the redundant ticket back to the desk, passing an equally redundant padre on his way into the chapel. I told the woman the ticket was no good and left, trying not to reveal the slump I felt inside and headed back to Immigration to meet Peter. I passed the sleeping warrior and took a seat again with my old friends. After about five minutes a minibus drew up outside. From it tumbled a football team's worth of crew going for shore leave. They came in all shapes and sizes. The tallest was the leader of the pack. He reported in to my friend. 'You must have a letter,' she said. Her most important line. 'I have a letter,' he said, used to the procedure. One by one she checked each ID of the eleven men. They shuffled round as if they were waiting in line to give blood, the topmost seat being filled as soon as it was vacated. Half way through, another minibus arrived. Two men came in with their agent. Still no sign of Peter and it was 6.50 pm. After the football team had been checked out I went over to the desk. 'I am going to the Seamen's Mission to see if I can get a lift to my ship *Palanpur*. If the agent arrives, please tell him I have gone back to the ship.' She nodded agreement. I thanked her and said goodbye. I left, assailing the sleeping warrior with a farewell. I headed back to the Seamen's Mission, that grim place. I wondered whether they knitted hats and scarves for seamen and provided sweets like they had at Norfolk, Virginia, United States of America. The minibus had been parked outside for some time, most of the time I had spent in the area. As I approached two men came out of the Seamen's Mission. One got into the passenger side; the other was climbing into the driver's seat. I was not having much luck. I ran across and tapped on the driver's window. 'I need to get to Landing Wall One,' I said. 'I will come back for you,' he said. I went back inside the Seamen's Mission and sat just inside the doorway on a bench. After around twenty minutes he returned. I stepped out and got into the minibus. We set off. Within five minutes he was returning to the Seamen's Mission with the last of my Rand, and I was skipping back towards *City of Adelaide* and

Palanpur with the same light feeling you get when you know you are going home. I smiled at the fine lines of her hull. As I went up the gangway, one of the rails collapsed. 'It was not me,' I called, laughing. Andriy K was on duty. I asked if Anatoliy was still on board. 'Yes,' he replied.

I went up to my cabin and dumped my small purchases and went to the galley for a sandwich. I was starving, having eaten only a chocolate bar with toffee and peanuts the whole day. In my place, a gift of silver. The new cook had left my supper for me covered in foil. I peeled it off like a chocolate coin off a Christmas tree, and found beneath chips and a chicken leg. I popped the chips in the microwave and annihilated a few of them. I left them in too long. I opened the fridge and helped myself to several slices of two different types of salami, German and Italian. I put a few slices of cheese beside the chicken that I had transferred to the foil in order to microwave the chips, and began to pull pieces off it and stuff them in my mouth. I was ravenous. I brought the chips across on the now very hot plate and put the slices of cheese on them to melt. I was halfway through picking out the last of the chicken meat when Anatoliy stepped into the mess. I was so glad to have the opportunity to say *goodbye* to him. I had been disappointed not to see him in the morning before I left for Cape Town. I told him I had gone to the galley to wish him well. He said at that time he would have been in his cabin for his coffee break. I had heard in the morning on the bridge that he and Chief Officer Igor, whom I had said goodbye to at that time, would likely be leaving around 4 pm. I thought I had missed Anatoliy, but with delays with bunkering partly due to some oil floating around *Palanpur*'s hull that had to be checked and cleared before we could take on fuel, his departure had been delayed. The oil around our hull turned out to be nothing to do with us. Anatoliy cracked open a beer for me and one for him and we chatted a while. I mentioned my supper. He had asked the new cook Oleksiy, to leave this for me. He was summoned by a phone call to his mobile. Peter Whitmore, had arrived to take him and Igor to stay a couple of nights in Cape Town till their flight to Paris on the 7th. We hugged and promised to stay in touch. Then he was gone.

It was around 9.30 pm after Anatoliy left. I went up to my cabin laden with a couple of beers from the fridge. I lay down and reflected on the day I had had on land. We were scheduled to leave around midnight. Nothing seemed to be happening so I did not go up to the bridge. When the engines came on I waited a bit for them to warm, then peeped out of my cabin window and saw a suckling stuck to the hull again, all lit up for night duty. The two tugs were back in action. I finished a beer and headed upstairs. On the bridge I was introduced to the new Chief Officer, Mykhailo Makushenko. The light was dimmed as it always is on the bridge at night, I suppose for the same reasons it is discouraged to use car interior lights at night. I had my camera and took photos of the tugs in action, some video and just watched the morning's proceedings in reverse. Everything went very smoothly. As we left Cape Town it twinkled astonishing beauty in the black of the night. The spread of lights was outstandingly clear, a testament to the pride felt in this City. The shadow of Table Mountain loomed above this sparkling skirt that followed us out to open sea. I was filled with great peace and satisfaction as I headed down to my cabin at 2.45 am.

DAY FORTY-TWO

September 22, 1864 – Thursday

A fine morning but showery afternoon. We practised some of the old Duetts. I am reading Macaulays Lays of Ancient Rome which are most interesting. The sun-set was very beautiful. We danced after tea till 11 P.M. We have been sailing about 8 knots nearly all day, but too much to the westward. We had some Shark for Breakfast which tasted very much like Sole.

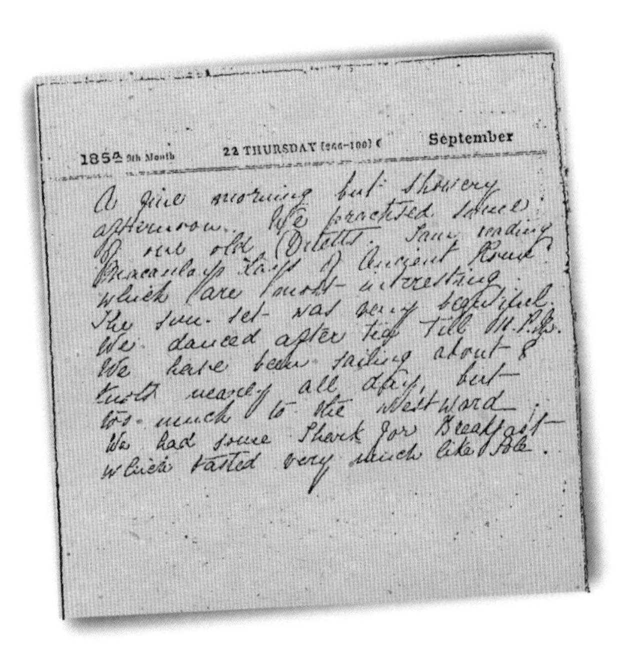

185[illegible] 9th Month 22 THURSDAY [266-100] September

A fine morning but showery
afternoon. We practised some
of the old Duetts. I am reading
Macaulays Lays of Ancient Rome
which are most interesting
The sun-set was very beautiful.
We danced after tea till 11 P.M.
We have been sailing about 8
knots nearly all day, but
too much to the Westward.
We had some Shark for Breakfast
which tasted very much like Sole.

6 January 2014 – Monday – Atlantic Ocean

A very rough night with *Palanpur* slammed by waves. At times it sounded like she would split in two. Looking out on the port side, there was a heavy swell and a strong wind. I could see seabirds playing above the waves, dark brown ones, and gulls.

I spent most of today in my cabin, even missing lunch. I was tired and had slept long. I began typing up notes from yesterday. I have now missed two days of readings, but I can take them from *Palanpur*'s log.

The weather is very rough and heavy booming echoes through the hull from the battering of waves. In the afternoon I looked out from my porthole. I rushed to get my camera. There was a little green fishing boat arguing bitterly with King Neptune, who was in a foul temper and throwing his weight around. I felt sick at the thought of how their stomachs were being flapped around like flaccid balloons. For sure there would be no food in them. I doubt whether they would be able to physically cook and eat food in those conditions, and if they were successful in doing so, it would be a miracle if they kept it from spewing out into Neptune's eye. I wondered at the hardships people face in the name of making a living and providing for others. I would not wish those conditions on anyone. When I went down for supper there was another silver offering in my place. I compared my luck to the men in the green fishing boat. I had already picked up supper from the galley, tinned tomatoes, pork fillet dressed in breadcrumbs and pasta with grated cheese. There was also a little side-salad. I enjoyed the food and picked cold potatoes from my uneaten lunch under the foil, augmenting what I had already eaten. There was a piece of fish also clad in breadcrumbs, that looked appetising, but not for eating cold. I could have microwaved it but I had eaten enough. I hate wasting food and I detected a wee down-mouth from Oleksiy as he cleared away my plate. German had been at the table when I arrived and he said, 'We missed you today,' *Sweet*, I thought.

I sent a couple of emails, one home and one to Ruth Currie asking her about the gap in Sarah's diary from 21 September to 3 October. I also told her I had been to Cape Town. We are at latitude 35°04.00'S, longitude 016°36.06'E.

I spent most of the day typing and had a couple of beers in the evening. I thought of reading a bit from *Master & Commander* but was not inclined to, and went to sleep early, around 9.30 pm.

DAY FORTY-THREE

September 23, 1864 – Friday

A fine day. Much colder than we have had it lately. I practised in the morning. Just six weeks to-day since we left Plymouth. We danced in the evening.

7 January 2014 – Tuesday – Atlantic Ocean

A rough, heavy swell wet night with *Palanpur* slamming through the waves to the thunder of cannonball and fuses burning, metal garage doors slamming shut and horses kicking out at the ramps of horseboxes.

A very slow start to the day for me. There had been a lot of waking through the night due to the wild pitching of *Palanpur*. At 3.15 am I felt my way through the cabin and looked out to see the ghostly hull of *City of Adelaide* staring back at me. *I'm okay*, she screamed through the wind, and winked with her dipping hull tango-ing with *Palanpur* in the craze of the night. I went for lunch though I had little appetite. I was glad I did, for there were mashed potatoes, pork escalope, salad and a very tasty minestrone soup to begin. Igor Ivanov from Crane 1 gave me his memory stick for me to copy my photos of him operating the crane on to it.

After lunch I had my shower. The shower cream that I was protecting so carefully fell from the wire rack in the corner of the shower and the already split cap cracked even more. I was gutted to find a fair amount of the cream had slewed across the outer shower floor. I was hoping this toiletry would hold out until Adelaide. I went up to the bridge to take readings. We were at latitude 36°54.48'S, longitude 023°28.95'E, course 114.3° on the gyro compass, and travelling at 10 knots in a gale force wind speed of 48 kilometres per hour. I asked Andriy V if he had seen the little green fishing boat yesterday. 'Yes,' he said. 'They phoned us to warn us of their trawling nets, to keep clear of them. We had already seen them.' We looked at the chart. I wanted to see if we had passed Cape Point. We had, the day before, and were now heading towards the Indian Ocean, expected arrival in those waters on Saturday. I noticed a yellow light was on on a panel of warning lights on the bridge control. It was the bilge water alarm. Andriy V explained the level was up, it was being collected and when it reached a certain volume, it would be pumped out to sea. I checked my emails and found I had a reply from Ruth Currie. She told me her copy of Sarah's diary was the same as mine. She said she would try and get in touch with her second cousin James Kerr, who has been documenting the family history. I had forgotten to say to Ruth I had seen in James Kerr's notes that there were several pages torn out from the diary. I also had an email from my son saying none of *The Three Craws* had a copy of the script needed for my *Craw Two*, Bob Mitchell's radio show commemorating Robert Burns' birthday that was being broadcast on 26 January 2014. I asked German, who had arrived on the bridge, whether it would be possible to send an email with this script attached. He agreed, so I went to my cabin to copy it onto a memory stick. I took it back up and he sent it off. I returned to my cabin to continue typing. Later he showed me it had arrived, as a *thank you* had been sent.

At supper of pork kebabs there was a salad with crab sticks cut through it. You know I am a bit queasy about shellfish. I ate a few, they were quite pleasant but enough was enough. I made for the bridge after my meal. German was sitting in his chair, watching the weather. This is a tricky area in the planet's oceans with a lot of swell and moody winds. We had some rough weather in the North Atlantic, but this is different, with much more spray and waves of around 3-4 metres so far. Mykhailo appeared wearing sparkly red trainers. I thought if he needed to get home in a hurry he could just click his heels together, like Dorothy in the Wizard of Oz, and find himself back at *no place like home*. He is very interested in *City of Adelaide*. He and German told me there is to be a crew gathering on Saturday. Cook Oleksiy wants a thousand pel'mini to be made. This is a pasta stuffed with ground meat, similar to ravioli. He wants the whole crew to be involved in making these, including me. I paled. We discussed this food and other Ukrainian fare. Mykhailo was surprised I knew about it. He asked me if I knew about borscht. At this point German told him that my father was Ukrainian. He looked puzzled by this. In time I will tell him how my father came to be in Scotland. I spent a good hour chatting with them, it was a relief to be out of my cabin. I took some photos of *City of Adelaide* in her tattering rags, spotting that her bow is thrusting through the plastic cover. *Soon she will be naked and she will be happy*, I said to myself. The wind is very strong, coming onto her sides and the cover is filling with Neptune's breath and splitting at the seams. I took some video of her pitching and heaving in the swell, then returned to my cabin feeling refreshed, had a couple of beers and finished reading *Master & Commander* with a sigh. The finishing of this book means I only have two anthologies of short stories and poetry books left to amuse me. I will begin to read through the next stage of the first twenty-eight chapters of this book before combining the next completed lot into those. A warm surge like a geyser in Yellowstone Park erupts in my chest.
If I keep my head down low and keep chipping away at the other sections of this book, I should have completed the first draft by the time we reach Adelaide.

Today is Ukrainian Christmas. Everyone is working as per normal. Celebrations will take place at the weekend, weather permitting, for there is no way in these heaving seas Oleksiy could cope with the extra work.

DAY FORTY-FOUR

September 24, 1864 – Saturday

A fine day and favorable wind. I practised and worked in the morning. We danced all the evening.

8 January 2014 – Wednesday – Atlantic Ocean

A similar night to last night, very noisy and uncomfortable.

Another very slow start for me, with another night of waking to the crash and thump of waves trying to break our hull. I had to secure cups and bottles away into jacket pockets and the fridge, jamming them tight so that they would not clank together, make a noise or even smash. It looked as though a great fat, black, slimy snake was slithering alongside *Palanpur*'s hull, waiting, waiting to strike. But she kept her nerve. She kept her eye on the course and modified it when necessary, to minimise roll and resultant stress on the lashings. *City of Adelaide* is losing her coat bit by bit, stripping back until now her deck is totally uncovered, the plastic rippling back towards her stern. The doorway on her top deck that was covered over with plywood is exposed. We can see with binoculars the grating that had been placed over the opening, probably at Irvine, to keep pigeons out. I wondered whether the letters sent from boys and girls in schools in Scotland that are inside *City of Adelaide* would hold out until we get to Adelaide. We have had quite some soakings. I think every day of what conditions Sarah and her family had had to cope with, and the brave, adventurous spirit of that family, and how this led to them becoming very wealthy. To take a family of four around Europe for the Grand Tour must have been very expensive, and no expense was spared. Sarah and her sister Blanche had Italian lessons in Boulogne, they visited numerous places of culture and stayed in upmarket residences as they went. The fact that Sarah's father went back to England every month for mail from Australia reinforces the wealth and business interests the family enjoyed.

This was another day of intense typing for me. I went to the ship's office to pick up emails after supper. I had one from my eldest daughter saying *The Three Craws* had been rehearsing. She also said things are going well with her music. I also had an email from Alan saying there is to be a party at my brother's to mark his fiftieth birthday, with all family present bar my granddaughter, who will be found a babysitter. I thought this a shame because she is a wee party animal. I felt a pang of guilt and loneliness that I would miss this special occasion for my wee brother.

I managed to eat both lunch and supper today, but will have to be a bit firmer about portions. Waistbands are getting tighter. Nothing to do with the chocolates I received for Christmas from the crew, or the one or two bottles of beer in the evenings, you understand. Supper was meatballs and a very nice salad made from celeriac, and my favourite, mashed potatoes. Soup at lunch had been vegetable. I ate more chocolates than I intended. In the evening I had a hot chocolate and went to sleep early. This has been another quiet day. I felt quite lonely for cuddles, and had a few tears.

DAY FORTY-FIVE

September 25, 1864 – Sunday

A cold and rather rough day. Prayers were read in the Saloon. In the afternoon (6 P.M.) we went to the Sailor's Service. A very good sermon was read from Genesis C. VII v.1. Come thou and all thy house into the ark. In the evening we had Music. We saw a ship in the distance.

is eaten, and thou shalt gather *it* to thee; and it shall be for food for thee, and for them.
22 Thus° did Noah; [p] according to all that God commanded him, so did he.

CHAPTER VII.

1 *Noah, with his family, and the living creatures, enter into the ark.* 17 *The beginning, increase, and continuance of the flood.* 21 *All flesh destroyed.*

AND the LORD said unto Noah, Come [a] thou and all thy house into the ark: for thee have I seen righteous [b] before me in this generation.
2 Of every [c] clean beast thou shalt take to thee by [1] sevens, the male and his female: and of beasts that *are* not clean by two, the male and his female.
3 Of fowls also of the air by sevens, the male and the female; to keep seed alive upon the face

9 January 2014 – Thursday – Atlantic Ocean

The sea is becoming more blue. The air is fresh, I opened one of my portholes but kept it on the latch, as there was a lot of spray and the wind is still quite fierce. I slept in again, having been unable to sleep until after 3.30 am tossing and turning like the waves outside. Eventually I ate some yoghurt and drank a glass of peach juice. I had been up till after midnight typing, then played computer games. I amused myself and put Sarah as a competitor. She has her name on the leader board for Pinball, though she is behind me by a couple of hundred-thousand points. During this voyage I have succeeded on getting onto the leader board. I have not played Pinball for years and my name was against the top five on the list. You cannot lose if you are the only player. I had been thinking a lot about Sarah on that evening whilst I was playing, and promised that if I managed to top one of my scores, I would put her name against it. I think it is hilarious that someone who was born in 1844 has her name on the list of high scorers on an electronic game of the 21st Century. She often mentions playing chess and quoits during her voyage, and quite often trailed the leader, but she clearly enjoyed a bit of competition, and having fun.

I awoke about 9.50 am then turned over for a few minutes. 11.40 am sneaked round very quickly. I had my shower and headed straight down for lunch. I was surprised that Eintopf was the soup of the day. Andriy K was in the mess. 'We are having Eintopf today? Is it Saturday?' I asked. 'I thought it was only Thursday.' He looked to the right, rolling his eyes upwards and began calculating. Eventually we concurred it is only Thursday, and laughed. I do not mind if Oleksiy makes Eintopf again on Saturday because it is probably my favourite soup. The rest of lunch was pork fillet, pasta and tinned tomatoes. German was just leaving as I arrived. He said they missed me again on the bridge. I explained I had a lot of typing to catch up on but would come up after supper. Immediately after lunch I mopped up the sliver of water that had been thrashed by the sea through my cracked-open porthole. It had trickled right to the cabin entrance door. I wiped down my soft holdall that had got wet and continued with more typing. I felt snoozy and lay down for what I intended would be around half-an-hour. Two hours later I awoke. With just an hour till supper, I typed some more.

When Andriy V came into supper he laughed when he found out I had fallen asleep for two hours, so had not made it to the bridge for readings. After supper I brought my camera and notebook to the bridge. I went outside for the second time in days, and took some photographs of *City of Adelaide* and the rays of sunshine behind her that echoed the spread of the cables of Crane 1. The salty slush was there again, and I remarked on it to German. He said it is the best salt for the table and for in a bath. Mykhailo was there. He told me I had an email. It was from Rosemary McKay, written in her familiar warm tone. She hoped I like Drambuie – do I! She wondered what foods I like as she is planning on taking me out to eat. She wondered how long I would be staying in Adelaide, as there are several events coming up she thought I would enjoy. She said she was disappointed I would not arrive in time for the Robert Burns event she would be compering on his birthday, 25 January. She told me everyone is getting really excited about the arrival of *City of Adelaide*, and will be there to greet her. They are not alone.

German went to get his memory stick for the web address of the school camps he told me about a few days ago that his daughter attends. He also showed me photographs of his daughter at the camps. They look a lot of fun. There were images of the Carpathian area where one of the camps had been held. It looks beautiful, very like Scotland. I was reminded of Pressmennan Lake, near my home. Valeriy told me he had been skiing in that area with his family. It looks very clean. There were photos of arts and crafts in a shop and I recognised the style, pointing out an embroidered runner similar to one I have at home.

I took some more photos of *City of Adelaide* as her plastic cover splits. At Cape Town a team had come from Netherlands to try to repair the rents the cover had already suffered, but it was not possible. Richard Smith will be at Port Hedland and he will decide what to do. The way things are looking she will have to go back to Dordrecht for a new cling-film to be fitted. That will not be, of course. I am sure the cover would have survived intact if we had not added extra miles, with consequent additional rough weather, to load cargo at Norfolk, Virginia, United States of America.

I took readings on the bridge and thought I would send a message to Jim Tildesley for the Education Officer at the Scottish Maritime Museum to diffuse to the schoolchildren who are following this final voyage of *City of Adelaide*.

I decided to leave it till tomorrow. At the present time we are three hours ahead of the United Kingdom, by tomorrow it will be four. We will be passing the island of Madagascar in a couple of days, to the west of Africa and south of the Mozambique Basin. I must send an email to my youngest daughter about this as my wee granddaughter is a great fan of the films in the Madagascar series. She will be amused. We are at latitude 39°06.09'S and longitude 034°21.50'E, speed 11.6 knots, wind speed 35 kph. Temperature is a cooler 22°C. I am having a couple of beers with the intention of having an early night so that I can go up to the bridge in the morning and look at *Palanpur*'s log and also the list of designated duties of each rank of seaman. Andriy K had returned his consent form to me with a remark that he is 'just a simple seaman'. His modesty astounds me. He takes charge of this enormous steel leviathan of 11,473 gross tonnage, and he is only twenty-five.

I asked German whether it would be okay if I got a bottle of whisky for the crew whilst we are making the pel'meni on Saturday. He said there is none left, with a twinkle in his eye. I have heard this before in relation to red wine. I said, 'There is, because I asked Andriy K.' We laughed. He said we will see what the weather conditions are like. I will get the whisky. Andriy K said I can have access to the slop chest anytime I like. I am told there is no vodka left, for that was my first choice thinking it would be the crew's favourite tipple. I will not be surprised if I find there is vodka on the table when we have our Ukrainian festive feast. I am getting wise to their ways. My father used to play these games too sometimes, this kidding on. Another thing I have noticed is how direct Ukrainians are when addressing you or responding to you. I used to take this hard, thinking my father was harsh, but now I find it is just the way of his people, possibly my over-sensitivity.

DAY FORTY-SIX

September 26, 1864 – Monday

A cold dull day. I was dressed rather earlier than usual and had about half an hour walk on the Deck before breakfast. We saw a great many porpoises jumping about in the water – also saw a Cape Pigeon. We danced for a short time in the evening but were obliged to go down on account of the rain. We tried a quadrille in the Saloon but there was scarcely room enough and some of the people objected to the noise. All the windows have been boarded up to-day as the Captain expects rough weather.

QUADRILLE

FASHIONABLE DANCE FOR EIGHT PEOPLE IN A SQUARE FORMATION, IMPORTED BY LADY JERSEY TO ENGLISH ARISTOCRATS IN 1816 FROM ELITE PARISIAN BALLROOMS

THE QUADRILLE WAS THE FORERUNNER OF THE MODERN AMERICAN "SQUARE DANCE".

Dancing the quadrille, English print circa 1820

10 January 2014 – Friday – Indian Ocean

Another grey sky this morning, with moderate seas of about 2.5 metres in height.

I woke up at 9.20 am this morning, had my shower and went to the bridge around 11 am to send the newsletter to Jim Tildesley.

> *'Hello girls and boys, A Happy New Year and greetings from City of Adelaide on board M/V (Motor Vessel) Palanpur. It is Friday morning at 11.15 am and you will probably just be tumbling out of bed because your time is 4 hours behind mine. We are going along at 11.7 knots per hour in a fresh breeze with swell of approximately 2.5 metres, which is better than the near gale conditions we had a couple of days ago with waves of 5.5 metres upwards. Our position is latitude 39°37.96'S and longitude 038°14.62'E. See if you can find this on your atlas, a wee clue is we are somewhere south of the island of Madagascar, off the east coast of Africa, south of the Mozambique Basin in the Indian Ocean. I am very excited to be on this journey with City of Adelaide. I have been passionate about this ship for many years, and am very lucky that my dream of going*

with her to Adelaide, Australia has come true. I keep pinching myself to make sure it is real! Every day I write a journal, which is like a diary, about what is happening on board Palanpur, what is happening on the deck, what we have had for our meals, chats I have had with the crew. There are seventeen men running the ship, from age about twenty to fifty-five. They are all Ukrainian except for two of them, who are Russian. They look after me very well, and we have had celebrations over Christmas and New Year. Since they operate from a different calendar to ours we will be celebrating again! See if you can find out about their calendar. I am sitting on the bridge of Palanpur where all the controls and computers are. It is very exciting, there is even some dance music going on in the background while the 3rd Officer and Master of the ship are doing some office administration. I have only been on a small roller-coaster once, and it is a bit like that standing on the bow (front) of the ship and diving into the waves. I will tell you about my visit inside the crane and the engine room in my next newsletter. Have a nice weekend. Best wishes. Rita Bradd'

I took information to Andriy K, about my equipment and serial numbers for Australian Immigration. He loaned me a manual so that I could see what duties the different seamen ranks carried with them, but it was more of a procedures manual. I found it interesting nonetheless. I was a bit horrified to read this in the manual and thought of Alan, a virtual stowaway on the 1864 maiden voyage of *City of Adelaide*:

MARITIME AND COASTGUARD AGENCY (MCA)
Code of Safe Working Practices for Merchant Seamen
Extract from Chapter 11
Security on Board
11.5 STOWAWAYS
11.5.1 If there is any likelihood of stowaways, a thorough search of the vessel should be made before departure. It is easiest to send stowaways ashore in the port where they boarded, and they may hide in places which are secured at sea and which may be deficient in oxygen so that they suffocate or starve, or in holds which may be fumigated.

Not much hope for him, since *City of Adelaide* was fumigated in Dordrecht, Netherlands, before she was towed on her barge to Mammoet Terminal, Rotterdam for loading on board *Palanpur*!

It is 6.15 pm, I have just returned from having beef stew with carrots, mushrooms, cauliflower on a bed of rice, with side salad of celeriac, green peppers, chunks of a soft cheese that are too salty for my palette. I heard the second announcement from German since I came on board. The 2nd and 3rd Officers are to go to the bridge. The weather is worsening. I will stay out of their way.

DAY FORTY-SEVEN

September 27, 1864 – Tuesday

A very rough day. The windows were fortunately boarded up yesterday, as today the waves have several times been over the Deck and the Cabins are very wet. We were reading and working this morning when a wave came over the Deck and into the Saloon. We were obliged to sit on the table and on the back of the seats while the water was being baled out. We went on Deck about half an hour. It was amusing at dinner time to see everyone holding on to their plates and glasses. In the evening we played at 'Old Maid'.

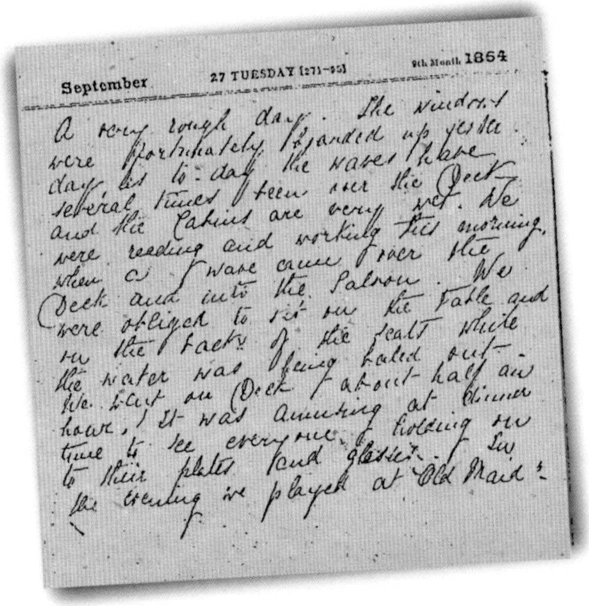

September 27 TUESDAY [271-95] 9th Month 1864

A very rough day. The windows were fortunately boarded up yesterday, as to-day the waves have several times been over the Deck and the Cabins are very wet. We were reading and working this morning when a wave came over the Deck and into the Saloon. We were obliged to sit on the table and on the back of the seats while the water was being baled out. We went on Deck about half an hour. It was amusing at dinner time to see every one holding on to their plates and glasses. In the evening we played at "Old Maid".

11 January 2014 – Saturday – Indian Ocean

It is a little brighter this morning. The sea was wild last night. Lying in bed it felt one minute I was in suspended animation, surfing along on the crest of a wave, the next slammed down with *Palanpur* throbbing with the violence of the thrust, so that everything shook. I tried not to think of her splitting in two. I peeped out at *City of Adelaide* at least three times during the night. The deck was lit up and she looked ghostly in her cradle, yet she pulsated with strength, determination and pride.

It is *Palanpur* Pel'meni Party day. I got up, showered and went to the bridge to give Andriy K my Customs form for Port Hedland, Australia. We swapped, he giving me the slop chest order form. Tick: one bottle of Grouse whisky, one milk chocolate Ritter Bar. He had none left that had nuts in, except the white chocolate one and that is too sweet for my palate. I checked my emails: one from Jim Tildesley thanking me for the newsletter, the other from Alan. He had installed a new oil storage tank at home and the old, rusty one had been uplifted by our usual scrap merchant, having been cut up first into manageable chunks as it had been very heavy. How he managed to fit the new one on his own I will find out when I get home.

I wrote an email to my youngest daughter asking her to send me my horoscope. I cannot believe how accurate Russell Grant is. I have had my daily horoscope sent to my email for the past few years and often look at it retrospectively and am amazed. I sometimes record what actually happened against his prediction.

Examples:
'Libra (Sept24-Oct23)
Fri 24 May 2013
Expanding your knowledge gives you renewed hope. Every time you acquire a new piece of information, you realise there is so much more to learn. This could be the beginning of a rewarding career. Teaching, writing, or doing research will bring you the intellectual stimulation you crave. If you've always wanted to write a book, now is the time to begin. You're particularly good at writing vivid adventure stories. Let your imagination run wild. Readers will eagerly respond to your romantic style.'

20/05/13: Recorded 1st take of *City of Adelaide : Farewell to Scotland* with Kevin Cadwallender.
30/05/13: East Coast FM *The Three Craws At The 3Harbours Festival.*
01/06/13: 3Harbours Festival, went to see Battle of Prestonpans Tapestry in Prestonpans Community Centre.

'Mon 03, June 2013
This is a great time to interview for a job that appeals to your creative side. If you've ever wanted to enter a glamorous industry like film, fashion, or photography, now is the time. You'll make a great impression on the powers that be. They're looking for someone with a distinct point of view who can work well with others. You possess both gifts and should be paid accordingly. Go ahead and take a chance on this exciting opportunity.

You're due for an adventure.'

04/06/13: Met Hannah Lavery to discuss her invitation to me to open Dunbar's Wee Festival of Words
30/06/13: Wrote to Gordon, Baron of Prestoungrange, re the trip to Bayeux with the Battle of Prestonpans Tapestry. Proposal presented on 15/07/13 to him and Arran Johnston for *The Three Craws* to take part in September

My daughter described arrangements for my brother's 50th birthday party on 18th January, four days after his actual birthday. I will try and phone on the day. She has updated my *City of Adelaide* Facebook page. An email from a friend said she is more excited about this trip than I am. Impossible!

Last night I spent hours on the Irvine section of this book and at last I have reached new notes, from the day I met Sarah's great-granddaughter Ruth, and saw *City of Adelaide* for the first time at Irvine on 20 March 2013. The impetus is growing. The crew are beginning to talk of when we arrive in Australia. Not long now. It struck home with great force that in less than three weeks we would be in Adelaide. I am full of excitement and awe at what will happen when we arrive. There will be crowds for sure. I want to stay on board until *City of Adelaide* is off-loaded from *Palanpur*, and will be left behind in Adelaide when she departs to unload further cargo up the east coast of Australia. By the time she does this, she will almost have circumnavigated the whole Continent, as she then heads for Brisbane, then Dampier.

I chatted a little to Andriy K, then noticed an instrument on the top curtain in the curtained off area on the bridge where charts, instruments, books, manuals, printers, computers, telephones, modem are all kept, all you need for navigation, communication and administration. He explained it is for recording air pressure, and is different to the thermometer outside that I take temperature readings from. It is around 11.30 am and we are right under the tip of Madagascar at latitude 40°04.31'S, longitude 044°45.63'E, 22°C in the shade. We are on course 090.5 at 11.7 knots and wind speed 12-16 knots.

I went for lunch, pork fillet, tinned tomatoes and pasta with cheese grated over. The soup was borscht and very tasty. I came back to my cabin to pick up where I had left off last night, when I am about to meet Ruth. My phone rang. In my ear, Andriy V. 'Rita, we have drill at 1 pm.' I had twenty minutes to get ready. I reached for my orange boiler suit, fed my legs into it one by one, pulled it up over my backside, slipped my arms into the holes for them to go down the sleeves and shrugged the rest of it over my shoulders. I smoothed it down and pulled up the zip. I sat on my bed, pulled on a pair of socks, put my pink bed socks over them, slipped my feet into the heavy-duty shoes, took my hardhat off its peg, put it on and clasped the chin strap into place. It was windy out there and my hair is slippery. I knew the hat would not stay on unless it was anchored to my head. The men have the knack of adjusting the plastic strap so that it bites into the back of the head, but it does not work for me. Last, but not least, I brought out from the locker above my wardrobe my lifejacket and immersion suit with bottled water in its carrying bag, and made my way to the mustering station on the weather deck. A few of the crew were already assembled, and one-by-one more of them ejected from the steel doors in the accommodation block. There was good-natured banter and serious talk too, but I did not know what they were saying. Andriy V arrived with his clipboard and took the roll call. We put on our lifejackets and tested that the torches and whistles were working. He then organised a fire safety drill. I was not needed. I made my way towards *City of Adelaide* to see her bare flesh that was becoming exposed by the plastic cover's deterioration with all the battering by wind, sea and sun it had recently undergone. I danced and leapt across the weather deck and looked up at my chalice, her fine timbers rippling strong in the daylight. On her port side a large piece of plastic had ripped and was flapping in the wind. My stomach churned to see the timbers of *City of Adelaide* I had last seen in Greenwich when she sat on the barge in the River Thames for the Renaming Ceremony before being towed to Dordrecht. I wanted to reach out and stroke the wood, but it was too high up, even when standing on tiptoes. I made my way back to my cabin, lugging the immersion suit and carrying the lifejacket up the stairs. Inside the cabin, I chucked them down, released the chin strap, took off the hardhat, heavy-duty shoes, socks, socks, boiler suit and put everything back where I had found them.

I was lying on my bed pumping two 2-litre bottles of water in the air, alternating the one in the left hand with the one in the right, exercising my upper arms when the phone rang again.

'Rita. Where are you?'

Well, I was answering the phone so it was obvious where I was. Nevertheless, 'I am in my cabin.'

Andriy V continued, 'But we are not finished with drill. We must go to lifeboat station now.'

'Okay. I will put my things back on and be there in a couple of minutes.'

I went through the procedure again in record time, mentally patting myself on the back for this and went to the mustering station. Andriy was scribbling on his clipboard, following procedure to make sure everyone was present following fire drill. Ivan Polskoy was one of the fire officers. I had seen him with his breathing apparatus earlier on my way back to my cabin. We all made our way to the stern. This was the third time since coming on board *Palanpur* I had been up the two flights of steps that led to the lifeboat pod. Mykhailo asked to go inside. I thought he was mad. Andriy V turned to me and said, 'We are not going inside capsule today. Next time.' I hoped *next time* would be after Adelaide. It is not a pleasant experience going inside that great orange bullet.

I made my way back to the accommodation block with Stepan Deli. Once again he showed care and attention to me descending the stairs at the lifeboat station. We chatted on the way back, and admired the fine, exposed timbers of *City of Adelaide*. She is breaking through the membrane of her re-birth. I went through the steel door leading off from the weather deck and through the internal door to the staircase. I paused on the other side to sort the straps that had come loose from the lifejacket I was carrying. Kostyantyn came through the door and started up the stairs in front of me. I just caught sight of his hand slipping through the handle of my immersion suit bag. He leapt effortlessly up the stairs with it and carried it right up to my deck level. I was so grateful, particularly because of the extra weight of two litres of water.

Back in my cabin I wondered what to do for the hour before it was time for the pel'meni party. I spent it thinking about Sarah and her family. It was 3 pm before I knew it, and made my way down to the crew mess.

'Please,' said Oleksiy, stretching out his arms in the direction of the crew mess. I opened the door. Today the word *mess* is appropriate. Several of the crew were standing round one of the tables. They were chatting away, and smiled when I stepped into the room. 'Come,' they said. On the table was a series of bowls and trays. I trod gently over, quickly stuffing the plastic shower cap I had got in the hotel in Rotterdam into a breast pocket. I had brought it in case I needed to tuck my hair out of the way. Inside the larger of two plastic bowls at the far end of the table was a great mound of ground pork: meat minced even more finely than what you would find in the United Kingdom. In the slightly smaller bowl was simple flour. Some of these contents had been decanted into two smaller opaque glass bowls at the near end of the table. There was an even smaller opaque glass bowl for moistening fingers. The men were taking little blobs of meat out of the bowls between thumbs and forefingers and manipulating them into small balls. These were then placed in the middle of a disk made of a flour and water dough. The disk was then folded over in the middle, trapping the meat inside, to meet the edge at the other side. Fingers pressed the edges together to form a semicircle with the meat hump in the middle. They then meticulously – some more than others – went round the edge and made little patterns that sealed the edges of the pel'meni together. The final episode in this process was to tuck one end of the folded disk under the other. Each was then placed on a tray in rows of about nine until it was covered. Oleksiy then carried them away to the kitchen. The procedure continued until all the ingredients were gone, and over one thousand pel'meni were ready to be cooked. They will be dropped into a huge pot of boiling water batch-by-batch. When they float to the surface, they are ready.

In the crew lounge through a fug of smoke, I saw three men armed with rolling pins. These were the oil of the engine that kept the machine slick and fluid. Young Serhii Strokach, one of the two apprentices was putting every last bead of energy into rolling out the dough. From a great dirty-white lump of flour and water he pressed and rolled, pressed and rolled, turned the dough round, pressed and rolled, pressed and rolled until it was the right thickness. He lifted it off the table draped over the rolling pin and carried it through to the mess for it to be cut into disks by fellow crew using the open end of a tumbler. If the men filling the disks with the ground meat were not ready for a

new supply of dough, the men in the lounge would cut the disks out and carry them through. Vitaliy came through with a pile of them. He dealt them out like a pack of cards in front of the men doing the filling. All that was missing were the hearts, diamonds, clubs and spades. There was an air of conviviality in the room. I heard a clatter from the lounge. Serhii was retrieving his rolling pin from the floor and slapping it back into the dough. Andriy K was sitting with his slop chest orders. He disappeared. Around twenty minutes later he arrived back. I whispered to him, 'My whisky?' 'Outside your cabin,' he said. I leapt out of the room, dived upstairs, grabbed it and came back down, hiding it behind my back as I stepped back into the crew mess.

'Now you have no excuse not to sing,' I said, holding up the litre bottle of Grouse. The men had told me before that the ready supply of beer was not strong enough for them to make them sing. I fetched a dozen or so glasses from the officers' mess, twisted the cap off the bottle, and began to pour. Not everyone wanted whisky. We toasted this afternoon's event several times during the course of production. The mood in the room became even more jovial. 'Three,' I said, holding up my three middle fingers indicating the tradition. I certainly had my three shots, but somewhere before the party was over, the bottle of whisky disappeared with a crowd of those that were in the lounge where I had left the bottle. I had indicated to the guys to help themselves, but did not expect that! It was a shame when Oleksiy, the orchestrator of this afternoon's ensemble, came looking for a dram and found that the bottle was gone. I think he had had one, at least. I had a wee blether with Stepan. I had taken several photos of the men making the pel'meni. Stepan asked me to copy them to his memory stick. Ihor Timoshytskyi, the other apprentice, had asked to see the photos. I toggled through them on my camera as he leaned over to look at them on the small screen. Then he asked me if I would like my photo taken making pel'meni. Would I? Thank you, young man. This is definitely one for the family album and website. He went away to wash his hands to take my camera. He took a few images of me leaning on a glass in the pel'meni dough, cutting out disks. Just after 4 pm the rest of us that had not scarpered with the whisky, dispersed. I came back to my cabin. I went back down to the officers' mess at 5.30 pm as per the usual suppertime, but Oleksiy said it was not time yet, had no one told me supper would be a 6 pm this evening. When I came back down at this time, I met German on the stairs with Mykhailo. German said, 'Good you are going down now when the pel'meni is still warm. It is a good one. It is better to eat it hot.' Oleksiy grabbed a plate and covered it with pel'meni when he saw me. 'Put over some vinegar, a little sour cream and some black pepper.' I followed his instructions to the 'T' and filled my belly with an economical, mass-produced by hand in just over an hour, delicious little pile of *Perfect Palanpur Party Pel'meni.*

Back in my cabin my brain was lubricated enough to write some poems. The words just seemed to drip off my pen. I have not looked at them yet today, so they may be just a bit of drivel. I had written about five when there was a knock at my door. I opened it. There stood Sergiy Fomin holding the consent form I had distributed the other day for permission from each crewmember to mention them in this book. He asked me if I could help him with the section outlining his duties. I was glad of this opportunity, I wanted to know what each crewmember's job entailed. Sergiy told me that his jobs include amongst others: welding; crane operating; painting; rudder control; mooring assistant. I had watched Sergiy throw the heaving line with the monkey's fist knot at the end to the stevedores on shore at Cape Town. The stevedores then dragged the mooring ropes ashore to secure the ship to the shore, looping the ends of the mooring ropes over the bollards. Sergiy told me his next contract will be as bridge cadet officer. He has already got his officer qualification but now needs practical experience to move to the next level in his chain of promotions. He has spent the required thirty-six months at sea and paid the required fee for making maximum of Second Officer status. In order to go on the bridge he needs to have two promotions. He already has one. This promotion is given by the captain, rank also known as master, and can be spread over two contracts with two different captains or masters. I remembered seeing the other ordinary seaman, Kostyantyn Portnyagin on the wheel at Norfolk, Virginia, United States of America as we left that port. I compared this transgression with what Anatoliy Letnyanka had been going through. He had to hold down the job as cook on board *Palanpur* and use his time in the afternoons between meals to observe and perform tasks in the engine room in his pursuit of becoming an Electrical Engineer, and have his record book signed off by the Chief Officer. 'Exactly,' was his reply. He said this Master is a good one. I got the impression he wished he had approached German for some bridge experience during this voyage before he departs from Adelaide for his holidays. Sergiy informed me that when at sea sailors receive a basic salary. When in port and carrying out cargo operations such as lashings, the crew receives overtime money. Captains are responsible for calculating salaries, and there is no consistency between captains as to how they work out money earned by the crew. Sergiy will receive enhanced salary as he progresses up the chain of command, rises through the ranks. Sergiy told me a bit about the Harren & Partner fleet, and mentioned their *Hanse Explorer* yacht that Andriy Kostenko has crewed. I will ask Andriy if he wishes to expand on this. Sergiy left my cabin and I made myself a hot chocolate and ate a few chunks of the first Ritter Bar I had had in a few weeks before tucking myself in for the night.

DAY FORTY-EIGHT

September 28, 1864 – Wednesday

A very rough day. We have not been able to go on Deck as it has rained incessantly and the waves keep coming over. It is very uncomfortable down stairs, as the Saloon is very wet and the water is floating in the Cabins. Two boys and the Stewards were baling the water out all night. We could not sleep as the water made a most dreadful noise. The Cabins are rather dark as the windows are boarded up. The waves are running mountains high – a regular Cape sea! There are a great many Cape pigeons about.

12 January 2014 – Sunday – Indian Ocean

A grey start to the day with some fog, a gentle sea and occasional rolling. This broke away to a lovely blue sky, the first in days with white puffy clouds dotted here and there.

A good sleep slipped me into the morning. I was in fine fettle and went for my shower. At lunch the soup looked as though it had boiled egg chopped into to it so I put the lid back on it and ate tinned tomatoes, rice and a chicken leg stuffed with garlic. Oleksiy is fond of this bulbous beast that makes your breath smell but is good for your stomach and digestion. It was very tasty. There were little chocolate cakes, and pancakes with ham, gherkins and melted cheese on top on the sideboard in the officers' mess, possibly leftovers from breakfast that I never go to. I took a savoury and wrapped it in a napkin, took a chocolate cake and headed with my booty to my cabin. I had awakened during the night at around 4 am and rolled about for a while before deciding to get up and type yesterday's entry. I had done this for about an hour before going back to sleep. I continued the story, picking up after the pel'mini party. I popped some washing in the machine and forgot about it. When I remembered it, it had been moved. What is it with Chief Officers? Mykhailo told me later on the bridge he was finished with the dryer and I could continue with my washed washing and put it in the dryer. I said I had already shifted it. I ate my wee snack around 4.15 pm and had a cup of coffee with it and a couple of chunks of Ritter Bar. At supper we had pork chops with a mushroom and cheddar cheese sauce melted on top. German had asked me at the table whether I had forgotten my way to the bridge. He said we have a bit more than two weeks left of this voyage to Adelaide. He said I would be leaving the ship. I told him I would be sad. He said that many sailors do not like being at sea. I said it is very hard to be apart from family. He looked down. I thought to myself I am a free agent to a certain degree, and can leave the ship at any port when I like, (except Norfolk, Virginia, United States of America!) but the crew are tied to several months contracts. Even if this means a four-month break between contracts, it is still a very long time to be away from home. German headed out of the mess. Valeriy was still at the table. I asked him if I could visit the engine room again to take some photos. 'Sometime this week,' he suggested. This will be good. I may not have another chance as time is running out. When Valeriy went out, Andriy K asked me about the value of my wedding band for the Customs form. I said about $140.

'What is the serial number?'

'L-O-V-E', I said.

'What does this mean?'

I said, 'I do not know. I have been trying to work it out for many years.'

We laughed. I showed him my other ring, a silver band embellished with paua shell. He looked at it. 'I do not think we need to record this,' he said, and left the room.

After supper I headed for the bridge to send a pile of emails. I sent one to Rory MacLean, a travel writer who tutored a writing course I did in 2006; another to the Society of Authors asking advice on publishers and agents; I sent one to Ruth Currie about her family photo; I sent one to my hairdresser as requested by him the last time I saw him, to say I am still alive and not been dying my hair; I sent one to Rosemary McKay; I sent one to my son. By the end of all this it felt like I had written a book. Mykhailo, German and Andriy K were on the bridge by the time I had finished my emails. I said I would pop down to my cabin and bring the photo of Sarah and her family up to show them. Mykhailo is very interested in the whole history of *City of Adelaide*. His wife and he have been looking at *Wikipedia* for information on her. He was talking to me about emails as well, how if you do not see one arriving for you in the system you wonder why no one is writing to you, and if you phone someone and they are not there, you wonder where they are. We all want to be loved and needed.

I played some Solitaire and Pinball before bed. I felt Sarah's presence very strongly. My score went through the roof of my previous record by 3,000. I awarded this top score to Sarah and wrote her name on the leader board. Visions of her playing chess against the Doctor on board *City of Adelaide* entered my head. I do believe she's better at playing Pinball.

DAY FORTY-NINE

September 29, 1864 – Thursday – St. Michaell. Michaelmas Day

A fine breeze. The sea not quite so rough. The ship still rolling about and shipping heavy seas. In the evening we had round games.

13 January 2014 – Monday – Indian Ocean

Another brighter morning. The sea is quite calm, and we are rolling along gently.

I awoke at 8.15 am quite refreshed. I got up and had my shower and a giant cup of liquorice and fennel tea. I had taken up some liquorice tea bags to the bridge last night. German and Mykhailo did not recognise the aroma and looked up in the dictionary the origin of the plant. I worked on poems I had written at the end of the pel'mini party and was surprised to find I had seventeen when I added those to ones I had already written. I went for lunch, pork fillet, tinned tomatoes and pasta with grated cheese over. Soup was vegetable with gherkins through it. I had a slice of white baguette with it.

After lunch I set up my video camera to take some footage that would demonstrate the rolling of *Palanpur*. I placed the cardboard tube of a toilet roll on the linoleum, parallel with *Palanpur*'s hull. It was reluctant, unstable and frankly, useless. I searched for something else. The coffee jar would not roll straight; the tin of sweets was uneven from its plastic lid and there was a chance the lid might come off and scatter it sugary contents everywhere. The can of beer was perfect. It rolled with the precision of an expensive motor car. The video was a wrap. Elated by this I went to the bridge to take some wind direction statistics and a few location readings as I had missed some over the last few days. Andriy V let me borrow the detailed ship's log and I sat in the bridge with the cup of tea he made me. I munched a couple of cream-filled biscuits whilst writing down a few details:

At noon on 06 January 2014 we had been at latitude 35°04.0'S, longitude 016°36.6'E, with wind speed a gentle 8.8 knots per hour. Readings are taken every two hours, but this limited extract from the ship's log gives an example of how the wind can change. Columns are headed up *Time, Wind Direction, Number on the Beaufort Wind Scale* (World Meteorological Organisation) and *Probable Wave Height in Metres.*

06/01/14			
0200	SE	Force 5 (Fresh Breeze)	2-2.5 metres
0600	SE	Force 8 (Gale)	5.5-7.5 metres
0900	Pitching and rolling, deck cargo (ie, *City of Adelaide*) sprayed by sea water		
2100	SSE	Force 7 (Near Gale)	4-5.5 metres

07/01/14 Wind direction continued to be from SSE until 0900 then it changed to from SE and at midnight it changed to ESE
08/01/14 ESE till 1000 till 2200, change to ENE
09/01/14 0600 change from ENE to NNE Force 7
0800 change from NEE to NE till midnight
10/01/14 NNE at latitude 39°39.2'S, longitude 038°24.5'E, change at 1400 from N, Force 6 Strong Breeze, 3-4 metre waves;
11/01/14 0200 change from N to NNW Force 6; 0600 Force 4 Moderate Breeze;
1000 W, Force 3 Gentle Breeze, 0.6-1 metre waves; noon latitude 40°04.3'S, longitude 044°48.9'E;
2200 change to SSW Force 5; midnight SW Force 5, steady until change on
13/01/14 1000 WNW Force 3
and so on.

Vadym was touching up paintwork outside on the bridge and we had a wee wave and a smile. Andriy V said he is my favourite. I said you are all my favourites. I asked him about my Equatorial name. 'It is in progress,' he said.

'Maybe I have broken with tradition. It is tradition is it not, to be given a name instead of choosing one?'

'This is normal,' he said.

'I am always breaking with tradition,' I said. 'You give me a name. Or make my name just *Seahorse*, instead of the full *Gypsy Dragon of the Ocean Moon*. Or give me a new name.'

He looked over at me. 'I think I have a name for you.'

I said, 'I hope it will be a good one. What is it?'

'Sea Nymph.'

I burst out laughing. We both went back to our studious ways. After a while Andriy asked me what I was doing so long. 'Just this,' I said holding up the nice new notebook he had given me. He needed the log book and took it away. I went over to him and said, 'Actually, I am spying.' He said,'This is not such closed information.'

German arrived as I began logging in to the computer for the two emails Andriy had told me I had. One from the system advising acceptance of my hairdresser's address, the other, a very speedy response from Rory MacLean replying to my request for some advice on book publishers. I thanked him, and added HarperCollins Sydney to my list of *must-dos* when I get to Australia. I showed the email to German and explained I had been on a writing course with this man. 'A writing course?' he said. 'I did a writing course when I was seven years old.' I dunted him, and we laughed.

Happy with my time on the bridge I came back to my cabin to work, leaving plans for a walk round the bridge on hold in case of colliding with wet paint.

I went to supper but could not eat much. Pork and chicken in aspic was presented in a large bowl. It was fresh out of the fridge and very cold. I picked out a few pieces of chicken. Russian salad was very tasty but…again, the dreaded boiled egg meant I could not shovel this tasty dish into my mouth. I painstakingly picked out what I could eat and devoured the baked potato with slice of bacon on top. I was glad German and Valeriy were not at the table with me to watch this dissection of Ukrainian traditional food. I managed to empty the left-overs into the food waste and think our new cook did not see this act of desecration.

I wrote a few poems, read a few and continued working on the Irvine section. I am enjoying the memories all this brings, and am looking forward to moving on. I went to the bridge to take some photographs of a stunning sunset, a golden crucible filled with liquid gold. German and Mykhailo were there. I returned to my cabin, played a few games of the usual three, and went to sleep around 12.30 am.

Neptune's Girls

Neptune roars and rolls,
shakes and slaps
the flat bottom of *Palanpur*.
He throws everything at her,
tries to silence the pounding
that drives her on through
the storm.

She is relentless.
The beat of her heart
is the guarantee of life
for seventeen sailors
and a grandmother
and a new beginning
for an old maiden
who brought new blood
to the City of Adelaide
whose name she bears.

We three girls are sisters renamed.
Hyundai Phoenix gave rise to *Palanpur*,
Carrick was burnt and shredded,
thrown to the murk of
the River Thames to refloat *City of Adelaide*
and I was baptised on the Equator,
named *Gypsy Dragon of the Ocean Moon*
and known to Neptune as *Seahorse*.

DAY FIFTY

September 30, 1864 – Friday

A squally day. The weather cold but bracing. We could not walk about so sat and had ropes fastened round us to prevent us from slipping.

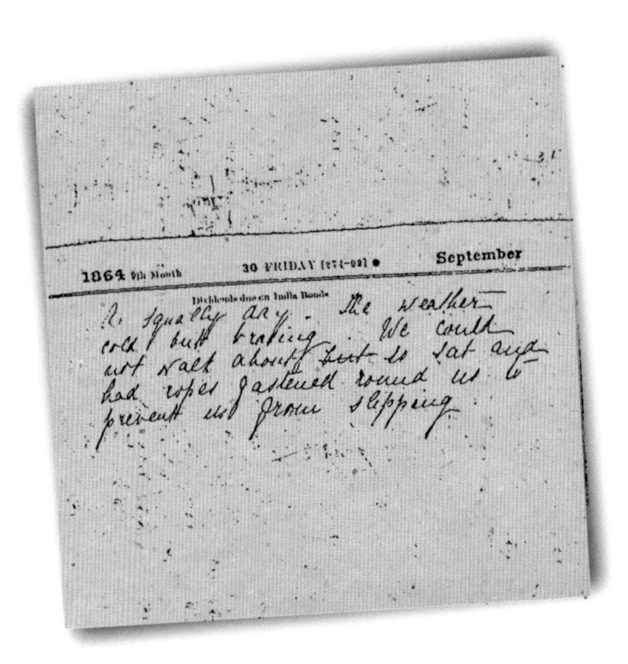

1864 9th Month 30 FRIDAY [274-92] September

Dividends due on India Bonds

A squally day. The weather cold but bracing. We could not walk about so sat and had ropes fastened round us to prevent us from slipping.

14 January 2014 – Tuesday – Indian Ocean

A grey start, a gentle sea and occasional rolling. This broke away to a lovely blue sky in the afternoon.

I awoke to my little brother on my mind. Today he is fifty years old. This is the fiftieth day of this voyage. One day for each of his years. I remember the day my father brought him and my mother home in a blue Ford Anglia, hired specifically for the occasion of the journey from Simpson Memorial Maternity Pavilion of the Royal Infirmary, Edinburgh. That building is now converted into exclusive apartments. Babies are now born in the modern, new Royal Infirmary at Little France further to the east of the city. A few months after he was born, I was dispatched to an all-girls boarding school and never saw the growing of him until we lost our big brother, aged 17, to suicide in 1968. I was allowed to come back home and finish schooling in my local grammar school where I felt uncomfortable in the presence of boys.

So here I am on *Palanpur* with *City of Adelaide* having had to overcome the inhibitions of being in the mass company of men, and men only. My hair is grey at the roots and I do not know if I will ever plaster hair dye on my head again. This voyage is not just about bringing *City of Adelaide* home safely. It gives an insight into her maiden voyage through the eyes of Sarah, and her final through mine. Through this unique experience I am shifting into a new phase in my life with an unknown destination. Those long-ago years at boarding school prepared me for separation from family. I ache at opening the old wound of everyone being at home except me, yet here on *Palanpur* I celebrate the lives of my family thriving in my absence. I am teaching my husband to cook, because I am not there to do it for him! I read somewhere that true love is letting a loved one go and do what they feel they must do to make them happy, and I believe it works for the benefit of all. It is different though when work separates a man or a woman from his family by necessity, not free choice. He provides for his family, but is not there to enjoy them.

After lunch I gave Stepan back his memory stick laden with some photos from the pel'meni party. I explained some of them were blurred. We had stir-fry beef with rice and salad, very tasty and a relief to have some different meat from pork. I went to check my emails. Four, two from Amos Connect saying my two new contacts had been accepted, one from Rory MacLean with an indicator of what to expect from a publisher in the way of payment, and one from the Society of Authors with advice on publishers and contract vetting, a service they will carry out when the time comes. I worked in the afternoon, and took a short nap of about an hour. There was a lot of activity on the deck again and the drill was going, but it did not seem to bother me. I had forgotten we had lost another hour of sleep with the crossing of another line of longitude. I did not envy the lads out there in the heat working with their backs bent de-rusting and painting the weather deck, wearing their gear whilst sitting on those cute wooden stools.

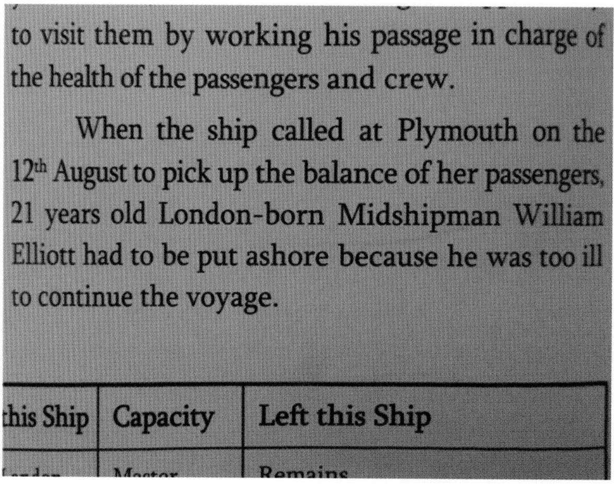

to visit them by working his passage in charge of the health of the passengers and crew.

When the ship called at Plymouth on the 12th August to pick up the balance of her passengers, 21 years old London-born Midshipman William Elliott had to be put ashore because he was too ill to continue the voyage.

this Ship	Capacity	Left this Ship

I decided to try to speak with my brother. I had been told there was a satellite phone in the hospital, where the young lad who had suffered so severely from seasickness and had to be flown home from Norfolk, Virginia, United States of America had lain. It is on the same deck level as the ship's office. I got the key from the bridge and put it into the lock.

'You have seven minutes left,' said the American voice at the end of the phone. This was the remnant of credit on the card I had used to try and phone my family on Hogmanay. It would be just enough for the purpose. I dialled the number. 'This number is not available at this time.' I thought our mother was perhaps on the phone to him. I might have to wait an hour before a possible connection. I tried again, putting the zero in after +44 just in case phoning a mobile in the United Kingdom was different to phoning a landline. 'This number is not available at this time,' she said again. I waited a few minutes. *Ring Ring Ring Ring Ring Ring Ring.* The phone went on and on. No connection to an answering machine.

'Hello.'

It was him.

In the background his wife was laughing. 'He wasn't going to answer the phone,' she said. *Laughter.* The phone was put on loud speaker.

'Where are you?' he asked.

'In the middle of the Indian Ocean,' I said. 'Happy birthday.'

It was exhilarating to hear their Scottish voices. It was strange for me to speak normally without the Ukrainian accent I had adopted. My brother told me they were headed up north to the mountains in their camper van with their three springer spaniels. There was snow on the grass verges. I was glad to be here in the sunshine in approximately 22°C. A few more words and we were cut off. I thought, *that was not seven minutes.* I tried the number again. 'This number is not available at this time,' she said in her jolly tone. I dialled one more time. Success. They had lost the signal driving into a dip in the road. Four minutes. Just enough time to hear about the party planned for the 18th, to wish my brother a happy birthday again, and to say how sorry I was when they told me my sister-in-law's mother had passed away.

I went back up to the bridge to give the hospital key back to Andriy V. Three heads were poring over a chart or some other document. German told me there were three ships ahead of us waiting to gain access to Port Hedland. He did not know how long we would have to wait for a berth. I had seen this scenario on the Live Marine Traffic website before I went to Rotterdam. There was a few days' delay before *Palanpur* could pick up steel at Bremen. We are at latitude 35°38.63'S, longitude 064°43.90'E, course 070, at 13.9 knots per hour, wind speed 15.5 knots. At supper there was a beef stew with potatoes through it, not unlike my own, and some gherkins with a hint of cloves in the flavour.

I wrote a few poems then went for an early night at 10.30 pm. I woke to a bright sheen flashing behind the curtains that were swaying in the swell. I pulled up the hem of one of them and saw a gleaming full moon. I wanted to rush to the bridge with my camera, but settled instead for a shot from the window of my cabin. It is very difficult to take a good picture of the moon on a moving ship, but I succeeded in getting a facsimile, with three moons beaming down on the skin of Neptune through a rainbow aura.

DAY FIFTY-ONE

October 01, 1864 – Saturday

Another rough day. In the morning we sighted the islands of Tristan d'Accuna, Nightingale and Inaccessible. Tristan d'Accuna is the only one inhabited. It belongs to the British. – There are about 700 people.

15 January 2014 – Wednesday – Indian Ocean

The bright moon last night made for an early dawn. It had peeped out from behind clouds and I remembered about the photograph I took through its rainbow halo round 5 am. Later, the sky was blue with popcorn clouds. All day the sea has been a blue satin quilt shaken in the sunshine, and diamond dust has landed back on it. We will never reach that dark streak of a horizon that is so elusive in this pure air.

I had an early-ish shower and got straight to work. I stripped my bed and found splinter number three under the mattress cover. I knew it. I pondered on how long it had taken to find its way there, being as these pesky pests are no more in size than a corn fly, and they move at less than snail's pace. *Squish.* I get that itching feeling again. After lunch of fish, tinned tomatoes and chips I went up to the bridge. I wanted to sit out in this amazing weather. Andriy V was very busy. He had a pile of paperwork stashed at the computer where the emails come and go. I logged on when he was in the small office area. Three emails: two from Ruth Currie both confirming and correcting the information I asked her for about Sarah's siblings, and for a recap on the identities of the children in the family photograph I had brought with me; and one from Alan. He told me some local gossip, and that he is picking up my mother to take her to my brother's party. All present and correct except for me and my wee granddaughter. I replied to Ruth, and to an earlier one from friends in Canada, and began one to my youngest daughter but had to cut that short as Andriy needed back on the computer. I printed off emails from yesterday that I needed to keep and went outside. Crewmember Vadym Gresco had been doing more touching up of the paintwork on the railings outside the bridge. It was almost dry, and I sat at the bow of *Palanpur* contemplating the incredible chocolate smoothness of the Indian Ocean. As I got up to leave and go back to work, I saw Vadym return from lunch armed with his paint pot and brush. He warned me the paintwork was touch dry, then he noticed an imprint from the palm of a glove on the curve on the top rail of the outside staircase. He looked at it with an expression of puzzlement and melancholy. An undercurrent of mirth rippled between us. I scratched my head. Then he said, 'It was me.' 'Aaaah,' I said with a gleam in my eye and a smile of relief. It was a pretty pattern of Solitaire, not the card game, but the one where you have to leap over little pegs to get to having only one left on the board.

We are at latitude 34°04.13'S, longitude 069°51.97'E, going at 12.3 knots on a course of 068-070. Wind speed is 3.5 knots. *Palanpur* is rolling smooth and wide, and *City of Adelaide* is echoing the dance. The thrill of glimpsing her planks, more than one hundred and fifty years in age, through the plastic cover is immense. It feels like I have swallowed a cup of acid and it has instantly evaporated at the thought of seeing her bared to the bright Australian sunshine.

I spent a productive afternoon looking back on the last few days' daily entries and wrote a couple of poems, whilst minding the load of bedding I had put on a 60° wash cycle. The dryer filter had an amazing amount of fluff from what are cotton sheets. I looked out of my cabin window as I hung the bedding up to air off over the lounge area table and chairs. The sea is developing moguls, like mounds of packed snow on ski slope black runs that I have seen but never experienced skiing over.

My dears, I am reeking of garlic. We had boiled beetroot salad and raw slices of that panacea for things gastric, garlic. I shall be well for a long time, and am glad I am these thousands of miles from Alan. He hates the smell of it. So do I for that matter, but when you are part of the garlic gobbling gang, *anti-social* is not in the vocabulary. The reek did not quite reach the other side of the officers' mess as I spoke to Andriy K about the Antarctic. Sergiy Fomin had indicated the other evening that Andriy had spent some time on board a small yacht that is part of the Harren & Partner fleet that did expeditions to Antarctica. I told him about Gavin Francis' book, *Empire Antarctica* and said I would let him see it. Andriy said he had spent two contracts on board this vessel. It had been in the Antarctic summer when temperatures were between -2 C and 10 C. Andriy V joined the conversation, sitting in the space next to his usual seat so that he would not obscure my line of vision to Andriy K. It had been a sociable supper, as prior to Andriy coming in Valeriy, German and I had a laugh about the story Alan had told me about a neighbour's run-in with the local constabulary, and this led to banter about *Palanpur* being a prison and when we get to Adelaide, I would need to wear a stripy uniform. When we talked about Richard Smith joining us at Port Hedland, it was decided he would also need to wear this attire, and both of us wear handcuffs. Jokingly, German asked me whether we should allow Richard aboard. With reluctance I said we should. I did not want to share my time with *City of Adelaide*, but he needed to make preparations for our arrival in Adelaide.

I was busy typing in my cabin when my phone rang several times. It is not quite at arms' length reach. It was German. 'Sorry to disturb you,' he said. 'There is a very bright, full rainbow at the front of *Palanpur*.'

I was touched at his thoughtfulness and said, 'I will be there right away.'

'Right away' it was not. I pulled on my jersey, put on sandals and fetched my camera. I looked out from the port side porthole and saw why he was excited. I was glad I did, for when I got to the bridge the clouds had already started to munch up the centre of the rainbow. Its brightness had faded, but I could see the faint beginning of a double one on the starboard. I took a couple of photos and a small video. German showed me the photos he had taken. He was really disappointed I had not seen the rainbow in its full glory. He asked me what took me so long. I replied I had to put on shoes and a jumper. We began to chat about education systems in our and other countries, the different ages children start kindergarten or nursery school, and the ages they begin more formal schooling. We agreed that the freedom of childhood is irrecoverable.

Andriy K came up for his shift. I went down for *Empire Antarctica* for him to look at. 'Woow,' he said. He flicked through the pages, looked at the index, then the photographs and showed me the area of Antarctica where he had spent two of his contracts with Harren & Partner. I invited him to borrow it.

German was sitting at his computer as I left.

'Thank you for the rainbow,' I said, and headed back to work.

DAY FIFTY-TWO

October 02, 1864 – Sunday

A rough but bright day. We were on Deck nearly all day. Prayers were read in the Saloon. After tea we went to the Sailor's Service. We had to walk through the water to get to the fore-part of the ship. We afterwards walked for a short time and then had some singing.

16 January 2014 – Thursday – Indian Ocean

The days are stretching out with early dawns. The sea is Morris dancing, flicking lace handkerchiefs at the flock of woolly sheep grazing in a heavenly azure meadow.

I woke at 8 am, turned over and found my eyelids peeling back to 9.30 am hands on the clock. I got straight to work. My main goal for today is to bring together Days 29 to 45 into the main body of this book. I set to the task straight away and felt a surge of elation when I saw how far it has come. The present word-count for the main body is over 91,000, a joyful number. I decided to work on the Irvine section. There is still much to write, the day when *City of Adelaide* was rolled off the slipway by the self-propelled modular transporter and onto the barge, and her leaving Irvine, Scotland for Chatham in England.

I went to lunch after my shower, Eintopf (not Saturday again), chicken legs, tinned tomatoes and rice. Oleksiy seemed a little less cheerful today. He is anticipating another loss of an hour's sleep. Last night he had spoken about the lack of wifi on board this modern ship. I agreed. I had assumed I would have internet access on board for blogging on my bare, new website and keeping my Facebook status up to date as well as sending photographs and information for the Australian *City of Adelaide* website. I had hoped to submit some articles for magazines and newspapers to help offset the cost of this voyage. This leaves me with some anxt, and I cannot emphasise enough how grateful I am for the generosity of Peter Christopher in offering me accommodation when I arrive in Adelaide. I will stay on board *Palanpur* until *City of Adelaide* is off-loaded on to the barge that will take her to the inner harbour. Oleksiy spoke about how he hoped to be able to communicate with his girlfriend other than by email. I supposed he meant by Skype or Facebook. He has set up his laptop in the galley to watch DVDs, mainly comedy. Anatoliy had his stereo system for listening to rock and even heavier than rock music when he was preparing meals. It makes it homely having these media with accompanying singing and laughter in the background.

Before I went into the galley I had bumped into Serhii. I took the opportunity of asking him for his form. I struck gold because I managed to waylay Kostyantyn

Portnyagin as well. Somehow Ihor Timoshytskyi slipped past, as did Vadym Gresko whilst I was talking to the other two. Kostyantyn could not find his form. I said I would give him another. Serhii said he already gave me his. I apologised, then remembered it was a contact address I needed from him. He said he would give me this. My good luck continued when Sergiy Fomin joined my little flock. I asked him if he would pop back to my cabin and run over what I had typed from the notes I took from him the other evening.

It feels good to be tying up loose ends. I found myself singing the chorus of *Bound for South Australia.* I joked with Andriy K at lunch, asking him if he had finished *Empire Antarctica* yet. He has left it on the bridge so that he can read it in the evenings when it is quieter.

I stormed on all afternoon with Irvine. I found I had forgotten things and it warmed me to the core to read about the times I had seen *City of Adelaide* at Irvine. She has left a huge hole on the western horizon of that town and will be mourned by many people who knew her as a hulk there, but also those who knew her as a club meeting place not so many miles north of Irvine at Glasgow, where she sank and was left for a year before Jim Tildesley, retired Director stepped in and offered £1 for her recovery and rescue to his place of work, the Scottish Maritime Museum. He did at one time manage to secure some funding for her, but it was nowhere near enough for anything major like preservation or restoration to be undertaken. It would be gratifying if the Australian descendants of those emigrants who travelled out from their respective countries on *City of Adelaide* would rally round and help or continue to help with her preservation; it would be a miracle if there was enough generosity in that great and prosperous land for her restoration. At any rate, she is in a place where there is more hope for her now than there has been for the last several years, and she has been spared demolition.

Supper came round really quickly and I was hungry. Oleksiy must have seen this in my eyes. He spread a huge dollop of mashed potatoes across a large plate, invited me to take the small bowl of side salad, and took my plate for a homemade pork burger: 'One,' I said, grinning and holding up one finger. He shook his head from side to side, weighing it up. On my way out Mykhailo said I would be going back home 'like this', holding out curved arms at his sides and blowing out his cheeks. I laughed, 'If this were so, it would mean divorce.' In the end I ate everything except the salty cheese in the salad, the second burger and a little potato. Oleksiy laughed when he saw I had not managed his defiance, and he scraped it into the food waste bin. I felt comfortable with what I had eaten but hate to see food uneaten.

'Don't worry,' he said.

'Don't worry, Rita,' said Kostyantyn.

'Don't worry, baby,' I sang. 'Do you know the Beach Boys?' I asked him.

'Yes,' he said, scraping his leftovers into the waste. The fish in the sea would be happy.

I had seen Valeriy at the table when I went for supper and almost spoke to him to make a time with him for the trip to the engine room. He got up with his plate so I decided to leave it. We have another couple of weeks for me to go with him and take some photos, and check on the information he had given me on my first visit.

Back in my cabin I could not face typing again. I had spent all day at it except for meals. I plugged earphones into my old laptop for the first time since I got it. I have had to get used to having earphones in, but I still do not like them. I listened to some music from *Karunesh*, grateful for the rags to riches difference in sound from listening through the laptop with the volume up. I found it very relaxing and it gently unwound my head. I thought Anatoliy would now be in the middle of written exams for his training to become an Electrical Engineer. I popped up to the bridge to take readings, and to look at the sunset. 'No rainbow tonight,' said German. He and Mykhailo were busy. I looked at the ship's tracking monitor. We have traversed the South East Indian Ridge and are at latitude 31°37.63'S, longitude 077°35.98'E, wind speed 23.7 knots, ship speed 15.4 knots. *City of Adelaide* has the sun on her back, a big pale disk you dare not look at for danger of blinding yourself. It is 24° at 7 pm on that thermometer in the shade.

I stepped outside and felt stickiness under my feet. Vadym is not going to be happy. He will see a pattern like the one he left on the handrail yesterday. But he will see the funny side of it. Mykhailo checked the soles of my sandals as I bent my knees to show them to him. There was a tiny speck of wet blue paint, I made sure it was not going to cause Andriy K any extra work in the morning so I took them off. My tongue is withering away with the lack of blethering today. I am concerned.

So concerned I went back up to the bridge to photograph the sunset and get those extra forms printed out. Andriy K came on Watch and I asked him to do this for me. I gave one copy to Mykhailo and explained about it. He will fill it out later. He said his wife had been asking about a t-shirt from the *City of Adelaide* merchandise shop. I said I would ask Peter Roberts about this for when we arrive in Adelaide. Discussion about speaking to Richard Smith about this when he comes on board at Port Hedland went on. I said Peter was the best one to ask about this as he runs the website. At any rate, t-shirts will be bought. German asked me if I had any questions. I said it is too late in the day for questions. Despite this we ended up talking about the Harren & Partner fleet. The computers on board are already out of date. It is easier to replace than repair if the need arose. The oldest ship German had been on was thirty years old, an age when scrapping takes place. German told me that there is competition now between *Palanpur* and another ship to be next in the queue to offload cargo at Port Hedland. If we do not get there in the evening of the 22nd we will be pipped at the post. The other ship anticipates arrival at 6 am on the 23rd. If we do not make it before then, there will be a delay of six days for us to get a berth in the port. This would add to shipping costs, and there would be a knock-on delay of our departure to Adelaide. This would muck things up rather for the planned celebrations down in that Port. Our luck may depend on what cargo the other ship has, and there may be berths for two ships. I now understood the upturn in our speed today. The race is on.

DAY FIFTY-THREE

October 03, 1864 – Monday

Not quite as rough as yesterday but very cold.

17 January 2014 – Friday – Indian Ocean

Last night the moon was full, forcing its way through a rainbow haze. It stole an hour from my sleep as I lay watching and filming it bouncing along with *Palanpur*, at first with the port porthole closed. I unscrewed the bolts securing it gently, to avoid them squealing in the silence of the night, and spread it wide open. The feeling of freedom and breathing in of this freshest, pure air is something I cannot find the words in the drawers of my brain to describe. I rummaged deep and wide, but they do not exist. The waves are gleaming under the moon. An occasional star made it through the cloud. *City of Adelaide* was bathed in milky white under its gaze. This morning the sea is tartan, cross-checked with blue hues and pinks.

I went to sleep after this wonderful experience with the moon. I found myself twirling the soft hair underneath my fringe. The silver moon had drifted back memories of my beautiful grey mare, Ginny, who was named Silver Moon when I first bought her. Another girl renamed. I felt my eyes sting and nipped my thoughts. I used to slip my fingers under her forelock and find those downy hairs at her poll between her ears, and rub it with circular motions with my finger ends. I kept thinking of her and Morgan, my other horse who was ten years younger than her, at twenty-three. I told you about Ginny earlier when I heard her snickering in my ear the first time I listened to Alan's MP3 player on the day I recorded her, the last day of her life. Fate throws cruel blows, and I was to lose Morgan within four weeks of her death, through mysterious circumstances, an unidentified cause. Fate also lays a soft hand on your shoulder, for I know that if I still had the commitment of those horses, I would have found it very difficult to make this journey because they needed looking after.

I slept longer in the morning with the interrupted sleep and woke with a tremendous feeling of well-being. I just had time for my shower and a cup of tea before lunch, a thin soup I crumbled a piece of bread into. Oleksiy is defeated. He has reduced my portions. I had some pasta twists with cheese on top, a pork fillet and tinned tomatoes. I put the plateful into the microwave to re-heat the food and enjoyed the melted cheese. I had taken a couple of forms down, one for him and one for Kostyantyn. I popped into the ship's office on the way to the officers' mess to paperclip them together and there sat Vadym. I gave him the blank form meant for Oleksiy as he had not returned his yet. He said he had it somewhere. He said he would fill it out, 'On one condition.'

'What is that?'

'That I am a hero.'

We laughed. 'Of course you are a hero,' I twinkled.

We were having a blether when Mykhailo came in and began to talk to him. I heard him mention the word *contract.* I took a form to Oleksiy who pinned it on his door to remind him to fill it out later.

I lay down for a short rest before going up to the bridge. I wanted to send the second newsletter to Jim Tildesley for the Education Officer at the Maritime Museum for the children. Andriy V was in a talkative mood. He asked if I knew the dance tune *Eins Zwei Drei Polizei.* I said 'No,' laughing, but I did know *Rhythm is a Dancer*, that had been on earlier. This led me to talk about how good my son is at moving to Dance music, and how he had record decks when he was a teenager, that were all the rage. I told him how I used to help supervise at the local youth club, checking the youngsters were not smuggling in alcohol and so on. He was amused by this. He asked more questions about my family and their musical interests. I asked him whether he would be increasing his family of one. 'Why not?' he commented. He told me about his sister, that she lives around 70 km from his house. She has two children. His parents are 40 km from him and his wife's parents are yards away. We discussed babysitting by grandparents, how the privilege of caring for the youngsters lights up the faces of the grandees. Andriy told me he had been a footballer at amateur level, even so he received good monthly pay. I felt he was torn up about this, just as Sergiy Forman is about his billiards playing. He mentioned some of his friends have gone on to professional football as part of the Black Sea team, or черное море (*Chernoe More*) in Russian, and another will be playing with *Olympic Lyon* in the spring.

German arrived on the bridge and greeted me. He went straight to the office area and printed off a lengthy what sounded like *Telex.* Andriy went back to work at the table with the couch, and I replied to an email from my youngest daughter. I breathed in some of the day air and went back to my cabin to continue with Irvine. It is stretching out with a couple of events that have been revived in my mind in the course of writing that section. I returned to the bridge. Readings for today are latitude 29°48.50'S, longitude 082°47.42'E. We are speeding along at 14.5 knots, almost maximum speed in violet-blue waves – remember there is a race on – and wind speed is 9.8 knots. The trajectory is Rosemary Island. I will email Rosemary McKay about this. Outside temperature in the shade is 22°C. Mykhailo arrived from his sleep, he looked shattered, and was not in good fettle. I did not hang about.

Soon it was suppertime, rice and a pork chop. Oleksiy had made Russian salad again. I checked about the egg. 'A little,' he said. I explained. He apologised, said he did not know. I think he has forgotten because in the beginning he told me Anatoliy had given him the rundown of what I do not eat. Oddly I can eat the dressing on the fillets he cooks. I think it is the texture, and also the distinct flavour of eggs that bothers me. Back in my cabin I lay down and listened to some *Karunesh*. I got back to work and heard a knock on my door, just about 8 pm. It was Sergiy. He said last night he had dozed off, and decided not to come up after 9 pm in case I was sleeping. I said I sleep when I am tired. I have to say this is a true luxury. He was holding his laptop and Kostyantyn's form and the contact information for young apprentice Serhii. Pronounced *Sergey* this name can be spelt two different ways. I offered Sergiy a cup of tea or a beer, but he declined. He looked at the typed notes of our chat the other day and gave them the thumbs up. I was relieved, because it was quite a bit of information to process. He showed me pictures of him helping develop and paint below decks of *Palanpur* in 2011 when she was just a year old and known as *Hyundai Phoenix*. He showed me some lovely photos of where he has been as an employee of Harren & Partner. He showed me photos of Seville and Rotterdam, he spoke of Dampier, he showed me a food market in Korea that looked absolutely disgusting with unrecognisable foods apart from clamshells, on sale. There was a tray of something that looked like boiled penises (sorry lads). I saw some photos of another ship in the Harren & Partner fleet, the *Palmyra*, and some showing precautions taken in certain areas to deter unwanted visitors, also known as pirates. There were many photos with the word *Fun* embedded in them. Sergiy's eyes welled up with pride when he showed me photos of his small son. The next time he goes home is in July. He will have been away for eight months. I wonder at how a marriage can stay intact in these circumstances when the couple are so young. It tears my heart to think of all the stages he is missing of his son's growing up. He told me his wife will send a new load of photographs to Harren & Partner. These will be brought on board by an unofficial delivery man in the form of a new Third Engineer who is coming on board at Adelaide. I told Sergiy our Captain German will be returning to *Palanpur* after his leave, and encouraged him in his aspirations. The battery on his laptop was fading. It was time to go. He thanked me for the chance to practise his knowledge of English. I thanked him for coming up, and said he was welcome anytime.

DAY FIFTY-FOUR

October 04, 1864 – Tuesday

The weather fine but the ship rolling very much. Early in the morning a man fell from the rigging and sprained his hand. Just after Breakfast a man smashed the middle finger of his right hand.

18 January 2014 – Saturday – Indian Ocean

Another beautiful blue sky and chopped jelly sea. There is a strong breeze but it is warm and fresh.

I awoke and spent an hour in my think tank until 10.30 am, then got up for the usual ablutions. I tried on my white three-quarter trousers I have been keeping for arrival in Adelaide. They fitted better than the last time I wore them. Happy days. Lunch was borscht, pork fillet, tinned tomatoes, gherkins sliced neatly and baked potatoes with a morsel of cured bacon on top. I ate the lot. After lunch I settled to reading over Day Forty-Seven to finalise it. It is slop chest day. I ordered a case of Budvar, a milk chocolate Ritter Bar and a carton of Mango juice. Andriy K has given me the first newsletter I have seen in days. I wished he had not. A little boy of three has gone missing in the neighbourhood where one of my daughters used to live. There was news of the birth of Princess Anne's daughter Zara Philips' first baby, a girl. The contrast of this baby's future life of privilege against the story I read of the death of a little girl of twenty months caused by her discharged soldier father, who had lost an eye in a gunfight in Afghanistan, made my insides churn. I cried for the little life, the harmless wee bundle that her mother had suckled from the warmth of her breast, nurtured and cared for in the eighteen months in the absence of her father. He had crumpled up her fragile body like a piece of paper.

A welcome interruption from penning morbid poetry came from my phone ringing. Andriy V spoke softly.

'Were you sleeping?'

'No, I am writing.'

'Rita, today we are having drill at 15.20 hours. We will do Man Over Board and Oil and Chemical Spillage. Please come to muster station for participation.'

Yay. Another chance to put on my orange boiler suit. I adjusted the plastic strap of my hardhat and discovered I can fit it against my head after all, removing the absolute necessity of using the chinstrap. I wish I had known this at the time Brian Oglanby was filming me in Rotterdam imitating the scene from *Titanic*. I am not looking forward to seeing that footage. I removed the two-litre bottle of water from the bag containing the immersion suit for the occasion and waited for the seven short, one long blasts on the hooter. I joined the segments and completed the satsuma. Andriy V took the roll call and asked the crew questions. He finished and said to me I did not need to take part in the next session, that he would talk me through it all in English once he had finished with the crew. I should wait somewhere, maybe in the muster station. I elected to go and stand in the shadow of *City of Adelaide*. I peered up at her planks on the bow. I went to her port side and peered up at her planks. I went back to her bow and sat on the spreader lying in front of her on the weather deck. German came out from the bridge and we waved to each other. I watched Andriy take the crew through the life raft drill and would later learn of the two types of raft, one stowed on the port side that automatically releases on removal of its pin, and when thrown overboard it self-inflates by a yank on the painter (a rope attached to the bow of a boat for tying it to a quay). Crew members could jump into this or access it by use of a ladder stowed beside it; the other on the starboard side is put over the side with the use of a davit. It is manipulated into place so that a capacity of twenty-four crew members can step into it at deck level. There is a red handle and a yellow handle that are used to manoeuvre the life raft out and away from the ship's side and to lower it into the sea when another handle, also painted red, releases the raft from the davit. Two men on deck hold the life raft steady in its descent with ropes, one at the inner side and one at the back to facilitate this operation. I asked about the rope stowage, was it a special way of winding and securing it. 'Yes,' he said. I have always been fascinated by the way ropes are stowed on sailing ships when I have seen them during the tall ships races. Food and water are stored inside the life rafts, refreshed regularly so that best before dates do not expire, and a knife is there to cut free from ropes attaching life rafts to the distressed ship.

I turned my back and faced *City of Adelaide*. I watched her shape swaying in tandem with *Palanpur*. I was right in her path. How lucky I am to be on this voyage. Home is very close now. I lay down in the sun for a while. The men went past me towards the stern, I assumed for oil and chemical spillage training. Some

sea spray moistened my cheeks and I licked my salty lips. I took a stroll around the weather deck and found the entrance to the rope stowage area for mooring *Palanpur*. I added a visit to that to my list of *must-dos* before I leave the ship. It looks a place of great interest and activity. I walked to the starboard side and saw the first flying fish I have seen since before Cape Town. I also saw rainbows in the spray again; complete ones this time. It would be impossible to take a photo of them from that angle as the spray would splash back and hit the camera.

Sometime later the men came back towards the accommodation block. Andriy came over to me. He said, 'Now I will show you *Man Over Board* drill.' We talked about the Williamson turn. This is a manouvre used to bring a vessel under power back to a point it previously passed through, often to recover a man overboard. He told me about the flares that automatically activate if the ship is sinking. He showed me the pictorial step-by-step guide to discharging the life rafts into the sea. Chief Officer Mykhailo appeared and began to reiterate some of what Andriy had already told me. We looked at the life raft that the Man Over Board team would use if the occasion ever arose. I asked Andriy if he had ever had to use these lifesaving facilities. 'Only in training,' he said. I asked whether, if the self-inflating ones are recovered, could they be used again. He said not. I suppose they will be recycled in some way or another.

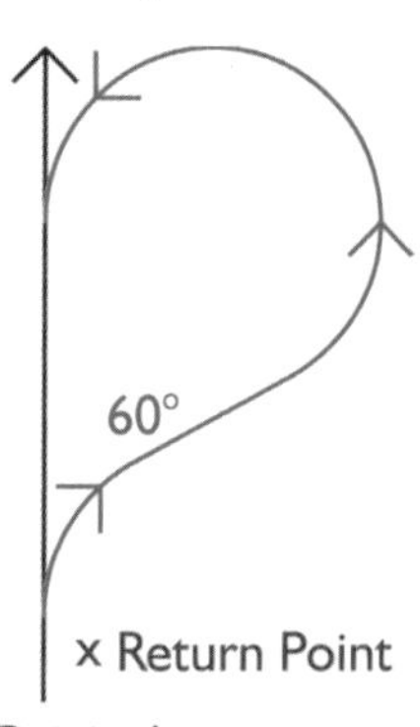

After drill I went to my cabin and stripped off to my shorts and top. I went up a deck to catch some sunshine, the first time I had sunbathed since before Cape Town. I had factor 40 on my upper chest, particularly since the skin in that area had been itching quite a bit over the last couple of weeks. I stopped putting Nivea on that bit, and began using the factor 40 instead and this seemed to help. I sat for about half-an-hour, enough in this latitude where the sun is powerful. I stood in the strong wind at the starboard side of *Palanpur* and almost got my cheeks to ripple the way they used to when Alan and I drove along in our old Triumph TR3 sports car with the windscreen removed, particularly in 1971 on the evening of 7 September after we were married in Edinburgh and drove back to Dunbar. Glamorous bride I was not. It took hours to remove the tangles from my long hair, and scrape dead insects off my face.

Suppertime. Beef and pork stew with carrots, mushrooms and tiny cauliflower florets. All was quiet. Nikolay Topilin, Third Engineer left more or less as I arrived. It was just me and Valeriy until Mykhailo came in. He took some borscht from lunchtime and was carrying his meal wrapped in aluminium foil. He asked me about the food we eat at home. I said it is much the same. We eat a lot of pork and beef, mainly pork because it is my favourite meat. He asked about mealtimes. I said they are about the same as on the ship but in my house they are never set. If I am absorbed in writing I do not cook. My husband and son will cook if I do not. They learned this self-survival skill when I went to Spain in 2002 for nearly a month during the tall ships race. Mykhailo asked me if we eat rabbit. I said not. I said people do, you can buy it in shops, but even if a rabbit is hit by the car or shot in the name of pest control, we do not eat it. I told them about when I was newly married and my husband and I were driving along in the dark. A hare had come out from nowhere. Hares are unpredictable. They come. They go. They dart back again. They stop. You have to give them time to find an opening where they can run safely into a field, and dip your headlights to help them do this. This hare had made its mind up. It disappeared. My husband accelerated the car. Wham! It had changed its mind. It was too late to miss it. We put it in the boot for our six year-old rescued German Shepherd to have for his supper the next day. I was young, only nineteen. I was a town girl. I stuffed the entire beast, fur, guts and all, into a pot and boiled it up for a few hours. I took it out and gave it to the dog who carried it off with glee. He scoffed the lot. There was no glee for us for the next few days. It was bad enough having the house stinking from the boiled hare. It was worse that we also had to suffer the stench from the dog trumpeting his gratitude via his rear end! The two lads had a good laugh at this. I stood up to take my plate to the galley and took it through. I headed up the stairs, then realised I had yet again left my cabin key on the table. I went back down. I met Valeriy at the bottom of the stairs. He said if I wanted to go to the engine room tomorrow morning, he would be working. I said this is his day off. He responded that he had some small jobs to do. What time would I want to go? I suggested after his coffee break. He said 9 am would be better as he hoped to be finished by the time coffee break came round. We would meet in the officers' mess, as we had the last time. I continued on my way for my key. I paused to take some salami and Emmental cheese from the fridge. I wrapped it in a napkin for later on to have on rye bread I still had from Anatoliy. I met Ivan and asked him about his permission form. 'I will bring you,' he said. The lads were gathering in the TV lounge. I went up to my cabin and deposited the goodies for later. I took the Peter Rabbit biscuit tin I had emptied earlier and took the last of the Quality Street chocolates I had been given for Christmas *From the Crew* from the fridge. I placed several packets of Haribo sweets I had bought for the crew in Cape Town and went back down to the TV lounge. The lads were all set up in front of the television, like they were in a mini-cinema. There was a lot of smoke. I stepped into the room. 'Some sweets from Cape Town.' I put the tin on a table, stepped back and left a room full of smiles.

DAY FIFTY-FIVE

October 05, 1864 – Wednesday

A beautiful day, light breeze. Doing very little. We have been on deck nearly all day. We each hemmed a scarf for the Sailor boys. I practised for a short time.

19 January 2014 – Sunday – Indian Ocean

A hazy start gave way to another beautiful day. It became very hot in the afternoon.

We are seven hours ahead and I bet they are still partying at my brother's house. It is 10.55 am and I am back from the engine room. I had gone down to the officer's mess as pre-arranged with Valeriy. I was there sharp at 9 am. I took a cup of coffee from the percolator then realised I had forgotten my notebook. I went back up to my cabin for it and returned downstairs. Ihor Timoshytskyi met me between the two messes, saying I was to go with him; Valeriy was waiting in the engine room. I grabbed my hardhat, camera, notebook and pen and went with him through the men's locker-room. It is like any other you would see: full of lockers. We passed these and he opened a door at the other end of the room. It connected to the passageway below the weather deck. We went to the port side corridor this time, through the hatchways where you have to duck or bump your head. Ihor opened the door to the engine room. There sat Vitaliy at a computer, Nikolay and Valeriy were standing. We immediately began the photoshoot. I took a few of each as individuals and in groups, and a couple of Ihor wearing safety goggles in the workshop before Valeriy, Nikolay and I went through to the engine rooms. Ihor plonked his ear defenders on my head. I already had in those funny wee orange plugs you can buy, but these were more effective and since he was leaving our company he did not need them anymore. Now we all looked like *The Fly*.

Inside the engine room communication was by hand gesture. There is no point in trying to talk over the noise of *Palanpur*'s heartbeat. Valeriy spread out his arms and stretched his mouth, silently asking where I would like pictures taken. We took some at the cylinders, at some dials, at the wall storage for oversized tools. Here we paused.

Nikolay handed me a large spanner about a metre long. He took one for himself. I tapped him, pointing at my spanner. I lifted it by its grasping end and put the open end towards his neck, and indicated for him to do the same to me. We put menacing looks on our faces as Valeriy clicked the camera button a couple of times. We moved on. I took a couple of those two standing one higher than the other using a laser beam to take the temperature of one of the engine parts. So it went on. It was great fun, and at the end Nikolay finished his minimal shift for a Sunday morning and escorted me back to the accommodation block. Oleksiy was busy in the galley. I spotted pel'mini in basins behind him. I asked him if I could take some photos of him and he had no hesitation in obliging. I stood where his array of ladles for dishing out soup, stews and so on would not obliterate his face. A few lovely smiles were set to the digital memory and he continued with his duties and I went up to my cabin and continued mine in the form of a lie-down. It had been an early start to the day for me, and the heat in the engine room was stifling. I had been sweaty again on this second visit but had been wiser and worn minimal clothing beneath my orange overalls.

At lunch I took a small amount of pel'mini. I covered them in tomato ketchup as Oleksiy had no soured cream left. They were tasty. A thin soup had preceded them and I told Valeriy and Mykhailo who were at lunch at the same time as me that at home we sometimes put tortellini into a thin soup. We also put Parmesan cheese over them. The Ukrainians are very fond of fresh ingredients and were unimpressed by my use of stock cubes.

I went to the bridge around 2.30 pm to take readings and to ask for another phone card. I checked how many hours we are ahead of Greenwich Mean Time. We had crossed another line of longitude so I had to wait another hour before phoning Scotland. Folk with hangovers need as much sleep as possible, and I did not want to cut into that. I had a good idea of what time my sister-in-law cooks breakfast after a heavy night, and therefore roughly when my family would emerge. I calculated back. 6.15 pm my time would be safe. I asked for the hospital key to use the satellite phone there to relax and not disturb workings on the bridge.

It was sometime after 3 pm. Readings were latitude 24°16.96'S, longitude 096°08.82'E. Andriy V told me I had five emails. 'You very popular,' he said. 'Some will be work,' I said. In the end, three from my youngest daughter, one was from Rosemary McKay, reading *We are all getting excited!* The final one was from Richard Smith who is joining *Palanpur* at Port Hedland, giving me details of his flight and hotel reservation.

Andriy came over. He showed me some seafaring cartoons on the computer. He tried to copy them to my flash drive without success. I pointed out that that particular one only has 1MB of memory. We had a good laugh at some of the images, in particular one where there were two floosies in the picture, one good-looking one with an ugly face, the other with a fabulous figure but ugly as sin. We began talking about the International Code of Signals where flags and pennants are raised. The Morse Code signs are printed after the colours and shapes of the flags. We joked about how to announce drunkenness:

Delta (dash dot dot) =	*keep clear of me: I am manoeuvring with difficulty*
Foxtrot (dot dot dash dot) =	*I am disabled: communicate with me*
Whisky (dot dash dash) =	*I require medical assistance*

I went down to the hospital and locked myself in. I dialled. A dozen rings or so later, my brother's voice bounced into my ear. I could tell he had had a skinful by the way his tongue swelled up his pronunciation. I asked how the party had been, how many were there and so on.

'About twenty.'

His wife in the background chipped in. 'Twenty-four to be precise.'

'The party was magic,' he said. 'My sister-in-law made me a cake of the trenches. It was amazing.'

My brother is pretty much an expert on WWI. He has been interested in the history of it for many years.

'It even had barbed wire on it and wee soldiers in the trenches.'

'Cool,' I said, wishing I had seen it for real.

'Do you want to speak to Alan?' he said. 'He's right here.'

Silence as the phone was passed over and we spoke briefly before I heard the voice of my youngest daughter. In the meantime the jungle drums beat that I was on the phone. Soon my little family was gathered round and I had a quick blether with each of them, including my mother. My son was breathing down her neck and she passed the phone to him. His girlfriend came into the room; she went back out to the camper van where my eldest daughter was asleep. She had not got the message I was phoning. She got to the phone in time for us to squeeze a minimal conversation in before the electronic American voice gave a minute warning that my phone credits would expire. We said goodbye. It had been a very fulfilling phone call and I whistled a wee tune on my way back to my cabin. My little brother. Fifty.

I went up to the bridge to give back the hospital key. Mykhailo came up shortly afterwards. He spoke of my washing in the machine that had finished its cycle. He said he had stuff in the drier. When he took that out he would move my washing up for me. I said, 'It is okay, I can do it myself, thanks.' We talked a little. He talked about something that a writer should have. I did not quite grasp what he meant. He asked if I would be asleep at 9 pm. I said not. He said he would knock on my door and 'give you'. I wondered what he meant, but said *okay* regardless. I made to go down to my cabin as there would be a handover between him and Andriy V.

He said, 'You are going to cabin now?'

'Yes.'

'I will come with you and give you this.'

We went down stairs. Mykhailo went into the open door of his cabin two doors from mine and stepped back out.

'This is for you.'

Into my hand he gently placed a feather.

'It is black goose feather. You must have. All writers must have a feather.' He gesticulated dipping a quill into an inkpot. 'It is not real pen, but you must have feather,' he said, quite animated.

I turned the soft, black feather over in my hand. It was beautiful and I felt warmth spread through me. I noticed a second, much smaller feather. It was tinged with spectacular royal blue fluffy down right at its point. Both were attached by a spring hook to a plastic ring with the words *Alpha Edition* printed on. Alpha Edition. I hope this is a good omen for this book.

'You can cut,' he said, scissoring his fore and middle fingers, meaning I could remove the plastic ring. I was really touched by his thoughtfulness, and wondered why he had such a thing with him.

After supper of pork chop, pasta and tinned tomatoes I went to the bridge again. German was there. He told me a couple of jokes:

'A master of a ship in distress calls the USA coastguard:

'We are sinking; we are sinking!'

'What do you mean you are thinking?'

'No. We are sinking we are sinking!

'Okay, your boat is thinking. What is it thinking about?'

'No! We are SINKING! Our ship is going down.!'

Then: 'A master is helming his ship. It is night time. He sees a light in the distance. The light is getting closer. And closer. The master signals for them to alter course. There is no response. The distant light gets closer and closer. The master signals again. Still no response. He takes his binoculars and puts them to his eyes. Only then does he see. The distant light is a lighthouse.'

I told German I had been back in the engine room to take some photos that morning. He asked Mykhailo to show me some photos of *Palanpur* and some other ships in the Harren & Partner fleet, where they had been and cargo they had taken. There was a huge tank weighing 600 tons; there was a photograph of a worker in India wearing a hardhat that was nothing more than a piece of plastic shaped to his head that would give none of the *egg box* protection fitted to our hardhats; there was a hold full of pipes of different diameters from quite thin to really wide, bent into shapes just like a pipe you would smoke, each piece carefully stacked and tied together to avoid movement during the voyage to their destination. It was an amazing sight, a tangle of steel tamed against wooden blocks with webbing straps. I was distressed to see an articulated lorry in Korea where a monkey was tethered to the trailer behind the cab. I hoped the owner brings it inside when the lorry is moving. There was one shot of this poor creature with crazed eyes drinking from a can of cola.

The three of us spoke on many topics, language again, how all official and legal paperwork is written in Ukrainian yet the majority of people communicate in Russian apart from in the west where 99-100% still use Ukrainian as their daily language. I was happy to hear that in recent years there is a resurgence in feeding the Ukrainian language into the mouths of youngsters, that there is a marked difference between a nine year-old's grasp of the language as compared to a sixteen year-old's. I spoke of pronunciation, how difficult it can be to understand a cultured English voice, or a voice from the Aberdeen region or from the Scottish Islands. We spoke of dialects, influences from other cultures, and how we are able to understand each other.

I asked again about the hour forward. German looked at a Marlow calendar. We spoke about this company, how it is a major employment agency for seafarers, with their largest office handling thousands of personnel being based in the Philippines. When I first came on board there was a notice on the main announcement board down by the messes, appealing for staff to donate to the relief of the after-effects of the awful hurricane they had suffered there just before I embarked on this voyage.

I had spent a couple of hours on the bridge.

I thanked everyone and went down to my cabin. It has been a full day filled with great laughs. I am going to miss these guys.

DAY FIFTY-SIX

October 06, 1864 – Thursday

A wet morning but very beautiful afternoon. We are sailing along much faster than yesterday. We worked and read in the Saloon all the morning and after lunch walked about the Deck.

20 January 2014 – Monday – Indian Ocean

A cloudy day with some blue sky. The wind is stronger, the waves shorter with little white flecks. This gave way in late afternoon to grey sky and rolling seas that made me sit down now and then for fear of losing my feet. The temperature dropped and I closed my porthole.

I awoke at 10.15 am feeling very sleepy. I did not get up straight away. When I did I went for my shower, cup of tea and then down to lunch of pasta with Parmesan cheese, tinned tomatoes and a breaded cutlet. Getting down at the start of mealtimes is better as the food is freshly cooked and not sat on a heater or placed beneath aluminium foil till folks come to eat. After lunch I lay down and slept some more. I awoke at 3 pm. The swell is getting up and the ship is rolling a lot. This will slow our pace down and we may not make it to Port Hedland ahead of the other ship that we are racing against. We still have about another 1000 miles to go and must get there on Wednesday evening to beat them to the queue. German told me last night that we need a specific berth because we must have a wide area to stack the sections of the weather deck onto as the crane lifts them off, like the apron at Norfolk, Virginia, United States of America. I went down to supper, beef risotto, very tasty. Oleksiy is back to his old ways of piling it on, but I managed. I enjoyed the sauerkraut as ever. I am writing this after supper, with a Bud beer to try and keep away a threatened migraine. I know. Not something the doctor would recommend, but I am giving it a go. I had a strong hot chocolate last night and three chunks of Ritter Bar. These could be the culprits that caused my sore head. After supper I felt like I did when I was at Guide camp again, when I was eleven. It was the first of my little brother's summers. We guiders were to be away from our families for a whole week. I hated it. I hated sleeping in a tent. I hated the food, especially the cabbage. I hated the chemical toilets. I hated the separation. Midweek on Wednesday our parents were allowed to pay us a visit. I packed my stuff and was ready. When my mother came with my wee brother, we all three went home together. I was never so relieved. I did not know it then, but just a few months later I would be sent to boarding school.

I am not quite sure when my trend of running away began. Probably when I was a toddler and disappeared from playing downstairs from our top floor flat with several other children. My mother eventually found me at the promenade, where I had dropped my doll down the cliff. It had landed on a grassy shelf. She got there just in time to stop me from trying to retrieve it. At boarding school I was always plotting. Plotting by myself and plotting with another girl who was also very unhappy. She left somewhere around third year. I began cross-country running after school, ducking under the school's boundary fence and heading off across the bog below the tennis courts, along the valley and up through the field at the other side of the hockey pitch and back into school boundaries. I had put on a lot of weight with the stodgy school food, and this was my cure for losing it. No one ever missed me. I had tried to get permission to become a weekly boarder and be allowed home at weekends, but the headmistress disallowed this because she reckoned it would unsettle the other girls whose homes were too far away for them to weekly board. I hatched a plan. There was a bus that brought girls from Berwick in to school each morning. They were picked up in the afternoon to go home. I sneaked onto the daygirls' bus one Friday afternoon, got into Berwick, took the train to Dunbar and surprised my mother. Of course she telephoned the school to say I was safe. Of course I got into trouble for being disobedient. It did not stop me from doing it again. And again. And again until the nuns finally gave in and made it official. My father was working in Italy at the time. Had he been home I would not have got away with this. I look back and think that although I was very unhappy at boarding school, it prepared me for being in confined spaces.

Lately I have been asked if I am not fed up with being at sea. 'I love it,' is my staunch reply. I have been at sea almost seven weeks since Norfolk, Virginia, United States of America, with only a few hours on shore at Cape Town. You would think it would be quite quiet here in the great wide ocean. The sea is constantly whispering, swishing, roaring. The air conditioner constantly hums. Men work. Crane hooks clank. The ship is power-washed on a regular basis. Occasionally you can hear the beat coming from the stern where the engine room is. There is certainly nothing silent about this voyage.

DAY FIFTY-SEVEN

October 07, 1864 – Friday

A showery day. We were on Deck nearly all the morning. I have finished reading 'Charles O'Malley', a very interesting tale by Charles Leser.

21 January 2014 – Tuesday – Indian Ocean

A grey morning, brightening up with the ageing of the day. I worked very hard and did not see much of the outside conditions. The Irvine section is just about finished now. It will be a relief to move on to write about Greenwich.

I was up at 9.30 am to press on with Irvine. I feel quite weary with it, and am determined to bring it to a close tomorrow. I had to study photographs to get the sequences of casting the lines off to free *City of Adelaide* on the barge into the Firth of Clyde. I passed Vadym at lunchtime. He said he had not forgotten about 'this piece of paper'. I still have a few permissions to be handed back. I also passed Ivan who had said he would give me his the other day. I just look at him in a certain way, and hope he gets the message. My head was buzzing when I went up to the bridge. Readings for the day are latitude 21°25.45'S, longitude 106°52.05'E, we are going at 14 knots, wind speed is 18 knots. Outside temperature is 27°C. Andriy pointed out his favourite band *Ocean Elsa* was on the player. He described it as soft, or romantic rock. He gave me his memory stick with photographs he talked of the other day. There are a fabulous lot of a baby whale coming right up to the hull of *Palanpur* with his mother standing off allowing the crew to *admire her baby*, as he put it. There were others of various ships and some striking ones of Table Mountain.

When German came up to the bridge I asked him about the promotion process. He explained there are different ways of progressing and different nationalities have their own system that ultimately leads to the same qualifications. Governments may sponsor places, individuals have to pay fees for college, you may gain practical experience on board a ship before college verification, but a standard entry test is undertaken to prove suitability for the vocation of a seaman. He gave me a large handbook, *Standards of Training, Certification and Watchkeeping for Seafarers*, shortened to STCW. The STCW Convention and STCW Code book includes amendments, and is stamped with the approval of the International Maritime Organisation. Chapter VIII covers *Standards regarding Watch-keeping*. It covers topics such as: fitness for duty; voyage planning; watch-keeping principles in general; watch-keeping at sea; protection of marine environment; principles to be observed in keeping a navigational Watch that covers for example, lookout by sight and hearing in addition to all other available means, appraising risk of collision, stranding and other dangers to navigation, detecting ship or aircraft in distress, shipwrecked persons, wrecks, debris and other hazards to safe navigation. When on duty the lookout will not undertake any other duties or be assigned them as this could interfere with that task. It goes on about how the helmsperson and lookout are separate. There are variants built into the rules such as for night watch, weather and sea conditions, traffic density, fitness of crew members on call, familiarity with ship's equipment, procedures and manoeuvring capability. It goes on at length covering all situations to do with watch-keeping under different conditions and in different areas; taking over the Watch where the officer handing over has to be satisfied that his relief is in a fit state to take over. If he is in doubt, he must notify the ship's master. The relief must familiarise himself with all conditions prevailing at the time of taking over the watch. It goes into every possible detail you could think of. There are also Principles to be observed in keeping an engineering watch; Principles to be observed in keeping a radio watch; Watch-keeping in port; Taking over the deck watch; Watch in port on ships carrying hazardous cargo; Cargo watch. This is just one small section of the handbook.

I asked German about the possibility of being present on mooring operations when we get to Port Hedland. Right away he said this is okay. He and Mykhailo both advised that I must wear my safety gear and keep a look out for my personal safety in respect of ropes springing back or coiling. The update on arrival at Port Hedland is we hope to make it by tomorrow evening at 8 pm in order to get a berth and not have to wait for six days at anchor, if the other ship beats us. It will be a long, boring wait at anchor in the heat if we do not make it. I had an email from Richard Smith asking about what socket points we have on board. I told him two-pinned European. He is flying up on Thursday on a lunchtime flight and staying two nights in a hotel at Port Hedland. German informed me that a project manager will be coming aboard at Port Hedland as well. Two cabins will be prepared for these new guests. I was dozing later in my cabin when Mykhailo knocked on my door hunting for extra bed sheets. I gave him my spare set. I lay down again after he went away and slept till after 8 pm. I continued working on Irvine, reading through from beginning to end.

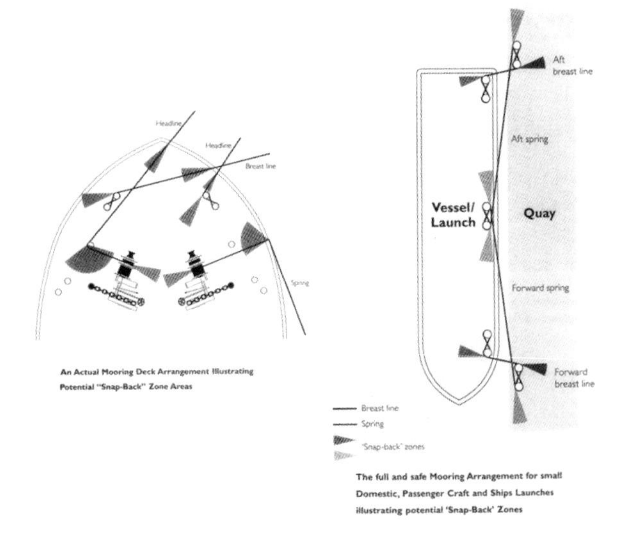

An Actual Mooring Deck Arrangement Illustrating Potential "Snap-Back" Zone Areas

The full and safe Mooring Arrangement for small Domestic, Passenger Craft and Ships Launches illustrating potential 'Snap-Back' Zones

I went to bed about 1.30 am, feeling a bit unwell. I have been overdoing it somewhat. There is a lot of rolling of the ship as well and although I am not nauseated, my head feels under terrific pressure, particularly above my eyes.

DAY FIFTY-EIGHT

October 08, 1864 – Saturday

A miserable day. It has scarcely ceased raining. We were unable to go on Deck. I practised a short time. Afterwards I played Backgammon with Doctor and won two games out of three. In the evening we had a little Music and singing. About 1 A.M. we rounded the Cape.

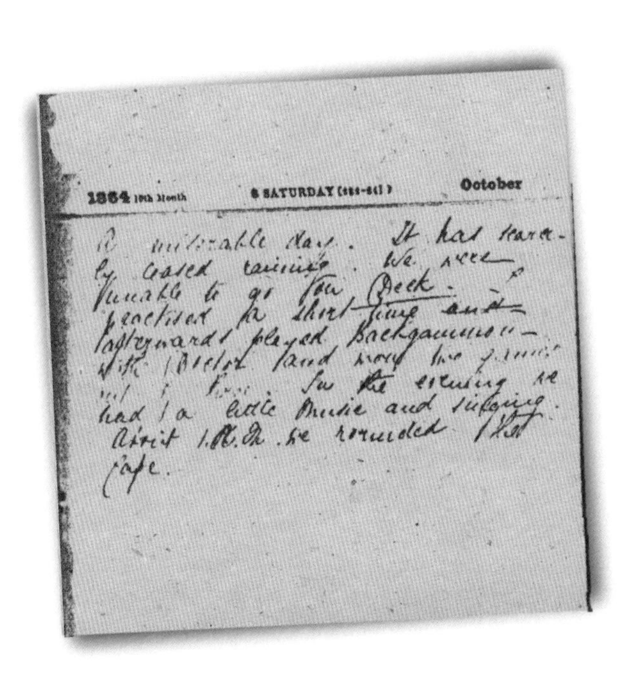

1864 10th Month 8 SATURDAY ([illegible]) October

A miserable day. It has scarcely ceased raining. We were
unable to go on Deck. I
practised a short time and
afterwards played Backgammon
with Doctor and won two games
out of three. In the evening we
had a little Music and singing.
About 1 A.M. we rounded the
Cape.

22 January 2014 – Wednesday – Indian Ocean

Another grey morning but getting very warm. I felt really unwell this morning when I awoke at 7 am. I had a long drink of water and some mango juice, then decided to take my bedcovers over to the lounge and lie at the same direction as the pitching of the ship. It is like lying on your back on a seesaw. I could feel the blood gushing from the soles of my feet to the topmost peak of the ripples in my brain. I slept for a couple of hours and felt much better. I decided not to use the computer this morning. Instead I washed my cabin floor. I wonder if I will have any hair left by the time I get to Adelaide. It all seems to be collecting on the cloth. I felt a bit better and went for an early lunch, chicken soup, chicken legs stuffed with garlic, rice and pale gherkins.

Valeriy was there. I told him I would upload photographs from the engine room to the ship's computer this afternoon.

Andriy K came in to lunch. I said to him I would be coming for him to 'show me the ropes' tonight. He said we were not arriving in Port Hedland until tomorrow about 11 am. *Mooring procedures*, to give the process the correct term, would not be until around 12 noon. 'You are very welcome,' he said. We talked some more about Antarctica. He said that there are cruisers exploring the region but with the small 47 metre motor yacht of the Harren & Partner fleet a trip is more exclusive, as this vessel can go into channels the larger cruisers cannot. This can make a very unique gift for those who can afford to charter the yacht for those special occasions. Confidentiality about who has chartered the yacht is vital, for obvious reasons. I told Andriy about our sailing experiences around the Greek Islands. We had been three times: once when I was five months pregnant with our first child; once when our children were teenagers, and the third time when it was Alan's sixtieth birthday and the whole family and their partners came along to share a 48' yacht. Andriy told me about some other ships, widths, lengths and so on. He had some paperwork with him. I had heard some mention of *safety meeting*, and guess they are preparing for tomorrow's discharging of the six locomotives back into Rob Carbon's care. I had seen German and Mykhailo from my window on my way to lunch checking the lashings of *City of Adelaide*. Mykhailo was taking notes. There are temporary guardrails erected all around the deck where the covers will be lifted off tomorrow.

I went up to the bridge just before 3 pm to see what our position is. We are at latitude 20°14.60'S, longitude 112°59.23'E, we are storming along at 16.3 knots, wind speed 27 knots, and it is 30°C. We are crossing the Exmouth Plateau. I gave Andriy V my memory stick with photos of the pel'mini party and the engine room and a few of me in various poses, e.g., Greenwich and the firewalk over hot coals I did to raise funds for local respite facility, Leuchie House. 'Rita, Rita,' he said, shaking his head. The sun is struggling through the clouds, it is very humid. I am going to sit out for a wee while. The atmosphere was not so great, with the fumes from the exhaust of the ship blowing forward, so I came back inside. I went down to the ship's office as the computer on the bridge is fully occupied today with preparations for tomorrow. I found an email from Richard Smith saying he has arranged for him and me to do a newspaper interview tomorrow. I was somewhat taken aback. He talked about sometime after 2 pm. I will need to tell him I have arranged to be on mooring stations at roughly 12.30 pm and will not be available until later in the afternoon.

I went back up to the bridge, then down to sunbathe. I did about ten minutes on each side. It is over 30°C, but the sea air is cooling. Back in my cabin I felt a bit peckish. I had a pot of yoghurt in the fridge and the pistachios I had bought from the very first slop chest. I cannot believe they have lasted this long. At supper I could only eat the pasta and sauerkraut. I just picked at the meatball. I am not in the mood for meat. Vitaliy, however, was. He came in with a giggle. His plate was piled higher than I thought ever possible. I said I was worried he would burst if he ate it all. Nikolay said it was a good amount of food for a hard-working man. Vitaliy added a slice of bread to the whole to make it perfect. Before all this, German had apprised me of the schedule for tomorrow. The pilot would arrive at 11 am to see us into port. Mooring would begin around one and a half hours after this. Walking in the port is not allowed, access is by vehicle only. The Seaman's Mission is only about 500 yards from where we will be moored, but the agent will be able to take me for wifi access. German also told me you can buy a modem so that wifi can be used on *Palanpur*. This will be very handy. Earlier German had told me about the project manager who would be coming aboard at Port Hedland, similar to those who had been on board in Rotterdam. They are ex-captains who take these jobs on so that the Captain or Master of the ship can concentrate on his regular duties and not be diverted by managing matters of cargo. There will be a meeting in the morning to discuss proceedings.

I went up to the bridge again to discuss this matter of a modem with German. I had not quite grasped what he meant. I took up my wireless dongle. He said it looks like that, and went to get his. I saw it has a slot for a sim card in it. Now I understand. I am a bit agitated I have not been able to get to a computer today for any length of time. I will welcome such a gadget, it will give me independence and privacy. I should also be able to send attachments with it. I am going to try at least to send an email to Richard this evening. I need to check when he is arriving. I think it is tomorrow but he talked of a lunchtime flight and if he wants a newspaper interview from 2 pm it will suit us both to have a later interview. I am not compromising my planned time being shown the ropes.

I began the Greenwich section of this book. At 10 pm I went to the bridge to send Richard an email about tomorrow. It was so dark and peaceful up there I backtracked and found the ship's office computer was free. I responded to an email from my youngest daughter, and got back to Richard, suggesting 3 pm.

DAY FIFTY-NINE

October 09, 1864 – Sunday

A beautiful day and going along well. We were on Deck all the morning. Prayers were read in the Saloon. In the evening we went to the Service at the forecastle. Harry read a Sermon – the jist of which was I am the way. We walked on the Deck for about an hour and afterwards sang till 10 P.M.

I am amused at Sarah's scant reference to the sermon.

23 January 2014 – Thursday – Indian Ocean

A beautiful day. We also are going along well. I drew my curtains back to see the seascape had completely changed. We are pushing through low, short waves of pale teal. No sign of land yet. I took my shower, popped in contact lenses for the first time in two months, and was up on deck just after 9 am. Andriy K is on Watch, no cheeky remarks about my earliness this morning. He is too busy concentrating on navigating *Palanpur*. The computer was free so I took my chance to see emails. There was one from my youngest daughter and one from Rosemary McKay reminiscing about her own arrival to Australia from Glasgow, Scotland thirty-five years ago. German called to me from his wee office area. 'Rita, I need your help.'

'What is it?'

He came over and handed me two sheets of paper stapled together. Peter Christopher has released a statement to the Press about *City of Adelaide* arriving at Port Hedland. The paper was from Combi-Lift – Operation:

'Hi German/Micki,
Looks like you guys are going to be famous ;)
Brgds, (best regards)
Micki'

Forwarded along with this message was Peter Christopher's Press release, with a covering message:

'Hello Simon
Just alerting you to growing media interest in the Palanpur arriving in Pt Hedland in case you wish to alert its Master. TV and print media photographers will be there. The following is the media release which we issued today. Thursday will be the first time in over 125 years that the City of Adelaide has been back in Australia.'

German and I discussed this, how it will be difficult to answer media questions without knowing what they are going to ask. He referred to me knowing the history of the ship. I said the CSCOAL Directors were the best people to speak on this, my strength lies in my obsession with *City of Adelaide*, and Sarah Ann Bray's connection with her, especially through her diary. He talked about the fame aspect, that I must have expected news interest. I knew we would have Press coverage, but did not expect it yet. He said I would need to put on makeup for the cameras. I said I would be wearing my safety gear. We joked it would be a good idea to put on hardhats, and even welding masks. I told him I had had a little experience of being interviewed for television, when John Riddell of *7News* spoke with me at Greenwich.

German advised me we are behind schedule a bit, estimated time of arrival is now 3.30 pm. This soon changed. We now expect to arrive at 5.30 pm. We will have to anchor in the bulk cargo area for approximately three hours. I soon found out what the bulk cargo area is. Ships, ships, everywhere! So much steel concentrated in this area. Some are with ballast, with a high freeboard, others you can see are laden to where the deck lies not so far from the waterline, possibly up to the Plimsoll line, the mark on the hull of ships that denotes the maximum safety limit for the weight of cargo carried. Ships can be at anchor for months waiting for cargo.

I was taking photographs of the ships unsuccessfully stapling the waves together and decided to go up to the top deck to photograph the Australian flag. I also managed to capture the Harren & Partner pennant before it was taken down from the main mast. The Combi-Lift one remains in place, proudly flapping in the wind. I noticed Harren & Partner's mission statement on headed paper on the bridge:

Zero injuries and spills
We believe in solutions

They have certainly fulfilled that on this voyage.

'Tak,' (Ukrainian for *yes*) and a long sigh came from the bridge.

I asked German what the yellow pennant up beside the Australian flag was. 'It is for quarantine. We will soon be able to remove this,' he said with a smile.

I can see land! Land ho! We are into shallower waters now, and I see pink patches ghosting amongst the pale teal. There are a couple of small black patches of what looks like oil skimming the water. All I can hear is the Australian flag flapping on the top deck, and *City of Adelaide*'s shredded shroud is flapping too. It is applauding her arrival into the waters of Australia.

It is time for silence. Communication is taking place between the bridge and shore, instructions being relayed and acknowledged by German. Andriy K is on the helm, German is look-out. We are bumping on the waves a bit. It is quite choppy. A roadmap of marker buoys leading to the channel stretches for miles towards land. Andriy V has come back to the bridge, his khaki overalls removed. He is now on Watch. Everyone is concentrating, peering down into screens showing readings that will bring us safely to our anchorage. At 12.15 pm we put our brakes on. *Palanpur* shuddered in her bridling. We have won the race.

We have come to a sharp halt at 12.20 pm. *Palanpur*'s tummy is rumbling with the sound of chains releasing the anchor to hook into the seabed. Plankton is drifting in soft pink clouds all around our hull. German checked the anchorage and spoke on the radio phone. He was calling Port Hedland. He gave our anchor position. A light has come on on the topmast indicating we are at anchor. I noticed a statistic that the port anchor has 11 shackles.

I went down for my lunch, for *Palanpur* was not alone in her tummy rumbling. Eintopf. Hooray. I took a piece of baguette and ate quickly. Beneath the aluminium foil lay a treat: mashed potatoes, pork stew with mushrooms and yellow gherkins. I made up a sandwich for later with some really dark brown bread, not quite Pumpernickel, not quite the paler rye grain bread Anatoliy had given me a while back. I am looking forward to tasting it later, with its filling of Emmental cheese and salami. I went to my cabin feeling somewhat shattered. It is becoming really emotional lying off the coast of Australia. It is all go with the locomotives being unloaded tomorrow. I lay down on my bed ruminating over what had happened in the last five hours. Soon my eyelids closed, I drew up a blanket and closed them again. I was almost asleep when my phone rang. I hoped it would not be for a drill warning. 'Rita,' Andriy V's voice spoke in my ear. 'Do you want to see a helicopter land on one very large vessel?' and, 'Pilot is coming on board in about five minutes.'

'I will be there straight away.'

I grabbed my cameras and headed up to the bridge. Within those five minutes sure enough a tiny black dot could be seen with binoculars away in the distance towards the land. Closer and closer it came to a huge ship moving slowly in the shipping channel. The helicopter came close to the deck, hovering like a bee gathering pollen from a flower. It finished its business and proceeded, tail in the air, nose to the deck of the huge ship as though seeking out more pollen. It lifted its head level then flew up back to invisibility. I was so grateful to Andriy for thinking of asking me to come and share, for me, this unique experience. I returned to my cabin armed with some amazing images in my camera.

Anchors a-weigh! Time to go!

I and my cameras returned to the bridge. In the distance a yellow pilot boat was approaching us at great speed. The life of an ex-captain or ex-chief officer is indeed racy. It is a life I think I would have enjoyed. In fact, a life at sea is one I know I would have enjoyed.

We weighed anchor at 3.15 pm and the pilots were on board at 3.25 pm. We left latitude 20°09.25'S and longitude 118°31.20'E in a wind speed of 12.8 knots. It is 30° in the shade. Andriy V put on the coffee. I took a half-cup and cooled it down with water. We are turning to starboard. I noticed the Harren & Partner pennant has been raised again. I took video of the yellow pilot boat approaching, and some photos. A huge dragonfly was flying about the bridge, but it was camera shy. Every time I tried to capture its image, if ducked away. It was actually bigger than the helicopter. Perspective plays nonsensical games with our vision.

We are to have only one tug for berthing. One of the two pilots who had boarded us quizzed German about all the checks that should have been carried out for arrival at Port Hedland. He was very assertive and German was able to answer in the positive. He was being addressed as Captain. We even sounded *Palanpur*'s horn to assure the pilot that it was in working order. The pilot advised German that if he had any concerns about anything he should speak to him. He said he is a pilot in training. If German had concerns about this, there is a second pilot on board who is qualified, and he would take over if German had objections. German had to sign off an agreement that he was happy with the arrangements in place. At 3.33 pm the pilot took over navigation of *Palanpur*.

There are dark patches in the now pale-green water. These bruises are not from cloud punch. They are not oil. They are rises in the sea bed that we must avoid. There are still a lot of pink patches around, plankton. Discussion was taking place around the mooring arrangements, two plus one plus one, whatever that meant. German mentioned what would be the situation for lights. This would be confirmed in the berth.

'Steer 162,' said the trainee pilot.

'162,' says German, acknowledging the order, repeats course information to confirm course.

I noticed Igor, Able Seaman, is on the helm. He looked different in the light where the bridge shades had been drawn. I asked Chief Officer Mykhailo who was on the helm, and he confirmed it was Igor, who normally operates Crane 1.

The pilot boat RT *Tough* has just attended our stern. I did not see the arriving of it.

I suddenly realised we were past the spit of the land and rapidly approaching Port Hedland. I could see trees! Palm trees, other trees and grass! My stomach lurched with excitement.

This is a very industrial area. There are steel constructions everywhere and ships, ships of all shapes and sizes. A great bowser of a green ship was to port of us. I thought we were going to moor up alongside or near her the way our ship was being manoeuvred, but our engines had stopped or almost stopped and we were being shoved towards the wharf. There are no train tracks to be seen. This means the six locomotives will be unloaded onto some form of road transport to carry them off to some distant mining area. Here there was no torrential rain like there had been at the loading of the locomotives in Norfolk, Virginia, United States of America, just sunshine and humidity. By the time we were being shoved against the wharf I realised I should be down at mooring stations. I confirmed with Mykhailo the time. It was 4 pm. He said we would moor at 4.15 pm. Time for me to get ready, he indicated. I high-tailed it to my cabin, slipped on the thin pair of socks, then the thick, glittery bed socks, white this time, not pink. I slipped my bare legs into the legs of my boiler suit, tucking down the shorts inside. I had changed from a shirt to a vest top. It was far too hot for anything else. I slipped my heavy boots on, grabbed my hardhat and made my way to the mooring deck. I stepped out of A Deck door and straight onto the weather deck. I could see no one in the mooring station where all the ropes were laid out perfectly so that they would not kink as they were drawn by the stevedores to shore for securing to the bollards. It was like the Marie Celeste. Action was evident, but there was not a soul around.

Andriy K appeared. I stuck to him like mud. I found our Bosun Anatolii, and Apprentice Serhii in the mustering station we go to when we are at drill, just sitting waiting. I went from port side to starboard and in doing so discovered Vadym and Sergiy in a tiny cabin with I think, four bunk beds and not much else. I asked what this was for, and jokingly suggested *stowaways*. I do not think I would have liked to stay in that accommodation, though it could well have been what I might have been given for this journey. I had left myself open to any eventuality in regard to accommodation conditions for this entire voyage. Eventually the whole team arrived for the action that was to come. I felt a bit awkward filming them, but found it easier now they have given their consent. I am never sure if Anatolii's big blue eyes are challenging me not to film or photograph him, or whether he is inviting me to. Sergiy was up the ladders from where we had had our barbecue, with Vadym throwing the lines with the monkey's fists out. This very heavy, dense knot gives weight to the line that could be confused with a painter because of its relative thinness. No one is singled out for their effort, everyone works hand in hand. I was not in a good position below this point to know exactly when the two guys were going to throw the lines and so missed them with my camera, but caught video of them landing and a lot of the stevedores handling them. When I was in Bermuda in 2000 I became fixated with all this rope throwing, when I watched a really efficient stevedore there.

Andriy K was in charge. He was directing the timing and what ropes should be passed to the shore. Once the monkey's fist line had been drawn up to the join with the loop of the thick mooring line, the stevedores lifted that over the bollard. Once it was secure, Anatolii pressed a button/pulled a lever that set a winder to whine and wind the rope back and length-by-length made it taught, securing *Palanpur* against the wharf. This was repeated two more times till three thick mooring lines were heaped over the bollard. I saw Serhii putting his all into hauling the hawser back inside *Palanpur.* Inside the mooring deck, the excess ropes were wound off the floor and neatly stored on huge steel capstans. Everyone helped, no one slacked. To my eyes the exercise was flawless and five men walked in front of my video camera justifiably proud of a job well done. The three stevedores gradually made their way from the bow to the opening for the gangplank. They laid our throwing ropes there and a forklift truck brought a gangplank to our port side. The first people to use the gangplank were the pilots. I took their photos with *City of Adelaide* in the background. The trainee pilot had paperwork with his name on it that he asked me to photograph; the qualified pilot's name I will have to get from the bridge. The qualified pilot and I had had a conversation on the bridge about *City of Adelaide.* I enthused as I do about her history. He said his ancestors had come to Australia in the 1860's. I suggested they might have come over on *City of Adelaide.*

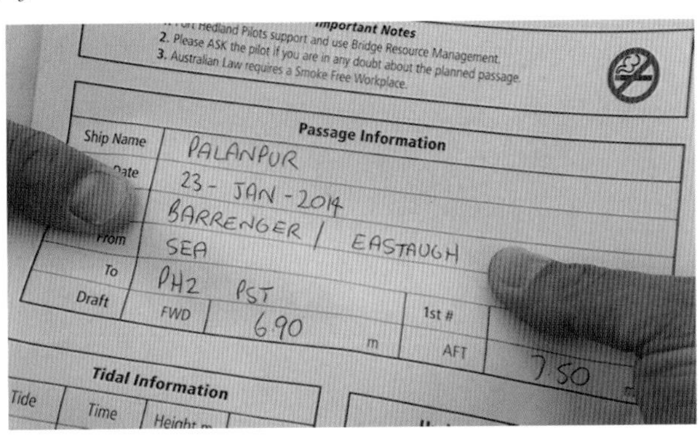

I went to my cabin for my shower. I did not know whether the Press would still be around. I noticed a helicopter buzz us a couple of times during mooring operations. I put on makeup and dressed in the cream top and blue and gold wraparound skirt I had worn on Old Year's Night, and texted Richard Smith. The text failed to send twice, so I phoned him. I was delighted when he invited me to dinner. I had heard Port Hedland accommodation and meals are very expensive. I packed $50 into my wallet to pay my share. Richard organised for the agent, Marius to pick me up. I fetched my passport from the bridge just in case, and headed for the weather deck. It is a relief to know I will not have any problem getting on shore in Australia. Richard had given me a ten-minute warning for the arrival of Marius. I waited for him on the weather deck for about five minutes. When he arrived he said I must wear a hi-vis jacket and hardhat. I had checked earlier about this, but he had a different opinion of what was required. I was so relieved. It gave me a chance to go back to my cabin and put some lippy on. I had forgotten this important aspect of my toilette.

Lippy and hardhat later, we proceeded to his truck. I got in and we passed security with no need for my passport. He had cleared everything. From my angle, this is the easiest of all three ports I have called into on this voyage. Richard was waiting outside his hotel, The Esplanade, when we arrived. It was a simple block of flats. We went through the entrance doors where the air-conditioning provided a welcome relief from the humidity. We walked through another set of doors. I laughed to myself when I saw the sign on the doors. *The Empire.* The same name as the café my parents had when I was a child. Beyond the doors, a garden with trees and people. Loads of people. Glamorous people scented with expensive perfumes melded with fat people, bearded men, folk with tattoos.

Richard spotted a table beneath a tree that reminded me of one in my own garden. We sat under it, me with my gin and tonic, he with his Johnnie Walker Black Label scotch on-the-rocks. He had suggested champagne, but I preferred to leave that for Adelaide. I said I would pay for the drinks, but when I said I only had American dollars he said he did not think they would accept them. I also mentioned my credit card, but he declined my offer. Richard had to go and ask for menus. He chose a fisherman's selection, I chose Chicken Parmigiana. The meals arrived in good time for us meeting Marius at 9 pm. Richard had chosen a lovely red wine, a full-bodied

Sauvignon Grenache, one of my favourite combinations. Our chat was very pleasant, covering all sorts of aspects of *City of Adelaide* and where the Directors are at currently. Richard told me he had given up a very lucrative part-time contract to go to Irvine and supervise proceedings there. So many people of different nationalities and regions have been bewitched by *City of Adelaide* and got involved with the recovery of this grand old lady at their own expense, even incurring debt through their obsession. It is vital to keep support and coordination going. I learned from our conversations what a tremendous negotiator Richard is. I think I should take some tips from him when negotiating a deal with a publisher. We talked about a publisher. We talked about his contracts, his employment, his days of being an employer and having to pull in the belt. He told me how he had required cooperation from people from the yacht club at Irvine to take their yachts off the moorings when it was decided to remove *City of Adelaide* a month ahead of schedule. This was to allow her passage from the slipway on the barge to beyond the Bridge of Scottish Invention that is split in the middle. He was given a list of over thirty people to contact and the one person who had at first been a bit reluctant over the exercise ended up telling people about *City of Adelaide*. Richard suspects his reluctance may have stemmed from perhaps he did not want *City of Adelaide* or *Carrick* as she was known there, to leave Irvine. I know from the glum, faraway look on many faces at Irvine that this person was not alone.

We will talk more over the next few days when he will be a shipmate between here and Adelaide. He is a very interesting, laid back, powerful man and I think he and German will hit it off, for they are quiet about their ways of people management. I was amazed to find he had read Eric Newby's *The Last Grain Race*. It had been a gift from his son-in-law. I told him *Moshulu*, the ship the story takes place on, is moored in Philadelphia as a floating restaurant, and I have the book with me.

Richard told me that Mark Caudwell is flying out from Lincolnshire in England to Adelaide tomorrow. He is a farmer who had read about the *City of Adelaide* project in an article in *Old Glory Magazine* by Hugh Dougherty. Mark volunteered for two weeks alongside Richard and a team of skilled local Scottish steelworkers. He also donated use of a tele-handler that gave mechanical support to help lift the components of the steel cradle. Some of these weighed over two tons.

At 9 pm I downed the last of my wine and we headed for the front entrance. Negotiating a time for uplift with Marius had been interesting. I said goodbye and thanked Richard for a lovely evening. Marius took me back through the security gate and to the car park. He asked me if I needed him to walk back to the ship with me. I said not, and thanked him anyway. We shook hands, he retrieved my hardhat and hi-vis jacket from the back seat of his truck and I got out.

The feeling of pride walking back towards *Palanpur* in the dark with her lights ablaze all around was the same as what I had in Cape Town after my one day ashore in over six weeks. She is indeed the prettiest cargo ship I have set eyes on and I am so lucky and privileged to be sailing with her. To see *City of Adelaide* nestling on her caused a tear to roll down my cheek. I noticed even more plastic had ripped from her port side flanks. I could see windows now, and recalled how I had clambered through one to be on board when Peter Maddison occupied her at Irvine.

Tomorrow I will try and photograph these.

I made my way up the gangplank. Andriy K is still on duty. He had seen me off the ship, he was seeing me back on. Two deck sections have been removed and the first three locomotives are seeing fresh air for the first time since 9 December 2013 when we left Norfolk, Virginia, United States of America. I spoke to Andriy for some time. I found out we do have a gym on board, in the workshop. All these dark secrets. We were joking and talking about this and that. I told him I had hair dye but am not going to use it. He talked about his girlfriend who dyes her hair five times in a month. I was horrified.

Andriy told me about the time there had been a stop in Morocco. Careful checks are always made before leaving a port to ensure no one has stowed away on board, with searches in all areas. After three days at sea they heard a knocking. They looked to see where it was coming from and found a stowaway. They were shocked and their captain had been furious that this had happened. Responsibility for such a person is very expensive. The ship was headed for Aberdeen, and luckily Scotland accepted this person. The police came and took him away, but not before Andriy had played some games with him, including cards, and he said this person had been very good at chess. He surely must have been better than Sarah, who was almost always losing to the Doctor. I told Andriy that Andriy V had given me a copy of the cartoon image of life on board a ship where the stowaway had been cramped right at the lower deck of the bow. I told him I was worried about my husband because I had bought him a stowaway ticket for this journey. We laughed.

I checked with Andriy what the stack of large loops of steel were called. 'They are grommets,' he said. 'Of course,' I said. 'I also worked with grommets when I worked in a factory a long time ago. They were rubber. They were like this.' I curled up my forefinger until it formed a very small circle against my thumb. We found the comparison hilarious. German came and joined our conversation. He asked if I had had a good evening. I told him all about it. I did not tell him that I had plugged that he should also be interviewed by Jasmine Bamford tomorrow for the local North West whatever newspaper she works for. Richard had asked me at the beginning of the evening whether I had seen him talking to the media as *Palanpur* and *City of Adelaide* arrived. I had said not. I was in the mooring deck. He said Jasmine wants to interview me tomorrow.

I asked German about his not drinking alcohol. He told me wine and beer do not agree with him. I knew Richard is bringing six bottles of wine on board tomorrow. He had asked me about mealtime arrangements. I told him dinner is at 5.30 – 6 pm. He had had to pay extra to bring those bottles of wine on board the plane. Richard had asked me in an indirect way how I was financing my trip. He seemed quite serious when I said my mother had given me her funeral fund for it. I assured him all was well, I took it as a guarantee she would be there to get it back on my return. I told him about the first harp I had bought that has become too heavy for me to handle and has too wide a reach, causing me pain in my shoulder. I will try and sell this on my return to Scotland. Richard was interested in my writing and harping histories that began in 2006 and 2009 respectively.

Mykhailo had come along after German. He said I looked twenty years younger with the makeup on. I said if I dye my hair I will look forty years younger, and we laughed. I had said to Richard earlier that I was making a statement for older women on this journey. I will be sixty-two this year. He told me he is over seventy. We older generation fair take a grasp on life. We had talked about his contract in Japan and how if Japanese people feel they have failed in life, they take their lives. I told him I knew about this.

I waved to Vadym and Serhii who are still working away. The lashings of the six locomotives are being melted away. I expect we will see Rob Carbon tomorrow. My fingers are tired, nearly 5,000 words today. I am unwinding now with my third bottle of Bud since I got back. Please remind me to remove my contact lenses before I shutter my eyes.

At 2.47 am I saw a small speed boat with two people on board crossing the port at our stern. Night night from Australia, from beneath the shadow of a heap of something white on shore that reminds me of the snowy peaks of Scotland.

DAY SIXTY

October 10, 1864 – Monday

A very fine day but the sea rather rough. As Papa and I were walking on the Deck a wave came over and wet us very much. I practised for about an hour. In the evening we walked on the Deck. The moon was very bright. There was a lunar rainbow.

24 January 2014 – Friday – Port Hedland

A gorgeous blue sky morning. Two locomotives have already been lifted out of the 'tween deck and been carted off on a huge lorry. It had a metal plate on its rear with the word *Oversized* printed on it. A ship has sneaked in across from us overnight. She is called *British Chivalry*.

I went up to the bridge with a slight hangover. I drank some Buds last night whilst writing up the day's events, and went to bed around 3 am. There are no more locomotives being offloaded today due to a hold up at the delivery site. The bridge was crawling with people. It looked like some maintenance was going on with the computers. And then I saw Rob Carbon, the agent for the locomotives. It was great to see him, we greeted each other warmly. We talked a little about my journey since Norfolk, Virginia, United States of America in between him carrying out tasks. He said his wife is from Cape Town, it is his most favourite city in the world, along with Sydney. He said talking about Cape Town is making him think of planning a trip there. I said it is a place I would like to return to and explore the surrounding area. I told him about the bus tour. He asked if I had gone up to the top of the mountain in the cable car. I explained I thought there would not have been enough time to break out from the city bus tour for this. Rob told me a bit about our current surrounding area. Space to build new houses in Port Hedland had become limited due to the shape of the area, so they developed a new place called South Hedland. He pointed it out to me. It sounded like there is more there than in Port Hedland, but I doubt I will make the excursion. He joked that people say there will be a huge hole in Port Hedland where the iron ore is being mined, and a huge mountain in China to where it is delivered for making steel. Practically all the iron ore mined here is destined for China. Without hesitation Rob offered me his laptop to go on the internet. I was happy about this because I would at last be able to check the internet and would not need to go to the Seafarers Centre yet. He had a mobile modem on it, different to German's. I am going to get one of those. After the emails and checking the CSCOAL website I managed to get onto Facebook for a couple of minutes before I heard his voice on the outside staircase. I answered a couple of messages to do with poetry events. I could not believe the amount of junk in my emails. I am definitely going to unsubscribe from some things when I get home.

Richard told me last night the local news reporter wanted to interview me today. I had a look at the CSCOAL website. It always impresses me. They have put up a photo of *City of Adelaide* in Port Hedland. I looked at the section on *Diary Extracts* and saw mention of Sarah's. This shocked me. I did not know it had been transcribed and was available to the public. The good thing was I also found some of her family history. This means I will need to continue research on her when I get to Adelaide.

I had another reunion on the bridge. Sanjay Rautela whom I had met at Rotterdam was there. Our greeting was friendly, and we chatted while he worked. German was answering points someone sitting at the bridge desk was asking him when I went for lunch. I met Vadym on the way. He was carrying a cup of tea. He had not heard me coming downstairs. 'You look tired, Vadym,' I said. His face cracked open a wide grin. 'I am a polar bear in the zoo in this heat. It is okay in the crane because it is air-conditioned.' The lads are all very cheerful today, even though they have to work in this terrific heat. Stepan heard me in the galley and called to me. 'Are you going to Port Hedland?' I mischievously replied, 'No, I am staying on board *Palanpur*.' This caused a great deal of laughter between him, Vitaliy and Oleksiy. Serhii came in for his lunch, and I went off to eat mine in the other mess. When I got there, Oleksiy directed me away from my usual place to sit opposite Vitaliy, who was eating soup. Nikoliy would be on my right. As I made my way to sit down, a man came in. He introduced himself. He clicked his heels together and bowed slightly before he shook my hand as I made my way from the table. He is Ralph Jacobsen, who deals with heavy cargo. He told me there is an inspection going on on *Palanpur*. This explains all the extra people and activity. He went to sit in my space. I remembered Vitaliy saying, 'That's my seat,' when I first came on board this ship. I would not be issuing that challenge to Mr Jacobsen. Where I was to sit meant I had my back to him. The seating arrangement you may remember does not feel sociable, with your back to people at the table behind. It is strange to try to talk to someone through the back of your head, but it may be something to do with rank.

What is the opposite of cabin fever? I cannot believe I am not yet out and about in Port Hedland. Maybe talk of high prices has scared me off going. My meal last night cost about forty dollars, kindly paid by Richard. After lunch I laid down for a while. There was some clanking going on. I looked out of my porthole but saw nothing. I had to shut the window as whenever I was almost asleep there was another clank and I nearly jumped out of my skin a couple of times. I was a bit annoyed with myself for having a couple of beers too many last night, not that I was drunk, but my head was dull and I had a slight headache. I took a couple of pills and hoped it would go away quickly. I noticed a fly had managed to sneak in to my cabin. It was one of those really annoying ones that buzz you all the time. I had seen a smaller fly earlier. It looked a bit like a Scottish midge, but bigger. Perish the thought. At around 3 pm I went down to the galley to make a sandwich like the one I had made last night. After this I went up to the bridge and went outside for some air. It was so lovely to have the sun consistently shining, and the heat on my body. German came out and asked me why

I was not at the Seafarers Centre. He said there is a bus running that picks people up at quarter to the hour. I did not know this. I said I had not wanted to bother the agent to take me such a short distance so late in the day. Tomorrow I will be up early and will go to town and try and get an appointment for my hair that has grown quite a bit since we left Rotterdam and needs shaping.

Richard came up to the bridge from the outside staircase. He introduced himself to German. He was lathered with sweat. He had been making a detailed list of all the things in the *City of Adelaide*'s container lashed to the deck of *Palanpur*, for customs in Adelaide. We chatted a while then he said to German he would get the agent to come and collect him. I told you my brain was dull today. It was German who suggested I go with Richard and the agent to the Seafarers Centre. This would mean I would get there around 5 pm instead of waiting for the next bus at 5.45 pm. I decided to go and get on the internet, as I would miss Rob's offer of using his laptop again tomorrow, with my plan to go into town. I nipped down to my cabin to freshen up and went back to meet Richard on the bridge. The agent had arranged the pick-up time and we had around twenty minutes to wait. We spent half of that blethering on the bridge then began to make our way towards the stern where the gangplank had been moved to from just by the accommodation block at the bow yesterday evening. Halfway along the deck I realised I did not have my hard hat and hi-vis vest, though I had seen some crew return from the Seafarers Centre without these items. Still, the agent yesterday had been quite firm about the need for them and so I complied. Andriy V was on Watch at the gangplank sitting in the shade with his dark glasses on. He introduced himself to Richard and said he would give him an induction of *Palanpur* tomorrow. Richard signed himself off the ship and Marius met us to escort us to his truck.

In the Seafarers Centre it was a wee bit of an Aladdin's Cave. Compared to Cape Town, it was a palace. There were trinkets made from beads, sliced opals, iron ore, some sparkly red stones I forget the name of. Amongst other things there were smart tote-bags with Aboriginal scenes on them, tea towels, fishing tackle, cosmetics, toiletries, perfumes, juice, crisps, sweets, nuts, postcards, cuddly toy kangaroos, cuddly toy koala bears, multi-packs of small ones of these that grip when you press their arms apart with the mechanism, and spring together on release, locking on to whatever you choose. It was just one such koala bear that an ex-colleague gave me years ago when she came back from a trip to Australia. I had gripped it onto a model sailing ship that had belonged to my father that is on display on bookshelves at home. I had no idea at the time that was an omen. I bought another t-shirt for my granddaughter with some wee koalas doing acrobatics through the trees. I bought a bag of jelly snakes and a

chocolate bar. I checked prices for the mobile modems German had told me about that you feed with a sim card. Rob had one stuck in his laptop this morning. To get set up it would cost around $50. I checked at the desk whether they accepted US dollars. Affirmative. They said they can exchange money as well. When I went to pay for my small purchases, including stamps for the postcards and get an hour's credit on the internet, my credit card was rejected. They tried it twice more. Nothing. It was coming up as not valid. It was lucky I had brought $50 US from the emergency cash my brother had loaned me.

The pleasant girl on the desk at the centre showed me where the computers are. There were plenty, and different areas you could choose to use them. Valeriy was sitting at the bar with his iPad talking on Skype with his family. He was glowing. I had already seen Andriy V at the desk when I was browsing the shelves. Then Oleksiy came in. I logged straight onto Facebook, updated my status and responded to messages I had received. Someone commented they now understood why I had been so quiet. I went onto my *Bound for South Australia* public page and updated that. I set up an event page for Bob Mitchell, my *Craw Two*'s Robert Burns show on Sunday that my *Three Craws* are appearing on. I hope Rosemary McKay will listen in as Bob is going to mention her and everyone in Adelaide. Jim Anderson from East Coast FM radio station had put up a cool message that he would play a tune for me. I was touched by this. I put a message on the Adelaide Pipe Band page, put a couple of comments on other pages of friends who are interested in or have been involved with *City of Adelaide*, including Peter Maddison. The hour seemed quite long. I had a brief chat with a friend who had told me before that his sister lives in Adelaide. I sent him my mobile number to give her, asking that she text me when we get there. It is amazing how many of my friends have relatives in Adelaide. I had also texted my number to one of our writers' group members who has a cousin there who are great sailors. I found out from Alan when I got into my emails that the bank had cancelled my bank card. There had been a letter from their fraud department alerting me to unusual activity on my card. I was puzzled. I had notified them I was going travelling. Purchases in foreign countries should not have been an issue. Now I worried what would happen when I got to Adelaide. The loan from my brother would not last forever.

After my time was up I still had well over an hour before the bus back to *Palanpur*. I decided to go outside and phone home. There were loads of people using the internet for Skype. I thought I would phone to arrange for Alan to put on Skype and I would call him. He was so excited about me calling we just kept blethering and the Skype idea was not brought into the conversation until after about fifteen expensive minutes. We had a laugh because I had literally caught him with his pants down in the toilet! I was sitting on a huge rock outside the centre. There were a couple of birds twittering away in a palm tree beside me, and there was a fantastic, huge pink candyfloss cloud above the sky that I photographed. It was quite noisy sitting there, some jumbo trucks were passing, towing three trailers behind them. I went back inside the centre and there were even more of our crew. I bought a bottle of Guinness and sat on a bar stool at a high table to write postcards I had bought, addressing one each to Hugh Loney and Adrian Small as well as family. Rob had apologised to me this morning that he had posted the postcards I had written in America in Australia. He had been tight for time for his flight, and could not get stamps from the shop near his accommodation. Ihor came through with some empty beer bottles. He asked me what I was doing and I told him. 'Very nice,' he said. While he was there the bus driver called out the name of our ship and that of another to go to the bus. When I boarded, I saw even more of our crew. Stepan was sitting across from me. I had not recognised him with glasses on. Ivan was there as well. When we got back to the ship the lads were very careful of me, young Serhii helped me over the rather cumbersome access from off the gangway. It involved stepping off the gangplank over a high set of sturdy wooden steps and then setting my foot onto the horizontal iron bars of *Palanpur*'s railings. Someone else took my bag. The ship *British Chivalry* was moored nearby, but this was a full helping of Ukrainian Chivalry. I was moved by their care of me.

On my way back to the accommodation block I was walking behind Ihor. He said to follow his feet. He had on gleaming white trainers. I asked if they were new. He said not. I said he looks after them very well. I asked what the D rings were lying down beside the remaining locomotive on the 'tween deck. He explained they are part of the lashings for welding the cargo to the decks that had been removed to release the locomotives. Richard and I had earlier discussed the wooden blocks the locomotives were sitting on and he examined and explained things to me through his engineer's eyes. I said he would be able to discuss this with Rob tomorrow when he returns to supervise the next unloading phase of his locomotives.

I spent about an hour in my cabin downloading photos and texting my youngest daughter. The fly made a re-appearance. I got the hand towel from my bathroom and flicked at it. 'Yes!' I rejoiced. But when I went to pick it up with toilet paper it took off from the couch where it had landed, but slowly. I flapped at it again and it disappeared. Then I saw it back on the couch, with one wing damaged. I gathered it up in the toilet paper, and flushed it down the toilet to feed the micro-organisms in the waste system. I heard the noise that had kept me awake earlier when I was trying to have a nap. I looked out of the window that looks over the deck towards *City of Adelaide*. Anatolii was throwing the D rings from off the 'tween deck up onto the top of a square block just below the weather-deck. I was glad to see the deck was nearly clear of them and there would be no more clanking today. I watched video of yesterday's mooring stations, and was amused at one of the stevedore's lack of skill in handling ropes.

I went down to the galley. My dinner was there (in my new place), covered with silver foil. I reheated the beef stew, pasta with melted cheese over, and sauerkraut in the microwave. It had looked a huge pile of food I thought I would never finish, but I did. I saw a corkscrew on my normal table and thought about the slop chest being empty of merlot. I am looking forward to tasting some of Richard's South Australian wine he is bringing on board tomorrow when he takes up his cabin. At least he will not need to use scissors to uncork his bottles, like I did.

It has been a strange day with all these extra people and activities. I look forward to exploring Port Hedland tomorrow. Today is William Pile's birthday (1823-1873).

DAY SIXTY-ONE

October 11, 1864 – Tuesday

A fine day but the wind very cold. We were on Deck for about an hour and a half in the morning but were obliged to walk all the time. Since noon yesterday till noon to-day we have made 266 miles.

25 January 2014 – Saturday – Port Hedland

A blue sky day with large, airy clouds. I awoke at 6 am and tried to doze, but with operations due to start at 7 am, it was impossible. I made a cup of tea and showered. I peeked through the curtains overlooking the deck and saw things were already starting. I dressed quickly and headed for the bridge. Harren & Partner inspectors are still working away. I greeted everyone on the bridge when I arrived and went to the starboard to film. Crane 1 was ready for action to offload locomotive three from the

'tween deck. It had already been unlashed, its welded joints melted to release its holding stays. The preying mantis spreader was hooked on. A huge steel grommet had been laid over the top of the spreader and wedged into one of a series of grooves along the top of it at each end to dangle on either side of it, forming four loops. Horseshoe shaped shackles with holes at either end had been hooked round the grommets. Through a series of shackles, alignment of holes against flattened wing shapes at each end of the topside of a 225 tonne bar and at the bottom, massive steel bolts fixing them together, huge nuts locking the shackles into place by sheer strength of hands, the locomotive was ready to be lifted. At the end of the loops long thin ropes and lengths of webbing had been attached to help guide the locomotive. Igor set Crane 1 to whine. The hook raised the spreader with all the lifting gear. He manoeuvred the crane arm away from the wharf until everything hovered above the locomotive in the hold. He gradually lowered the lifting gear down into the hold where deck hands were waiting. They took hold of each of the four dangling ropes and guided the grommets to loop them round huge steel buttons at each side of the fore and rear of the locomotive. The spreader spanned nearly the entire length of it. Igor operated the crane with precision. The last of six locomotives was hoisted from what had been its shelter for more than seven weeks.

A massive green and silver lorry had arrived from over the bridge at right angles to *Palanpur*. It had the words *Over* on the right of the front bumper and *Size* on the left, and was further inscribed with the logo *NO Foolin with Doolan* spanning the engine cover in front of the windscreen. It was parked alongside us, waiting to carry away the emerging locomotive that was destined for a life in the iron ore mining industry. I watched men un-hoop the grommets, snip off some plastic ties, remove wooden packing blocks in preparation for the onward journey. I saw steel chains being threaded between gaps in the lower side of the locomotive and tightened into securing rings fixed into the flat bed of the multi-wheeled trailer. I counted thirteen wheels on the side closest to me, and ten rows from the back, making 130 in all. The lorry drew forward to begin reversing back across the bridge to drive away, and I saw again the plaque at the back of the trailer with the word *Oversize* on it. They are not kidding.

Watching this entire operation, the reverse of what I had seen in Norfolk, Virginia, United States of America was mission accomplished. Now for my hair. German told me the bus to the Seafarers Centre that would connect with the bus that went every second hour to the shops in Port Hedland would arrive in fifteen minutes. I met Rob on the outside staircase en route to my cabin. He again offered me access to the internet on his laptop. I thanked him, but said I was going into town. I rushed down to change my clothes and met a freshly-showered Andriy V coming out from his cabin. He asked me if I was going to the City.

I said, 'Yes.'

'I will meet you. I am going to Seafarers Centre.'

'Okay,' I said. Ideally I would have put in contact lenses, applied makeup and so on. There was not time for pampering so I stripped off my shorts and vest top and put on jeans and a stripy top. I met Andriy at the gangplank. We chatted to Serhii who was on Watch till the bus arrived ten minutes later and we drove to the Seafarers Centre, where I exchanged some US dollars. My credit card was still barred. I remarked at the difference between this Mission and that in Cape Town. They said many missions are struggling.

On the connecting bus to Port Hedland there were masses of steel everywhere. There were great big rust-coloured oil storage vats with the words *combustible liquid* just visible, rusted steel towers, pale green and fawn steel houses designed to look as though they had been made using wooden planks. I could see no windows; they were all shuttered up to keep the sun at bay. There were attempts at gardens, but it is so dry here the terrain looks scrubby. I recognised a few plants you can buy in garden centres in Scotland. From the windows of the speeding minibus everything was the colour of dried blood on a white bandage. I saw an animal farm of steel wire: a cow, pigs, chickens. There was a family of rusted steel kangaroos on one bend. We arrived at Port Hedland to a row of shops. There was the local newspaper office, the North West Telegraph. I tried the handle of the door. It was locked, and I remembered it was Saturday. There was a recruitment agency, a newsagent, and a clothes shop whose window went round the corner to the entrance of the mall. Inside, I found the hairdressing salon right away. There were two men having their hair trimmed. I waited, but no one acknowledged my presence. I went across to another newsagent and thought about buying a card for Andriy V who is 30 today. He had said he does not like a fuss, so I decided I would make him one, like those I had made at Christmas and for Andriy Kostenko's 25th birthday. I bought a newspaper that had headlines for Australia Day celebrations on the coming Monday. I had a good browse in the shop. I found Time magazine, a special edition on Nelson Mandela, but resisted buying it. I returned to the salon. A woman came over straight away. I asked for a dry cut. She had a space at 3.30 pm, so I booked myself into it.

I browsed some clothing on what was meant to be a bargain rail and moved on swiftly. I had been warned as to how expensive things are in Port Hedland. My hair cut was to cost $50, slightly more expensive than at home. I went into a well-stocked supermarket and bought a chilled cappuccino in a plastic container. I bought some assorted cakes for the crew, thinking if there is to be a party before Adelaide they would be good for that. I looked for a mobile modem but found none so went into an electronics shop and had another browse. I asked about a mobile modem but they did not have any that would be useful outwith Australia's networks. I took the bus back to the Seafarers Centre where I bought a few items to take home before returning to the ship for lunch. Oleksiy was hyper. He told me about news he had seen on the Russian website *Koribila.* I went through to see it. There was a photograph of *City of Adelaide* taken from the port side! Unbelievable! What a coincidence! I glued my eyes to the screen. *Palanpur* looked really smart with her twin towers of strength. We felt immense pride to be part of this story, written in Russian, but I knew what the article was saying. 'You are famous!' I said to Oleksiy. He was really excited.

I watched a documentary on KC TV of the *Olive May,* a one hundred and thirty-year-old cutter based in Tasmania. She has been fully restored and her owner has put her back to the use she had in her working life, collecting local produce such as apples and grapes and taking them to market. It seemed the owner was pretty well-off, and I would suggest to CSCOAL it might be worth getting in touch with him. Germaine Greer, who is 77, was making some kind of statement of making a fight back for older people by getting involved in some planting to help poor areas somewhere. I did not catch the whole bulletin as someone was talking to me, but I recognised we have something in common. Being older does not mean an end to opportunity and adventure.

After lunch of fish, baked potatoes and sauerkraut I typed a little of this morning's events. I headed to the gangway to pick up transport back to Port Hedland at 1.45 pm. It was great to see *City of Adelaide* close up again. More and more of her wrapping is coming off. I thought her timbers looked dry, and felt concern.

Back at Port Hedland I had plenty time to kill before my hair appointment. I went into a supermarket completely stocked with alcohol. It had a fantastic range of beers, wines, spirits, vermouths, sherries, ports. There were amazing label designs. I asked an attendant if it would be okay to take some photographs of them. He gave a definitive 'No'. I had seen a sign in the Seafarers Centre warning sailors that photography of any sort was forbidden in the shopping mall. He explained there had been inappropriate photography of children, resulting in the ban. I bought a bottle of sparkling mead I thought would be interesting, a bottle of crushed apple cider and a bottle of very dark beer. I went to the other supermarket again and bought a couple of peaches, two bananas, a huge mango, a *Picnic*. A Picnic! I had not seen these chocolate, peanut and wafer bars for years. I bought a box of six seashell chocolates. There were long queues at the checkouts and when I looked at the supermarket clock it was just a few minutes to my appointment.

The lady asked me what I wanted done with my hair. Now girls, you know what it is like when you put your head in the hands of a stranger. I expected her to spray my hair with water, normal procedure for a dry cut in my experience. She just took her time, snipping here, snipping there. I had asked her to leave a bit of length so that I could still put my hair up. When she was finished with the body of my hair, she took my fringe between her fingers and swooped the scissors into it and dropped it. No tweaking or anything. The strangest thing of all was she began lifting sections of my hair up and pointed the tips of her scissors really close to my scalp, then snipped just a few hairs right in at the roots. I have never experienced this. I could only think this was a way to give my thin hair some lift. I wondered what my hair would be like in a couple of weeks. I could imagine spikes of hair sprouting from my head. Afterwards I sat on a bench and drank some water I had bought. There was an ATM machine. I wandered over to see what cards it took. A cheery man came to use the machine and I backed away. He began to chat to me, asking me where I was from. I said I had come to Port Hedland with *Palanpur*. 'Really?' he said. He asked me to tell him more. I said I was going for the bus back to the Seafarers Centre, but he said there was time for a chat. He said, 'I am the Port Captain, I know how things work. You know I should put you in handcuffs.' He had a twinkle in his eye. 'There are not supposed to be passengers on cargo ships.' I laughed, and explained I am writing a book. I asked his name. He is Lyon Seyyels, from South Africa. Through our chat I was able to confirm we are leaving at midnight. He said I should go for my bus. We shook hands and I got on a coach full of crew from other ships.

Back at the mission, I bought half an hour of internet connection for my phone to download nine weeks of emails. I had seen them on Rob's computer but wanted to bring my phone up to date. I took an hour on the big computers with the intention of using Skype. I had texted my youngest daughter to watch out for a call. It is months since I used it. I tried all manner of usernames and passwords, but could not get connected. I tried to re-register, but with not having an Australian postcode it was useless. I went to buy the mobile modem, the one with the booster. At least with that I should be able to connect from the ship. I would need help to get it going, you can see I am hopeless with technology and instructions. As the lad at the desk was putting the credits onto the sim card, the bus was about to leave. Fingers crossed all will work out.

I went up to the bridge when I got back. All the locomotives were gone and the deck was almost completely sealed again. Everyone was in good form. 'Did you get hair cut okay?' Mykhailo asked. 'Yes,' I said. Several pairs of eyes looked at me in disbelief.

There are still no emails in the ship's Amos Connect system. I spoke to Mykhailo about it. He had a look. He said to speak to German, he would give me another card if there was nothing he could do to sort it. Down in my cabin I got on with some typing and downloading of film and photos. I was restless. I find I always am when we are about to take off from moorings. I was not really hungry but decided to go and have my evening meal. I had just taken a few mouthfuls when Richard appeared. We greeted each other and chatted till about 9 pm when he said he would go for a nap so that he would be fresh enough to stay awake for our departure from Port Hedland.

I also went to my cabin but could not sleep. I worked, went up to the bridge at 10.30 pm to find it deserted. I went back again about 11 pm. It was still deserted. Shortly after I went back and found German, Richard, Mykhailo and Andriy V, who was on his routine watch.

One tug boat appeared to our starboard and latched on beneath *City of Adelaide*. One by one I saw our mooring ropes cast off from the bollards by stevedores. The stern line went, we were adrift controlled by the tug. Proceedings had begun shortly after 12.30 am. The pilot came out onto the outside of the bridge and I removed myself from being in the way. Both Richard and I filmed our exodus from Port Hedland. It was pitch black. The lights were pretty, but Cape Town was undoubtedly the most spectacular departure on this voyage. Port Hedland would be my last.

Palanpur reversed away from the wharf, then did a three-point turn to face down the channel that would lead us to open waters. The channel was lit with the usual starboard green and port side red guide lights, but ahead there was a chain of Christmas lights twinkling us back to the Indian Ocean. We passed again the city of tankers tramping off Port Hedland, waiting for their next orders. They were lit with the endless blocks of orange lights we left in our wake. I went down to my cabin at just before 3 am. I lay down in my bed and knew nothing more until a few hours later.

DAY SIXTY-TWO

October 12, 1864 – Wednesday

A very rough and rainy day. We were not able to go on Deck. The Doctor played Chess with me and won. In the evening we played round games.

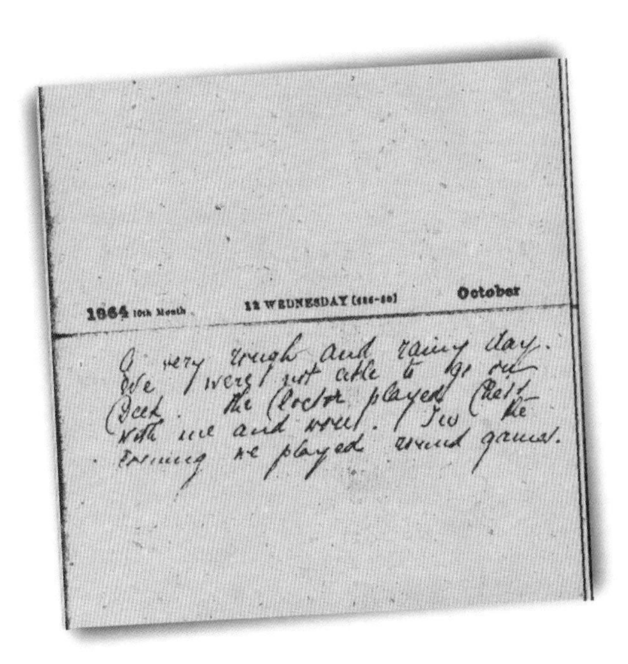
1864 10th Month 12 WEDNESDAY October

A very rough and rainy day. We were not able to go on Deck. The Doctor played Chess with me and won. In the evening we played round games.

26 January 2014 – Sunday – Indian Ocean

The sea is that pale teal shade again. The waves are small.

I took a long time to come to this morning with all the shore activity yesterday. The ground had seemed to sway a few times when I went on shore, and although I did not walk much, it was novel for my system to be on steady land instead of sitting at a desk on a constantly mobile platform. I kept my head down and got as much written as I could. If I do not keep up the momentum it is so easy to fall behind. I am feeling quite exhausted with the constant focus on keeping this diary.

After lunch I phoned Valeriy. I asked him if he would help me understand the mobile modem. I had uploaded it but was not able to activate it. He agreed to come to my cabin at 1 pm. I apologised for interrupting his quiet Sunday. He said, 'It is okay.' He brought a piece of paper with him he had picked up in the Seafarers Centre with instructions of how to connect. He sat down at my desk and began the process.

I showed him the little book that had come with the modem and pointed to the instructions in it. He began to get up and said, 'If you want to do it…' I said, 'No, no. You do it.' I was not sure if he was annoyed or whether he was giving me the option of putting in the instructions under his supervision. At any rate, he got it working. I was delighted. He pointed out that as soon as we were any distance from the coast there would be no signal. This somewhat defeated the purpose of me getting it. I invited Valeriy to sit at the table so I could fill in some blanks in my notes from the visit to the engine room. I went through the list I had prepared and soon we were done. I then asked him about freedom fighters for Ukraine during WWII, and present day attitudes. He responded that it depended on where in Ukraine I was referring to. He explained that in western Ukraine freedom fighters were considered heroes. In the south and east, they were not. A choice had to be made on whether to support Communism or Germany. It depended on where Communism was strongest. He said that there had been attempts to eradicate the Ukrainian language as some sort of ethnic cleansing. When he left I was a bit overcome.

I went up to the bridge and put some washing in the machine on the way. We are at latitude 20°27.22'S, longitude 115°13.19'E. We are going along at 13.1 knots in the Indian Ocean with wind speed 22.6 knots. Richard appeared on the bridge with his gift of six bottles of wine. There was debate with German as to when these would be drunk. He announced we should have a party and spoke of pel'mini. We will see what Oleksiy thinks. In the end German suggested we take a bottle or two to supper and give Andriy V a glass to celebrate yesterday's birthday. Andriy looked up from his duties. 'I am on Watch,' he said. German suggested he enjoy a glass with his meal. German talked about his parents' house in the countryside. They have a flat, but love to escape to this house where his grandmother, his mother, and he had been born in. He said his children love to go there. Four generations. Just like *City of Adelaide*.

I went down a deck and removed my washing from the machine, put it in the drier and put a second load on. Richard and I then went down to the officers' mess, he opened a bottle of wine and poured us each a glass. Vitaliy was offered one, at first declined, but then he came over with a big grin on his face, glass in his hand. I flicked my neck just below the jaw line and everyone laughed.

Richard and I spoke till around 9 pm. I took my washing out from the drier and wondered who had been waiting to move their laundry from the washing machine up into it. I went back to my cabin and could not get into typing, so shut off with some Pinball and Solitaire, and drank the small bottle of cider I had bought yesterday.

I am so excited to be in Australian waters. We are on the home stretch now.

DAY SIXTY-THREE

October 13, 1864 – Thursday

A rough day. We were able to go on Deck for almost an hour. I practised. In the evening we had music.

27 January 2014 – Monday – Indian Ocean

A lot of cloud in the blue sky. There are short waves with flecks on their crests. I saw a few seabirds in the distance.

I awoke at 8.15am and realised it was *my* washing that had been in the machine last night. I am really losing the plot. I popped some clothes on to go up and move it to the drier. I met Richard in the stairwell. He was coming down from the bridge and told me he had been showing the crew photographs of Greenwich, including some of me. I went up and sorted the washing and came down again and began typing more of Saturday's entry. Washing down of *Palanpur* was taking place. Igor was dressed in a waterproof suit with a hood. It is surprising how much dust he was washing off. We waved to each other then he pelted my window with water.

Before I knew it it was lunchtime. We had breaded pork escalope with plain rice. I tarted up the rice with some chilli sauce and put some German mustard on the side of my plate. I stayed a while chatting to Richard. He told me he had tried on his immersion suit. It sounded hilarious. He said he had intended photographing himself, but could not find his mobile phone. He discovered it when he pushed one foot to the bottom of the suit and felt a hard lump. It was impossible for him to take a photograph of anyone, never mind of himself in these suits. Once you are in them, you are swallowed up and your hands become like golf drivers. I went to continue writing and spent about half-an-hour before feeling sleepy, I ate some chocolate and the Picnic bar, washed down with a cup of coffee. I saw someone cleaning inside Crane 1 as I lay down. Two hours later I was awake again. It was 4.15 pm. I took a shower and went up to the bridge to take readings: latitude 24°35.45'S, longitude 112°47.53'E. We are going along at 11.6 knots in the Indian Ocean with wind speed 33 knots. Richard had told me we had passed the Tropic of Capricorn this morning. We are passing Point Quobba to port, approaching Geographe Channel, Shark Bay, Naturaliste Channel, Denham Sound, Steep Point and further south Pepper Point. My email is still not working. I went round the outside of the bridge to take the air and a few photographs. It was lovely on the port side, but as soon as I rounded to the bow of the ship the wind was fierce. I had to hang on to my glasses perched on the top of my head to avoid them being whisked away into the Indian Ocean. I saw a couple of fish attempting a flypast, but they failed miserably in the swell. I passed the midpoint at the bow where *Palanpur*'s mast is and thought of turning back, but persisted. I clung to the railings for fear of being blown overboard as I approached the starboard side.

We are pitching along in waves around 3.5 metres high. The wind was absolutely howling, and I took some video when I turned from starboard to face *City of Adelaide*. The waves were piling against *Palanpur*'s hull. I went back inside. Andriy V is very busy, but when he had finished what he was doing he came over to the computer and tried the *Leave Vessel* menu to get my emails going again. Apparently also, by activating this, my emails will be forwarded my private address. It was hopeless. He said we can try again in a while. This delayed me by about ten minutes for supper. I popped into the galley and Oleksiy told me German and Richard were at the table. German had finished his meal. Richard had not started his. He had been waiting for me. It was shishlaki on plain rice with grated celeriac and carrot salad. Richard had opened a nine year-old award-winning bottle of wine. It was very heavy, 14.5%, almost like a port. It really hit the spot. Richard says Australians in general drink less wine, their's is stronger than the average wine drunk in Scotland. We had just one glass, and when Andriy V came for his supper, he accepted a glass. He tested its nose and gave it immediate approval. 'Better than last night,' he said. Andriy was joined by Sergiy Fomin. They soon were in deep discussion.

Richard and I spent about an hour or so chatting about our families, how long I will stay in Adelaide, locations of the homes of Peter Christopher, Rosemary McKay and his own. Peter stays in an area where grapes and apples are grown, a bit away from the centre of Adelaide. He told me about Sydney, because I had mentioned I would like to go there. It is not so far or expensive to get there by plane, and a half-day tourist boat trip would give me the prettiest view of the city. He said a flight to Melbourne from Adelaide would be around $90AUS if I took a last minute one, for I had expressed an interest in going there too. He was not enthusiastic about rail travel, it being fairly limited. He described where he used to live, near the hills to the west of Adelaide, but he and his wife had moved nearer to the city. We chatted in general, but specifically about how much of our time has been consumed by *City of Adelaide*. I asked him about the Committee members: Creagh O'Connor of the cricketing world is Chairman, and Peter Christopher, Peter Roberts, Mark Gilbert, Richard Smith and Tom Chapman are the five Directors, with support from Rosemary McKay, Tom's wife Wendy, and Peter Roberts' wife Harbinda.

I could see a pretty, deep pink light coming in through the porthole. The other portholes in the mess remained sealed against the sea from the last rough weather. Suddenly a wave crashed over the glass. It is getting even rougher with the ageing of the day. I got up to look at the sunset, but it had passed. Richard had a look, then we talked a little more. I gathered my dishes and washed them. He asked if I was going to the bridge. I said I would be. He said he would see me up there.

German and Mykhailo were talking when I arrived. Richard was standing to port side watching the seascape over the deck. I sat down to see if there was any change with my emails, but it was situation *status quo.* I mentioned it to Mykhailo when he was free. He set me up with another card. I doubt if I will memorise the codes at this late stage in the voyage. I feel I am coming to saturation point with extra conversations and the very full day on Saturday in Port Hedland. Richard talked about the wind on the nose of *Palanpur* vis-à-vis the waves, speed of the ship, and the wind speed across the deck. It took me a while but I think I have grasped it. He is happy to help me with any technical terms. German confirmed at supper that there is to be another pel'mini party so that Richard can see what happens. This is when the rest of the wine he brought on board will be drunk. I feel another bottle of whisky or maybe gin this time, coming on. Another party! Hooray! It will also give me a chance to get some more photographs of the lads throwing the dough around, as about half of those from the first party were blurred due to the movement of the ship. I will take video this time.

I said *goodnight* to Mykhailo and went over to German in the chart room to bid him goodnight. He wanted to show me Kalinengrad as we had been talking about it and how it is a Russian state that can only be accessed via the sea, or through Poland or Bulgaria or Belarus. I had got muddled with Stalingrad, so he showed me where this was. He swiped the page over to the west and I saw Szczecin. I told him my mother had been born in Stettin or Szczecin as it is known as now. He said, 'Then she is Polish.' I said not, that that part of Germany had been given to Poland as war reparations after WWII. She is German. She had grown up in Posen, now named Poznan, and my grandfather had been shot there by the Russians in January 1945. I apologised for raising this. He waved his hand and said, 'This is the past,' and I agreed. If only everyone could be as accepting. I told German I had gone with my mother to Szczecin in 2007 when the Tall Ships Race visited there. We travelled over sea and land so she could share her childhood memories with me. We had always talked of making this trip, and I know that if it had not been for the tall ships going there, we never would have done it.

German told me about the islands where Aleksandr Isayevich Solzhenitsyn, Russian Nobel Prize Winner for Literature in1970, had been incarcerated. Amongst his other non-fiction works, he has written of the horrors of living under that Gulag, or 'Chief Administration of Corrective Labour Camps'. German told me the islands are very fertile and monks built a monastery there. The Gulag has become a great tourist attraction. Modern life is juxtaposed with the lookout towers, huts and barbed wire fencing that evoke the appalling conditions and barbaric practices that were rife in the Gulag.

I found Richard sitting on the couch just watching the dials and drinking in the atmosphere of the bridge. I love being up there as well. It is really relaxing and always calm. We chatted briefly and he said he was going down to bed to read for a bit, though he said would probably fall asleep after a couple of pages. I went off to my cabin and finished this day's work with lots of yawns, and booming thuds on the hull with the biggest spray we have had yet, sweeping right over C Deck. *City of Adelaide*'s cover is really split right down the bow now. Richard had said he thought her plastic cover would not make it to Adelaide. I said I thought the crowds would like that. I know I will.

It is 12.40 am. I heard an almighty crack from the deck. We have just had a thrashing from King Neptune who has been placid for a remarkable length of time. He is taking revenge that we have been out of his grasp during our stay in Port Hedland. The hull of *Palanpur* was slammed down by a huge wave, with a resounding thud. I looked out of my window towards the stern. *City of Adelaide* is being stripped of her cover. It is completely ripped. Her bow is thrusting itself into this storm. Her nose is well and truly poked through. She is freeing herself. She has caught the scent of home.

DAY SIXTY-FOUR

October 14, 1864 – Friday

A fine day but scarcely any wind – the ship still rolling and very cold. The thermometer at 8.30 A.M. in the Saloon 44 ½ Fahrenheit. I played Chess with the Doctor. In the evening we had round games.

28 January 2014 – Tuesday – Indian Ocean

We passed a really wild night with *Palanpur* rolling about in agony from the thuds and thumps Neptune was dealing her belly. She groaned and moaned, slammed down on the waves, hovered on top of them trying to avoid the next blow. I could not sleep and went to check on *City of Adelaide*. The rent in her cover at her bow was spreading further and further towards her keel, revealing more and more of her fine, proud, determined prow. I knew she would do it. I knew she would want to come to Adelaide in her fine, faded glory and not wrapped in some alien fabric that never existed in her great days of sail. She had sweated under that cover, yet it had protected her through the horrors of the Atlantic and rounding of the Cape of Good Hope. Now she was breathing. She was drinking in salt water to quench the thirst she had built up since approaching Port Hedland and from having sat there in relentless heat with that plastic raincoat on. No need for that in these southern waters. It is not cold, just really, really wild. I said to Andriy K this morning, who passed no comment about me arriving on the bridge at 7.30 am, that I thought these conditions were as bad, if not worse than those we had endured round the Cape of Good Hope. He swithered, and demonstrated the different wind directions that had prevailed in each circumstance. I am ignorant of this to a degree, even though I have crewed small yachts; I just do what I am told. It is something I would need to sit down and study books about, let the information sink in to the anaemic coral of my brain. I took loads of photos and film with *City of Adelaide* posing in this gale force condition. She does it well, even commanding rainbows from the spray and early morning sunshine.

It was perfect beauty and sheer ecstasy for me to see her in these conditions where there was a lot of cloud in the blue sky, strong winds of over 44 mph and temperature of 25°C. There are short waves with flecks on their crests. The seabirds are still tagging along with us. I thought of *City of Adelaide* crossing these waters one hundred and fifty years ago. I thought of Sarah and her family coping with 44½° Fahrenheit, equivalent to 7° Celsius; the wet; no central heating and hot water on tap, like we have on *Palanpur*, perhaps just a stove and uncertain food. Their journey from mid-summer August in London to late spring November in Adelaide, meant functioning by candlelight until 10 or 11 pm, entertaining themselves with music, piano practise, reading literature that indicates her level of education at her young age of twenty. She is very cultured, brave and full of good spirit and strength. She has not yet met the man who would become her husband, but I see she has a very good relationship with the Doctor, with whom she spends time playing chess, exercising her mind in strategy. Richard told me today that Pamela Whittle, the great-granddaughter of Captain David Bruce, has the very piano Sarah played, and is donating it to the *City of Adelaide*. I find it extremely moving that this piano has survived, and it will be reunited with *City of Adelaide*. I will try to see it and even play it. The thought of my fingers touching the same keys Sarah touched one and a half centuries ago is astounding.

I have to abandon writing now due to serious rolling of *Palanpur*. The first thing to go sliding around was the chair at the table in the lounge area. It screeched across my cabin towards me, then sledged down from starboard to port side, groaning all the way. It groaned its way back again. I got up to try and secure it. The chair I had been sitting on then took off across the room, following in the wake of its twin. Chairs were on the attack. I was thrown against the cabin door, then my feet went out of control and headed towards my bed on the opposite side of my cabin. I turned my back to the wall in time. The dip in the wooden frame that holds the mattress in place allowed me to land on my backside and I just managed to avoid bashing the back of my head on the wall with the force of the throw by catching it with my left shoulder blade. My legs went up in a flying V. I struggled to my feet again and staggered across to the desk at the end of my bed and unlocked the drawer. The top, free-running drawer came out and almost struck me. The second and third drawers below it have a block on them to stop them from flying open. To open them you have to lift them slightly by the handle and then pull them from their housing. The power of the throw of *Palanpur*'s rolling was so great that they became unlatched. My books on the lounge table flew off around the room despite the elephant skin. I pushed the drawers back into place and locked them down. I gathered up the scattered books. I unlocked the drawers again, being careful to push my legs against the second and third ones to keep them secure. I kept the top drawer in place with my right hand and placed the books into it with the left, closed it and turned the key. I wrapped my netbook up in a shirt and put it in the wardrobe. I wrapped this laptop in a duvet cover and put it in the wardrobe. I put my mugs into the pockets of the coat I had not worn since Rotterdam. All the while, the chairs were taking off at every opportunity. I looked around for something to lash them down. Yes! I lay the first chair on its side and shoved it under the lounge table, legs sticking out pointing towards the cabin door. I thought about pulling the laces from my trainers or my heavy-duty boots, but this would cause a major problem in the worst-case scenario of *Abandon Ship* that I seriously thought might happen. I spied the belt of my satiny dressing gown and pulled it from its loops. I wound it round one of the chair legs a couple of times, then secured it with a pretty bow to one of the steel legs of the lounge table. But how could I secure the second chair? My sandals were strewn across the cabin floor. I gathered them up, opened out the ankle straps, matched the Velcro pads of the right sandal to those on the left to make a length, then secured the arm of each chair together by wrapping the length of leather ankle straps round them and pressing the two remaining Velcro pads together, leaving my sandals dangling out at the back of the upright chair. I tucked pads of elephant skin that had not been strong enough to hold the chairs from sliding around beneath the chairs where they had touch points with the floor and tested, pushing my weight against them. I gave myself a score of 10/10. They would not move again. I looked around the room. It was bare apart from the various jackets, boiler suit, hi-vis vest, hardhat, winter coat, dressing gown swinging around on the two pegs by the cabin door. The curtains on the window overlooking *City of Adelaide* swayed from side to side. The ones on the two portholes beside my bed secured to rails by hooks at their tops, yawned out to the maximum at the hems away from them, then slapped back. The coffee jar stood firm, but the plastic honey one had flown off the top of the fridge twice before I laid it flat. Three apples in the bowl stayed wedged together, though one of them sported a bruise from a previous collision with the floor. All that was left on the surfaces apart from these was the desk lamp, kettle, towel and bedding: all I had been supplied with when I arrived.

Even in these circumstances a dark cloud descended from the top of my head at the thought that in a few days' time I would be leaving this space that has been my home for nearly ten weeks.

DAY SIXTY-FIVE

October 15, 1864 – Saturday

A fine cold day. We played 'Puss' on the Deck in the afternoon. Blanche and I practised some Duetts. In the evening we had some music – walked on Deck from 9 to 10 P.M. A beautiful moonlight night.

29 January 2014 – Wednesday – Indian Ocean

A beautiful blue sky morning followed last night's sunset of copper on the horizon when it looked like a huge Paiste gong was descending into the blue. As soon as I drew back the curtains the heat belted onto my body. We are still rolling about and *Palanpur*'s speed has been reduced to compensate for the long swell of the waves. Sure enough, this morning *City of Adelaide* is naked. Her cover is flapping about in tatters. One of the plastic banners with *City of Adelaide* emblazoned on it has come free at one end and every now and again the name is turned by the wind towards the bow of *Palanpur*. Anatolii and Kostyantyn had tucked in two large sections of the cover that were hanging by a thread ready to take off into the Indian Ocean, to be secured against one of the supports for *City of Adelaide*, and also underneath her.

I awoke this morning at 9.45 am, feeling exhausted. I could not even be bothered putting on any clothes. I could not be bothered going down for lunch. I rang Oleksiy and got no reply. He would be in the thick of dishing out lunches. After fifteen minutes I realised he *would* be in the thick of dishing out lunches, and not in his cabin. I got him in the galley, of course.

'Yes Rita.'

'I am not coming to lunch just now. Please let Richard know this in case he is waiting for me.'

'I understand, yes.'

I went up to my cabin and began typing, sitting on my bed with my back in the corner propped up by pillows. My laptop was on the mattress between my legs, not the best position for posture, but the only safe place to be in the unsafe pitch and fall of *Palanpur*. Soon I found my eyes closed and my hands had rested on the keyboard, producing gibberish. I gave in and went for a snooze. Two hours later I emerged. It was 4.15 pm. We were still rolling about and serious care had to be taken when navigating round the cabin. I was ready to grab hold of anything to keep me upright. In the shower I cursed a few times as my feet were almost taken from me. I even had to hold on to the grab rail, a thoughtful addition by *Palanpur*'s designer that saved me more than once. I washed my hair with one hand on the grab rail, the other working my hair into a lather. You get used to the rhythm of the ship and can feel the build up to a massive roll. Nevertheless it is easy to get caught out. I ate some crackers, my own version of ship's biscuits I had bought in Port Hedland. I was hungry from having no breakfast or lunch. I typed until suppertime. Pork fillet again, crunchy root crop salad with chunks of that cheese I find too salty, and pasta with grated cheese sprinkled over. German and Valeriy were there when I arrived, and Vitaliy was at his place at the next table. I asked Vitaliy if he had heard my chairs scraping around yesterday evening. He grinned and said he had. I told them all about my lashings to keep the chairs in place. They laughed. Valeriy's shoulders rose and fell like *Palanpur*, his mouth was stretched, he was reverse-sniffing and his eyes were glinting. It was great to see him so amused. Richard appeared. He joined us and poured me half of the last of the finest wine he had opened the day before yesterday. Due to the severe rolling of *Palanpur* last night he decided not to pour any in case it spilled. We chatted quite a while. He has been working on points that need attended to in Adelaide before our arrival, mostly to do with the barge. He had sent his sketch for t-shirts to CSCOAL. I had been surprised there were no t-shirts available, as the website advertises them for sale. Mykhailo had been keen to buy one for his wife and I had asked on his behalf. I had also asked Peter Christopher a couple of weeks ago whether it would be possible to provide each of the seventeen crewmembers with a t-shirt free in recognition of the part they have played in bringing *City of Adelaide* home. I will ask if they can have some other token.

Andriy K had left my slop chest order list. I picked a bar of milk chocolate and a carton of mango juice. I felt awful when it occurred to me Richard might have liked to order something. I asked him later if he would like something. After a while he said he would like a bar of chocolate. 'Is that all?' I said. 'No juice?'

'I usually have juice at breakfast-time, but no thanks.'

'Just one bar of chocolate?' I tempted.

'Well, make it two then,' he said. He asked me if I would like *The Stump Jump* bottle to take home. I thanked him. We discussed baggage allowance so I took it to my room and photographed it, and peeled off the award label from it to keep. He is very proud of the Adelaide wines, and rightly so judging by what I have tasted so far.

Richard told me CSCOAL are striving to have *City of Adelaide* permanently slipped on Fletcher's Slip in the inner port. There she would be away behind a gate and sheds alongside could be used as workshops and for storage. He mentioned the Maritime Museum in Port Adelaide. I told Richard about Britain's oldest historic fighting ship HMS *Trincomalee*, a Leda-class sailing frigate built just after the Napoleonic War that is a floating museum in the Borough of Hartlepool in County Durham, North-East England. About twenty years ago I had accompanied Dunbar Sea Cadets on a bus trip there. They had recreated a whole dockside scene with memorabilia from the time, informative film showing life how it was then with re-enactment and sound effects of cannon fire from ships, gory scenes, food that was consumed, press-ganging, punishment; all this centring round the fully-rigged ship standing in its wet dock for added effect. I told him I had been to Lerwick on Shetland in 2011. This was to be my last visit to an International Sail Training Association Tall Ships Race as I began focussing entirely on *City of Adelaide* from then on. I told him of the horror that struck the island and the race fleet when news of shootings in Norway spread that a lone gunman had killed at least 85 people at a youth camp on the island of Utoya. It was pouring with rain. It was miserable. The flags of the fleet were lowered to half-mast as a mark of respect. Norwegian ships *Statsraad Lehmkuhl*, *Sorlandet* and *Christian Radich* were all berthed together for the first time since their visit to Lerwick in 1999, where they had gone after Greenock, where I first found out about *City of Adelaide*, then known as *Carrick*.

I could see *City of Adelaide* becoming a tourist attraction, and indeed the Dutch Barque *Europa* that takes part in the Tall Ships Races, had sent a message to CSCOAL that they would visit *City of Adelaide* in 2013 when they were in the southern seas, but the clipper ship had not arrived at the time of her visit. United Kingdom's *Lord Nelson* that is adapted for young people with disabilities, made its first round-the-world voyage and called in to Port Adelaide at the same time, thereby joining two other Dutch ships, *Tecla* and *Oosterschelde* and Port Adelaide's own tall ships *One-And-All* and *Falie* for a Festival of Maritime Trades organised by the South Australian Maritime Museum. Richard said there are thousands of pieces of artefacts closed away from the public eye, just kept in storage. I wondered if anything had come off *City of Adelaide*. He told me of the stripping out of buildings that could have been brought into commission in his opinion. It sounded to me like there is huge potential for collaboration between the museum, *City of Adelaide* and all these things that could emulate what Hartlepool has done. I will try to have a look at all the places and things Richard mentioned, and gain a full insight into the potential. Richard said he would introduce me to people when I am in Adelaide. I am looking forward to this. I mentioned to him that I had read in the brochure he had given to German about the planned dinner in Adelaide on 7 November 2014 to commemorate the arrival of *City of Adelaide* on 7 November 1864. If I do not make it back to Australia for *City of Adelaide*'s one hundred and fiftieth birthday party in May, I shall be back in November, and hope Alan will come too.

After supper I went up to the bridge. German asked me where Richard was. I said he was working in the officers' mess. He said, 'Why does he not use the conference room?' He sent Andriy K down to tell him about this space I had also been offered when I first came on board *Palanpur*. I had not used it much, working in my cabin was comfortable. Andriy re-appeared and said Richard felt fine where he was. It is a good space, and tea and coffee are on hand if he wanted it.

I had a variety of questions relating to previous diary entries of events I needed clarification of. Andriy K was on Watch and German was there, as was Mykhailo.

I said to German I had some questions. He said to Andriy that I wanted to interview him. He laughed. German showed me the management structure of Harren & Partner. I had been interested in the inspections that had taken place when we were in Port Hedland. I had met again Sanjay Rautela, and Ralph Jacobsen who had introduced himself to me at supper. German told me he had been his teacher, and he had sailed with him for seven years. He inspects ships and trains boarding teams. External and internal audits take place regularly. When I had been on the bridge while these inspectors were on board, they continually asked questions of the officers to ensure everything was understood and in order.

When I was on the mooring deck I noticed the port anchor had markings on the chain. German and Andriy explained the links are numbered in sets of five. There is a red anchor shackle, next to this is the first link of the first section that is painted white, the next four links are not painted and they are numbered 1-5; the next red anchor shackle is painted red, the link next to it is painted white and the next one to that is also painted white, they are numbered 6-10; the third shackle is painted red and the next three links to it are painted white, and so on. The port anchor has 11 shackles and a length of 27.5 metres. The links between the shackles are manufactured without joints for strength. Once the shackles are fitted, every five links are sealed with molten lead for strength. The lead is melted when it is required to be released. When the anchor is released the Bosun is so familiar with the chains that it is possible for him to count the length just by sound.

I asked Andriy about the mooring arrangements in Port Hedland. I had heard mention of 2 + 1 + 1. He explained this meant we would be using two headlines, one breast line for strong wind, and one spring line that has a length of 220 metres. We talked about the material the ropes are made from; there is polypropylene that is submersible, more flexible, cheaper and easier to make that manilla that is made from banana trees. I asked Andriy what the line with the monkey's fist is called. He said it is the heaving line that can be thrown 15-30 metres to shore. I asked him about the machine Anatolii the Bosun had been operating on the mooring deck. He said it is a winch; he pushes a lever to wind/unwind the moving ropes. The access holes for the ropes are called leads. There are storm anchors to port and starboard. Andriy K told me about the Life Line Throwing Appliance that is stored in a cylinder with a handle on it. When I saw it I thought it would be thrown to wherever it was needed. Not so. There are four units on board, stored in the Fore Mooring Station.

> ***'Self-contained rocket propelled line throwing appliance***
> *A self-contained line-throwing appliance consisting of a plastic case with an end cap and 250m of line, an integral striker mechanism plus a rocket. Fired by a twist grip and used for passing a 4mm dia. line from ship to ship, ship to shore, shore to ship, and shore based rescue service, or for rescuing a swimmer in distress. Ships typically have to carry 4 units to comply with SOLAS regulations.'*
> (Compiled from www.PainsWessex.com and www.Dräger.com)

Andriy told me that there are great dangers on the mooring deck, such as water that comes on board when the ropes are dragged in. The stevedores on shore drop them and they fall into the water before they are brought onto the mooring deck. Safety glasses must be worn when hauling in the anchor because of dirt, flakes of metal and other debris flying off the chain that is stored in what is called the *chain locker*. Andriy K and German spoke about windlasses, capstans, bollards. If a sailor is found sitting on one of these, they are told to *stand up from the head of the bosun.* I said we need to put bandanas on them, since our Bosun wears one. The mood was jocular. We laughed about the time when a stevedore had thrown the monkey's fist on board and it had hit Andriy on his hardhat. Had he not had this on, he would have been injured. As we spoke, German was asking Andriy questions as if testing him. I teased he was using his position of power to get Andriy to answer questions he himself probably could not answer. We laughed. We talked about the pronunciation of *Greenwich*, German saying it as it is spelt, phonetically; he modified it to *Grenache*, this is a variety of grape wine is made from; and then the way it is supposed to be spoken: *Grenitch.* We discussed language yet again, and its idiosyncrasies.

There was a beautiful sunset. I had not brought my camera, but watched the golden gong of Ra summon the darkness, as it slipped from sight beyond the horizon. Richard was at the starboard with his camera, recording its descent. At 8 pm we are west of Perth. Our latitude is 32°07.32'S, longitude 113°42.35'E. The wind speed is 29 knots. There are two readings for wind speed, True and Relative. The True speed is the actual speed of the wind, the Relative reading gives the speed of the wind according to the speed of the ship, so that if we are travelling at 10 knots, the Relative reading would be 39 knots by today's speed.

Andriy showed me a photograph on his phone of *Hanse Explorer*, a luxury yacht in the Harren & Partner fleet. He has spent two contracts on board her in the Antarctic, and has driven private and professional clients in its Zodiac RIB (reinforced inflatable boat) to get them to less accessible areas, such as narrow channels surrounded by ice. I mentioned the Southern Cross. He teased I need to look to the south to see it. I stepped outside the bridge to the walkway. I rounded the corner on the port side and my breath was taken from me. I was startled by the Milky Way. It was as though a bucket of bright white milk had been splashed across the pitch black velvet sky, the stars dazzling points of diamonds jutting through it. Andriy came outside behind me. I showed him Orion's Belt, how it is the opposite way round to the way it is in Scotland. Andriy followed me to the bow of *Palanpur* and pointed to the Southern Cross, those four dots in the sky I was overcome by on Christmas night when I lay in front of the bridge. I was mesmerised by the sheer beauty and vastness of the firmament. We went back inside. I thanked him for all his help with information. He said he was happy about it, being good revision for him and making time pass quickly. I was glad, always worrying about being a nuisance.

The magic over for now, Andriy printed off diagrams and labels for equipment on the mooring deck for me. I checked emails, one from my youngest daughter, one from Alan, who is worried about my credit card being frozen. I asked him to send the bank's phone number so that I can call them from the Sat phone on board, though this would be expensive. I told them Peter Christopher had mentioned me to the Press when he updated them on the progress of *City of Adelaide*:

> *'By the way, a Scottish woman from Dunbar, Rita Bradd, has travelled out with the ship, and will have an interesting story to tell.'*

He had received a response from the reporter saying he would be very interested to speak with me.

The ship's radio crackled into life.

'May Day…May Day…we are taking on water.'

This sobered our mood. Some poor souls were out there in a yacht that was sinking. We heard the coastguard ask all vessels to keep a look out for it, adding gloomily that they had no co-ordinates for the yacht's position. German arrived on the bridge. He and Andriy looked at the radar. I saw a flashing blue light at the top of the mast before us. Andriy was clicking this on and off. A pulse of hope in the black of the night.

DAY SIXTY-SIX

October 16, 1864 – Sunday

A beautiful morning but rather showery afternoon. We were on Deck nearly all day. Prayers were read in the Saloon. In the evening we went to the Service at the Forecastle and read a very good Sermon. The text was "Therefore be ye also ready". We saw a whale spouting. It looked like a ship in the distance. We stayed on Deck till 9 P.M. and then had music.

30 January 2014 – Thursday – Indian Ocean

Another beautiful morning with a clear blue sky and teal sea. The night passage had been a little less aggressive. I kept the chairs lashed together and continued to use my bed as my office.

I looked at my phone this morning and found I had a signal. A couple of messages came through, one from the sister of a musician friend back home. She invited me to meet her in Adelaide or in Glenelg where she lives. I mentioned this to Richard at lunchtime. He said Glenelg is a very smart area on the coast. Adelaide lies behind it then the hills are behind Adelaide. I will show her photos of her brother at some of our music gigs, and from their parents' fiftieth wedding anniversary when I played harp for them. I am looking forward to meeting her.

I showered early and got some typing done before lunch. We had very nice chicken and pasta with cheese. The pel'mini making for Richard's wine was scheduled for 1 pm; this gave me ten minutes to go up to my cabin and then back down again to the crew mess. Kostyantyn and Serhii were there first, then Vadym joined us. He said, 'Do you know what means pel'mini? It is *ear*.' German came in, he wondered where everyone was. Eventually a few more folk arrived; Anatolii, Sergiy, Igor and Ihor. There was a lack-lustre air, the lads may have been tired. Oleksiy had been disgruntled at losing his afternoon nap and that we would be losing another hour's sleep tonight. There was some discussion about the troubles in Ukraine. Things were getting ugly. Oleksiy had given me his form a couple of days before. He was quite wild that he had to use this spelling of his name. When he had received his Ukrainian passport his name had been changed from his birth spelling of Alexiy, the Russian way of spelling it. Even though he is Ukrainian he was blazing that this change had been made. He was named after his father and now their names are spelled differently. I wondered if it was legal to have your name spelled one way on your birth certificate and another on your passport.

There was not the celebratory atmosphere that I remembered from 1 January, but this is not Saturday. Richard arrived with his camera. I had already taken a few photos.

He began recording the lads. They kept their heads down, perhaps they were shy. I asked Igor if I could have a go at making a pel'meni. I had cut a disk out at the last party and this would complete the cycle. Andriy V joined us. Richard continued to take photos, he took some of me with my camera and I took some of him having a go at making them with his. He had not sealed his two attempts properly and Vadym said to him, 'My friend this is no good.' They were re-formed and everyone was happy. I said to Richard I was going to my cabin to leave them to it. He decided to go and do some work. The lads were chatting away, relaxed in the social occasion it was. Sergiy asked me if he could come to my cabin to ask about some English language queries he had. I left as Serhii was carrying a tray full of pel'meni in the wake of Oleksiy, who was showing him where to store them. I noticed two beautiful baked breads in the kitchen, fresh out of the oven. Out came my camera again.

Back in my cabin I did some typing then went for a snooze. I awoke at 5 pm, so had an hour. I went down at 5.30 pm for supper. The pel'meni were very tasty, though German thought they were not as good as the last ones. There is no sour cream to have with them, I did what I did the last time and sprinkled fresh ground black pepper onto a splash of white vinegar and put a dollop of tomato sauce on the side to dip them in. Oleksiy had put loads of melted butter on the pel'meni so I did not dip much. They are very filling. Richard told me they had again made one thousand of them. He poured me a small measure of red wine that was tasty, but it would take a lot to beat last night's *Stump Jump*, but that was exclusive wine. He offered me some white wine, but I declined; other people had not yet had a taste of his Adelaide wines. I left him chatting with Valeriy and went aloft to my cabin to work. I decided to pop up to the bridge before settling down, to take readings. I had not a clue where we were, but Richard had mentioned how changing course had improved comfort on board *Palanpur*.

We have rounded the south-west corner of Australia. We are on the home stretch. We are at latitude 35°23.61'S, longitude 116°31.33'E, wind speed 17.5 knots, ship speed 13.8 knots, and it is 27° early evening temperature. We are level with Point Nuyts in the Southern Ocean, to the south-west below sea level is Broke Canyon, to the south-east is Wilson Canyon. I decided to take a little sun and went down to put on Factor 40. I sat on the deck below the bridge for about ten minutes each side then went up to chat. I checked my emails. One from Alan saying I obviously had not received his earlier emails concerning my credit card. He again provided the bank number for me, saying I should call them reverse charge as soon as I can use a landline.

German came over. He was so happy because his wife had emailed to let him know that an acorn he had picked up in a famous botanical garden had sprouted. He had picked up two but there was no sign of anything happening with the other one yet. He said there is a saying:

A man is not a real man unless he has three things:

A home

A tree

A son

He is rejoicing because now he has all three. He is so happy, he extolled the virtues of oak trees, their mighty strength and the great age they can grow to. I said the Ukrainian emblem has oak leaves in it. I said I have a poem I would give him. I told him about the Sassine Oak near my home that had been occupied by tree dwellers when they had wanted to fell them for use in Windsor Castle after part of it was destroyed by fire, to keep the new timbers authentic with the original age of the building. We had quite a discussion about trees, German consulting the dictionary to indicate where necessary the ones he was talking about. We discussed the problem in the United Kingdom with ash trees, where ash dieback disease is causing the splitting of bark that leads to the death of the tree. Andriy K knew the tree I was talking about when I described the seed. We talked about sycamore trees. We talked about cedar with its needles instead of leaves. We talked about juniper, the gin tree, and I said how its berries are good to put in your pillow to combat stress. He told me about wormwood that absinthe is made from and how it is good to sprinkle around to get rid of and keep fleas out of the house. I knew its best use is as a disinfectant. *The green fairy.* That is one alcoholic drink I cannot abide.

German raised the topic of my father. He said I was right, that history is written by the victors. I did not coin that phrase, I just aired it. He asked me if I would visit Ukraine. I said I wanted to. He said around L'viv is beautiful. He had shown me photos of this before. He said my father had been right to fight for what he believed in. Richard arrived. He asked if I had seen the sunset. I said I had managed to record it but my battery had died just before it totally disappeared under the horizon. It was not as spectacular as last night's but I have three more nights for further attempts before we reach Adelaide. We are due to arrive on Monday, early morning. I have said again I wish to remain on board *Palanpur* until *City of Adelaide* is discharged, even though this could take a couple of days with all the lashings she is held together with. Richard told me Peter Christopher had held a gathering last night that Captain Bruce's great-granddaughter, Pam Whittle had attended, along with CSCOAL members. He is talking of having a barbecue when we get in. Wiebbe Bonsink from Hebo will be there to supervise discharge of *City of Adelaide* off *Palanpur*. Richard wants me to meet Mark Caudwell who had provided the tele-lift at Irvine that had saved an enormous amount of money for CSCOAL. Together with this and the time he had put in volunteering had made him the person in the United Kingdom that had contributed most towards the recovery of *City of Adelaide*. German had asked whether I have prepared a Press statement for our arrival. He would direct Press to me if he is asked to speak to them. I said *City of Adelaide* is the star of the show.

DAY SIXTY-SEVEN

October 17, 1864 – Monday

A very wet day. I read 'Rienzi' till noon and afterwards played two games of Chess with the Doctor which lasted till 3 P.M.

31 January 2014 – Friday – Southern Ocean

The clock struck its loud ticks and pushed us forward another hour at 1.15 am. I typed until 5.30 am that would have been 4.30 am. At last I am up to date with the daily entries. I still have to go back to Greenwich and Rotterdam, but that can be done later. I am getting excited at the prospect of arriving at Adelaide.

I awoke at 10 am and turned over. The clock was at 11.50 am when I next looked. I did not feel like eating any lunch and lay for a while, thinking about thank-you emails and marketing. I stayed in my cabin until about 4 pm, then began a clear up. I went down to supper where Richard had opened another bottle of red wine, Penfolds, a wine stocked in Scotland. It was a 2005 bottle, and on the label was the year of the start of the winery. 1844. This is the year that Sarah was born. I am going to get her as much into modern times as possible. I think Penfolds should name a wine after her. It was a very rich, full-bodied wine. I must say Richard has good taste.

Richard and I chatted about lifestyles, in particular houses. He told me of some building projects he has carried out, and concepts for buildings he had been recognised for. Otherwise there was not much conversation today. I am still tired, but must try and get that email to Combi-Lift off. I will go up to German and see whether he can give me direct email addresses for Combi-Lift and Harren & Partner.

I have just come back from the bridge. German does not know the specific person who requested that I be permitted to make this voyage. He encouraged me to wait till Monday since it is the weekend. I am happy to go along with that. We chatted a while about arrival times. He does not think *City of Adelaide* will be discharged before Wednesday morning. German mentioned there is a cruise boat that people have paid to come on board to escort *City of Adelaide* into Port Adelaide. He does not think the Australian Maritime Safety Authority will allow people to disembark from that to board *Palanpur*. We discussed logistics and agreed it was doubtful this would be allowed. I found Richard had met the same restrictions I had about sending attachments to emails.

There is a long, long swell in front of *Palanpur*'s bow. We are almost into the Great Australian Bight. I am really excited. It will be hard to resist going ashore in Port Adelaide, but if I do I will come back and spend the last couple of nights here in my cabin.

DAY SIXTY-EIGHT

October 18, 1864 – Tuesday

A beautiful morning but very rough afternoon. There was snow for the first time during the voyage. We were on Deck till lunch. There were a great many birds flying about.

01 February 2014 – Saturday – Southern Ocean

A pale grey sky all day with short, low waves swishing us along. *City of Adelaide* has been soaked, her entire bow is visible from my cabin window.

I heard a loud thunderclap at 6 am and awoke with a start. It was still quite dark. I saw something had been pushed under my door. I put the light on. It was my certificate with my new name given by King 'Neptun' for crossing the Equator. At last! Andriy V had hand-written it out, and kept it to a simple *Ocean Moon*. We had talked about *Gypsy Dragon of the Ocean Moon*, *Seahorse*, and just few days ago he mentioned *Sea Nymph*. I thought about the video I had taken the other night when the beautiful moon was full and streaming through the port side window beside my bed. I thought of my old horse Ginny, originally named *Silver Moon*, and was content. I went back to sleep until around 10 am, got up and hand-washed a couple of items in my en suite basin. I spent time looking over the poems I have written and typed up the remaining ones from the *Black and Red* book my mother had given me for the journey. She had had it for more than a dozen years, authenticated by its musky odour. Before I knew it it was lunchtime and I had not had my shower. I decided to have a cat wash rather than be late for the meal. Oleksiy was in the store when I arrived. He came out, 'Rita, Rita,' he said, and put his hand on my shoulder. I reciprocated with, 'Oleksiy, Oleksiy' and used the same gesture. He dished up pork fillet, pasta and grated cheese. I took some borscht that was tasty as ever. Richard was at the table. He said that the guys are going to miss me. I sure am going to miss them. I am very emotional today, and already had some tears flow this morning, my shoulders shuddering them to land on the bed-sheet where they transformed to dark blue. It is the whole experience I have had with *City of Adelaide* since 1999. Where did it come from, this obsession with a ship built

one hundred and fifty years ago in Sunderland? Why did she keep scratching at me, making me research her, drawing me to see her at Irvine far from my home? Why did I look at the CSCOAL website just at the right time when something important was happening? Why did I look at the donors' page and find out about Sarah Ann Bray being on the maiden voyage, subsequently meeting her great-granddaughter Ruth Currie who gave me the copy of her diary and family papers that steeled my determination to escort *City of Adelaide* back to Australia? Why was Peter Roberts so helpful in getting me on board this Harren & Partner ship chartered by Combi-Lift heavy-lift ship *Palanpur*? Why is the crew Ukrainian, giving another dimension to this story? Everyone has been so co-operative and generous. Every day I speak with Sarah and wonder what she thinks of all this. I believe she is here with us, inside *City of Adelaide*'s belly.

After lunch I planned to start work on a *thank you* for the lads for the way they have made me feel so comfortable, and giving me so many laughs on this voyage. I thought I might do a cartoon but then when I was looking at poems again I came across one of my *Palanpur* poems *Whisky Sours* that pays tribute to these men of the sea. It is sentimental, but I thought it appropriate. I began to work through it using the dictionary Anatoliy our previous cook had uploaded into my computer. I wanted to present it in Ukrainian as well as English. I also plan to write their names round the edges of the paper once it is done. I will ask Sergiy to come to my cabin tonight to deal with the questions about English he has. I will ask him if he will help me with my project.

I felt *City of Adelaide* call me from my cabin. There are not many chances to go down and be close to her. The sea is too rough; men are working on the weather deck; the wind is too strong; cargo is being loaded; cargo is being off-loaded. I put on my heavy-duty boots, sparkly fluffy bed-socks, hi-vis Combi-Lift jacket, and hardhat. I put on a winter jumper as it is a bit cool today. I headed for the weather deck, deciding at the last minute to take my camera. Images provide inspiration for writing, particularly poetry. Her immensity never ceases to amaze me. I stuck my nose into the timbers at her bow and inhaled her essence. One and a half centuries filled my senses. I smelled the sweat of men sawing planks that were clad against her iron ribs beneath. I saw gleaming copper nails embed into timber, heard the dull rhythmic tap-tapping of steel hitting wood echoing round William Pile & Hay's Shipbuilding Yard in Sunderland. I heard men curse when the aim of their hammer was not true; I saw blood spurting from a bashed thumb and dripping to the ground, turning the pure wood dust ruby red, and a thumbnail turning black to fall off days later. I saw rolled up shirt sleeves, woollen waistcoats, flat caps, pipes, heavy boots. I saw grey smog hanging over tall brick chimneys spewing exhausted fumes into the air above. I heard a dog yapping, the sea lapping, a hooter signalling a break for the men to eat whatever morsels they had brought to fuel their output.

I began to take close-up photos; gaps between the planks, barnacles at the stern, dowels, huge copper nails, clusters of smaller nails. It helps if you keep your lens clean. I noticed it had some salt spray dotted on it, and gave it a wipe. I photographed the iron eyes that were not clasping *City of Adelaide*'s missing rudder to the stern. I took a few shots through the bottom ring looking up through the others to the sky. *City of Adelaide*'s rudder had been appropriated over a year before she made this journey, and had been taken to Australia. It was a replacement from when she had lost her rudder and ran aground off Kangaroo Island in 1877. I remember Peter Maddison asking the question, 'Where is the rudder?' These Australians have done nothing without stealth and determination.

I picked up a few pieces of debris that had blown off *City of Adelaide* in the weather she met after Port Hedland. I walked round to the port side for more photos. When I first came on the deck Richard had been outside the bridge using the Sat phone. His voice had carried on the wind. Now he was examining *City of Adelaide*'s bow, his camera slung round his neck. I took a few more photos, including some of the large dowels. Several smaller ones have come loose in the journey, perhaps with shrinkage of the planks in the hot sun at Port Hedland. These dowels would probably have been hammered in with the use of mallets, making a deep, soft thud-thud sound. Richard took a few photos of me looking up at *City of Adelaide*. I took some of him with his camera. It is far superior to mine, and the wide-angle facility is a definite advantage. I left Richard and came up to have that delayed shower. Serhii helped me close the deck door. He is always looking to help me. At supper Oleksiy dished out his tasty beef risotto. I popped my head in to the crew mess to see if Sergiy was there. He was. Vadym, Stefan and a few others were having their meal. 'Bon appetite,' I said. I went over to Sergiy and asked him if he would come to my cabin at 7 pm for the help he had asked for with his English. He was hesitant so I suggested 8 pm. He readily agreed to this. I found out from Valeriy in the officers' mess when I went through that some of the crew were playing football on the 'tween deck. Really? Another surprise. So that's how the lads keep in shape. It must be great for them to have those locomotives out of the way so that they can let off steam as an alternative to working out in their gym. Ten weeks with these lads, yet there were still surprises.

Oleksiy had given me two bottles of still water and one of sparkling after lunch. There is no point in my asking for a pack of six when I will be leaving the ship in four days' time. We are due to dock in Port Adelaide the day after tomorrow in the early morning and off-loading *City of Adelaide* will take a couple of days. I went up to check our position. German and Mykhailo were working in the office area. I had no emails. I chatted a while with German. I said I would like to photograph the bridge crew tomorrow before lunch. Mykhailo may not comply as this is sleep time for him and it is Sunday, when everyone has an easier day. I then found I had some photos of three of the bridge crew. They do smile for me.

I went back down to my cabin for the appointment at 8 pm with Sergiy. I expected him to have loads of writing for me to look at. He had a second email address to add to my permission form, and three words he asked for help with pronunciation of. It is really an honour to be asked by the lads to help progress their grasp of English. I asked Sergiy if he would help me with translating *Whisky Sours*. He readily agreed. Whenever I feel I am putting them out with my conversation or requests, they insist I am helping them practise their English. Sergiy asked if I could get a printout of the poem in English. 'I will go to the bridge and get this,' I said. He came back for it at 9 pm and I gave him a memory stick with a few photos I had of him with some other crew, and the document I had prepared of the Ukrainian translation. He said it might be difficult to do this, and I explained it is very difficult to translate poetry and keep the flow and metaphor. I apologised for it being so long but he said he is happy to practise his English. He also said he writes songs and poems sometimes.

Since then I have typed. I popped down to the mess to make a sandwich with black bread with coriander seed in it. A couple of days ago I had asked Valeriy if the seeds were caraway; he corrected me, they are cumin. I put on cheese and salami, ate it back in my cabin and washed it down with a beer. I had a look at the CSCOAL website extract to refresh my memory of donors. There is a great mix of international donors, many from Scotland and Australia. I am glad to see names of people with memories of when *City of Adelaide* was named *Carrick*. I shall try to contact some of them when I get home, along with several people I met in Irvine to hear their memories.

The clock ticks forward another half hour. We have about sixteen hours till Adelaide.

DAY SIXTY-NINE

October 19, 1864 – Wednesday

A rough, cold day – several snow storms. We should not have gone on Deck but the Captain called us to see a Whale. There were three but all of a small size.

02 February 2014 – Sunday – Southern Ocean

A beautiful blue sky with scant shallow clouds. Sunlight is glistening on wavelets, dazzling like new fallen snow sparkled into life by Apollo.

I wrote a poem this morning, inspired by the shadow of the radar burling on the deck before the bow of *City of Adelaide*. It is a rallying call to the people of Australia to back the arrival of this beautiful clipper ship and support her in memory of their ancestors. There is a lot of activity on the weather deck this morning, preparations for the start of cutting *City of Adelaide* free tomorrow. I saw Kostyantyn removing rust with a grinder, Anatolii, German observing the clipper ship's hull, and Mykhailo inspecting.

Richard came up to the bridge just after 11.45 am. None of the bridge crew were there except for Andriy K and Andriy V who were just ending and just starting their watches respectively. He had been taking photographs of the crew in action. We went down to lunch, chicken noodle soup, chicken leg, rice with melted butter. I spied mushrooms simmering in a pot and asked if they were for supper. Oleksiy said they were and, 'Would you like some?' Yum. There was ice cream to follow and I took the last chocolate one. After lunch I came to my cabin and began drafting an email to the Press enquiry I had received from Peter Christopher via Richard the other day. I added *Andy Philip* of Press Association to my Address Book and will wait for Amos Connect to acknowledge this, probably in a few hours.

I was really emotional last night with this journey coming to an end, but very excited and not a little apprehensive about arrival in Adelaide. It sounds a beautiful place from what Richard has told me and I am looking forward to experiencing its delights and meeting the directors of Clipper Ship City Of Adelaide Ltd and Rosemary McKay again, and new people. My phone is receiving a weak signal on and off, nothing strong enough for it to be of use. I need to hear my family's voices.

I went out on the weather deck for some air. Just after, some of the crew followed me with Richard, wearing a hard hat, in their wake. There was a large cardboard box. Inside was a banner for *7News*. The crew were going to attempt to put it on the deck of *Palanpur*.

Andriy V said, 'Hello, Ocean Moon.'

I said, 'Hello, Whale.'

I watched as first Kostyantyn, then Ihor threw the line over the deck. It was supposed to reach across the deck and come over the other side. The wind was not favourable. I asked Richard if he would take a photo of me at the bow of *City of Adelaide*. He agreed so I went up for my camera. When I got back work was in progress. I saw Kostyantyn and Ihor up in Crane 2 tower, throwing the line from that great height. I took a few photos. Richard was by this time well engrossed in trying to get some way of having the banner fixed so that when helicopters fly over in the morning, *7News* will be seen from the air. Quite a number of the crew were involved in operations, and Mykhailo came down and took charge. He and Richard discussed options. Andriy V and Mykhailo had Harren & Partner fawn boiler suits on, the rest of the crew were Combi-Lift. It took quite a while to tether the large banner for *7News* down, and not so much for the Combi-Lift one. Richard went to his cabin and brought down the cityofadelaide.org.au website banner and began fixing it to the cradle at the starboard side of *City of Adelaide*. As he was busy I asked Ihor to take a photograph of me at *City of Adelaide*'s hull. He had been at the muster station with a couple of the guys so I was not distracting him from work. The crew are necessarily single-minded about their work. I went back to my cabin to get ready for supper. Not long after, everyone began arriving for their meal, pork fillet with mushrooms and cheese and chips. Richard brought in a bottle of rosé wine. I looked at the label. It has a tall ship on it exactly like the design on the soundboard of my Bohemian harp *Gypsy Rose*, but without the topgallant and royals sails set. I told Richard about the building of the harp and the shocks I gave Christoph Locherbach, chamfering the edges of the pillar and saddle, staining it pink, carving a horse head. I told him about the rallying poem I wrote this morning. He said I should read it to the people on the boat that are sailing out to see *City of Adelaide* tomorrow at 5 pm. There will be around four hundred people on board. Daunting! He said he would make sure I could come on board. He also said Peter Christopher has taken a week off his work. He will want to participate

in the celebrations of this wonderful achievement. After supper Richard showed me his design for the exhibition centre for *City of Adelaide*. It is rather stunning and expensive. He showed me photos of his two-month trip to Darwin with his wife. They too were stunning. I would have looked at more, but Sergiy was coming to let me know how he got on with the poem translation.

I took film of the sunset, *City of Adelaide*'s and my last one. There were rolling clouds across the sky above her and the sunset was liquid gold. Sergiy arrived. He read out what he has translated so far and it sounded beautiful. He was concerned though that it was pure text, and with having had to work today he had not had time to take it into poetic form. He asked if I would leave it with him and he would pass it to the crew once he had completed it. I agreed to this. He took my Skype, email and website addresses and asked me to include a message to his family in this book:
I love my wife and son very much.

After he was gone I went to the bridge to give Andriy K my passport for the morning's immigration. German had asked at supper if I had packed. I said not. German told me I could stay on the ship as it was circumnavigating Australia. He said *Palanpur* is heading to Singapore to pick up cabling for off-shore cable laying and then heading for the south coast of England. Oh, to stay on board, but Adelaide and Sarah call. I am ready now to leave Palanpur and move to the next phase in *City of Adelaide*'s life. These last couple of weeks have been really full on. I feel there is still so much to learn, but with spending so much time writing, this has been prohibitive. One thing I am looking forward to is being able to communicate electronically at will.

We are passing north of Kangaroo Island at latitude 35°30.00'S and longitude 136°30.88'E, travelling at 12.3 knots. Not long now.

DAY SEVENTY

October 20, 1864 – Thursday

A very rough day and snowing almost incessantly. We were on deck for about a quarter of an hour. The wind which was from the south was dreadfully cold. I finished reading Rienzi by Sir E Bulwer Lytton.

03 February 2014 – Monday – Southern Ocean/Port Adelaide

I crawled to the end of my bed and pulled back the curtains hiding the portholes on the port side of *Palanpur*. Dawn was festooned with swathes of pink-rose over a calm blue sea. A red cargo ship bobbed not far away. It was the fourth ship I had seen at sea during the whole ten weeks of this voyage. In the far distance I could just make out dark lumps on the horizon. Huge waves? I looked again. Land! Adelaide? It had to be!

I jumped off the bed to look at *City of Adelaide* from the deck window. She was now almost completely stripped of any covering. A different horizon was behind her, the morning sun burst out and began to follow her. She looked magnificent. She was full of anticipation. She could smell home. I showered, dressed, grabbed every recording device I could lay my hands on, and bounded up to the bridge. It was 06.40 am. I greeted the crew member on duty. I failed to register who it was in my excitement. I slipped outside onto the walkway. In front of us was a magnificent spectacle. A pot of gold dripped through a break in the grey clouds above. Behind it the whole of that lumpy coastline was on fire, back-lit by the crimson dawn. A cluster of lights glowed in the distance. Combi-Lift and Harren & Partner flags flapped with the sound of whips cracking as we ran before the wind. A cargo ship passed in front of our bow, while above a helicopter whisked up the air. Out of nowhere a green and yellow boat marked *Pilot* appeared on our port side. Its red hull pitched and tossed in the

ever-increasing wild waves. A man came out from the cabin as the boat accelerated to *Palanpur*'s stern, making for starboard. It continued on to position itself in front of us. He was preparing to lead us into the mouth of the river that would bring us to *City of Adelaide*'s final destination: Port Adelaide. I watched the boat roll one moment, then saw its bow rise steeply from the waves, only to fall again. I was glad I had not had any breakfast, and hoped they had not either.

The coastline was becoming clearer as we approached. Now I could see tall buildings appear in the mix. Looking back at *City of Adelaide* and the twin Liebherr cranes, spray was coming off the eager waves. They were like wild horse, their manes flailing out from their arched necks. The remnants of *City of Adelaide*'s raincoat streamed out in harmony with them. Now the sky spread a pink fan over the land. There were two tall chimneys, more buildings and many, many spiky objects that became trees as we got closer to the river mouth. We followed the pilot boat between post guides to port and starboard. A couple of motor boats had come out to greet us. I saw huge steel cranes on the spit of land, and a bird glanced over the waves below. We entered the channel formed by breakwaters we would sail between, the first marked by a post with a red triangle. As we approached the end of the breakwater where it met land, a flotilla of yachts and motor boats sailed towards us. Richard appeared. He pointed to one of the yachts that had many pennants on it. 'That's my boat,' he said with pride. His family had come to meet him. We both waved. The land was sandy, edged by a beach. On the deck below, Sergiy was preparing the lead line with the monkey's fist knot at the end. He lowered the free end of it, weighted by a shackle, to those beneath him in the mooring deck. I became aware of lights flashing at the edge of the land. A slow realisation spread through me. Here were rows of people who had come to watch the arrival of *City of Adelaide*. They were taking pictures. I felt an inexplicable sensation run through me. We were near the end of this fantastic voyage. I did not want it to end. A murmur of panic rumbled through me.

I broke out of my reflection when the dark blue of the Scottish flag, the *Saltire*, waved its diagonal cross at us. My heart soared. Someone from Scotland was in the crowd. There was a park stuffed with cars glinting in the rising day. A pilot boat was moored on the river's bank. The flotilla of boats was following us, now joined by a police boat. *Palanpur* let out a loud hoot that jumped me out of my skin. More and more steel structures lined the edge where land met the river, conveyors for cargo stood alongside an army of giant cranes. There were storage tanks, huge and round; silos, pylons, and radio masts. On the port side things were much greener, with trees and bushes amongst pools of water that mirrored the sky. Sergiy continued on rope duty, Serhii joined him. The ropes were laid out in neat bundles, and planks of wood were placed on top to weigh them down from being disrupted by the wind. Sergiy waved at me as he disappeared down the hatch to join the rest of the crew on the mooring deck. We meandered round bends in the river, and passed a large shed with the letters *ASC* printed on it. Outside, mounted on strong wooden blocks, was a submarine. Some men were watching us from the coning tower. Nearby in dry dock was a naval vessel. Another long blast on the hooter, my skin on the floor again. The tug *Svitzer* appeared. She was between us and the shore. She manoeuvred behind our stern and passed to our starboard side, where she flanked us, escorted us on the last leg of our voyage. We passed what I think is a cement factory, and I knew when I saw two cargo ships moored up round the bend, that we were close to the end of the line. At the *Guides SA* I saw a black and white collie dog, the first dog I remember seeing since I left Scotland. There were more people, more houses, and a myriad of yachts tied up at a yacht club with a gantry, and a sign nearby, *Port River Marine.* As we got closer to the first cargo ship moored up in front of a building with *Viterra* printed high up on it, I saw it was called *Primrose.* The second one was AS *Valeria,* from Monrovia.

All this time I was filming, taking pictures and flitting past Richard on the bridge while he was doing the same. We spoke little in our excitement. Then we saw a green shed, behind it the blue shed of Dock 2, where we would be mooring up alongside. In yards behind the sheds lay rows of huge parts for wind turbines, and I could see stacks and stacks of logs piled alongside stacks and stacks of scrap metal. Ahead lay the Diver Derrick Bridge that Richard told me breaks in the middle and lifts, to allow ships to pass through on a twice-daily basis. As we approached, one of the tug boats connected with our hull and nosed us round to face the opposite direction, so that we were reversing alongside the wharf. I quelled my emotions, trying to keep as steady a hand as possible with all the movement of operations on board, in the river, on the wharf, and within me. I swear a smile spread across *City of Adelaide*'s bow, and she winked at me. Overhead, the helicopter continued to eyeball us. Things were moving slowly, yet too quickly. There was a massive ship that matched the colour of its cargo that looked like sand, or lime on the other side of the Port River. Mykhailo stepped out from the bridge into the sunshine and posed for me to take his picture. He looked sleepy and relaxed, gave no hint of the enormous responsibility he faced of helping manage the off-loading of *City of Adelaide* from *Palanpur. 7News* and Combi-Lift banners lay glinting from the deck in front of *City of Adelaide* in the early sun as we were pushed closer and closer to the edge of Dock 2. A crowd of cars spilled out their contents, and soon cameras were clicking and flashing again. German came out onto the bridge walkway with the pilot, and below, a single stevedore walked on the wharf. Mykhailo reappeared, wearing his orange boilersuit. He lifted one foot and placed it on the guardrail, tying the laces of each boot, one after the other. People were emerging from inside the blue shed. I captured a very proud, happy and relieved Richard in my camera. What an achievement by the *City of Adelaide* team. His face said it all.

But it was not over yet. Docking *Palanpur* was the easy part. The challenge of lifting *City of Adelaide* off from *Palanpur* lay ahead.

I placed photographs of Sarah and her family against my cabin window that overlooked the ship, along with the SCARF menu card featuring Peter Maddison waving the red ensign from the top deck of *Carrick* that *City of Adelaide* was known as at the time that picture was taken. I was deep in thought, going over the unbelievable hand of cards Fate had dealt me that gave me this whole journey with *City of Adelaide*: being a tall ships groupie that took me to the tall ships race in Greenock in 1999, the sea cadet handing me that flyer with the image of the forlorn *Carrick*, desolate on the slipway at the Scottish Maritime Museum at Irvine; finding the *Clipper Ship City of Adelaide Ltd* website, discovering Ruth Currie and tracking her down with the help of CSCOAL, meeting her and receiving the copy of the diary of her great-grandmother, Sarah Ann Bray, being granted permission to accompany *City of Adelaide* on her absolute final voyage, and being in the right family, my fantastic, amazing, tolerant family, who supported me, albeit somewhat with reluctance, all the way. All this fitted together and made my dream of making that voyage come true. But I still needed to know why, what in the universe brought all this to me.

My reverie was broken by my phone ringing. German spoke in my ear. 'There is someone below who wants to see you.' Who could it be. I paused, hesitated. I did not want this dream to end. My cabin had become a safe haven, a world away from a world full of chaos and reality. I sat on my bed and sobbed. Time slipped by. My phone rang again. 'Rita, are you not going down to meet your friend?'

I dragged myself out of my sadness, raised myself off my bed and made for the stairway, dabbing at my eyes all the way. My feet found each stair with a heavy sole. As I opened the steel door and stepped into the sunshine, I spread a smile over my face. As I saw the flaming red hair of Rosemary gleam in the sunlight, the smile became genuine. I was dazed by the light, dazed by the land, and dazed by the warm welcome she gave me. She was carrying the Scottish Saltire. I became overwhelmed as Peter Roberts and Peter Christopher greeted me. Everything was surreal. I saw Brian Oglanby, whom I had met when I sneaked on board *City of Adelaide* at Irvine behind his camera set up on a tripod. John Riddell of *7News* was there with his assistant I had met in Greenwich. The two Peters, Rosemary and I posed for cameras. Soon she stuffed the Saltire round my neck. I was taken into the blue shed to give an interview

Left to right: Peter Roberts, the author, Rosemary McKay, Peter Christopher

for the Press. People all around were welcoming me with hugs and words of congratulations. From somewhere inside the shed Mark Gilbert appeared. He gave me a huge hug. I will never forget what he said. 'It's a marvellous thing you have done. You have given a human touch to the story of *City of Adelaide*'s final voyage home.'

Above, left to right: Mark Gilbert, Peter Christopher, Mark Caudwell

Left: Captain German Koltakov. Right: Chris Antony, Marine Pilot at Flinders Port

Above, left to right: Wiebbe Bonsink, the author, Peter Christopher

Right, left to right: German Koltakov, Mykhailo Makushenko

Members of Clipper Ship City of Adelaide Ltd and friends

Andrew Chapman

Des Ross

City of Adelaide on the Radar

Palanpur takes the waves on the Great Australian Bight
blue, blue everywhere. We surge through jelly waves,
twelve knots per hour and the men are working,
preparing to release lashings that curb the cradle
of *City of Adelaide* to the weather deck.

Sparks fly from the grinder as the Ordinary Seaman
presses it into action seated on a wee wooden stool
made on board this steel leviathan just for this purpose:
to work with minimum strain on his knees and spine.

City of Adelaide is bristling with excitement.
She has seen these waters before, never expected
to see them again as she languished in solitude
on a dismal slipway in Scotland, forlorn
like the driftwood beached at her stern.

The blade of the radar on the monkey deck spins
at her bows in shadow from the morning southern sun,
winds her up, laughs in the breeze for it has picked up
she is close, close to the port she visited so many times
more than a century ago, discharging the Spirit of the North
onto its opposite shores of South Australia.

She is vibrant today, her planking washed and swelled
by a salt bath and shower of relief that at last hope
is on the horizon that the lifeblood of emigrants
she brought to these shores lives on, will take her
to their bosoms in memory of their ancestors
who braved the voyage into the unknown in a quest
for adventure and a better way of life, enduring wind and rain,
storm and snow, sickness, small heat, little light, sodden clothing,
poor diet for more than at least two months.

This pretty clipper ship has a little sister, you know.
She is spit-and-polished into hearts all over the world,
this *Cutty Sark* at Greenwich, London –
a tea-clipper and sometimes cargo carrier
her role was not so much that of carer holding safe
passengers embracing intrepid spirit and adventure

it is this that has kept *City of Adelaide* alive
these one hundred and fifty years;
it is this that has brought her home to you;
it is this that is pressed into the fibre of her soul.

Epilogue

When the excitement settled down with the Press and public, I found myself wrapped in the bosom of a new family – my *City of Adelaide* family. Meeting again the Directors of 'Clipper Ship City of Adelaide Ltd' on their own turf, and some of those who had been at Greenwich, was mind-blowing, stupendous.

I cannot find the words to describe how it felt to have arrived safely in Port Adelaide after ten weeks at sea with my amazing shipmates. It was all surreal. I had fallen down a rabbit hole and landed on the other side of the world. Since I first heard of Australia in primary school aged about seven years, I was fascinated by that Continent. I never, ever expected to set foot on her soil. I never, ever expected to arrive in the way that I did, in the footsteps of a complete stranger, Sarah Ann Bray who broke into my life so unexpectedly in 2012 and fascinated me.

I was surprised by a text on the way up the Port River sent by Linda Strachan, a writer friend who lives not fifteen miles from me. She and her husband had taken a spontaneous break to Adelaide. Peter Christopher later took me to meet them for coffee and cake, then we took them to Dock 2 to see the two ships.

I was whisked away to join the party of hundreds gathered on board pleasure cruiser *Dolphin Explorer* to sail down the Port River and view *City of Adelaide* still lashed to the decks of *Palanpur* in Dock 2. The enthusiasm of the crowd as they were piped on board by *City of Adelaide* honorary piper Des Ross was intense with pride and achievement, that the ship that was built one hundred and fifty years previous was at last home in the Port she had voyaged from London to on twenty-three occasions from 1864 and gone on to have such a varied life. Here was the ship that had survived two floodings, a sinking and threat of demolition in Scotland. Here was the most iconic representation of the birth of the State of South Australia, the ship that had cradled ancestors to free settle in the State, the only State in Australia that has not been built on the blood, sweat and tears of those transported there in the early days of discovery. People could see for themselves and cherish the vessel their forebears had endured months at sea in at a time when ships were literally at the mercy of the vagaries of nature, out in a limb in the middle of oceans where there was little or no chance of rescue and no meaningful means of communication in the face of disaster. As we passed the ship loud cheers erupted, tears rolled down cheeks and arms waved warm greeting to *City of Adelaide*. She had come home at last.

Rosemary McKay introduced me to Captain David Bruce's great-granddaughter, Pamela Whittle and her two daughters, Julia (left to right Carol & Richard Smith, Mark Caudwell, Pamela and Julia Whittle, the author) and Meredith Reardon, (in bottom image L-R Margaret and Dr Alan Platt, Meredith and the author). They took me right into their arms and into their family. I truly felt I had finally arrived, belonged. The night was black when guests began to depart. I left the company. I would not go to take up Peter Christopher's offer of accommodation. Not until *City of Adelaide* was offloaded from *Palanpur*. I would stay with my charge until she was craned off *Palanpur* and onto barge *Bradley* that had been bought specifically as the temporary home for *City of Adelaide*. A permanent site had been promised by the State Government, but this had not yet been chosen from several options mooted.

I remained on board throughout operations to discharge *City of Adelaide* on to barge *Bradley*. Things were manic over the next few days and I had no time to write up the fantastic events that took place.

Sarah's voyage from Plymouth to Adelaide lasted seventeen days longer than mine. She arrived on 7 November 1864. Her diary continued in much the same vein as many of her previous daily recordings – there is only so much you can do in the restricted environment of a ship! There was a squally, very cold day that meant spending a short time on deck. Piano playing with Blanche continued, as did playing chess with Mr Ringwood. Within twenty-four hours she recorded a 'beautiful day' when they spent the morning on deck. In that time *City of Adelaide* had sailed two hundred and twenty-six miles. On Sunday 23 October the weather was showery. Prayers were read as usual, but in the afternoon, and in the evening Sarah writes, 'one of the sailors, Harry read a very good sermon from *Mark c vi v 12* – And they went out and preached that men should repent'. The next day she refers to a journal that 'Jack' wrote on his passage to Adelaide and found that 'he spent his time nearly in the same manner as we do'. More chess, mostly losing, and round games, walks on deck, whilst the ship was becalmed nearly all day was recorded, and on the Tuesday they were only going about 6 knots an hour. Wet weather seemed to prevail, sometimes preventing walks on deck.

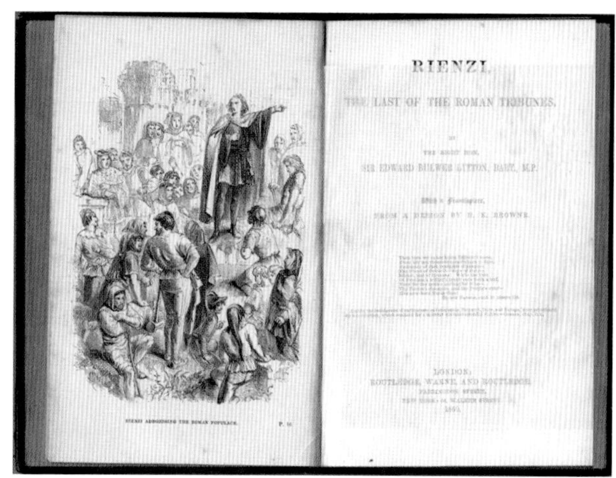
RIENZI.
THE LAST OF THE ROMAN TRIBUNES.
SIR EDWARD BULWER LYTTON, BART, M.P.
LONDON:
ROUTLEDGE, WARNE, AND ROUTLEDGE

Sarah was an avid reader of books such as *The Ingoldsby Legends*, *Rienzi*, *Macaulays Essays*, that I am enjoying collecting. An east wind drives *City of Adelaide* on and fine weather sees her taking up walks on the deck again.

A few days before arrival in Adelaide, Sarah and Blanche have read *Two Gentleman of Verona* (where I enjoyed many holidays in my teens when my father worked there). Four days before arrival, Sarah refers to the crew being 'busy cleaning the paint and varnishing', just as crew on *Palanpur* did before arrival in each port.

I was so glad I remained on board *Palanpur* for those extra days. It helped me come to terms with the fact that I was leaving this incredible ship that had been my home for ten weeks. It had carried me away from the day-to-day responsibilities of home and family. I enjoyed the minimalist, practical comfort of my cabin. I loved the adventure. I adored being at sea. I had become fond of the crew. In the whole time I never once felt threatened or unwelcome, quite the reverse. When we overcame our shyness, we relaxed into a place where we could share our language, culture, politics, religion and most of all, banter. We shared many stories that raked out memories and emotions long hidden by the passage of time.

I watched *City of Adelaide* being skidded off her own temporary home. Rather than crane her into the air, she would be slid off the deck. Those steel plates that baffled me were welded on to it to provide a surface that facilitated her being dragged by chains. Millimetre by millimetre she moved painstakingly between the two cranes of *Palanpur* that took her weight, till she dangled in her slings. Everyone stopped breathing as she was lowered onto barge *Bradley*. Each move was scrupulously inspected before the order for the next step was given. Men crouched and flattened themselves against *Bradley*'s deck to ensure effective, accurate execution of paper and computer plans were realised. Finally, she docked.

Cheers, tears, embraces, smiles, handshakes brought to a close this epic, unbelievable fairy story. I looked at the empty deck of *Palanpur*. I looked at my photo of Sarah Ann Bray. I knew that she had come home.

Poor Peter Christopher. When he offered me accommodation on arrival in Adelaide, I bet he never expected me to stay for five weeks! It took me around a week to recover from separation from *Palanpur* and become a land-lubber again. His hospitality and generosity was immeasurable. I was often whisked away by Rosemary McKay, who introduced me to Port Adelaide Caledonian Society, and in general I was astonished at how many Scots folk I met. Their warmth in welcoming me was overwhelming. I was invited to speak of my voyage on a radio programme for Scottish communities worldwide (www.5ebi.com.au), and was interviewed by *7News* as well as Adelaide newspapers. When I got home, I received coverage from the Press Association and spoke on several community radio shows. It is my goal to make the story of *City of Adelaide* and her fight for survival one that will capture hearts around the world. She is truly a remarkable ship, a survivor against all odds.

As for dear Sarah, who crossed one and a half centuries to give me this unique, fantastic adventure, I was astonished beyond belief to find she is buried in Greenock, Scotland where my story began in 1999. I am convinced that that day I boarded *City of Adelaide* in 2012 her spirit became one with mine, and she made me the vessel that would bring her home to Adelaide.

I continue my research. The story goes on. Watch out for the next instalment!
I really hope you enjoyed our story! If you wish to join my mailing list, please contact me through my website www.ritabradd.com or email me at ritabradd@ritabradd.com. Many thanks.

October 30, 1864 – Sunday

A fine morning but very wet afternoon. We all thought last week that we should have been in Adelaide today. We were on Deck till lunch. Prayers were read in the saloon at a quarter to One. A breeze sprang up at 4 P.M. and lasted till 10 P.M. During that time we went about 14 knots. It then suddenly changed and the ship rolled about dreadfully. We could not go to the Sailors Service. We were off King George's Sound about the middle of the night.

November 6, 1864 – Sunday

An unpleasant day, the winds hot. We walked about the deck in the morning. There was service as usual in the morning but my head ached so dreadfully that I was unable to attend. At 11.30 P.M. land was seen and about half an hour after the light at Kangaroo Island.

November 7, 1864 – Monday

A beautiful day. I woke about 5 A.M. and saw the land from the porthole. We were on deck about an hour before breakfast. The land at first looked rather low and barren. We were busy packing in the morning. After lunch addresses were presented to the Captain and Doctor. We anchored about noon. The health officer came on board immediately. Jack and Mr Lewis arrived about 4.30 P.M. There was to have been a dance in the evening and the Captain wished Jack to stay on board but as Mr Lewis was with him we thought it advisable to land. We went in a boat to the Semaphore, drove to the station and came to town by 6.15 P.M. train. We proceeded immediately to St Lukes Parsonage, which Jack has taken furnished for two months. Mr and Mrs Lewis Mr and Mrs Suter (?) dined with us. There was a letter from Elisa.

THE TIMES | Friday December 26 2014 1SM

13

News

Oldest clipper's final perilous voyage retraced

Scotland Staff

The last voyage of the world's oldest surviving clipper ship is to be retraced in a book.

The *City of Adelaide* took thousands of people from Europe to Australia in the 19th century but after a long and adventurous life she was left to rot on a slipway in Irvine, North Ayrshire.

After a successful restoration campaign, Rita Bradd, a Scottish writer, was granted exclusive access to accompany the 150-year-old vessel on her final 14,000-mile journey. Bradd joined the crew of the cargo ship MV *Palanpur*, which carried the clipper from Rotterdam in the Netherlands to her resting place in Port Adelaide in south Australia, where she arrived in February.

A tall ships enthusiast, Bradd kept a diary in tandem with that of a young woman who made the maiden voyage in 1864, charting the ups and downs of the trip — from Christmas Day on the equator to surviving a cyclone.

Researchers estimate that a quarter of a million south Australians can trace their origins back to passengers who travelled on the *City of Adelaide*.

Her sailing days ended in 1893 and she was used as a hospital ship, renamed *Carrick* as a training boat and a clubhouse before being raised and kept on a slipway at the Scottish Maritime Museum in Irvine after sinking in the River Clyde in 1991.

A charity called Clipper Ship City of Adelaide led a campaign to save and relocate the ship to become part of a maritime heritage park in south Australia. The group beat a rival bid from Sunderland, where the ship was built.

"The ship is a people's ship," said Bradd, who will give a percentage of the book's profits towards the ship's upkeep. "It's an incredible story, not just my part in it, but the whole ship and the people who have been involved with her and the passion that bubbles out from everybody." The 70-day voyage took the ship from Rotterdam to Norfolk in Virginia and on to Port Hedland, western Australia, via the Cape of Good Hope, following the historic route she would have taken in her heyday.

Recalling the final and most precarious leg of the journey, Bradd said: "We hit the tail end of a cyclone and it was really wild ... I was always imagining what it would have been like being inside the ship in storm-force winds, it must have been awful.

"When I saw the land, I was so relieved. I was overcome with joy at the safe arrival of the ship and for that wonderful engineering experience to have been such a success."

Rita Bradd, right, was on a cargo ship that took the City of Adelaide back to Australia

Pamela Whittle, Captain David Bruce's great-granddaughter

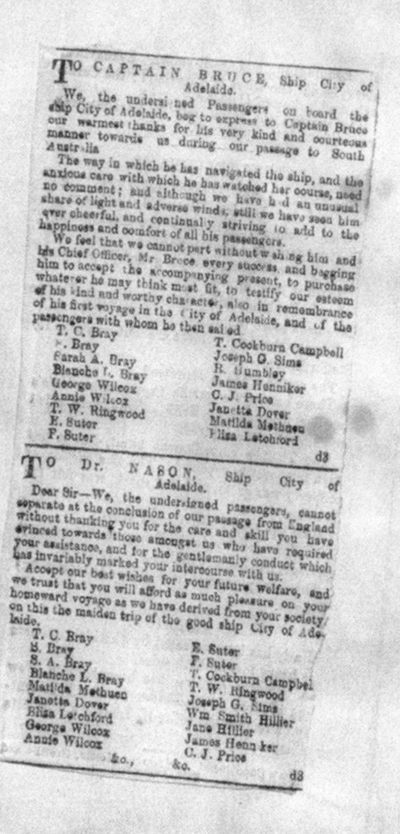

TO CAPTAIN BRUCE, Ship City of Adelaide.

We, the undersigned Passengers on board the ship City of Adelaide, beg to express to Captain Bruce our warmest thanks for his very kind and courteous manner towards us during our passage to South Australia

The way in which he has navigated the ship, and the anxious care with which he has watched her course, need no comment; and although we have had an unusual share of light and adverse winds, still we have seen him ever cheerful, and continually striving to add to the happiness and comfort of all his passengers.

We feel that we cannot part without wishing him and his Chief Officer, Mr Bruce, every success, and begging him to accept the accompanying present, to purchase whatever he may think most fit, to testify our esteem of his kind and worthy character, also in remembrance of his first voyage in the City of Adelaide, and of the passengers with whom he then sailed.

T. C. Bray	
. Bray	T. Cockburn Campbell
Sarah A. Bray	Joseph G. Sims
Blanche L. Bray	R. Humbley
George Wilcox	James Henniker
Annie Wilcox	C. J. Price
T. W. Ringwood	Janetta Dover
E. Suter	Matilda Methuen
F. Suter	Eliza Letchford

d3

TO Dr. NASON, Ship City of Adelaide.

Dear Sir—We, the undersigned passengers, cannot separate at the conclusion of our passage from England without thanking you for the care and skill you have evinced towards those amongst us who have required your assistance, and for the gentlemanly conduct which has invariably marked your intercourse with us.

Accept our best wishes for your future welfare, and we trust that you will afford as much pleasure on your homeward voyage as we have derived from your society on this the maiden trip of the good ship City of Adelaide.

T. C. Bray	
S. Bray	E. Suter
S. A. Bray	F. Suter
Blanche L. Bray	T. Cockburn Campbell
Matilda Methuen	T. W. Ringwood
Janetta Dover	Joseph G. Sims
Eliza Letchford	Wm Smith Hillier
George Wilcox	Jane Hillier
Annie Wilcox	James Henniker
	C. J. Price

&c., &c.

d3

The South Australian Register
November 8 1864

THE *CITY OF ADELAIDE* – It is many years ago since Captain Bruce took up his station on the berth from Adelaide to London, and after giving general satisfaction in the *Irene* he resolved to build expressly for the trade a new vessel in which all the requirements his experience could suggest should be met. The order was given to Messrs. Pile & Co., the eminent shipbuilders of Sunderland, and the result has been the production of a ship of which the colony may well be proud. The frame is of iron, with teakwood planking, 195 feet over all, 19 feet depth of hold, and 33 feet 6 inches beam, with lines and proportions which will ensure fast sailing.

Nor is speedy progress the only aim, for in her passenger appointments every means have been taken to ensure perfection. The main saloon is a handsome appointment decorated with white and gold, and furnished with settees, tables and sideboard of solid teak. Mirrors and pianoforte add to the general effect; while a visit to the state-rooms, of which there are six on each side, show at a glance that nothing is wanting to promote the comfort of voyageurs, even down to hot water warming apparatus.

While in tropical regions there are large ports to afford ventilation and light, and two excellent bath-rooms for ladies and gentlemen provided – one under the break of the poop; and the other abaft the main saloon. Her appearance to a nautical man is extremely pleasing; for while possessing the fine lines of a clipper vessel, there is a neatness about the spars and rigging which adds materially to her appearance. In the matter of people it was a mere facsimile of the old *Irene* – Captain Bruce on the poop, his son in the waist, and the same providore (Mr. Claxton) in the cabin; indeed it seemed from this but a resuscitation of the old blue-sided trader, though at a glance at the craft decided her superiority and aroused pleasurable feelings that the Port Adelaide trade warranted the building of such a ship.

Patent steering gear, patent topsails, windlass and pumps were adopted, and it also seems as if Captain Bruce had served his time but to produce the beau ideal of what an Adelaide trader should be – in cargo space liberal and ample for wool freight; in second cabin 30 and in saloon accommodation 35 passengers will find ample space. The excellence of the arrangement is highly eulogized by the passengers, of whom a number are very old colonists, who return with pleasure to Australia, and testify to the merits of captain and ship in our advertising columns.

She left London on August 6, and touched afterwards at Plymouth, from which port she has made a passage of 87 days, having had light and fair winds from the Channel to the Bay of Biscay, but in the early trades instead of a continuation of favourable weather it blew but three days from the N.E. Thirty-three days elapsed before crossing the Line, and the meridian of the Cape was passed on October 8, without a single incident to break the monotony of a trip beyond a hurricane which assailed the ship when off the Cape Verde Islands, in which she behaved admirably, she reached the lightship on Monday afternoon, but as her draught of water is over 17 feet some days will elapse before she can cross the bar.

Acknowledgements

There is no way to measure how much of a pleasure it has been working literally side-by-side with my long-time friend, Bob Randall on this book. His eagerness, expertise, patience and obligement have mastered my research, writing and images into this exceptional creation. I could not be more proud.

This odyssey has come about with the generosity of spirit of a myriad of people.

The Scottish Maritime Museum Jim Tildesley, former Director of the Scottish Maritime Museum and member of the UK National Historic Ships Committee (Author of 'I Am Determined To Live Or Die On Board My Ship'), with initial contact in 2005; the serendipitous meeting with his successor David Mann when I spontaneously took notes that inadvertently cemented the foundation for this book; Matthew Bellhouse Moran, Curator for assistance with cover image (www.scottishmaritimemuseum.org)

Clipper Ship City of Adelaide Ltd Peter Christopher, Peter Roberts, Mark Gilbert, Richard Smith, Tom Chapman, Creagh O'Connor (www.cityofadelaide.org.au)

Sunderland *City of Adelaide* Recovery Foundation particularly Peter Maddison

The Voyage Peters & May, in particular Simon Judson (www.petersandmay.com), Harren & Partner (www.harren-partner.de), Combi-Lift (www.combi-lift.net)

Palanpur Crew *Master* German Koltakov, *Chief Officers (1)* Igor Boltov *(2)* Mykhailo Makushenko, *2nd Officer* Andriy Vyshnyakov, *3rd Officer* Andriy Kostenko, *Chief Engineer* Valeriy Zastup, *2nd Engineer* Vitaliy Poplavs'kyy, *3rd Engineer* Nikolay

Topilin, *Bosun* Anatolii Prudchenko, *AB-1* Igor Ivanov, *AB-2* Vadym Gresko, *OS-1* Kostyantyn Portnyagin, *OS-2* Sergiy Fomin, *Wiper* Ivan Polskoi, *Oiler* Stepan Deli, *Apprentice-1* Ihor Timoshytskyi, *Apprentice-2* Serhii Strokach, *Chief Cook-1* Anatoliy Letnyanka *Chief Cook-2* Oleksiy Klochko

Russell Grant (www.russellgrant.com)

Friends who helped – Hilda Hermann (www.linkedin.com/in/hilda-hermann) and Margaret Skea (www.margaretskea.com) who inspired me to self-publish; Catherine Simpson (www.catherine-simpson.co.uk), Dr Claire Askew (www.scottishbooktrust.com/profile-author/32495), Dr Russell Penney, David Bradford, Bob Mitchell BA MSc, King's Bookshop, Callander, Scotland (www.librarything.com), Rory MacLean and others I may have missed. Particular thanks go to artist Hugh Loney for his unstinting support and encouragement, to Rosemary McKay and Peter Christopher for their kind hospitality in Adelaide, and last but not least, Ruth Currie, great-granddaughter of my heroine, Sarah Ann Bray.

Images Permission has been sought for use of images/text or has been received. Thanks to www.cityofadelaide.org.au, www.battleofprestonpans1745.org *p45*, Peter Kormylo, author of 'Robert Burns Selected Works', *p197, 198.* Southern Cross ESO/José Francisco (josefrancisco.org) *p211.* Most images are mine, if you wish to acquire any, please contact me on the form at www.ritabradd.com.

Further reading www.cityofadelaide.org.au/publications by Meredith Reardon and Ron Roberts

Research Most research has been carried out in person or via individual websites including www.cityofadelaide.org.au and www.en.wikipedia.org (donation made)

Family Enormous thanks and huge love to my awesome, wonderful family who supported me throughout my adventures and in making of this book, particularly my dear mother, kleine Mutterlein, Anneliese and 'long-suffering' husband, Alan.

Donations Lionel Elmore set up a stall to raise funds from the ship within a few days of our arrival. He has devoted most of his time to ensure her success as a visitor attraction at Dock One in Port Adelaide. Please help the ongoing success of the ship at www.cityofadelaide.org.au

Endorsements

"Casually listening to the radio one day I was intrigued by an interview with one of the Directors of 'Clipper Ship City Of Adelaide Ltd'. I quickly looked at their website, wrote a comment about my family connection and sent a small donation and thought that would be the end of the story for me. Not so! Rita was in touch and we soon met. Her enthusiasm for the ship and the impossibly illegible diary of my great grandmother has known no bounds. Rita's sail on the 'Palanpur' carrying the 'City of Adelaide' on her final journey is a remarkable story. I feel proud to have had great-grandmother who recorded the maiden voyage of the 'City of Adelaide'. She could never have conceived of what it would turn into a century and a half later. And I am very proud to have met Rita who has recorded her final voyage and brought the ship so much to life." Ruth Currie

"Her fascination with the Clipper Ship, 'City of Adelaide', and all those who sailed on her more than a one hundred and fifty years ago, takes Rita Bradd on a journey of a lifetime. Rita was determined to escort the vessel on her final voyage home, high on the main deck of a heavy lift ship. The only passenger with a crew of Ukrainian seamen on a trip from Rotterdam to Port Adelaide via Virginia, South Africa and Port Headland in Western Australia; Rita's captivating diary chronicles the voyage, her thoughts and emotions and reflects on the experiences of the original passengers heading for a new life in a very distant South Australia." Jim Tildesley

"I'll never forget my first encounter with Rita Bradd! She had just arrived on the 'Palanpur' bringing the Clipper ship 'City of Adelaide'. She was brimming with emotion and joy when we met. She realised that my family is descended from Captain David Bruce. Our bond was immediate – her story is captivating. I encourage you to read her story and feel her passion." Meredith Reardon*

"I had the great pleasure of meeting Rita when she arrived in Adelaide in February 2014 after her voyage bringing 'City of Adelaide' to her final home. She wrote a diary on her travels to coincide with the diary written on the first voyage. What an extraordinary adventure. Congratulations Rita!" Julia Whittle*

"I knew nothing of my family history until my husband and I toured 'Cutty Sark' at Greenwich. She looked similar to the lithograph of 'City of Adelaide' we have at home. We discovered she was afloat on the Clyde in Glasgow, known as 'Carrick'. We were sailing home to Adelaide the next day, so rushed to the Scottish Maritime Museum to get some information. On return visits to Irvine, I was distressed to see her looking so forlorn. I became a member of a committee formed to bring her home to Adelaide. I still visit her regularly, at the age of nearly 92. I love going on board to see the latest work being done by our wonderful volunteers." Pamela Whittle**

*great-granddaughters of Capt. David Bruce **granddaughter of Capt. David Bruce